T0330220

The Science of Science Policy

INNOVATION AND TECHNOLOGY IN THE WORLD ECONOMY

Martin Kenney, Editor
University of California, Davis/Berkeley Round Table on the International Economy

Other titles in the series:

Sally H. Clarke, Naomi R. Lamoreaux, and Steven W. Usselman
The Challenge of Remaining Innovative: Insights from Twentieth-Century American Business

John Zysman and Abraham Newman, eds.
How Revolutionary Was the Revolution? National Responses and Global Technology in the Digital Era

Martin Fransman, ed.
Global Broadband Battles: Why the U.S. and Europe Lag Behind While Asia Leads

David C. Mowery, Richard P. Nelson, Bhaven N. Sampat, and Arvids A. Siedonis
Ivory Tower and Industrial Innovation: University-Industry Technology Transfer Before and After the Bayh-Doyle Act in the United States

Gary Fields
Territories of Profit: Communications, Capitalist Development, and the Innovative Enterprises of G.F. Swift and Dell Computer

Martin Kenney and Bruce Kogut, eds.
Locating Global Advantage: Industry Dynamics in the International Economy

Urs von Burg
The Triumph of Ethernet: Technological Communities and the Battle for the LAN Standard

The Science of Science Policy
A Handbook

Edited by Kaye Husbands Fealing, Julia I. Lane,
John H. Marburger III, and Stephanie S. Shipp

STANFORD BUSINESS BOOKS
An Imprint of Stanford University Press
Stanford, California

Stanford University Press
Stanford, California

Special discounts for bulk quantities of Stanford Business Books are available to corporations, professional associations, and other organizations. For details and discount information, contact the special sales department of Stanford University Press. Tel: (650) 736-1782, Fax: (650) 736-1784

Any opinion, finding, and conclusion or recommendation expressed in this book are those of the authors and do not necessarily reflect the institutions they represent.

Printed in the United States of America on acid-free, archival-quality paper

Library of Congress Cataloging-in-Publication Data

The science of science policy : a handbook / edited by Kaye Husbands Fealing . . . [et al.].
   p. cm.
  Includes bibliographical references and index.
  ISBN 978-0-8047-7078-1 (cloth : alk. paper)
 1. Science and state—United States.   I. Fealing, Kaye Husbands.
  Q127.U6S3189 2011
  338.9'26—dc22   2010035621

Typeset by Westchester Book Group in 10/15 Minion Pro

Contents

Acknowledgments

The editors would like to acknowledge the contributions of Bill Valdez, who provided valuable insights and contributed greatly to the editing and structure of this book. We are also grateful to the National Science and Technology Committee's NSTC's Science of Science Policy Interagency group, whose continued support of and engagement with the very real practical issues have been critical to the revitalization of the field.

We would also like to recognize the invaluable assistance of the editorial staff at Stanford University Press, Margo Beth Crouppen and Jessica Walsh, as well as of Laura Yerhot, who did an enormous amount of work to help us prepare the manuscript.

Jim Thomas passed away suddenly while the book was being produced. We are deeply saddened by the loss of a visionary researcher, a colleague, and a friend. We are honored that his vision of the application of Visual Analytics to the Science of Science Policy is part of this book.

The Science of Science Policy

Editors' Introduction

*Kaye Husbands Fealing, Julia I. Lane, John H. Marburger III,
and Stephanie S. Shipp*

1. Introduction

Federally funded basic and applied scientific research has had an enormous impact on innovation, economic growth, and social well-being—but some has not. Determining which federally funded research projects yield results and which do not would seem to be a subject of high national interest, particularly since the government invests more than $140 billion annually in basic and applied research. Yet science policy debates are typically dominated not by a thoughtful, evidence-based analysis of the likely merits of different investments but by advocates for particular scientific fields or missions. Policy decisions are strongly influenced by past practice or data trends that may be out of date or have limited relevance to the current situation. In the absence of a deeper understanding of the changing framework in which innovation occurs, policymakers do not have the capacity to predict how best to make and manage investments to exploit the most promising and important opportunities.

This lack of analytical capacity in science policy sits in sharp contrast to other policy fields, such as workforce, health, and education. Debate in these fields is informed by the rich availability of data, high-quality analysis of the relative impact of different interventions, and often computational models that allow for prospective analyses. The results have been impressive. For example, in workforce policy, the evaluation of the impact of education and training programs has been transformed by careful attention to issues such as selection bias and the development of appropriate counterfactuals. The analysis of data about geographic differences in health care costs and health care outcomes has featured prominently in guiding health policy debates. And education policy has moved from a "spend more money" and "launch a thousand pilot projects" imperative to a more systematic analysis of programs that work and that could promote local and national reform efforts.

Each of those efforts, however, has benefited from an understanding of the systems that are being analyzed. In the case of science policy, no such agreement currently exists. Past efforts to analyze the innovation system and the effect that federal research has on it have typically focused on institutions (federal agencies, universities, companies, etc.) and/or outputs (bibliometrics, patents, funding levels, production of PhDs, etc.). Absent is a systems-level construct that those institutions and outputs function within and a failure to understand that science and technology innovations are created not by institutions but by people, often working in complex social networks. This social dynamic, as well as the complex system-level interactions that result, is the subject of increasing academic scrutiny. *Science* magazine recently devoted a special section to "complex systems and networks" and referenced studies that examined complex socioeconomic systems, meta-network analysis, scale-free networks, and other analytical techniques that could be used to understand the innovation system.[1]

There is no fundamental reason why it is impossible to develop a science policy infrastructure that is similarly grounded in evidence and analysis as the workforce, health, and education domains. It is true that it is difficult: the institutional and political environment is complex, and the scientific discovery process is noisy and uncertain. Yet scientists should be excited, not deterred, by interesting but hard problems. And the history of the scientific advancement of other policy fields, with their studies of equally complex, noisy, and uncertain processes, is evidence that such efforts can succeed. Indeed, an interdisciplinary and international community of practice is emerging to advance the scientific basis of science policy through the development of data collection, theoretical frameworks, models, and tools. Its advocates envision that they can make future policy decisions based on empirically validated hypotheses and informed judgment.

There are fundamental reasons why it is becoming critical to develop such an evidence basis. One is that the White House is requiring agencies to do so: the joint Office of Management and Budget (OMB)/Office of Science and Technology Policy (OSTP) R&D Priorities memo issued in preparation for the FY2011 budget asks agencies to "develop outcome-oriented goals for their science and technology activities, establish procedures and timelines for evaluating the performance of these activities, and target investments toward high-performing programs. Agencies should develop 'science of science policy' tools that can improve management of their research and development portfolios and better assess the impact of their science and technology investments. Sound science should inform policy decisions, and agencies should invest in relevant science and technology as appropriate."[2]

Another is the looming imperative to document the impact of the nearly \$20 billion in R&D investments embodied in the 2009 American Recovery and Reinvestment Act (ARRA). As Kei Koizumi points out in his chapter:

> Policymakers and evaluators can demonstrate easily the short-term economic effects of highway projects, of which there are billions of dollars worth in the Recovery Act; miles of asphalt poured, construction jobs created, and dollars introduced into local economies are well developed and easily produced measures for these investments. But what are the similar indicators for R&D investments?

Finally, the federal budget environment is likely to be extremely competitive for the foreseeable future. For a case to be made that investments in science have value relative to investments in education, health, or the workforce, an analytical and empirical link has to be made between those investments and policy-relevant outcomes. It is likely that that link will need to be made at multiple levels, since the macro link between R&D investments and economic growth is less convincing given the international evidence provided by the Japanese and Swedish experience.[3]

The federal agencies have begun to respond in two ways. One is to advance the theoretical and empirical research frontier through investigator-initiated research and new data collection. The second is to develop a federal community of practice among the seventeen science agencies involved in funding and administering science research.

In the former case, by mid-2010, the National Science Foundation's (NSF) Science of Science & Innovation Policy (SciSIP) program has made over ninety awards to social scientists and domain scientists. Ten of these are explicitly to use the ARRA stimulus as a way to examine the impact of science investments. The SciSIP program, through the Division of Science Resources Statistics, is also investing in the development and collection of new surveys to better inform the biennial Science and Engineering Indicators that are the basis for many policy decisions. This includes the new Business R&D Innovation Survey, which involves a complete redesign of the collection of R&D data, as well as the collection of innovation data.

In the second case, the National Science and Technology Council (NSTC) established, under the Social, Behavioral and Economic Sciences Subcommittee of the Committee on Science, a federal interagency task group on the Science of Science Policy interagency task group (SOSP ITG). This task group produced a road map for federal investments[4] and held a major international conference to highlight the findings in that road map.

Both the SciSIP program and the SOSP subcommittee have worked to foster a community of practice in a number of ways. The interagency group has organized major annual workshops on the implementation of science policy. A flourishing Listserv for the exchange of ideas and information has been established. And a new SOSP ITG/SciSIP website has been developed,[5] which has begun to provide an institutional basis for the development of a community of practice.

Of course, SOSP will not solve all science policy problems. It is intended to provide an intellectual framework upon which to make decisions. Indeed, as Goldston notes in his chapter:

> Science of Science Policy research will never be definitive, and Congress certainly always would and should draw on more than social science results in making its decisions. But there is plenty of room to improve the current state of affairs. In other areas of policy—macroeconomics, health care, environmental protection, to name a few—there is at least a semblance of an ability to project the outputs that will result from a given set of inputs, and a range of studies to draw on in discussing what has worked and what has failed. Reaching a similar level of understanding for science policy would be a welcome change, if hardly a panacea.

2. What the Science of Science Policy Entails

One of the aims of recent science of science policy activities is to develop the evidentiary basis for decision making by policy practitioners. There is also an organic development or reshaping of frameworks that pushes the boundaries of discovery in several fields and disciplines. While some debate whether the science of science policy is itself a discipline, there is wide agreement that there is a coalescing community of practice, which Feller, in his chapter, describes as a distributed association of policymakers (public and private) and researchers in a variety of fields and disciplines. This community is interdisciplinary and includes economics, engineering, the history of science, operations research, physics, political science, psychology, and sociology—and this list is not exhaustive.[6]

Federal science investments are driven by a political context, so the insights provided by political scientists are critical. Sapolsky and Taylor argue in their chapter that

> governments support the advancement of science and technology (S&T) mostly through their support of specific missions such as defense or health, and it is the politics of these missions, and the many contextual goals of government, that determines the rate and direction of its research and development investments.

Governments can also affect the supply and demand conditions for science and technology outside the budgetary process via regulatory regimes, anti-trust, taxes, standards, etc.

Understanding the institutional and sociological environment is also critical, which is why sociologists make an important contribution. Powell, Owen-Smith, and Smith-Doerr indicate in their chapter that the "sociological science of science policy will theorize the link between the origins and later trajectories of social systems that will provide guidance for policymakers eager to intervene."

The economics of science policy is evolving beyond the initial constructs of macroeconomic linkages of inputs and productivity outcomes. Recent models utilize network analysis, bibliometric tools, and behavioral models to uncover latent relationships between the levels and rates of new scientific discoveries and the financial, human capital, organizational, and infrastructural inputs. While these models have historically made important contributions to policy decisions, Feller, Jaffe, and Freeman each caution in this volume that there is a need to understand the limitations of incentive structures and the requirement for careful empirical analysis to understand the system of scientific knowledge creation. Morgan, in his chapter, describes several systems modeling approaches, some of which originate outside of the social sciences. This migration and synthesis of ideas is precisely what creates a dynamic community of practice.

One area of the science of science policy that is often overlooked is that conceptualization of scientific development at the cognitive level. This very micro-examination of science policy is an emerging field, with collaboration between psychologists and engineers. Both disciplines are eager to understand the elements of the creative process. Gero describes frameworks that are used to understand creative cognitive processes, which may lead to new ideas that are marketable—innovation.

And, of course, science investments are ultimately predicated on contributing to innovation. Gault's chapter connects the work on the understanding of the science system to the need for work on delivering value to the market in the form of new goods and services and contributing to economic growth and social welfare.

3. The Need for the Handbook

Our review of the science policy curricula and syllabi in major research programs suggests that the emerging field lacks a cornerstone document that describes the current state of the art from both a practitioner and an academic point of view.

This handbook is intended to fill this gap by providing in-depth, scholarly essays authored by leading scientists and policy practitioners. We recognize that the field has multiple dimensions, and as such, this book is divided into three sections: theoretical issues, data and measurement, and policy in practice. Each author has been asked to provide a survey of a different aspect of the field, based on his or her domain expertise, which explores the plausible foundations of an evidence-based platform for science policy. The interdisciplinary nature of such a platform is evident from the nature of the questions asked by the authors: What are the essential elements of creativity and innovation, and how can they be defined to serve a truly scientific approach to policy? How can the technical workforce be quantified and modeled—what is its likely future, and how does it respond to the multiple forces that could be targets of policy? What is the impact of globalization on creativity and productivity in the science and engineering fields? What are the optimal roles of government and private investments in R&D, and how do their different outcomes influence R&D and innovative activities? As such, the contributors span a variety of disciplines, including economics, sociology, psychology, and political science.

It is worth noting that this handbook focuses on the science of science policy, which we feel is an understudied and underresearched area. There has been a great deal more research on the science of innovation policy, although, inevitably, some of that research is alluded to in different chapters. In addition, the focus is on U.S. federal science policy. We recognize that there are vibrant and important research areas that study both business R&D investments and regional science and innovation policies. And while managers of large research enterprises, such as Microsoft, and state agencies face substantial resource allocation decisions, our sense is that these decisions are fundamentally different from those in the federal science arena. And, although the science of science policy has garnered important attention on the international stage, it is impossible to do full justice to the complexity of the international issues—that deserves another volume in its own right

4. Concluding Goals

We hope that this handbook will contribute to the overarching goal for science policy, namely, the development of "common, high-quality data resources and interpretive frameworks, a corps of professionals trained in science policy methods and issues, and a network of high-quality communication and discussion that can encompass all science policy stakeholders."[7] As such, the purpose of the book is to provide

1. an overview of the current state of the science of science policy in four key social science areas: economics, sociology, political science, and psychology;
2. a perspective from the broader social and behavioral science community on the interesting scientific challenges and opportunities in this emerging field;
3. a review of the empirical—measurement and data—challenges inherent in describing and assessing the scientific enterprise; and
4. a perspective from the federal science and policy community on the critical science policy questions that create the demand for a science of science policy.

Notes

1. *Science*, July 24, 2009, pp. 405–432.

2. M-09-27, Memorandum for the Heads of Executive Departments and Agencies, August 4, 2009.

3. Julia Lane, "Assessing the Impact of Science Funding," *Science* 5 (June 2009), vol. 324, no. 5932, pp. 1273–1275, DOI: 10.1126/science.1175335.

4. "The Science of Science Policy: A Federal Research Roadmap," November 2008.

5. See http://scienceofsciencepolicy.net.

6. For example, all of these areas are represented among the SciSIP awardees; see www.scienceofsciencepolicy.net/scisipmembers.aspx.

7. See Marburger, Chap. 2, in this book.

Topical Guide to This Handbook

Topic	Chapter 2	3	4	5	6	7	8	9	10	11	12	13	14	15	16	17	18
Agent-Based Models and Decision Analysis					X	X						X					
Competitiveness	X							X									X
Culture of Science and Institutions	X	X	X					X				X		X	X	X	X
Data Development and Exploration	X						X		X	X	X	X	X				
Discovery and Knowledge Creation				X	X		X	X		X		X		X		X	X
Disruptive Technologies and Transformational Discoveries		X	X		X						X				X		
Diversity			X					X									
Economic Growth, Wealth Creation, and Productivity	X		X	X				X			X						X
Economic Models	X			X	X	X	X										
Education	X			X							X				X		
Energy and the Environment															X	X	
Ethics			X														
Evaluation Studies								X					X				
Federal R&D Labs	X	X						X					X	X	X	X	
Funding Strategies and Incentive Structures		X		X			X	X					X	X	X	X	X
Health Sciences			X														
History of Science Policy	X							X									
Indicators and Metrics			X	X	X		X	X	X	X					X		
Innovation		X	X		X		X	X	X	X	X				X	X	X
Measuring Intangible Assets				X				X		X		X					
Institutional Networks, Including Inter- and Intramural Cooperation		X	X								X	X		X	X		
Interdisciplinarity			X				X	X				X					X
International Partnerships		X						X									X
Job Creation and Retention				X							X				X		
Organizations		X											X				
Political Design Model and the Influence of Political Institutions	X	X						X				X		X	X		X
Prospective and Retrospective Approaches						X	X						X				
Risk Models						X											
Quantitative Methods			X		X	X	X		X								
R&D Rate of Return			X				X	X	X	X			X				
Science Administration and Budgets	X	X		X				X									X
Science and Technology Education and Training			X	X											X		
Spillovers and Clusters		X	X														
Stakeholders and Power Relationships		X	X	X				X				X					X
Sustainable Growth, Including Wealth Creation								X									X
Systems Models and Applications					X							X					
Technology Commercialization/Diffusion, Including Bridging the "Valley of Death"					X						X			X			
Transformational Practices		X						X					X				X
Triple Helix–Partnerships Between Academic, Industry and Government Entities										X				X			
Value-based Decision-making–Economic and Public Value				X	X	X									X	X	
Visual Analytics													X				
Workforce (S&E)	X	X		X						X	X						

Why Policy Implementation Needs a Science of Science Policy

John H. Marburger III

2

1. Introduction

My perspective on the needs of science policymakers was strongly influenced by my experience as science advisor to the president and director of the Office of Science and Technology Policy (OSTP) during the two terms of President George W. Bush's administration (2001–2009). Watching policy evolve during an era of dramatic economic change, deep political divisions, and high-visibility science issues made me aware of weaknesses in the process that will not be remedied by simple measures. Science policy studies will illuminate the problems and undoubtedly propose options for addressing them but will not by themselves solve them. The growth of science policy studies as an academic discipline nevertheless provides intriguing opportunities for steady improvement in the management of the national science and technology enterprise.

2. Science Policy Challenges in the Executive Branch

The structure and responsibilities of the OSTP have changed very little since the office was established by Congress in 1976, and its basic form had been in place since President Eisenhower appointed the first full-time science advisor in 1957. The advisors have always played two roles: (1) advising the president and his other senior policy officials on all technical matters that reach the executive level, and (2) coordinating, prioritizing, and evaluating science and technology programs throughout the executive branch of government. A third responsibility is obvious but rarely discussed: the responsibility, shared with many others, of seeing policies through to their successful implementation. Each of these roles and responsibilities has its challenges, but none is more difficult than the third. The nature of this difficulty severely constrains strategies to overcome it, but the "science of science policy" movement is a potentially powerful tool for policy implementation. To appreciate why requires some background on the federal decision-making machinery. Science policy has many dimensions, but here I will focus specifically on the implementation of initiatives that require authorization and appropriations by Congress.

Policies are guides to action. Therefore strategies for implementation are nearly always embedded in policy proposals, often implicitly. The actions required to transform a policy idea into a desired result occur in stages. The early stages are successive expansions of the group of agents and stakeholders whose endorsement is needed to launch the initiative. Later stages focus on the management of the program, feedback of information about its success or failure to the policy level, and subsequent policy actions responsive to the feedback. Together these stages comprise the natural cycle of planning, implementation, evaluation, and improvement that applies to all systematic efforts to accomplish defined objectives. Science projects normally occur within a larger framework administered by an organization or a governmental agency. My interest here is in frameworks for science and technology programs at the highest policy level and the early-stage actions required to launch them.

The complexity of the U.S. federal science establishment is notorious. The executive branch carries out the business of government through a large number of departments and agencies, many of which today have a research arm and an employee in the role of chief scientist. Nineteen of these organizations are designated by an executive order as members of the interagency National Science and Technology Council (NSTC), managed by the OSTP. Twenty-five of them participate in the interagency National Nanotechnology Initiative (NNI), and thirteen each participate in the Global Change Research Program (GCRP) and the Networking and Information Technology Research and Development (NITRD) program.[1] Among the fifteen departments and fifty-six "Independent Establishments and Government Corporations" listed in the current edition of the *U.S. Government Manual*, only one, the National Science Foundation (NSF), is fully devoted to the conduct of science, including research fellowships and science education.[2] All of the other science organizations are therefore embedded within larger departments in which they compete with other functions for money, space, personnel, and the attention of their department secretary or administrator. Two of the largest science agencies, NASA (National Aeronautics and Space Administration) and NSF, do not report to a cabinet-level administrator and rely on the OSTP to make their case in White House policy-making processes.

The dispersion of research through such a large number of agencies was a weakness already recognized in the 1940s by Vannevar Bush, who urged consolidation into a single basic research agency.[3] That effort led ultimately to the creation of the National Science Foundation in 1950, but the consolidation included only a small fraction of the then-existing federal research portfolio. The bureaus that became the National Institutes of Health (NIH), NASA, the Department of Energy (DOE), and the Department of Defense (DOD) research entities remained separate and today have research budgets comparable to or greater than the NSF. Many smaller science agencies within cabinet departments, such as Commerce, Agriculture, and Interior, also remained separate. The challenge of managing multiple science enterprises in the executive branch motivated the development of bureaucratic machinery in the 1950s to avoid duplication, fill gaps, and preserve capabilities serving multiple agencies.[4] The White House Office of Management and Budget (OMB) has the greatest authority in this role, and the OSTP works with the OMB to establish priorities and develop programs and budgets for the science and technology portions of all of the agencies.

The OMB itself is divided into five relatively independent divisions (four during my service), each of which manages a significant portion of the overall science and technology activity.[5] This creates a challenge within the executive branch for initiatives that cut across the major science agencies. The NIH, NSF, DOE, and DOD research budgets are each developed in separate OMB divisions. Budget officials work hard to protect their independence, and they attempt to insulate their decisions from other White House policy offices. Major policy decisions are made through a deliberative process among White House and cabinet officials—always including the OMB—that narrows issues and choices for ultimate action by the president. Only a few issues, however, can receive such high-level attention, and most decisions about science and technology policy are negotiated within agencies and among the various White House policy offices.

This executive branch machinery is complex but reasonably well defined and understood by the bureaucracy. However, it is not always well understood by the political appointees in each agency whose tenure is often less than a single four-year presidential term. Their involvement in the process adds to the element of randomness always present in agency responsiveness to presidential direction, but the political appointees also reduce the impedance mismatch between the volatile political leadership and the cultural inertia of the bureaucracy. Designing high-level policies within the executive branch so they will actually be implemented requires detailed knowledge of the political and bureaucratic cultures of the agencies that will be responsible for implementation. Because these cultures depend on personal qualities of the agency leadership and specific historical tracks to the present state of the agencies, policy analysis and design are not well defined. For this and other reasons

common to complex organizations, the behavior of the agencies is not sufficiently predictable to guarantee that a policy, once launched by presidential
directive or executive order, will follow an anticipated trajectory. The usual
government remedy for the consequences of this uncertainty is to establish
stronger coordinating organizations at the top, such as national coordinating
offices (e.g., for the NNI and the NITRD), "czars," or presidential commissions. The OSTP itself has become increasingly effective in this role through
refinement of the NSTC structure over several administrations. Notwithstanding these arrangements, the agency line management is on the job continually and has more resources than the relatively small executive office of
the president to influence the action environment. I had this phenomenon in
mind when I described the origins of the Bush administration's vision for
space exploration to the 2009 "Augustine Committee" that reviewed NASA's
human space flight plans: "[T]he final [space] policy document was a compromise between contrasting policy perspectives offered by NASA and by the
White House policy advisors. In subsequent presentations to Congress and to
the public, NASA representatives emphasized the NASA view of the *Vision*,
which began to appear even during the policy formation process through leaks
to the media serving the space community."[6]

3. Legislative Impact on Science Policy Implementation

The legislative branch has no executive machinery to resolve the random
forces that influence its own operations. It responds to the president's budget
proposals with two dozen very independent appropriations subcommittees,
as well as a large number of authorizing committees and subcommittees. No
organization, such as the OMB or the OSTP, monitors or attempts to enforce
policy consistency across the hundreds of bills passed in each Congress, much
less the thousands of bills that are introduced and debated. Offices such as the
Congressional Budget Office (CBO), the General Accountability Office (GAO),
and the Congressional Research Service (CRS) are informational only and
have no authority over the 535 members of Congress. These offices are influential, however, through the quality and perceived objectivity of the information and analyses they produce. The CBO analyses are particularly successful
in fostering a consensus on the financial aspects of legislative proposals.

Legislative funding for science and technology programs originates in
nine of the twelve different appropriations subcommittees in each chamber,
for none of which is science the sole or even the majority category of funding. The "big five" science agencies—NIH, NSF, DOE, NASA, and DOD—are
funded by four different appropriations subcommittees. Each subcommittee

has its own staff, whose members' voices are more influential than many executive branch policymakers in establishing priorities and programs among the executive agencies. And each subcommittee is a target for its own army of advocates, lobbyists, and activist individuals whose influence is difficult to trace but highly significant.[7] Sections of bills are often drafted by lobbyists or constituents of a subcommittee member or the chairperson. The subcommittees are substantially "stovepiped," with little incentive to coordinate action except on highly visible multiagency issues such as climate change or energy policy. The authorization and appropriations bills give surprisingly specific and sometimes conflicting direction to agencies, substantially and routinely invading the president's constitutional prerogative to manage the executive branch.

This complex and unpredictable field of action leads to inefficiencies and perverse distributions of resources that create a continual irritant, if not a threat, to America's otherwise very strong research and development (R&D) enterprise. One extreme example is the tortuous history of the initiative to enhance U.S. economic competitiveness in the second Bush administration. In 2005 a wide consensus developed within the U.S. science and technology community that U.S. economic competitiveness was threatened by neglect of the nation's "innovation ecology."[8] The president responded with the "American Competitiveness Initiative" (ACI) in his 2006 budget proposal to Congress.[9] The 110th Congress authorized its own response (largely consistent with but more generous than the ACI) in the "America COMPETES Act of 2007 (ACA)."[10] Congress, to the great surprise and consternation of the community, failed to fund the program because of a stalemate with the president regarding his insistence that the total budget (not just for R&D) not exceed his top line. For three years the initiative languished until the Bush administration expired and the 111th Congress substantially funded the initiative, and much more, along with the American Recovery and Reinvestment Act of 2009. In subsequent budget submissions, the Obama administration has generally supported the main provisions of the ACI and the ACA. During the final Bush administration years, science budgets reflected the priorities of the appropriations committees, not the executive branch and its scientific advisory panels. Politics played a dominant role in this saga, but other factors also were significant, including the fact that the ACI and, to a lesser extent, the ACA identified explicit priorities. Major science agencies such as NASA and the NIH were not included in the initiative. Consequently, Congress was somewhat insulated from criticism for its failure to act because important science constituencies excluded from the initiative remained silent. During this period

Congress continued to add large earmarked amounts to the R&D budgets, but few were in the prioritized programs.

In the longer run the "competitiveness campaign" resulted in important changes in the pattern of appropriations for science, as did the earlier campaign to double the NIH budget in the 1990s. In both cases the late stages played out in a new administration affiliated with a different political party, which suggests that a sufficiently broad, bipartisan campaign can succeed regardless of which party is in power. Such broad consensus is difficult to achieve, which is why it usually occurs only in the face of a national crisis: notable federal R&D funding spikes occurred during World War II and after the 1957 Soviet Sputnik launch, while others followed the oil embargo in the 1970s and perceived cold war urgencies (e.g., President Reagan's Strategic Defense Initiative) in the 1980s. The NIH and competitiveness initiatives were not propelled by similarly dramatic events, but champions for both campaigns developed cases based on "disturbing trends," including lagging rates of R&D investment compared to other countries, discouragement or lack of preparation of potential young scientists, and shortsighted abandonment of basic research in favor of applied research and development.[11] These and similar arguments were taken up by advocacy organizations of which some, such as Research America[12] and the Task Force on the Future of American Innovation,[13] were formed for the purpose. Prominent figures were recruited, op-eds were written, conferences and "summits" were held, and, ultimately, government responded. In the absence of a precipitating event, the advocacy communities worked to create a sense of national crisis to motivate the process.

4. Toward a Firmer Foundation for Science Policy

I too participated in the competitiveness campaign in my official capacity, encouraging an early report by the President's Council of Advisors for Science and Technology in 2002, overseeing the OSTP's role in crafting the ACI, and giving many supporting speeches. My direct experience with basic and applied research programs in diverse fields over four decades convinced me of the importance of these goals, but I was uneasy regarding the case put forward by the advocacy community. I thought the "disturbing trends" needed attention, but I was not convinced either that they would lead to the feared consequences or that the proposed remedies would work as advertised. On some issues, such as the status and future of the scientific workforce, there were deep uncertainties ("Do we have too many scientists/engineers in field X, or too few?").[14] My policy speeches from 2005 and thereafter expressed my frustration over the inadequacy of data and analytical tools commensurate with science policymaking in a rapidly changing environment.[15]

Given the complex and unpredictable systems of executive branch agencies and congressional subcommittees, no deployment of czars, commissions, or congressional offices will guarantee that rational and coherent policy proposals will be implemented. Congress departs reliably from the status quo only in response to widely perceived national crises, or when impressed with a broad consensus among multiple constituencies. If the consensus is created by advocacy alone, then there is no assurance that the proposed solution will achieve the desired end, even if the problems it addresses are real. Moreover, advocacy-based consensus has never reached across all of the fields of technical endeavor that draw funding from the overall R&D pot. Attempts to prioritize among fields or agencies are extremely rare and never well received by the scientific community. Past campaigns focused on selected fields that were perceived to be relevant to the crisis at hand and ignored the others.

Can a sustained science policy consensus develop that is strong enough to influence the government machinery and wide enough to encompass all of the disparate but linked technical endeavors that federal funds support? There is some hope. The National Academies (NAS) offer high-quality advice in every relevant technical field, and the products of the National Research Council (NRC) carry substantial weight with all of the actors in the complex process described earlier. The NRC reports avoid blind advocacy but are nevertheless assembled by teams of scientists and engineers, nearly always in response to a specific narrow charter negotiated by the agency requesting, and funding, the study. Even a report as focused as "Gathering Storm" avoided specificity regarding the relative importance of different fields of science. When NAS president Frank Press urged his colleagues in 1988 not to leave key priority decisions to Congress, he was roundly criticized by his own community.[16] The only source of high-level policy analysis that is relatively free of the biases of advocacy and self-interest is the community of social scientists and others who analyze science and technology policy as an academic field of study. And it is in the growth of this community and its products that the greatest hope lies for developing rational and objective policy perspectives that all parties to the national process can draw upon. The collective endeavor of this community is what I understand to be the science of science policy.

I became acutely aware of the inadequacy of available science policy tools following the terrorist attacks of September 11, 2001. These actions sparked a strong patriotic response in the science and engineering communities. Along with the desire to respond aggressively to terrorism came a wave of uneasiness about the impact on science of demands for increased homeland security. These included an immediate tightening of visas for students and visiting scientists, regulations on handling "select agents," or substances of likely interest to terrorists, concern over the release even of nonclassified research results that might assist terrorism, and the possible diversion of funds from existing science programs to new efforts related to homeland security. All of this was new to the nation's technical communities, and sorting out the issues and options consumed huge amounts of time in studies and meetings. Among many other policy questions I was asked at the time was one raised by the National Science Board (NSB).

The NSB's Task Force on National Workforce Policies for Science and Engineering invited me to address its June 2002 meeting on the topic "Impact of Security Policies on the Science and Engineering Workforce." This was a reasonable request given the nature of the new policies, but it created a dilemma for me. Although I had no information on which to estimate the impact, the prevailing wisdom in the academic community was that it would be negative. I could think of reasons to reinforce that conclusion, but I was also aware of the complexity of the technical workforce picture that was changing rapidly because of globalization and profound development in China and India. Should I speculate? My extensive experience in research university and national laboratory administration gave me the confidence to offer an opinion. Or should I point to the much larger issue of our ignorance about such impacts and what we would need to remove it? To quote directly from my notes for that meeting:

> The fact is, I do not know what the impact of security policies will be on the science and engineering workforce. Part of the reason for this—the least important part—is that the security policies are in a state of flux. Another part is that the impact will be psychological as well as instrumental, and psychology is not part of our predictive model. The most important factor, however, is that there is no reliable predictive model for workforce response to any particular driving force, such as a change in policy affecting student visas.
>
> If there are such models, they seem to be implicit in the types of data we collect and the manner we choose to portray them. When I see graphs and tables relating to workforce, I have the impression they are answers to questions whose significance is either so well known to experts that no further discussion is required, or so completely buried in history that no further discussion is possible. I understand the need to collect the same data year after year so comparisons can be made and changes depicted accurately in the course of time. But I am not at all

confident that the right questions are being asked or answered to provide guidance for action. We have workforce data that I do not understand how to use, and we have workforce questions whose answers would seem to require more than merely data.

My idea at the time was that the National Science Board, which oversees the production of the important *Science and Engineering Indicators* report,[17] should consider the task of building a new workforce model that might make it possible to answer questions such as the one they asked me: "What do we expect from a technical workforce model?" My response to the board follows:

> I know what I expect from a model. I expect it to give policy guidance. I want to be able to assess the impact of a change of policy on the technical workforce. . . . What is the impact of a student loan forgiveness program? Of a scholarship program? Of a change in the compensation structure for researchers, faculty members, technical staff? Of an increase in sponsored research funds in some field? Of a change in graduation rates in certain fields among certain sociological groups? Ask all these questions with respect to area of technical skill, and with respect to the nation in which the changes are postulated to occur. It must be a global model, because the workforce we are speaking of has global mobility. It must take into account the effect of incentives, and the correlation of this effect with sociological parameters.
>
> Above all, the model cannot be simply an extrapolation based on historical time-series data. The technical workforce is responding to factors that are changing too rapidly to be captured by historical data. And yet the model does not have to predict everything with perfect accuracy. What we need is the ability to estimate specific effects from specific causes under reasonable assumptions about the future. . . . Does it make sense for us to launch a project to model the global workforce with the aim of producing policy guidance? We need an action-oriented *workforce project* that seeks to define the technical workforce problem in a broad way, and to exploit the power of modern information technology to produce tools for policy guidance.[18]

I knew at the time that this was not a task the National Science Board was prepared to undertake, but I wanted to signal my concern about an issue that seemed to threaten the credibility of all policy advice. In the face of grave national challenges we were relying on anecdotes and intuitions and data disconnected from all but the most primitive interpretive frameworks. While I was prepared to accept responsibility for my policy recommendations, the scientist in me recoiled from the methodological weakness of this approach. If we think empirically based research is essential for learning about nature, or making useful products, then why should we not encourage research to build empirically validated foundations for effective science policy?

5. A New Mandate for Science Policy Studies

By 2005 I had concluded that no single project or study would address the need for better science policy tools. My keynote speech to that year's American Association for the Advancement of Science (AAAS) Science Policy Forum compared our situation to that of economic policymakers who

> have available . . . a rich variety of econometric models, and a base of academic research. Much of the available literature on science policy is being produced piecemeal by scientists who are experts in their fields, but not necessarily in the methods and literature of the relevant social science disciplines needed to define appropriate data elements and create econometric models that can be useful to policy experts. . . . These are not items that you can just go out and buy because research is necessary even to frame an approach. This is a task for a new interdisciplinary field of quantitative science policy studies.[19]

The following year I addressed the "Blue Sky II" conference of the Organization for Economic Cooperation and Development (OECD) on "What Indicators for Science, Technology and Innovation Policies in the 21st Century?" Once again I drew a comparison with economic models:

> Unfortunately, in our era of dynamic change, the empirical correlations that inform the excellent OECD analyses of economic performance are not very useful to science policymakers as guides to the future. They are not models in the sense that they capture the microeconomic behaviors that lead to the trends and correlations we can discover in empirical data. Take, for example, the production of technically trained personnel in China. China is producing scientists, mathematicians, and engineers at a prodigious rate. As a scientist and an educator, I tend to approve of such intellectual proliferation. As a policy advisor, I have many questions about it. How long, for example, can we expect this growth rate to be sustained? Where will this burgeoning technical workforce find jobs? What will its effect be on the global technical workforce market? Is it launching a massive cycle of boom and bust in the global technology workforce? Historical trends and correlations do not help here. Nor, I am afraid, does simply asking the Chinese policymakers what they intend. They also need better tools to manage the extraordinary energy of their society. We need models—economists would call them microeconomic models—that simulate social behaviors and that feed into macroeconomic

models that we can exercise to make intelligent guesses at what we might expect the future to bring and how we should prepare for it.[20]

By the time of Blue Sky II, the National Science Foundation had already held workshops and issued a prospectus announcing the formation of a new program in the social science of science and innovation policy (SciSIP) and solicited proposals the following year.[21,22] The president's FY2007 budget proposal to Congress included funds to launch the program, and several awards were distributed beginning in calendar year 2006. The current (2010) synopsis of the program indicates support for "research designed to advance the scientific basis of science and innovation policy," which therefore "develops, improves and expands models, analytical tools, data and metrics that can be applied in the science policy decision making process." No single study or single organization will have the broad and lasting impact needed to rationalize policy implementation. But I do believe it is a realistic goal to build a new specialty within the social science community—complete with journals, annual conferences, academic degrees, and chaired professorships— that focuses on the quantitative needs of science policy. This is a good time to encourage such ventures, for at least three reasons.

First, the dramatic influence of information technology on almost every aspect of daily life, from entertainment to global trade, has made it very clear that technical issues will be an important dimension of nearly all future economies. In this context, science and technology policy acquires an unprecedented significance. Post–World War II science policy, at least in the United States, focused on cold war issues until the late 1980s. The decade of the 1990s was a transition decade. Since the turn of the century all science policy eyes have been on technology-based innovation and how to sustain it. Studies of government science investment strategies have a long history, but the increased demand for economic effectiveness creates a dynamic in which new approaches to science policy studies will flourish.

Second, in the face of rapid global change, old correlations do not have predictive value. The technical workforce today is highly mobile, and information technology has not only dramatically altered the working conditions for technical labor but has also transformed and even eradicated the functions of entire categories of technical personnel. Distributed manufacturing, supply-chain management, and outsourcing of ancillary functions have undermined the usefulness of old taxonomies classifying work. The conduct of scientific research itself has been transformed, with extensive laboratory automation, Internet communication and publication, and massive computational and data processing power. The Great Recession of 2008–2009 has, if anything, accelerated the pace of change. We simply must have better tools that do not rely on historical data series. They do not work anymore. Microeconomic reality has inundated macroeconomic tradition with a flood of new behaviors.

Third, the same rapidly advancing technologies that created these new conditions also bring new tools that are particularly empowering for the social sciences. Large databases and complex models are inherent in social science research. The vast articulation of Internet applications makes possible the gathering of socioeconomically relevant data with unprecedented speed and affordability, and access to massive, inexpensive computing power makes it possible to process and visualize data in ways unimagined twenty years ago. New capabilities for direct visualization of large data sets in multiple dimensions may render traditional statistical methods obsolete. A growing community of scientists from many different fields is inventing data mining and data visualization techniques that I believe will transform traditional approaches to analysis and model building. These new tools and opportunities can be an invigorating stimulus for all of the social sciences, including the social science of science policy.

If the science of science policy succeeds in establishing itself as a well-defined field and becomes a recognized academic subject, then it is likely to produce three resources that can substantially improve science policy implementation: common, high-quality data resources and interpretive frameworks, a corps of professionals trained in science policy methods and issues, and a network of high-quality communication and discussion that can encompass all science policy stakeholders. Subfields of science policy studies that focus on issues such as energy, climate change, and public health already exist and provide these resources in increasing measure. Climate change controversies notwithstanding, the growth of climate science as an academic field of study, complete with official recognition by international organizations, has manifestly strengthened a consensus for action that did not exist two decades ago. Health policy studies have been around much longer, without which exaggerated or baseless arguments about this or that impact of a given policy would carry much more weight than they do. The existence of a body of peer-reviewed, empirically based analyses makes it possible for news media and Internet-based services to intervene effectively in public policy debate. In the absence of such a resource, the Internet is an advocacy magnifier that adds little substantive value to the public discourse.

Government bears a heavy responsibility to manage the technical resources on which our collective future depends. Some nations, but not ours, provide this management through expert ministries with little public input. Our democracy balances the wasteful entropic forces of public process against the progressive forces of public enlightenment. The inevitable absence of policy discipline in U.S. federal government decision making creates an imperative for some system of public education that fosters rational policy outcomes. The existence of an academic field of science of science policy is a necessary precondition for such a system. Policies can be formed and carried through rationally only when a sufficient number of men and women follow them in a deep, thoughtful, and open way. Science policy, in its broadest sense, has become so important that it deserves the enduring scrutiny from a profession of its own. This is the promise of the academic discipline of the science of science policy.

Notes

1. See the OSTP website at www.ostp.gov for a description of these programs.

2. The U.S. Government Manual is available at www.gpoaccess.gov/gmanual/.

3. "Science: The Endless Frontier," chap. 6. See www.nsf.gov/about/history/vbush1945.htm.

4. For the early history of White House coordination of science, see "Impacts of the Early Cold War on the Formulation of U.S. Science Policy: Selected Memoranda of William T. Golden, October 1950–April 1951," W. Blanpied, ed., at www.aaas.org/spp/cstc/pne/pubs/golden/golden.pdf.

5. For OMB organization, see www.whitehouse.gov/omb/assets/about_omb/omb_org_chart.pdf.

6. These remarks, as well as other supporting documentation, may be found on the website for the "Review of Human Space Flight Plans Committee" at www.nasa.gov/offices/hsf/meetings/08_05_meeting.html.

7. One measure of external influence is the number of earmarks on the appropriations bills. The OMB counted 11,524 earmarks on the 2008 budget bills. See earmarks.omb.gov/2009-appropriations-by-spendcom/summary.html.

8. See the National Academy of Science report, "Rising Above the Gathering Storm," available at www.nap.edu/catalog.php?record_id=11463.

9. A brochure describing the ACI is available at www.nist.gov/director/reports/ACIBooklet.pdf.

10. The ACA is summarized on the House Science Committee website at science.house.gov/legislation/leg_highlights_detail.aspx?NewsID=1938.

11. See note 8 and J. M. Bishop, M. Kirschner, and H. Varmus, *Science* 259, 444 (1993).

12. See www.researchamerica.org.

13. See www.futureofinnovation.org.

14. D. Kennedy, J. Austin, K. Urquhart, and C. Taylor, *Science* 303, 1105 (2004).

15. See J. H. Marburger, *Science* 308, 1087 (2005).

16. A useful review of priority setting in science, including remarks on Press's 1988 Annual President's Address, is contained in chap. 5 of U.S. Congress, Office of Technology Assessment, *Federally Funded Research: Decisions for a Decade,* OTA-SET-490 (Washington, DC: U.S. Government Printing Office, May 1991).

17. See, for example, National Science Board, *Science and Engineering Indicators 2010* (Arlington, VA: National Science Foundation [NSB 10-01], 2010).

18. Prepared remarks for the Meeting of National Science Board Task Force on National Workforce Policies for Science and Engineering, June 28, 2002. Quoted in my Pegram Lectures, Brookhaven National Laboratory, November 18, 2008.

19. Keynote Address, 2005 AAAS Forum on Science and Technology Policy. See complete text at www.aaas.org/news/releases/2005/0421marburgerText.shtml.

20. "Science, Technology and Innovation Indicators in a Changing World: Responding to Policy Needs," ISBN 978-92-64-03965-0, OECD, 2007.

21. NSF Workshop on Social Organization of Science and Science Policy, July 13, 2006. The workshop report may be found at www.nsf.gov/sbe/scisip/ses_sosp_wksp_rpt.pdf.

22. "Science of Science and Innovation Policy: A Prospectus," NSF Social, Behavioral, and Economic Science division, September 2006, available at www.nsf.gov/sbe/scisip/scisip_prospec.pdf.

The Theory of Science Policy
Editors' Overview

The foundations of the evidence-based platform of science policy span several disciplines. For decades, the core social science disciplines of economics, sociology, and political science have given us frameworks that attempt to explain the dynamics of science and innovation activities. Together their methodologies provide an understanding of the stocks and flows of inputs and outputs in the system, the institutional structures that promote or impede scientific progress, and the power relationships that determine distributional outcomes. Recent calls for a social science of science policy have provided the impetus for a resurgence of researchers collaborating across disciplinary boundaries in search of a systems approach to answering age-old science policy questions. Engaged in this process as well are psychologists, whose frameworks add necessary dimensions to developing an understanding of the creativity process leading to scientific discoveries and downstream innovations. Complexity theorists and modelers have also expanded our view of the science and innovation enterprise, with architectural frameworks that provide scaffolding for policy simulations. Such empirical exercises complement those that are developed in the core social science disciplines. The following chapters synthesize the theoretical knowledge bases from which the science of science policy emerges and for which there is call for an engaged community of practice.

The politics of distribution related to scientific and technological endeavors is the focus of the Harvey M. Sapolsky and Mark Zachary Taylor chapter. While economists evoke the public good rational for government funding of R&D (see Richard B. Freeman's chapter), Sapolsky and Taylor describe a different concept of science *for* the public good. They argue that "science and technology create winners and losers, especially in the long run." In their paradigm, the "losers" are endowed with assets such as skills, capital, land, and other resources. Distributive innovation hurts them because it changes the status quo. If the potential "losers" are also power holders, then they have an incentive to create institutions and to exercise policy mechanisms that enable them to retain power. Sapolsky and Taylor conclude that this potential for redistribution of wealth and power could slow technological change—but not in every case. Interestingly, political leaders who couple the technological enterprise with national security concerns or to nationalistic economic competitiveness races are able to forestall the drag on technological progress by stakeholders who stand to lose ground in a new technological equilibrium. The evolutionary nature of science and technological innovation necessarily means realignment of power. Understanding these dynamics is critical to our understanding of the ecological system of innovation.

Sapolsky and Taylor avoid reference to the traditional parlance of "national innovation system." Instead, they discuss the role of government in a globalizing world. They posit two different scenarios for developing and developed countries. Governments in developing countries, they argue, must be strategic in their capital investments (including human capital). With far-flung functions of corporations, policymakers in developing countries should move away from targeting entire industries to targeting specific functions within a given industry. In the developed country context—presumed to be lead innovating nations—the authors argue for the importance of technological modularity and interoperability with global technical infrastructures. Globalization, therefore, requires technological and managerial flexibility within industry and government. Science and technology policy decisions will follow paths quite different from those in the mid-twentieth century.

Institutions are the focus of the chapter by Walter W. Powell, Jason Owen-Smith, and Laurel Smith-Doerr. This chapter focuses on the importance of social systems to the study of science and innovation policy. Identifiable linkages between inputs and outcomes in the science and innovation system channel through ethical, political, environmental, and other social constructs. Even if a causal link is empirically established between, say, human capital inputs and productivity in an industry, in a specific region, at a certain point in time, it would not be necessarily true that the same results would be obtained if any of the structural factors were changed.

Ethical, power, and network relationships critically determine outcomes. Powell, Owen-Smith, and Smith-Doerr give specific examples to make their point. In the case of stem cell research, the authors show how changes in presidential administrations affected the methods that researchers could use to extract, store, and use embryonic stem cells in laboratory experiments. Federal funding of research in this area allows politics (a derivative of social ethics and power) to affect lab science practices. The authors take this argument even farther. Since institutions vary by nation, international competition in science and innovation is appreciably affected by established institutions and institutional change. This is an important dimension to the science of science policy. Many countries use a benchmark rate of 3 percent of GDP for R&D funding. Since the institutional structures of these countries vary, it is not likely that a one-size-fits-all rule should apply. The authors also use this reasoning to explain why technology clusters form in some cities and not in others.

Power relationships, institutional contexts, and network structures, therefore, impact behavior in fields of research. The authors discuss the importance of this triad on the balance of basic and translational research at funding agencies, such as the National Institutes of Health. Additionally, they highlight the debate about the need for interdisciplinary research to achieve transformative outcomes. Lastly, they link the work on interdisciplinarity to gender and racial diversity in the sciences. The institutional frameworks determine differences in access and, therefore, contribution of individuals from a variety of backgrounds. If increased variety is super-additive (as Martin Weitzman shows in his journal article "On Diversity"[1]), then institutional barriers to diversity in science and innovation networks could reduce the efficacy of R&D funding.

The economics of science policy has several contributing fields and areas. Freeman's chapter focuses on the market for labor—the supply and demand for scientists and engineers, particularly under uncertainty. In an effort to answer the question of how to facilitate a market for scientific output, Freeman turns to a fundamental neoclassical tool—incentive structure. Pecuniary and nonpecuniary incentives can be used to encourage welfare—improving redistributions of human capital inputs into various scientific fields. Incentives can also be used to encourage various types of research initiatives, including the balancing of incremental and potentially transformative projects. Here Freeman embraces the sociology literature, acknowledging that the incentive structure must be cognizant of social networks. Networks can be intradisciplinary and interdisciplinary, as well as intramural and extramural (e.g., linkages between the academy and industry). One obvious question is whether the tournament nature of competition for scientists and engineers affects all demographic groups the same way. Freeman addresses this question with respect to women and immigrant scientists.

Government expenditures on scientific and technological development affect outcomes directly and indirectly. Awards and grants are direct dispensations to scientists and engineers at universities and other research institutions, while investment tax credits and other R&D subsidies may increase yields through businesses (crowding out notwithstanding). Freeman suggests that government's demand for science should comprise a diversified portfolio. More importantly, government funding institutions must recognize the impact that uncertainty has on their decision making, but also that fluctuations in their decisions have measurable effects on the development of R&D infrastructure, on the supply of human capital, and on the achievement of social goals.

Freeman highlights a critical aspect of science funding decisions—the uncertainty of outcomes. He draws on finance-based analytical tools for policy guidance. Options models and other portfolio allocation tools traditionally used to develop private-sector financial strategies have powerful applications in the context of the science of science policy. Research portfolios at large federal R&D labs or at academic institutions are likely test beds for such models. Freeman asserts that modeling the supply and demand of scientists and engineers—and the incentive structures that close the loop—requires a systems approach with options modeling to capture decision making under uncertainty. Measuring causal outcomes is not an exact science. The knotty problem is how to measure R&D spillovers—the externalities not only to society from new discoveries and innovations, but also to other scientific endeavors. Establishing metrics on these linkages is critical to weighing the economic returns to R&D, but it is precisely the uncertainty in the system that makes measurement difficult yet highly sought after.

The economics, sociology, and political science chapters have focused on understanding the science and technology enterprise at a mezzo or macro level. John S. Gero's chapter focuses instead on the extreme micro level—human cognition and innovation. He distinguishes creativity from innovation, in much the same way other social scientists writing in this section have done. Creativity is the process that yields new and useful ideas, while innovation is the process that turns creative ideas into products or processes.[2] The exploration of innovation and innovation policy is a relatively recent area of exploration in neuroscience. As such, this chapter gives an overview of the emerging field, including a thorough mapping from traditional literature and nomenclature on cognition to the application of technological innovation.

There is a clear theoretical link to the other chapters in this section of the science of science policy handbook. Gero directly links the cognitive definition of innovation to Schumpeter's concept of "creative destruction," where innovation displaces existing products or processes. In his rubric, there are three types of innovation: "augmentation, partial substitution, and displacement through total substitution." The latter is Schumpeterian. This is a powerful connection. Using a computational sociology technique, cognitive scientists can test the behavioral interaction between innovators and adopters of innovation. This is not only the development of neural networks but the evolution of social networks in the creativity-cum-innovation process. In these experiments, the impetus for change is the science of innovation policy. Analyzing behavioral responses to policy decisions is critical to understanding linkages and the dynamics within science and innovation systems.

M. Granger Morgan's chapter outlines a wide range of analytical models used in the science policy arena. The main emphasis of his chapter is that policy tools are not one-size-fits-all. Policy problems—particularly science and technology policy conundrums—require expertise in techniques that are more commonly utilized in operations research, decision analysis, technology assessment, options modeling, benefit-cost analysis, and life-cycle analysis. Morgan introduces the reader to the canonical literature in these areas and draws liberally on examples from energy and environmental policy. This chapter is particularly useful for pedagogical purposes. It also highlights the agencies and think tanks that are leaders in the development and use of systems modeling approaches.

Irwin Feller introduces the theoretical paradigms of the new science of science policy, defining the science (and art) of science policy, cautioning the builders and users of the enterprise about the limitations of models, tools, and data that currently exist, and encouraging researchers and policymakers to cultivate a dynamic community of practice. Feller draws linkages between disciplines and across generations that contribute to the understanding of how priorities should be set as organizations fund scientific discovery and technological innovation. The primary utility of this chapter, therefore, is the collection of works and the relationships among the works by thought leaders on evidence-based science policy.

Predictability is often demanded by decision makers. Purveyors of science policy models and tools are required to supply the best estimates under a variety of conditions, including uncertainty. Feller addresses the precarious dance between knowns and unknowns, highlighting what has been shown to be most effective but cautioning against ignoring the possibility of Type I or Type II errors. This is an important point, particularly in an era of increased dependency on empirically driven decision making. Noted in this chapter, however, is the need for concurrent data on the science and engineering enterprise, particularly data that are consistent across countries. Feller recognizes the recent efforts at the National Science Foundation to measure R&D and innovation separately, but he notes that measurements of the related inputs and outcomes require new and distributed vantage points.

Feller cautions researchers not to refine their models and tools or to develop new data sets in a vacuum. A community of practice, where researchers and practitioners engage in periodic discourse about new paradigms and outcomes, should minimize, as Feller puts it, "buyer's remorse." This is not to say that all social science of science policy belongs in Pasteur's Quadrant. But researchers and practitioners alike may increase respective utilities from such engagement. Referring to Bozeman and Sarewitz, Feller acknowledges that these activities are not merely to achieve increased economic efficiencies but to enhance social value.

Fred Gault's chapter provides a history of how innovation is measured and the components of innovation strategies (markets, people, activities, and public and international institutions). Gault identifies how innovation strategies inform policymaking as well as actions that can be taken to advance innovation. International organizations, such as the Organization for Economic Cooperation and Development (OECD), United Nations Educational, Scientific, and Cultural Organization (UNESCO), and New Partnership for Africa's Development (NEPAD) (all described in this chapter), facilitate this coordination and evaluation, which involves multiple dimensions such as the characteristics of the population, the history of the country, and the type of policy to be undertaken. Involving stakeholders at each stage of policymaking ensures the implementation of policies relevant to a country or a group of countries. International organizations provide assistance with coordination and evaluation, including the creation and analysis of survey data and case studies, the dissemination of these findings, and the formulation and review of policies. The ultimate goal of this support is to build a country's capacity "to identify, find, acquire, adapt, and adopt" knowledge and to incorporate this knowledge as an "indispensable component" to create and implement a science and technology innovation strategy.

All of these chapters have some mention of a system of science and innovation activities. Morgan's chapter describes the use of operations research tools for policy analysis. This is an important addition to the benefit-cost models and options models described in Freeman's chapter, the social network model alluded to in the chapter by Powell, Owen-Smith, and Smith-Doerr, the stakeholder analysis discussed in Sapolsky and Taylor's chapter, and the computational sociology model mentioned by Gero. Feller and Gault define the spaces of the science of science policy and the science of innovation policy, respectively. Taken together, these chapters outline the critical questions and emerging frameworks, tools, and data (both quantitative and qualitative) that are the mainstay of the science of science and innovation policy's community of practice.

Notes

1. Martin Weitzman, "On Diversity." *Quarterly Journal of Economics*, vol. 107, no. 2 (1992): 363–405.

2. Business model innovation is typically included in the definition as well.

Politics and the Science of Science Policy

3

Harvey M. Sapolsky and Mark Zachary Taylor

1. Introduction

Politics is the main obstacle to the development and application of a science of science policy (SOSP). Scientists and engineers need patrons. Government is the richest of all patrons but also the most difficult with which to deal. Several authors in this volume grieve the fact that those who want to plan research and development investments can control neither the level of government allocations nor their purpose. We argue that this is because governments support the advancement of science and technology (S&T) mostly through their support of specific missions such as defense or health, and it is the politics of these missions, and the many contextual goals of government, that determines the rate and direction of its research and development investments [1]. Governments can also affect the supply and demand conditions for science and technology outside of the budgetary process via regulatory regimes, anti-trust, taxes, standards, and so on. These politically imposed limits do not necessarily hinder rapid advances in knowledge or useful societal application or major innovation, but they do impede the quest for a science of science policy and the rational management of science and technology.

This chapter will describe the politics of government patronage of research and development activities, focusing on the main missions and searching for the guiding principles. It will also explain how political scientists theorize public support for, and opposition to, science and technology. The changing role of government in the face of globalization is part of this discussion. It begins, however, with a discussion of innovation and the politics that underlie the process of bringing significant change to society. In modern society, and most especially contemporary America, all claim to be promoters of innovation, seeing it as progress and primarily beneficial. But innovation always has costs and opponents among those who are to bear them. The success of the opponents relates very little to the outcome of a disinterested cost-benefit analysis of any given innovation, something that advocates of a science of science policy might favor, and much more to their ability to punch back politically. The opponents are not properly labeled the delayers of progress but, rather, the defenders of legitimate rights and interests. And contrary to popular perception, globalization is not decreasing these political dynamics but changing them, along with the role of government in S&T policy.

Finally, we should recognize that cross-national comparisons are useful, but only to a limited extent [2]. In the United States, the main governmental missions that science and technology serve are national security, health, economic prosperity, and safety and environmental regulation. Most other nations concentrate their S&T investments on economic development goals to the extent that they support research domestically, while free riding on the need for larger nations to tend to a broader array of public concerns. In fact no nation approaches anywhere near the investments the United States makes on either defense or health care research. We are truly the guardians of the global commons, invited or not [3].

2. The Politics of Innovation

Although specific definitions of "innovation" vary across scholars [4–9], most political scientists argue that innovation is not just creating something new, not just discovery or invention. Innovation requires at least the implementation of an idea, the placement into practice of something new. Following James Q. Wilson, however, we see innovation as involving more than implementing simple change [10]. Innovation is change that has significant impact on an organization's main tasks and personnel incentives. It changes the organization, what it does, and who leads it.

Take aircraft for an example. The U.S. Air Force believes in the centralized management of air power and is dominated at its highest levels by pilots, usually fighter or bomber pilots. A faster aircraft, one that has a longer range, or one that has a larger payload, generally, is not innovative because, such a craft, although an improvement, would likely do little to change significantly the doctrine of the Air Force. The switch to unmanned aircraft, however, would likely alter dramatically the Air Force's doctrine and hierarchy, even if it did not itself lead the innovation. The Air Force is already feeling the pressure of the U.S. Army's interest in unmanned craft for battlefield surveillance and its use of enlisted soldiers as unmanned system controllers. If the Army independently can see and target enemy forces far beyond the next hill, then the Air Force's combat role is threatened.

It is this aspect of innovation—change that threatens some groups and favors others—that is often ignored in discussions of the development of a science of science policy. Such threats are at the core of Joseph Schumpeter's insights into innovation. He called innovation "creative destruction," the killing off of the old by the new [11]. The destruction element is crucial for Schumpeter as it clears the path for the new. Airlines killed off intercity passenger railroads and ocean liners in the process of improving commercial and recreational travel. The premium people were willing to pay for faster travel gradually ate away alternative transport as airliner safety and comfort improved. Schumpeter's insight explains the opposition to innovation. The losers see their fate. Innovation may benefit society, but it has its victims, and these victims fight back.

Government is never the neutral observer in these upheavals but, rather, is pursued by both sides in the hope of gaining policy advantages in their mortal conflict [12–16]. These politics are often neglected by SOSP and innovation researchers, who tend to assume widespread support for progress in science and technology and then ask which types of policies will achieve the best results. Yet political resistance to technological change can obstruct or warp otherwise "good" S&T policy [17, 18]. Recent examples in the United States include resistance to nuclear power [19, 20], stem cell research [21], alternative energy [22, 23], HIV-safe blood products [24, 25], and even new weapons systems [26]. In each of these cases, the losing interest groups created by scientific or technological change were able to convince politicians to block, slow, or alter government support for scientific and technological progress. Therefore, in order to create a science of science policy, we also need to have an understanding of how domestic politics can affect the design, passage, and implementation of science and technology policy.

Science and technology change the power relations within a society by a variety of mechanisms, any of which can trigger political action to obstruct them. For example, sociologists and historians have focused on how new technologies can be designed to empower or disadvantage one social group over others [27],[1] or how science and technology can change the nature of human activity (in work, communications, war, etc.) and thereby fundamentally alter the roles or identities of the people performing these activities, and hence their social, economic, or political standing [28].[2]

Perhaps the most potent form of redistribution caused by S&T is economic. Technological innovation is economically distributive in that it allows people to perform entirely new activities or to perform established activities with increased efficiency. It therefore gives its adopters a competitive advantage by increasing their productivity or through factor accumulation. Perhaps more subtly, but equally important, new technology can also completely change the factor inputs to, and resource requirements for, various economic activities. In doing so, technological change can fundamentally alter the supply and demand conditions for these inputs and resources, increasing the value of some relative to others.

For example, the advent of steam-powered railroads changed the relative values of land, coal, lumber, and various metals and drastically increased the demand for engineering skills. The subsequent appearance of the internal combustion engine increased the value of oil relative to coal, while the rise of modern fuel-cell technologies may in the future decrease the value of both commodities as well as put a premium on hydrogen production and storage [29]. More famously, in the now stock cliché, the advent of the automobile destroyed the demand for products and services associated with the horse-and-buggy industries [30]. Further examples of the distributive nature of technological change can be cited ad nauseam; the point is that technological innovation creates winners and losers,[3] especially in the long run.

Exactly who are these "losers"? Depending on the form it takes and the economic and political environment in which it appears, technological change can threaten labor, corporations, consumers, governments, and so on. Losers can be skilled labor defending their jobs; owners of natural resources who seek to prevent their destruction or degradation; producers of competing technologies who seek to retain market share and profitability; consumers with large sunk costs in existing technologies; and even investors in stocks, bonds, or physical capital who seek to maximize their return on investment. But regardless of their individual characteristics, they are often holders of assets (skills, capital, land, resources, etc.) whose value will be hurt due to the effects of technological change on supply and demand conditions.

Moreover, these losers may seek to resist threatening scientific research or technological change by influencing or capturing government policy in order to slow or obstruct such change. Resisters can organize and use their financial or electoral clout to influence government to slow technological change via a range of mechanisms: taxes, tariffs, anti-trust litigation, licensing, standards setting and regulations, manipulation of guidelines for research, and so on.

Take, for example, the advent of modern shipping containers, which are a mixture of advanced transportation technologies and computer software. According to Marc Levinson's recent analysis, containerization drastically changed the demand for, and therefore the relative prices and incomes of, expensive inputs, especially dock labor [31]. Before containerization, the relatively short time that a ship spent at dock might account for three-quarters of its voyage costs [31]. During the 1960s, dockworkers understood this well and, realizing that containers threatened demand for their labor, organized against them. In some ports, labor opposition prevented containerization for years. Furthermore, not only were dock unions powerful but the major ports they dominated were a vital source of jobs and business for local economies and hence political support for state- and city-level politicians. Containerization at new or union-weak port facilities would eventually create competition, drawing work away from heavily unionized ports such as New York City and forcing compromises between container shippers and labor unions. However, labor resistance led to years of strikes and negotiations, eventually involving the Kennedy and Johnson administrations as well as Congress. This discouraged many shippers and ports from experimenting with containers, and bankrupting a few that did.

But labor was not alone. Fearing competition, the railroad corporations also fought containers into the 1970s, both legally, through regulatory bodies and legislative action, and illegally, through service disruptions and slow-downs for any customer using containers. Some railroads feared that containerization represented a redistribution of shipping to a technological mode in which they could not profitably compete. Other railroad interests resisted walking away from recent major investments into infrastructure for handling trucks and trailers, or expending yet more investment on container-friendly cranes and storage facilities. The costs of switching technology were just too high.

Hence the speed of innovation and diffusion of container shipping depended, in part, on political considerations. Around the world, those national and local governments able to compensate or coerce the losers saw their ports (e.g., Singapore, Shanghai, Los Angeles, Newark, Tilbury) and transportation firms (e.g., Sea-Land, Evergreen, Maersk) become leaders in modern container-based shipping, while governments unable to resolve political resistance to containers saw their ports shrink (e.g., London, Liverpool, New York) and corporations fall (e.g., Grace).

Which "losers" will act to resist new technology, and what determines the scope of resistance? Resistance is not simply a matter of labor groups or technophobes fighting progress but can also be a strategy pursued by corporations, scientists, or even the very interest groups an innovation is supposed to help [32].[4] One theory of resistance is based on asset specificity [33]. Those economic assets for which the costs of switching technologies (from established to new) are relatively high are said to be "specific" to a particular technology. Those assets for which the costs of switching technologies are relatively low are defined as "mobile." Factor specificity matters because if all economic actors were perfectly mobile between existing and new technologies then there would be no distributive effects: everyone would simply switch to the new technology when its return on investment (ROI) exceeded that of the existing technology. However, all actors are not equally mobile. For example, the skills of a nuclear engineer are more specific to the technology of nuclear power than, say, an Entergy Corporation[5] bond held by an investor. Hence, that investor might support new clean fuel innovation (such as windmills, tidal generators, solar power), since he can easily sell his bond and reinvest in the new technologies in order to receive the higher ROIs they promise. However, the engineer should be more likely to resist these new technologies, and to favor politicians and policies that support nuclear power, since her skills are tied to the fate of that technology. Thus the more mobile one's assets are relative to a particular existing technology, the less resistant and more supportive one will be to scientific and technological changes that threaten it. Conversely, the more specific one's assets are to an existing technology or scientific research program, the more resistant and less supportive one will be to changes that threaten it.

Culture, ideology, and religion also interact with economic interests to foment opposition to scientific research and technological change (e.g., computerized medical records, stem cells, genetically modified foods). As John Gero shows in Chapter 6, innovation threatens change in the value systems of both producers and adopters. For our purposes, this means that if the economic disruptions caused by technological change are linked to existing tensions between domestic identity groups (ethnic, religious, regional, etc.), then resistance to new technology can take on additional fervor due to the prior conflicts. For example, historically the economic "losers" created by innovations in birth control technologies over the past two centuries have generally consisted of physicians who sought to prevent nonprofessional medical providers from entering their markets. While the physicians could possibly have obstructed these innovations alone, their political resistance was considerably strengthened by alliances with religious and other groups that felt culturally threatened by contraception [34]. Likewise, current political debates about contraceptive technologies, and the medical research to develop them, are built upon religious, racial, and generational divides and their conflicting value systems.

The politics of distribution alone does not determine national innovation rates. Such logic would suggest that national innovation rates are simply a result of cost-benefit calculation: the more "losers" created by technological change, and the deeper the losses, the more political resistance should occur, and the slower innovation rates should be. But this is not always the case. There are many instances of minor technological change that have been thwarted by a handful of "losers" and many instances of major technological revolutions that proceeded despite massive economic, political, and even cultural displacements. Therefore, political scientists have begun to incorporate security concerns into their theories of science and technology, especially when explaining S&T competitiveness in other nations. Specifically, only when policymakers need to simultaneously address external security threats and domestic political pressures, but lack easily accessible resources with which to do so, will they be forced to promote S&T policies as a means to grow the national economy out of trouble [35]. Likewise, inward-oriented leaders who resist integration into the global economy tend to put national S&T development on a heavily military, especially nuclear, trajectory. In contrast, more internationalist leaders stake their political survival on economic growth and will orient national S&T policies toward the civilian economy [36].

Finally, although much of this section has focused on the resistance to technological change, scholarship on interest groups using politics to interfere in the "science" side of S&T is equally substantial, stretching back at least forty years, but it is often ignored in SOSP-style research. Science is regularly created and customized to fit the goals of particular industries or interest groups, with scientific studies designed to confirm preselected outcomes. These studies are then presented to regulatory bodies, courts, and legislators as evidence in support of favorable actions. Meanwhile, unfavorable science is often buried, diluted, or modified, sometimes by the very government agencies tasked with producing it. The credibility of unpopular research, or even of the scientists who produce it, is frequently attacked for purely political reasons. This occurs not merely in media statements but through legislative hearings and threats of costly, time-consuming lawsuits. One well-known tactic is for politicians to pack federal science advisory panels with experts loyal to particular economic interests or specific political ideologies. Examples of the aforementioned can be found across the scientific spectrum, in the cases of tobacco, asbestos, silicon breast implants, climate change, stem cell research, alar, genetically modified organisms, and myriad medicines and environmental contaminants [37–45].

3. Getting Beyond Opposition

Innovation does occur. Opposition can be overcome, but the process isn't always a pretty one. Politics often involves what science must abhor, although scientists may not—the manipulation of the truth. Consider how big projects may start. Albert Hirschman reviewed a large set of overseas economic development projects, most of which failed to achieve their goals. He wondered how they were approved in the first place and discovered a persistent pattern of proponents exaggerating the likely benefits and underestimating the likely costs [46]. Hirschman later compared economic assistance projects with research and development projects and observed the same pattern [46]. The way to needed resources is by overpromising. This is clearly the case in major aerospace programs such as strategic bombers [47], the Shuttle [48], and ballistic missiles [49].

The break on exaggeration is the development of knowledgeable staffs. Successful organizations, ones noted for their innovations, rarely stay innovative. As Clayton Christensen reports in his study of computer electronics, *The Innovator's Dilemma*, innovators hire staffs who then block future innovation because they worry over its costs and effects on current business [50]. The better the staffs, the more likely the exaggerations will be caught. In government, project overruns and schedule slippage, the constant companion of risk taking, are followed by demands for the insertion of independent evaluators, cost estimators, and testers into the government's decision-making process so that these errors will not be repeated.

James Q. Wilson captures well what we might call the "Science Policy Planner's Dilemma" in his analysis of organizational innovation. You can, he argues, increase the capacity of an organization to generate innovative ideas by increasing the diversity of organization as measured in terms of the variety of different professions it employs. Different specialists have different perspectives on the organization's tasks and needs. Wilson next argues that the more diverse the organization is, the more likely proposals for innovation will be presented. Fearing disadvantage, subunits seeing others offer ideas for change will offer their own proposals for change. But diversity has the opposite effect on the ability of the organization to implement innovation. Diversity in terms of tasks and incentives increases organizational decentralization and makes decision making very slow and difficult. Wilson studied city administrations. The nondiverse Chicago machine encouraged few proposals but could make binding decisions as the powerful mayor controlled all relevant agencies and boards. In New York City the mayor is relatively weak, but the many independent agencies and departments had many suggestions about how to improve government while advantaging their own programs. Decentralization, the complement of organization task and incentive diversity, promotes the presentation of innovative ideas but frustrates the adoption of innovation. Centralization does the opposite [10].

Science policy often increases creativity through its advocacy of research funding and the establishment of interdisciplinary centers but usually offers little encouragement to the centralization that aids implementation. Research agencies, most attached to mission-focused departments, proliferated in the United States after the Second World War, as science gained in public stature because of the wartime contributions of scientists, especially those associated with the Manhattan Project [51]. The support for science, though, was made vulnerable to the demands for greater mission accomplishments.

Comparing the experience of government research agencies, Sanford L. Weiner saw the potential for an innovation advantage, however, in the mission link. The agencies that did best in terms of both gaining resources for their grantees and producing science had what he described as "constrained autonomy" [52]. They were under pressure from their departments for mission-relevant results but had sufficient autonomy to develop ideas to the point at which their value was obvious. Autonomy bought time but did not remove the pressure for results, the fear that unless they produced there would be reorganization or termination. The less protected had no time to produce, and the most protected succumbed to the somnolent dangers of tenure.

Still, there is a difference between producing interesting ideas and generating significant innovations. The research agencies that had constrained autonomy may be the most productive, but innovation requires paying an organizational price, the destruction of part of the organization to allow replacement by the new. A clear way of seeing the politics involved is to examine the three main theories of military innovation.

One theory argues that because innovation is so painful, it has to be imposed from outside. The leadership of military organizations is drawn from the dominant communities within the service and is committed to particular doctrines—ways of employing forces built around those communities, often called platform communities because of their link to a special type of aircraft, ship, or weapon system. Their resistance to change in doctrine that would undermine the dominance of their platform community is well known if not entirely accurate, for example, the battleship admirals' supposed resistance to carrier strike aviation. Civilian officials are usually uncomfortable in interfering with military priorities, but faced with waging war with what they perceive to be a faulty doctrine, they will intervene to select a better one. The specific example that Barry Posen offers is the British government's decision on the eve of the Second World War to force the Royal Air Force to build an air defense system rather than pursue its preferred strategic bombing doctrine [4].

A second, contrasting view comes from Stephen P. Rosen, who argues that military innovation is a long, generational process in which junior officers see the need for innovation but require patrons to survive until they reach the senior ranks of their service to bring about true doctrinal change. Civilian intervention is largely useless. The pace of change is slow as organizational opportunities and allies are won and lost in a struggle to define the service's future. He finds supporting examples in the years between the First World War and Second World War, when carrier aviation and amphibious warfare were developed [8].

A third theoretical perspective on military innovation is offered by Owen Cote Jr., and one of us [53–55]. It argues that interservice rivalry is the driver of military innovation in the United States. The services in this view are indeed dominated by particular platform communities, but they also worry about their relative position in warfare. If a new technology appears or a major strategic threat develops, then the services will compete to gain advantage in the nation's defense. This perspective is a synthetic one, because it depends in part on a willingness of civilians to encourage the competition, which can be intense, and offers service leaders a powerful incentive to accelerate the advancement of new concepts internally. Dire circumstances, such as an approaching war, certainly can force civilian leaders to accept the degree of governmental disarray that interservice competition involves and service leaders to do the same within their organizations. The cold war offers examples of the power of interservice competition in the development of ballistic missiles and strategic defenses. Despite recent attempts to limit service competition via structural changes within the Department of Defense favoring joint activities both in the field and in acquisitions, the development of unmanned aerial systems seems to have benefited from the quest of individual services to control their own combat operations in Iraq and Afghanistan.

What is evolutionary at best, the acceptance by an organization of new ideas and an accompanying realignment of power within the organization, can get accelerated only with upheaval. Outsiders must intervene in the most important parts of the organization—its doctrine and power relationships—or organizations must be pitted against one another in a struggle for budget and prominence. Ballistic missile innovation essentially killed off the air force's bomber force and brought submarine officers, accounting for less than 10 percent of naval officers, to the top rungs of the navy. Planning usually gets pushed aside by the politics. Once again, the desirability of change is not viewed equally by all those involved, and some will fight to protect their interests.

4. Government Patronage of R&D

A fundamental need of planners is to set priorities, to choose some goals consistently over others in allocating scarce resources. As William B. Bonvillian and David Goldston detail in Chapters 15 and 16, respectively, politics is the process of setting priorities in the allocation of public resources and rarely involves a deep concern about consistency or scarcity. Science policy planners presumably would want to consider the resources available across government in developing their research investment plans to gain the greatest societal benefits. Sector politics has Balkanized research allocations, ignored assertions of societal priorities, and has no patience with the prescriptions of planners and yet likely offers science more resources and thus better opportunities for major advances than planners' fondest hopes.

The search for patrons leads to promises about the practical value of the work to be done. Public patrons, like private ones, can be convinced of the need to advance basic knowledge and of the prestige that goes with supporting the best in their fields, but mostly there is a desire to solve immediate problems or aid in the development of the local economy. Thus the first federal research grant was to help in the regulation of steam engines, which had a habit of exploding, and the earliest federal effort to aid higher education, the Land Grant Act, produced a lot of colleges and universities with technology, agriculture, mining, and industry in their names [56, 57].

Given dramatic examples of technology-based prosperity, such as Silicon Valley, the Research Triangle, and Route 128, modern governments are easily convinced of the economic rewards of increased research investments. But the task of selecting which locations and industries to support is one that strains governments. The pressure to assist declining regions or fading industries often overwhelms the intent to be strategic with research investments. The investments then become less of a stimulus to economic growth and more of a subsidy seeking to stabilize or preserve the places and firms slated for a Schumpeterian demise.

Defense has been an even greater source of support for research investments than economic development. Much of the interest has been a steady increase in the application of science and technology to warfare that has gradually changed the nature of warfare from a professional enterprise to an industrial undertaking to its current high-technology version.[6] Major punctuations in this chain are the U.S. Civil War reinforced by the First World War, which demonstrated the advantages of mass armies and industrialization, the Second World War, which included on the Allied side at least a full mobilization of science for warfare, and the cold war, which centered on an arms race involving jet aircraft, nuclear weapons, ballistic missiles, and nuclear-powered submarines and saw in the United States the development of systems engineering capabilities in both defense contracting firms and specialized not-for-profit organizations dedicated to serve public needs [58].

The latter organizations, which include the major national laboratories of the Department of Energy and the Federally Funded Research and Development Centers (FFRDCs), for example, Lincoln Laboratory, MITRE Corporation, and Aerospace Corporation, supported by the Department of Defense, have played a crucial role in the cold war by providing the government with a source of independent advice and technical assistance in managing the development of vital strategic systems. The federal government's own defense research facilities grew during the cold war, but most of the effort to develop and produce weapons became increasingly concentrated in the hands of defense contractors who were flexible in structure and could attract better technical talent because of being able to offer higher salaries than the civil service schedule. The FFRDCs and similar organizations became the government's check on the contractors because of their higher status (many were affiliated with universities), competitive salaries, and independence [59].

Through agencies like the Office of Naval Research, the Department of Defense pioneered federal support of academic science. This support helped place U.S. universities at the top of the international rankings in science and engineering. The allocations that favored a few universities on both coasts of the United States were the source of concern for congressmen and senators from other regions who thought correctly that their institutions would not share in the largesse offered by the Department of Defense [60]. Military claims about the need to use the most qualified researchers allowed for the concentration of defense agency research investments in just a handful of East Coast and West Coast elite institutions. Over time, however, the normal geographic equity pressures built into democratic politics led to the enactment of programs in the National Science Foundation and other civilian agencies to assist less endowed regions by earmarking laboratory construction and research support to develop new science and engineering capabilities. Moreover, defense contractors seeking to ensure strong congressional interest in their projects tended to favor states in these regions for the location of development and production facilities.

Even after the end of the cold war, America has maintained high levels of defense expenditures. Much more than any ally or rival, the United States emphasizes investment in advanced military technologies in its defense strategy. Consider that total U.S. defense expenditures are essentially equal that of the rest of world combined, but total U.S. defense research and development expenditures are several times larger than the rest of the world's total. And this level of research and development investment has been near constant for more than a half century. Although the use of off-the-shelf technology, applying commercial advances, is increasingly significant in warfare, the military advantages the United States has acquired through emphasizing defense research and development are difficult to negate [61].

Continuing privatization, encouraged on a bipartisan basis since the end of the cold war, however, has created rather inflexible dependencies. The government has lost much of its technical and management capabilities for building complex systems to private contractors, which are in turn nearly totally dependent upon the government for their revenues. The checks and balances that FFRDCs and similar organizations provided weaken as public management weakens. The dependencies are most visible in the creation of Lead System Integrators, contractors managing networks of other contractors and being responsible for nearly all aspects of program design and acquisition for several major public programs, which isolates research and development planning efforts almost totally from the broad societal concerns advocated by science policy planners and intertwines it instead with private interests. Lockheed Martin or Boeing, or some partnership between them, becomes the manager of big chunks of public research and development activities [62].

Health care research also has a powerful draw on federal funds. We are as individuals all time limited in a fundamental sense for death will do us part. Through some combination of our genes, our bad habits and misjudgments, and/or the actions of others, we will discover the precise limit that awaits us. Our relatively affluent and increasingly democratic government responds with more and more investments in medical and related research to our obvious unwillingness to accept our fate, seeking both to extend our time and make it as pain free and unencumbered as possible. There is essentially no definable limit to these investments. Like in defense, technology promises victory in our quest, but unlike in defense, it cannot deliver. The truth notwithstanding, we cannot resist the promise.

Spending on medical research is politically buttressed in several ways. One way is through the pressure for national health insurance. Americans have been debating the structure of their national health care system for nearly a century. The debate became more intense after the Second World War, when Democrats sought to enact a national health insurance scheme as the unfinished element in a social welfare agenda that President Franklin Delano Roosevelt had offered during the Great Depression. To defuse the political pressure that had been building for such a scheme, Republicans pressed for increased allocations to the budget of the National Institutes of Health based on the argument that medical research was the best insurance scheme of them all. Better knowledge of the causes and cures for disease would be better than more money for inadequate treatments [63]. Ever since then the major political parties have competed to provide increased resources for medical research as a demonstration of their party's better stewardship of the nation's health.[7]

Geography also works to advantage medical research. Medical schools have a large research focus not unlike the nation's research universities to which many are affiliated, but unlike the research universities, high-quality medical schools are spread relatively evenly with the population across the nation. High-quality medical schools are not concentrated in the Northeast or on the West Coast. Rather, they tend to closely follow the distribution of the population, because both physician training and medical research need what is euphemistically called "clinical material," patients well, ill, and dying. State legislatures easily are persuaded to support local medical training in the hope of gaining quality medical care locally. Medical research is viewed as a marker for quality, thus the marketing advantage of teaching hospitals with large specialty research and training programs.

A third political impetus for medical research funding is the lobbying efforts of disease advocacy groups that seek special recognition and increased funding for work that appears focused on their affliction. Congressional appropriations for medical research are made by disease or patient category rather than by scientific discipline. The political judgment is that the crusade to conquer breast cancer or AIDS deserves more support, not the promise of immunology or endocrinology. Despite the perhaps perfunctory protest of research managers, the National Institutes of Health has dozens of institutes and centers devoted to one special cause or another, with more being continually added [64]. Public fears likely increase overall support for medical research by ensuring a continuing contest for preferred attention among disease and victims. The stealthy redirection of the funds for actual scientific progress becomes the prime task of medical research managers [64].

The politicization of science has a fourth front—what is often called regulatory science, the effort to ensure the safety and efficacy of products. The government that once worried about the safety of steam boilers now worries about the safety of automobiles and electrical transmissions networks. We require tests of drugs to see if they work as promised and examine workplaces to determine if hazardous materials are properly used and stored. Behind this and much more, regulation is a large research effort that is partially mandated and partially the result of legal prudence to avoid product safety suits.

Regulatory science is problematic because it is often very difficult to describe the exposures and risks involved. Substances that are toxic at high levels of exposure may require exposure beyond certain threshold levels to have health implications. It is difficult to develop accurate models. What is toxic for one species may be harmless for another. What kills laboratory mice may not kill laboratory rats. Impacts may involve long gestation periods. Individual lifetime exposure levels may be very hard to measure, especially for substances that appear in low doses. Scientists chip away at these problems but never fast enough for regulators who are required at times to make society-affecting decisions with the limited evidence at hand.

Given the significant economic and ideological interests involved, the temptation is to claim that the science supports what are necessarily political judgments. Limited evidence means wide regulatory discretion that becomes politically palatable only through exaggeration or politicization. Consider sidestream smoking, for example. The overwhelming evidence that cigarette smoking causes high mortality and morbidity, publicized by public health officials, produced major reductions in smoking among Americans, reducing adult levels of smoking from nearly 50 percent in the 1950s to the low 30s in the 1980s. The remaining smokers were apparently undeterred. Public health officials then began promoting studies that seemed to show that nonsmokers, especially spouses and children of smokers, had adverse health effects from their exposure to sidestream smoke, creating further pressure on smokers to quit and greater regulatory opportunity to force them to do so. Nonsmokers, fearing the risks, have supported widespread bans on smoking in public. Smoking dropped to around 20 percent of the adult population and recruited fewer and fewer teenagers. It still remained difficult to measure exposure level or health effects of sidestream smoking, but few scientists dare object [65–67]. Parallels exist with the regulation of asbestos, lead, some food additives, and various pesticides [68].

5. Globalization, Fragmentation, and the Role of Government

Political economists argue that globalization has fundamentally altered the ways in which governments must approach S&T policy. Much like the sociological approach discussed in Chapter 4, these scholars are concerned with power and institutions; but political scientists tend to focus on institutions (and policies) with more formal structures than those considered by sociologists, such as the institutions that comprise a nation's strategy for economic development. Interestingly, they tend to agree with sociologists that networks play a major role in determining S&T success. Also, contrary to the conventional wisdom that ever-larger international markets are shrinking government options, they find that globalization has instead increased policy choices by fragmenting production processes (aka the supply-chain or value-chain) into dozens of pieces for any given industry or even a product line. Hence, nations seeking to compete in high-technology production must choose not only which industry but also which entry point on which to compete [7, 69–72]. Therefore, governments must alter their traditional top-down approach toward S&T and instead coordinate with other S&T relevant actors to customize policy with an eye toward selecting which kinds of activities their firms will compete on, not which industries.

Globalization can be defined as the "increasingly freer movement of goods, services, labor, capital, [and information] across borders, towards a single market in inputs and outputs" [73]. Science and technology have enabled globalization, but politics and competition drive it. During the 1990s, both proponents and critics argued that globalization severely weakened government's ability to make effective S&T, or any, policies. They hypothesized that competitive market forces would drive governments out of the business of managing their own economies, or at least narrow the policy choices available to them. Indeed, even in the government's traditional sphere of defense, civilian science and technology seemed to be taking the lead [61]. Proponents cheered these developments, arguing that economic actors were now forced to embrace innovation in order to compete. Critics decried the freer reign being taken by large Western corporations to dominate the production of new science and technology, against whom small, new, or developing innovators could never compete.

However, recent research in political economy has shown that neither scenario is occurring [7, 71, 74]. Globalization is changing the role of government in science and technology and is increasing, not diminishing or constraining, its choices. Nor can nations performing at the technological frontier comfortably assume away competitive threats from new innovators in developing or small countries. Globalization has radically transformed national approaches toward science and technology by fragmenting industrial production. Countries, and even subnational regions, now specialize not in particular high-tech industries but in particular stages of high-tech production [75]. New product innovations are now sourced globally, allowing firms and policymakers to choose which mode of innovation will provide them with the greatest competitive advantage.

Take, for example, Apple's iPhone. Its central processors and video chips are manufactured by Samsung in Singapore, where the German firm Infineon also produces the iPhone's communication hardware. Meanwhile, much of the iPhone circuitry is designed and manufactured by several companies in Taiwan, where its digital camera hardware is also produced. U.S. firms domestically produce the touch-screen controllers and 802.11 wireless specific parts, while manufacturers in Japan and Germany provide further touch-screen and base-band technologies. Finally, Apple's facility in Shenzhen, China, handles assembly, inventory, packing, and shipping [76, 77].

The role of government has therefore changed. During the previous century, successful science and technology policy often meant one of two approaches: one for developing countries and another for lead innovators. For developing countries, it meant patriarchal technocrats picking winners in the style of Japan's technological miracle. This "catch-up" path was fairly straightforward: first, imitation of basic Western manufacturing products and processes, followed by the use of economies of scope and scale to slowly climb up the value chain. The key policy prescriptions were heavy S&T education, subsidized finance, reverse engineering, joint ventures, technology licensing, inward foreign direct investment (FDI), and, above all, export orientation [78–80]. However, this policy strategy assumed an economy of vertically integrated industries producing a relatively stable set of products, preferably located in the same country, if not the same metropolitan area. Globalization has changed this dynamic.

Instead, in order to succeed at science and technology, governments in developing countries must now act more like management consultants. They must become more adaptable, acting as needed to facilitate long-term commitments to high-technology industries, not as custodians or commanders. On the one hand, this means that successful S&T policymakers in the developing world must be willing to delegate increasing degrees of decision-making power to industry as it grows and matures. On the other hand, state action is still necessary. As Breznitz puts it "states . . . should not wait idly hoping that the miraculous power of the market will throw some economic growth their way" [7]. Specifically, the state must foster national capacities in financial and human capital, not just in S&T but also among the technocrats who devise and implement policy.

For lead innovating nations, during the past century the keys to successful science and high-tech were either defense innovation or civilian national champions. In the United States, national security concerns motivated massive R&D investments, which laid the foundations for the American aircraft, digital computer, software, telecommunications, and satellite industries, to name but a few. Some technologies were driven forward for military reasons and then later realized substantial commercial applications. In other cases, the military was a useful justification to win resources for R&D that was essentially commercial or academic in focus. Meanwhile, in Europe and Japan, companies such as Airbus, Mitsubishi, and Siemens endured as high-tech competitors under the aegis of government largesse and protection [81–86].

But tendencies toward pork-barrel politics, technological monopolies, and national control of particular global S&T markets now threaten twentieth-century policy strategies. Therefore, in order to maintain their nations at the technological frontier, political scientists argue that policymakers in advanced countries must foster technological modularity: the ability of different technologies to interoperate with each other (like Lego blocks), regardless of their manufacturer, internal structure, or capabilities [87]. Modularity encourages innovation in individual technologies (e.g., cell phones, computers, software) without the natural tendency toward monopoly control and the stagnation that attends it. Modularity reinforces competition, but it also demands rules that balance globalization efficiencies with legitimate domestic preferences. Hence, both domestic commercial and international trade policy should foster localism, pluralism, and diversity, as long as interoperability with national and global technical infrastructures is maintained. The emphasis here is on flexibility and allowance for hybrid solutions. Finally, a focus on promoting modularity requires that policymakers focus on strengthening technological infrastructure (e.g., computer networks, genetic libraries, electrical grids) and enhancing ubiquity of access.

A further consensus among many political economists is that for the United States to have a high-tech entrepreneurial society, policymakers need go beyond S&T policy and engineer broader political-economic conditions [88]. First, policymakers must establish low barriers to entry and exit for firms. This requires a strong and stable financial system in order to provide investment capital to new firms. But it also requires flexible labor markets, since new high-technology firms cannot survive long if the capital and S&T labor they need are tied up in obsolete sectors supported by political benefactors. In other words, freedom to succeed is conditional on freedom to fail. Second, institutions must reward high-tech entrepreneurial activity and discourage nonproductive entrepreneurship, or rent seeking (i.e., criminal behavior, frivolous litigation, lobbying, and political transfers). This means designing policies and institutions that will reduce the "losers" to technological change by either preventing, coercing, or compensating them. Third, there must be incentives for the technological "winners" to keep innovating—low barriers to entry, openness to foreign competition, a competitive market system at home, and strong anti-trust laws. Otherwise, today's innovative victors merely mature to become tomorrow's innovation-resistant losers.

Finally, historical experience suggests that politicians and policymakers need to support an environment that blends larger firms and small entrepreneurial companies. Larger firms have consistently demonstrated their ability to replicate, refine, and mass-produce inventions, but they can be stultifying and run out of ideas over time (often due to labor resistance). Moreover, large firms have historically not excelled at producing the radical innovations that create new high-tech industries. Rather, this appears to be the competitive advantage of small entrepreneurial companies, which have a history of producing radical innovations with huge positive externalities [88].

6. Conclusions

Throughout this volume, practitioners and scholars alike look forward to the day when SOSP scholarship will aid in the design of policies by which investments in scientific research and technological development can produce broad societal advances. Ironically, the efforts to implement such S&T policies will likely be opposed by significant numbers of scientists and engineers who surely recognize that the decentralized, interest-driven, mission-based system that currently generates most of the funds for government-sponsored research in the United States is quite generous.

To be sure, there are prices to pay for this support. Failing industries gain more attention than some might want. Defense-related topics are especially well funded. Medical researchers link their work to specific diseases, even when links are remote. Threats of all types, from foreign challenges to the wrath of nature for our wasteful ways, are exaggerated and converted into support for more research and laboratory equipment. And the truth is not always told, especially when it contradicts positions popular with influential groups. But without the costs, the benefits likely would be smaller than they are today.

Even basic research, which feeds on our desire to learn the fundamental principles of our existence, claims the cloak of the practical. The National Science Foundation now promises national prosperity and did best in terms of budget growth in the national response to Sputnik [60]. The Department of Energy supports physicists who hint about the possible path to the next bomb when they seek the funds to construct a new physics machine and climatologists who warn darkly about the need for changes in energy consumption as they attempt to build ever-more accurate models of climate effects. And as we pointed out, the National Institutes of Health is cluttered with special programs for this or that cause, despite the common desire to advance basic knowledge.

Science policy specialists want also to serve national missions. The science they want to develop is intended to be more productive, offering efficient investments in the advancement of science and technology for society's benefit. With careful analysis, we can learn about ways to simulate best the pace and direction of new knowledge. We can reap collectively the results of the long-term investment in science.

But more likely scientists themselves will prefer to gain their money the old-fashioned way. The scares about Soviet nuclear weapons buildups, Japan's competition, energy shortages, and the rise of China got those billions. What about the global warming crisis, the aging of America, the rise of India, and our continuing decline in manufacturing? Surely a fearful patron is a generous one. We are always on some edge [89]. Thus while SOSP analysis may proceed briskly, the practical applications of a science of science policy may be slow to be adopted and at times stoutly opposed.

References

[1] H. M. Sapolsky. The Truly Endless Frontier. Technology Review (00401692), 98;1995;37.

[2] I. Spiegel-Rosing, D. de Solla Price. Science, Technology and Society: A Cross-Disciplinary Perspective. London: Sage Publications; 1976.

[3] B. R. Posen. Command of the Commons: The Military Foundation of U.S. Hegemony. International Security, 28;2003;5–46.

[4] B. R. Posen. The Sources of Military Doctrine: France, Britain and Germany Between the World Wars. Ithaca (NY): Cornell University Press; 1984.

[5] D. Doner. The Politics of Uneven Development: Thailand's Economic Growth in Comparative Perspective. New York: Cambridge University Press; 2009.

[6] M. Z. Taylor. Empirical Evidence Against Varieties of Capitalism's Theory of Technological Innovation. International Organization, 58;2004;601–631.

[7] D. Breznitz. Innovation and the State: Political Choice and Strategies for Growth in Israel, Taiwan, and Ireland. New Haven (CT), London: Yale University Press; 2007.

[8] S. P. Rosen. Winning the Next War: Innovation and the Modern Military. Ithaca (NY): Cornell University Press; 1991.

[9] H. Sapolsky, B. H. Friedman, B. Rittenhouse. US Military Innovation Since the Cold War: Creation Without Destruction. London, New York: Routledge; 2009.

[10] J. Q. Wilson. Notes Toward a Theory of Innovation. In: J. D. Thompson (Ed.), Organizational Design and Research: Approaches to Organizational Design. Pittsburgh (PA): University of Pittsburgh Press; 1971.

[11] J. A. Schumpeter. Capitalism, Socialism and Democracy. New York: Harper; 1942.

[12] J. Mokyr. Technological Inertia in Economic History. The Journal of Economic History, 52;1992;325–338.

[13] S. L. Parente, E. C. Prescott. Barriers to Technology Adoption and Development. The Journal of Political Economy, 102;1994;298–321.

[14] P. Krusell, J. -V. Ríos-Rull. Vested Interests in a Positive Theory of Stagnation and Growth. The Review of Economic Studies, 63;1996;301–329.

[15] D. Comin, B. Hobijn. Lobbies and Technology Diffusion. Review of Economics and Statistics, 91;2009;229–244.

[16] D. Acemoglu, J. A. Robinson. Political Losers as a Barrier to Economic Development. The American Economic Review, 90;2000;126–130.

[17] M. W. Bauer. Resistance to New Technology: Nuclear Power, Information Technology and Biotechnology. Cambridge: Cambridge University Press; 1995.

[18] L. Cohen, R. Noll. The Technology Pork Barrel. Washington (DC): Brookings Institution; 1991.

[19] K. A. Rogers, M. G. Kingsley. Calculated Risks: Highly Radioactive Waste and Homeland Security. Burlington (VT): Ashgate Publishing; 2007.

[20] R. J. Duffy. Nuclear Politics in America: A History and Theory of Government Regulation. Lawrence: University Press of Kansas; 1997.

[21] T. Banchoff. Path Dependence and Value-Driven Issues: The Comparative Politics of Stem Cell Research. World Politics, 57;2005;200–230.

[22] R. Hahn, C. Cecot. The Benefits and Costs of Ethanol: An Evaluation of the Government's Analysis. Journal of Regulatory Economics, 35;2009;275–295.

[23] G. Gamboa, G. Munda. The Problem of Windfarm Location: A Social Multicriteria Evaluation Framework. Energy Policy, 35;2007;1564–1583.

[24] S. Epstein. Impure Science: AIDS, Activism, and the Politics of Knowledge. Berkeley: University of California Press; 1996.

[25] M. Z. Taylor. Federalism and Technological Change in Blood Products. Journal of Health Politics Policy and Law, 34;2009;863–898.

[26] J. Sweezy, A. Long. From Concept to Combat: Tomahawk Cruise Missile Program History and Reference Guide, 1972–2004. Patuxent River (MD): Naval Air Systems Command; 2005.

[27] R. A. Caro. The Power Broker: Robert Moses and the Fall of New York. New York: Vintage Press; 1974.

[28] R. S. Cowan. More Work for Mother: The Ironies of Household Technology from the Open Hearth to the Microwave. New York: Basic Books; 1983.

[29] D. R. Beasley. The Suppression of the Automobile: Skulduggery at the Crossroads. New York: Greenwood Press; 1988.

[30] T. A. Kinney. The Carriage Trade: Making Horse-Drawn Vehicles in America. Baltimore (MD): Johns Hopkins University Press; 2004.

[31] M. Levinson. The Box: How the Shipping Container Made the World Smaller and the World Economy Bigger. Princeton (NJ): Princeton University Press; 2006.

[32] R. Shilts. And the Band Played On: Politics, People, and the AIDS Epidemic. New York: St. Martin's Press; 1987.

[33] J. Mokyr. The Lever of Riches: Technological Creativity and Economic Progress. New York: Oxford University Press; 1990.

[34] L. Gordon. Woman's Body, Woman's Right: A Social History of Birth Control in America. New York: Penguin Press; 1990.

[35] R. F. Doner, B. K. Ritchie, D. Slater. Systemic Vulnerability and the Origins of Developmental States: Northeast and Southeast Asia in Comparative Perspective. International Organization, 59;2005;327–361.

[36] E. Solingen. Nuclear Logics: Contrasting Paths in East Asia and the Middle East. Princeton (NJ): Princeton University Press; 2007.

[37] S. Epstein. Inclusion: The Politics of Difference in Medical Research. Chicago: University of Chicago Press; 2007.

[38] D. Greenberg. The Politics of Pure Science. New York: New American Library; 1967.

[39] R. Bell, R. L. Park. Impure Science: Fraud, Compromise and Political Influence in Scientific Research. Physics Today, 45;1992;90–92.

[40] S. Milloy, M. Gough. Silencing Silence. Washington (DC): Cato Institute; 1999.

[41] M. Nestle. Food Politics: How the Food Industry Influences Nutrition and Health. Berkeley: University of California Press; 2002.

[42] W. Wagner, R. Steinzor. Rescuing Science from Politics: Regulation and the Distortion of Scientific Research. Cambridge: Cambridge University Press; 2006.

[43] K. F. Greif, J. F. Merz. Current Controversies in the Biological Sciences. Cambridge (MA): MIT Press; 2007.

[44] T. O. McGarity, W. E. Wagner. Bending Science: How Special Interests Corrupt Public Health Research. Cambridge (MA): Harvard University Press; 2008.

[45] R. Paarlberg. Starved for Science: How Biotechnology Is Being Kept Out of Africa. Cambridge (MA): Harvard University Press; 2009.

[46] A. O. Hirschman. Development Projects Observed. Washington (DC): The Brookings Institution; 1967.

[47] M. Brown. Flying: The Politics of the U.S. Strategic Bomber Program. Ithaca (NY): Cornell University Press; 1992.

[48] J. G. Mahler. Learning at NASA: The Challenger & Columbia Accidents. Washington (DC): Georgetown University Press; 2009.

[49] H. Sapolsky. Polaris System Development: Bureaucratic and Programmatic Success in Government. Cambridge (MA): Harvard University Press; 1972.

[50] C. M. Christensen. The Innovator's Dilemma: When New Technologies Cause Great Firms to Fail. Boston (MA): Harvard Business School Press; 1997.

[51] H. Sapolsky. Science and the Navy: The History of the Office of Naval Research. Princeton (NJ): Princeton University Press; 1990.

[52] S. L. Weiner. Resource Allocation in Basic Research and Organizational Design. Public Policy, 20;1972;227–255.

[53] H. Sapolsky. On the Theory of Military Innovation, Breakthroughs, IX;1;Spring 2000;35–39.

[54] J. O. Cote. The Politics of Innovative Military Doctrine. Cambridge: Massachusetts Institute of Technology; 1996.

[55] H. Sapolsky. The Interservice Competition Solution. Joint Forces Quarterly, Spring 1996.

[56] H. DuPree. Science in the Federal Government. New York: Harper Torchbooks; 1957.

[57] H. S. Miller. Dollars for Research. Seattle: University of Washington; 1970.

[58] H. Sapolsky. Inventing Systems Integration. In: A. Prencipe, A. Davies (Eds.), The Business of Systems Management. Oxford: Oxford University Press; 2003, pp. 15–34.

[59] E. Gholz. Systems Integration in the US Defense Industry: Who Does It and Why Is It Important. In: A. Prencipe, A. Davies (Eds.), The Business of Systems Management. Oxford: Oxford University Press; 2003, pp. 279–306.

[60] H. Sapolsky. Science and the Navy: The History of the Office of Naval Research. Princeton (NJ): Princeton University Press; 1991.

[61] P. Dombrowski, E. Gholz. Buying Military Transformation: Technological Innovation and the Defense Industry. New York: Columbia University Press; 2006.

[62] G. Ben-Ari, P. A. Chao. Organizing for a Complex World: Developing Tomorrow's Defense and Net-Centric Systems. Washington (DC): Center for Strategic & International Studies; 2009.

[63] S. P. Strickland. Politics, Science and Dread Disease: A Short History of United States Medical Research Policy. Cambridge (MA): Harvard University Press; 1972.

[64] H. Varmus. The Art and Politics of Science. New York: W. W. Norton; 2009.

[65] H. Sapolsky. Consuming Fears: The Politics of Product Risks. New York: Basic Books; 1986.

[66] W. K. Viscusi. Secondhand Smoke: Fact and Fantasy. Regulation, 3;1995;42–49.

[67] M. Angell. Science on Trial: The Clash of Medical Evidence and the Law in the Breast Implant Case. New York: W. W. Norton; 1996.

[68] M. Gough. Agent Orange: The Facts. New York: Plenum Press; 1986.

[69] D. Breznitz and M. Murphree. The Run of the Red Queen: Government, Innovation, Globalization, and Economic Growth in China. New Haven (CT): Yale University Press; 2011.

[70] D. Rodrik. One Economics, Many Recipes: Globalization, Institutions, and Economic Growth. Princeton (NJ): Princeton University Press; 2007.

[71] S. Berger. How We Compete: What Companies Around the World Are Doing to Make It in Today's Global Economy. New York: Doubleday; 2006.

[72] P. F. Cowhey, J. D. Aronson. Global Information and Communication Markets: The Political Economy of Innovation. Cambridge (MA): MIT Press; 2009.

[73] M. Wolf. Why Globalization Works. New Haven (CT): Yale University Press; 2004.

[74] D. Rodrik. Why Do More Open Economies Have Bigger Governments? The Journal of Political Economy, 106;1998;997–1032.

[75] D. Breznitz, M. Z. Taylor. Special Issue on National Institutions and the Globalized Political Economy of Technological Change. Review of Policy Research, 26;2009.

[76] P. Abila. The Apple iPhone Supply Chain. Available from http://www.shmula.com/304/the-apple-iphone-supply-chain.

[77] R. Brubaker. All Roads Lead to China. 2007. Article available from http://www
      .allroadsleadtochina.com/index.php/2007/08/15/iphone-made-in-shenzen/.

[78] A. H. Amsden. The Rise of "The Rest": Challenges to the West from Late-
      Industrializing Economies. New York: Oxford University Press; 2001.

[79] M. Woo-Cumings. The Developmental State. Ithaca (NY): Cornell University
      Press; 1999.

[80] C. A. Johnson. MITI and the Japanese Miracle: The Growth of Industrial Policy,
      1925–1975. Stanford (CA): Stanford University Press; 1982.

[81] W. W. Keller, R. J. Samuels. Crisis and Innovation in Asian Technology. New
      York: Cambridge University Press; 2003.

[82] S. T. Anwar. Creating a National Champion or a Global Pharmaceutical Com-
      pany: A Tale of French Connection. Journal of Business & Industrial Marketing,
      23;2008;586–596.

[83] J. I. Jenssen, G. Jorgensen. How Do Corporate Champions Promote Innovation?
      International Journal of Innovation Management. Hackensack (NJ): World Sci-
      entific Publishing Company; 2004, pp. 63–86.

[84] A. Alesina, F. Giavazzi. Future of Europe: Reform or Decline. Cambridge (MA):
      MIT Press; 2006.

[85] P. A. Hall. Governing the Economy: The Politics of State Intervention in Britain
      and France. New York: Oxford University Press; 1986.

[86] R. J. Samuels. Rich Nation, Strong Army: National Security and the Technologi-
      cal Transformation of Japan. Ithaca (NY): Cornell University Press; 1994.

[87] P. F. Cowhey, J. D. Aronson. Transforming Global Information and Communica-
      tion Markets: The Political Economy of Innovation. Cambridge (MA): MIT
      Press; 2009.

[88] W. J. Baumol, R. E. Litan, C. J. Schramm. Good Capitalism, Bad Capitalism, and
      the Economics of Growth and Prosperity. New Haven (CT): Yale University
      Press; 2007.

[89] W. B. Bonvillian. The Innovative State: Why Federal Support for Science Is Es-
      sential for American Prosperity. American Interest, July–August 2009;67–78.

Notes

1. For example, Robert Moses, the designer of New York's expressways and state parks, deliberately used bridge, road, and even pool design to restrict usage by poor and lower-middle class families, especially African Americans. The battles over birth control technologies might also be appropriate here.

2. See, for example, Ruth Schwartz Cowan, *More Work for Mother* (New York: Basic Books, 1983).

3. Or, in the language of economics, it is neither Pareto superior nor Pareto optimal.

4. For example, many of those interest groups most affected by the AIDS threat (blood banks, gays, hemophiliacs) ironically sought to impede the innovation and diffusion of HIV-safe blood products and HIV tests.

5. Entergy Corporation is a New Orleans-based firm, involved in electric power production, which owns and operates ten U.S. nuclear power plants. It is one of the largest generators of nuclear power in the Western Hemisphere.

6. Barry Posen likes to call the change the "Thorough Exploitation of Science and Technology (TEST)."

7. Harvey M. Sapolsky, *Science and Navy: The History of the Office of Naval Research* (Princeton, NJ: Princeton University Press, 1991).

4

Sociology and the Science of Science Policy

Walter W. Powell, Jason Owen-Smith, and Laurel Smith-Doerr

1. Introduction

Science is a fundamentally social endeavor [1–3]. To sociologically trained eyes, the richest questions for a science of science policy are those that address the interplay of three general concepts: *networks, power,* and *institutions.* We argue that these three concepts illuminate social dynamics—the often complicated processes by which established systems take root, reproduce themselves, and change. These ideas are thus central to understanding the efficacy and consequences of policy changes and to providing insight into where new interventions might yield desired results. The interplay of networks, power, and institutions provides a lens to examine critical areas for policymakers. Most notably, a sociological approach to science policy offers new insights into *unanticipated consequences*, the unforeseen and often negative effects of deliberate policy changes.

Networks are patterned relationships that connect both individual and organizational participants in a field. Social, scientific, and economic ties influence behavior and outcomes through several general mechanisms. Networks channel resources and information, such that participants with more (and more diverse) connections are better positioned to accomplish their goals than are their more peripheral rivals [4]. Investigators who are central in the informal networks of their fields are more likely to succeed in research efforts that require them to stay abreast of the latest findings and methods. Networks also signal status and in turn reduce decision makers' uncertainty when they are faced with choices where it is difficult to establish quality a priori [5]. Reviewers and program officers seeking to evaluate the potential of a grant from a first-time applicant often use that scientist's network ties to mentors, collaborators, and employing institutions as a proxy for her or his scientific acumen.

Power relations are particular, asymmetric forms of network ties [6]. An individual or organization gains *power* over another by controlling access to either the tangible or intangible resources that another participant requires. In Weber's language, power is the ability to carry out one's will "despite resistance" [7]. Power most commonly accrues through the accumulation of status and control of sought-after resources or allocation procedures. In this view, both an investigator who is the sole source of a new reagent and the program officer who can exercise some discretion over the funded budgets of grants have power. Networks stitch far-flung parts of the scientific field into a unified whole, whereas power accounts for why particular individuals occupy gatekeeper or brokerage points in the system. Networks and power relations jointly explain why efforts to change complex social arrangements by policy fiat often go awry, spawning *unanticipated consequences* [8].[1]

Finally, *institutions* are the formal and informal rules and conventions that guide a great deal of social life. Institutions are also a double-edged sword: they constrain some activities but generate possibilities for other actions in particular contexts [9, 10]. Institutions are self-replicating, largely uncontested, and durable features of the social world. In science, for instance, the formal rules and informal expectations associated with peer review and the academic tenure process are highly institutionalized and often taken for granted. Institutions create a link between networks and power by delimiting the types of connections and actions that are appropriate in particular contexts. Institutions form the rules of the game and establish how particular relationships and resources translate into sources of individual or collective power [11]. Consider, for instance, the ways in which the practice of single-blind and double-blind peer review rules might lead differently positioned investigators to be more or less successful in grant competitions and in efforts to publish novel findings.

In short, science is a social system, one that is structured by networks of relationships linking individuals and organizations into overarching structures that are the terrain on which competition takes place. Institutions define the rules of the game, whereas differential access to power enables some individuals to exert their will or flout the rules. Our approach to the sociology of science policy focuses on specifying how networks, power, and institutions combine to constitute particular social systems that are more or less resistant to change. Put simply, science policy is an effort to alter the trajectory, workings, and content of the social system of science with the relatively weak lever of control over some, largely formal, aspects of institutions.

Reproduction and transformation are primary challenges in both academic life and the exercise of science policy. To explore this claim, we examine four issues for science and innovation policy: (1) ethics education in biomedical science; (2) federal funding for human embryonic stem cell (hESC) research; (3) regional science-based economic growth; and (4) interdisciplinarity in pursuit of transformative discoveries. These examples are drawn from our current research programs. In each instance, we outline the sources of power, the structure of networks, and the force of institutional arrangements in a brief examination of processes of social reproduction and transformation. We use our analyses, in turn, to consider some of the unintended consequences of policy interventions.

The first topic represents a policy mandate, as requirements for ethics education have become standard at granting agencies around the world. The second arena highlights a policy restriction. For nearly a decade, federally funded hESC research was limited by executive order to a handful of cell lines. The third and fourth areas pose potent challenges. Intensive efforts at regional economic development through seeding high-technology clusters present a conundrum in which local, state, and federal policies have often had limited effect or worked at cross-purposes. Finally, the recent push toward interdisciplinary research centers in U.S. colleges and universities represents an indissoluble mix of all three—policy mandates, restrictions, and conundrums. We draw attention to the features of each example that relate most directly to core questions for the sociology of science and technology policy. We believe this approach both informs the consequences of policy mandates and prescriptions and offers new insights into intractable or contentious problems. Our empirical examples are skewed toward the life sciences, as this is the main arena of our empirical research. We view the life sciences as an illustrative case for science policy—an area rife with political ferment, high-stakes funding decisions, pronounced geographic clustering, thorny ethical issues, and interdisciplinary innovation. At the same time, the institutional, network, and power mechanisms at work in these life science examples have wider implications for legitimacy claims, labor market processes, industrial clustering, and race/gender inequalities that span many fields of science.

2. Policy Mandate: Sociology of Ethics in Science

A familiar cycle to observers of science and culture is one in which a scientist's unethical behavior—often a highly visible scandal—triggers public mistrust of science, followed in turn by increased regulation of the scientific community. The blame for such failings is often laid at the feet of individual investigators who are presumed to be immoral and whose lack of scruples is taken to precede their entry into the lab. Few popular accounts of unethical behavior, however, assess the pressures toward questionable "shortcuts" that intense competition can bring to academic research [12]. Consider a highly institutionalized feature of science: the pressure of priority [13]. In both commercial and academic research, even though the lion's share of interesting, high-profile problems is pursued by multiple teams, the first investigator or organization to report a hotly contested finding reaps most of the rewards. Such competitive dynamics are a spur for novelty in science. These same pressures, however, can push researchers toward secrecy [14] or outright scientific fraud [15]. In one notable example, Woo Suk Hwang, the Seoul National University professor who was dismissed in 2006, not only falsely claimed to have been the first to clone a human blastocyst but also misappropriated funds and apparently persuaded junior researchers in his lab to "donate" their eggs for research [16]. Even though purportedly "oddball" personalities dominate the headlines on ethical lapses, the everyday pressures on scientists (e.g., to avoid sharing research findings or to exploit postdocs' labor rather than mentor them) are less visible. The social dynamics and allocation mechanisms of science strongly shape its ethical culture, a core sociological insight that is often perilously unrecognized.

2.1. Institutions

Since 2000, in the United States and Europe, an increasing number of requirements for ethics education and training have become a mandated requirement of governmental funding of science. Those policies, the codes of conduct they seek to formalize, and the often unexamined expectations about scientists' behavior that underpin them are part and parcel of what social scientists term institutions, that is, the formal and informal rules of the game. These ethics education policies have been viewed as an intervention into the cycle of scandal-mistrust-regulation. But a focus on "fixing" individuals seems to us a misplaced target. Interestingly, when this kind of "deficit model" is used in discussions of public participation in science, it has been viewed as misguided and patronizing [17]. So if claims that laypeople simply need to be educated about a particular scientific or technical fact are inadequate, then why do we turn to a similar "fix" for scientific misconduct?

Top-down policies for the ethics education of scientists and engineers operate on a deficit model that is one-dimensional and unidirectional—researchers are treated as if they fail to understand the rules and must be educated about them. Surveys of scientists find that this kind of traditional ethics training has little effect on whether individuals engage in "questionable practices" [18].[2] Formal instruction in the rules, it seems, does not equate to following them. What is missing, from a sociological perspective, is a critical assessment of the context of science in which ethical lapses occur [19].

In the domain of the life sciences, sociologists have analyzed the development of an increasingly institutionalized profession of bioethics. Unlike engineering ethics, where practicing engineers have been major contributors to the literature, bioethics has largely been the domain of specialists—ethicists and applied philosophers. The focus on ethical principles rather than on lived practices has led to a "thinning" of the discourse around major bioethics topics, such as the human genome project [20]. Not only have intellectual discussions become narrower, but the regulation of practices such as the use of human subjects has become more institutionalized, as has been seen in research on institutional review boards [21]. In sociological parlance, *institutionalization* is the process by which a practice, structure, or belief becomes a widely accepted, taken-for-granted, and (formally or informally) enforceable expectation for a field. The expectation that findings should be vetted through peer review and the requirement that research involving human subjects be evaluated by institutional review boards are two examples. The institutionalization of ethics (or "ethicization") in science can be seen in the international establishment of new structures and formalized policies.

But those arrangements have had significant unintended consequences as researchers have responded to new mandates in unexpected but not inexplicable ways. In interviews that explored variation in the responses of life scientists to policies originating in the United Kingdom, the European Union, and the United States between 2000 and 2003, Smith-Doerr found that scientists consistently reported dislike of the ways in which ethics policies and programs are implemented, but with some variation by country [22–24]. In the United Kingdom, life scientists skeptically regarded the policies tied to Research Council funding, anticipating that policies would change with leadership. Italian life scientists noted the lack of funding (and policy) at the national level and appeared frustrated by what they saw as overly complex requirements at the European level, where successful grantees reportedly employed outside consultants to complete sections of applications related to ethical issues. U.S. life scientists expressed distaste for the implementation of the National Institutes of Health (NIH) policy on human subjects in the form of web-based ethics training modules.[3] A considerable portion of the unease, we suggest, stems from misaligned efforts to mandate an individual-level solution to a problem lodged in the larger structure and dynamics of a field.

Life scientists who do feel strongly about ethical issues (e.g., allocating more resources to research on diseases of poverty rather than wealth) view the shallow implementation of ethics requirements tied to their funding as counterproductive to addressing "real" issues. In personal narratives, scientists discuss ethical issues in a much broader way than research misconduct (e.g., falsification, fabrication, and plagiarism). The importance of having a positive impact (rather than avoiding a negative impact)—such as working to solve global problems—seems more salient to how scientists talk about ethical issues in their everyday research and teaching [23]. Research suggests that the introduction of new, shallow routines, separated from daily research and educational practices, may be no more effective than no training at all [18, 24]. A life scientist must often balance, for example, teaching graduate students about increasing funding pressures and the need to pursue hot, trendy topics, while instructing them to refrain from "fudging" data. Ethics education requirements that fail to speak to these competing pressures, or to concerns about social justice issues in scientific work, can quickly become decoupled from what scientists consider the "real" work of science.

If ethics education becomes an unreflective (and distasteful) routine that has little connection to daily research practices, then it is unlikely to help with complexities and may even have the *unanticipated consequence* of diminishing fresh thinking and practice around ethical issues. Another unanticipated consequence (suggested by anecdotes among the scientific community) is that the stand-alone, noninteractive, web-based ethics training modules in the United States may have led to unethical behavior (e.g., department secretaries provided with the multiple-choice answer keys and asked to fill in the answers for all of the researchers in a department). Ever since the writings of Max Weber [25], sociologists have noted the dangers of bureaucratization and applying impersonal routines in circumstances where efficiency should not be the ultimate value. In this case, the rationalization of ethics training seems to have succeeded primarily in separating the increasingly specialized world of bioethics from the daily procedures and pressures of bioscience research. Here we see that the development of informal norms that clash with formal science policy reveals the tensions between the social forces of transformation and reproduction inherent in institutions.

2.2. Networks

Where ethical issues are viewed in a more positive light in the scientific community, one usually finds grassroots interactions as the source of engagement rather than top-down, imposed policy implementation. Those interactions can profitably be understood as networks that make some individuals more important for the success of new mandates than others. For example, Huff et al.'s research in the United States and Europe on computer scientists finds that "moral exemplars" are those individuals in the scientific community looked up to for fostering one of two moral ecologies [26]. Moral exemplars either developed the craft of computing (such as making it more inclusive for users with disabilities) or worked toward reform (such as new thinking about privacy issues). This kind of positive discussion on ethical issues and leadership in the scientific community arises from peer-based social networks—the webs of informal ties among scientists that develop with frequent and/or durable social interaction.

To be sure, networks are not a panacea—these webs of relationships often hold tensions within them that are difficult to resolve. For example, trust is part of the glue that holds networks together. Trust may also hide malfeasance, however, which can open the door for lapses in ethical research conduct among scientists and engineers. In sociological analyses of science and technology, we also note tensions between social change and reproduction. In ethics education, routinization is dangerous if innovative pedagogical methods and content are stifled; however, standardized elements can serve as foundations on which to build knowledge.

2.3. Power

Power relationships also play a role for, as some sociologists have warned, many of the ethical conundrums that beset contemporary science originate in the dependence of some people on resources controlled by others. An interesting question for science and engineering is how ethical issues are connected to broader social stratification categories, such as gender [27]. Tying ethics education to networks, attending to systematic pressures created by competitive pressures and allocation mechanisms, and paying keen attention to the role of power may pay dividends in more effective training, and may also set the stage for broader participation in science and engineering among persons with disabilities, women, and underrepresented minorities.

2.4. Implications

In sum, strong policies that carry mandates for behavior (such as universal requirements for ethics training) but attend solely to the individual knowledge and foibles of scientists will be less effective and more easily evaded than those that address the social system of science itself. Scientists' resistance to (and even co-optation of) ethics training in several nations stems from resistance to controls on individual professional autonomy, a growing separation between the guidelines developed by professional bioethicists and daily practices at the bench, and power differentials that make it difficult for concerned scientists or administrators to shape the behavior and attitudes of peers. Policies that dictate individual fixes for systemic problems only exacerbate these challenges. If the efficacy and attractiveness of policy guidelines depend on features of the scientific edifice, then so too do the consequences and reach of policy restrictions.

3. Policy Restriction: Funding Human Embryonic Stem Cell Research

Research using human embryonic stem cells (hESCs) is among the most controversial and promising in contemporary biomedicine; hESCs were *Science* magazine's 1999 breakthrough of the year and, a full decade later, held prominent (and incommensurable) positions in the 2008 platforms of both the Democratic and the Republican parties.[4] Three presidential administrations have struggled to balance the potential and the divisiveness of hESC research. The flashpoint of debate is seemingly innocuous—cultured cell lines kept alive and dividing in a dish. The key to both the politics and science of stem cells is the materials necessary for research at the bench.

Stem cell policy became a battleground, as activists linked it to some of the themes from the abortion debate. On one side, people with passionate hopes to alleviate suffering via new cell therapies advocate for expansive, publicly funded hESC research; on the other, those with fervently held beliefs about the origins and sanctity of life lobby to forbid research they find morally abhorrent. In the mid-1990s, extensive research on nonhuman primates and human models raised the possibility of therapeutic applications in people. In 1995, a research team led by James Thomson at the University of Wisconsin isolated embryonic stem cell lines from rhesus monkeys [28]. In 1996, the first passage of the Dickey-Wicker amendment to a Health and Human Services Appropriations bill banned federally funded research that damages or destroys human embryos. That ban necessitated that Thomson's efforts to derive human embryonic stem cells move off campus. In 1998, with private funding from Geron—a Menlo Park, California-based biotechnology firm—and the Wisconsin Alumni Research Foundation (WARF)—the independent nonprofit technology transfer arm of the University of Wisconsin—Thomson's team won the race to culture hESCs [28]. WARF filed for and won broad patent protection for both the techniques necessary to derive primate cell lines and the particular lines themselves. Geron was granted an exclusive license to develop products based on neural, cardiovascular, and pancreatic cells, along with nonexclusive rights to other types of tissue [29].

In early 1999 the Department of Health and Human Services issued an opinion to the effect that research using (but not creating) human embryonic stem cell lines was eligible for federal R&D support. A Clinton administration executive order implemented that opinion by allowing research to be conducted using existing stem cell lines. Upon taking office in 2001, George W. Bush revoked the Clinton executive order. Academic hESC research was in limbo for several months until, on August 9, 2001, President Bush issued a policy that re-opened federally funded research on a small set of existing cell lines, including the WARF-owned lines derived by Thomson. In March 2009, President Barack Obama rescinded the Bush-era funding restrictions and directed the NIH to develop new policy guidelines.

The final NIH guidelines were announced and took effect on July 7, 2009. Whether the new NIH policy succeeds in its stated goal of getting more diverse but responsibly derived cell lines into investigators' hands to speed clinical developments will depend in large part on successfully identifying and reacting to the complicated and, we believe, largely unintended legacy of the Bush era [30].

3.1. Institutions

The seemingly simple compromise offered by President Bush was institutionalized as policy via an executive order and shaped the development of hESC science in unexpected and complicated ways. Note first that both the Bush and Obama policies are defined by restrictions placed on the technical decisions that investigators have to make at the lab bench. This represents a significant institutional change in the relationship between federal agencies and the scientists they support. At least since the end of World War II, federal funding of academic research has progressed in a fairly decentralized fashion. This "fragile contract" emphasizes public support of research by investigators who are largely allowed to make autonomous decisions about what questions to pursue and how to pursue them [31, 32].

The hESC funding policies that governed research for more than a decade altered the institutional arrangements that have largely been taken for granted in the investigator-initiated, peer-reviewed grants system. That simple institutional change has had significant consequences, shifting the relative power of different players in the scientific field. These changes led to new, fragmented, and challenging regulatory and oversight regimes and recast the networks of affiliation and collaboration that are the skeleton of modern, team-based science. These three shifts—in *power relations*, *institutional contexts*, and *network structures*—in turn altered the decisions and practices of scientists, activists, businesspeople, philanthropists, and patients. While we lack space to systematically trace out all of the ramifications of these policies, consider a few high points.

3.2. Power: Shifting the Balance

A first implication of the restrictive federal policies was to dramatically empower corporate and other private funders of research and development (R&D). The NIH, normally the primary funder of basic academic biomedical research, could not support many stem cell studies. Moreover, hESC experiments could not be conducted with instruments or materials purchased with federal funds or in infrastructure constructed or maintained with federal money. Thus researchers interested in pursuing human embryonic stem cell investigations using newer materials were forced to either leave the United States or to seek alternative sources of support and to construct parallel laboratory infrastructures independent of their academic laboratories. This left a void that foundations and corporations rushed to fill, and other countries also attempted to lure leading U.S. researchers to work in less-contested settings.

Recall that Thomson's original derivation of hESCs was accomplished off campus, with funding from Geron and WARF. The resulting intellectual property lacked the government march-in rights that accompany federally funded intellectual property. As a result, the government had little formal recourse when it came time to insist that WARF loosen restrictions on the use of its proprietary materials for academic purposes. For its part, Geron received expansive and exclusive rights to develop cell therapies in three of the most high-profile and remunerative disease categories.

3.3. Networks

Even after the Bush policy made possible federally funded research with a limited number of cell lines, technical difficulties with "approved lines" and a lack of genetic diversity in these materials led scientists who were concerned with clinical applications to seek alternatives. One of the highest profile and most successful of those scientists, Douglas Melton, has derived and made publicly available twenty-eight new cell lines (which can now be federally funded for limited uses under the Obama policy). Those lines were created and distributed via the Harvard Stem Cell Institute (HSCI), a private, nonprofit institute funded by Harvard University, the Howard Hughes Medical Institute, and individual and foundation donors. The HSCI has been incredibly successful in its work of distributing cell lines and conducting cutting-edge research [30], but its institutional model differs from most academic or corporate settings in that its rationales and budgets are tightly tied to the concerns of patients and the search for cures for specific diseases.

Finally, U.S. national stem cell policies have opened the door for international competition in what might become a key clinical and commercial field [33, 34]. Research on hESCs is alive and well in the United States [35], but other nations, such as Britain, Sweden, Singapore, Korea, Israel, and even Iran, have dedicated significant national resources to the pursuit of stem cell science as a means to economic development and international competitiveness [36, 37]. In addition to shifting much of the action toward quick and specific clinical applications and commercially oriented development efforts, restrictive policies in the United States have altered the international research landscape. In at least one case, a developing country's move to treat stem cell research as a spur to economic growth had further unanticipated consequences. Sociologists Andrew Schrank and Cheol Song Lee argue that the scientific fraud perpetrated by Woo Suk Hwang and his colleagues was a direct result of Korean national policies that provided immense incentives for success but were ill equipped to evaluate nonindustrial development models [38].

3.4. Implications: A "Patchwork of Patchworks"

Varied national- and state-level ethical standards, policy stances, and regulatory regimes have created a complicated patchwork of cobbled-together standards for the conduct and oversight of hESC research [39]. The state and private funding options that grew up in the wake of the Bush order created dramatic fragmentation in regulatory and ethical oversight [40], imposing significant administrative burdens and even legal uncertainties on scientists seeking to conduct research on new lines or to access materials created under rules different than those they must follow [41].

One practical result of this fragmented, conflictual policy environment has been that researchers appear to make conservative choices in selecting well-known and already widely used research materials, with the unanticipated effect of concentrating hESC research on a very small number of cell lines that are less than ideal for many research purposes. In both the national and the international arenas, there is some evidence that scientists are "voting with their feet" by leaving more restrictive states and nations for locales that are more conducive to the pursuit of their research [34]. The Bush-era restrictions may also have altered the calculus by which researchers select collaborators, as papers published by international research teams, including U.S. scientists, became more common than is typical in biomedicine in the wake of the August 2001 executive order [33]. In addition to shifting the balance of power between key (public-sector and market) institutions for directing and rewarding science, the Bush administration policy altered the networks of materials sharing, collaboration, and hiring that are central to the daily work of science and that direct the evolution of new fields.

3.5. Unanticipated Consequences

The Bush-era policy, then, has had implications far beyond its seemingly clear content. Restrictions on investigators' choices of materials shifted power in the field toward the private sector, patient groups, and foreign scientists. Those changes remade both the physical and institutional landscape for research as some states responded to federal policies with tighter restrictions and others promulgated less restrictive policies [35]. Scientists voted with their feet, both by moving research efforts to more propitious locales physically and by changing patterns of collaboration. Some investigators stepped completely off the NIH funding track to pursue research using nonapproved cell lines under alternative private funding scenarios.

Those researchers who continued to work with federal funds and approved cell lines quickly converged on a very small number of lines that became the dominant reference materials in the field, despite their apparent insufficiency for some therapeutic and scientific uses. International moves to aggressively pursue economic development on the back of stem cell research contributed to a major case of fraud whose discovery set the field back in terms both of public approval and technical development.

Efforts to avoid both controversy and restrictions may have accelerated attempts to develop new methods for inducing pluripotency from adult cells that might have been less actively or effectively pursued without dual public and political spurs. Early dominance of the patent field by a few players has led to conflict between states, firms, and universities, as public initiatives such as California's Proposition 71 run afoul of broad private rights held by WARF. One result of those conflicts has been a costly, contentious, and eventually unsuccessful effort to challenge the Thomson patents. Finally, the increasing engagement of patient groups in funding and directing research more tightly yoked the prospects for stem cell science to quick, successful development of therapies, a very high bar for any field in its first decades.

We do not mean to suggest that all of the consequences of these policies are negative. Stronger, more widely accepted rules for ethical research at this sometimes discomfiting frontier, greater engagement by patients and the public, widely researched and well-characterized reference materials, and an influx of support from nonfederal sources are all potentially beneficial developments. We are less concerned that a given policy prescription is all good or all bad than we are with demonstrating that even fairly simple rules can have far-reaching and complicated outcomes because of their often unintended ramifications for resources and power, networks, and institutional arrangements. Here too a policy designed as a compromise between contradictory interests had significant unanticipated consequences. By dramatically reducing the power of the NIH in this emerging field, Bush-era policies led to a proliferation of alternatives that complicated the professional lives of scientists, placed more power in the hands of commercial and international interests, and may have actually lessened the ability of federal agencies to exert control over the trajectory of the field. New policy efforts confront the same ethical dilemma that shaped the old, with the added complication of administratively complex and difficult-to-reconcile policy and funding environments. The effect of the shifts in the role played by powerful actors at the center of evolving communities is also key to our next example, a policy conundrum that has yet to be cracked.

4. Policy Conundrum: Regional High-Tech Clusters

The growth of U.S. high-tech clusters in the life sciences over the past thirty years provides a number of interesting puzzles for science policy analysts.[5] At one level, the pronounced spatial concentration of the U.S. biotech industry seems to cast doubt on the efficacy of formal planning and policy initiatives. Hundreds of cities and almost every state have ponied up millions in taxpayer dollars to build research parks and laboratories with the hope of forming a biotech cluster. But more than 50 percent of the companies and considerably more of the critical outputs—scientific papers, patents, employment, and novel medicines—are found in just three locales: the San Francisco Bay Area, Cambridge and Boston, Massachusetts, and North San Diego County in La Jolla, California. Such a geographic concentration very much belies the efforts of municipal, state, and national governments to build science-based clusters.

But not so fast. A careful study of the emergence and development of biotechnology suggests that an array of policy initiatives played a critical role in this industry's history, albeit often with *unanticipated consequences*.

4.1. Unanticipated Consequences

Perhaps most notable is the central role of research funding by the NIH in supporting the basic research that led to the scientific breakthroughs that made the industry possible and sustained its continued development. At a

Chemical Heritage Foundation conference on the emergence of biotechnology in 1997, Nobel Laureate Arthur Kornberg emphasized to the crowd, "I don't want it to be lost that the explosive growth of basic biomedical science is due to the NIH, and these discoveries were made exclusively in academic labs supported almost entirely by the NIH" [42]. Federal research funding for the life sciences was a key component in biotech's emergence. The NIH increased support for recombinant DNA research by 34 percent a year from 1978 to 1982 [43]. Again, in the 1990s, research support for the life sciences mushroomed as the NIH budget rose from $8.9 billion in 1992 to $17.8 billion in 2000. The NIH funding provided both the wherewithal to conduct basic science and support significant interactions among the producers of fundamental biological knowledge and those involved in clinical research and drug development at public research centers, universities, and companies. The expansive role of the NIH, complemented by additional public research organizations, including hospitals, nonprofit institutes, and disease foundations, enabled the United States to have both a scale and diversity of basic and translational research unmatched by any other advanced industrial nation [44].

4.2. Institutions

Numerous other government policies also contributed to the development of biotechnology in the United States. At the NIH in the 1970s, then director Don Fredrickson steered a complex discussion of safety guidelines for recombinant DNA research and their application to investigators who had NIH grants, developing practices that simultaneously were safe and tractable [45]. Outside of the NIH, legal, legislative, and tax policies proved to be crucial to the emergence of the commercial life sciences. Legislation that reduced the capital gains tax and permitted pension funds to invest in venture capital opened the door for investment in start-up companies [46]. The close 5 to 4 decision by the U.S. Supreme Court in 1980 in the *Diamond v. Chakrabarty* case distinguished between a product of nature and a patentable genetically modified bacteria that did not exist in nature, enabling human-made and genetically modified microorganisms to be patentable [47, 48]. In 1987, the U.S. Patent and Trade Office expanded the range of patentable items to include any biological material that involved human intervention.

The U.S. Congress passed the Bayh-Dole Patent and Trademarks Act in 1980, authorizing federally funded researchers to file for patents on research findings with commercial applications and to grant licenses for those patents to companies. This legislation encouraged university patenting and licensing of research results and replaced previously customized agreements between funding agencies, universities, and companies with a uniform policy [49]. One result of that change was a period of dramatic mobility as universities with early leads in commercialization parlayed gains from patenting and licensing into stronger, more competitive basic research programs [50]. Moreover, the act signaled congressional support for the commercialization of university science. The Orphan Drug Act of 1983 was passed by Congress to encourage research on rare diseases by biopharmaceutical companies, granting them seven years of market exclusivity and tax credits. All of these moves created a policy environment that supported and encouraged university research to be an engine of economic growth.

Nonetheless, the extensive role of the U.S. government in supporting biotechnology tells us very little about why the industry developed in so few places. Indeed, given the wide-ranging scope of the judicial and legislative decisions and the political nature of federal research funding, one might have expected that federal policies would foster a broad distribution of companies across the nation. Couple the considerable federal support with widespread local initiatives and one might expect that biotech would blossom in many different regions, as the basic science undergirding the industry was being pursued at top universities throughout the country.

4.3. Networks

The three clusters—the Bay Area, Boston, and San Diego—that have become the centers of biotech in the United States are characterized by a number of distinctive organizational features [51]. These clusters have high rates of firm formation *and* dissolution. Unlike many of the unsuccessful or nascent clusters, which never catalyzed, organizational foundings and disbandings occur at a high rate. This ferment has several consequences. One, labor market mobility becomes relatively easy in these regions. For example, the extensive involvement of early employees of Genentech in South San Francisco and Hybritech in La Jolla in starting dozens of subsequent new companies is quite notable [52, 53]. Two, these networks of personnel flows and referrals are indicators of the creation of a closely knit regional technological community. This connectivity, coupled with the presence of a number of public research organizations (PROs) in each cluster, greatly lessens the risk of starting new firms. Three, high rates of founding and turnover point to experimentation with both new scientific ideas and business models, which further sustains a cluster by raising the bar of accomplishment and spreading best practices across the local community.

The regions where biotech flourished and grew into a robust local community possessed a considerable diversity of types of organizations, as well as central anchor tenant organizations that fostered interactions among disparate parties. In the Boston area, public research organizations, including MIT, Harvard, Tufts, and elite research hospitals, including Dana Farber, Brigham and Women's, and Massachusetts General, played this role [54]. In the Bay Area, venture capital firms, the interdisciplinary makeup of the medical school at the University of California, San Francisco (UCSF), the new technology transfer office at Stanford, and first-generation companies, most notably Genentech and Chiron, which operated according to "invisible college" principles, helped create a robust community [52]. In San Diego, the combination of research institutes such as Scripps, Salk, and Burnham, along with the new university at the University of California, San Diego (UCSD), and the first-generation company Hybritech, served as anchors [53]. Most importantly, as new entrants joined the scene in each of these regions, the anchor tenants remained active and protected the value of openness. As a consequence, the norms that characterized interorganizational relations in the three clusters bore the signatures of the anchor tenants.

Consequently, in the active clusters, biotech firms collaborated with other ostensible competing biotech firms in product development; older biotech firms joined in as investors in new start-ups. Established biotech companies took on some of the features of both venture capital (VC) firms and public research organizations, while VC firms and PROs in the successful clusters became intensively involved in starting new companies. Universities facilitated the licensing of university science and took equity positions in biotech start-ups. Employees at VC firms moved to biotech firms to take on founder or chief executive roles, and biotech company veterans founded VC firms. The VC firms established entrepreneur-in-residence programs, and companies began postdoctoral fellowship programs. In the three regions where robust biotech communities developed, there has been a thorough mixing of the participants and practices from formerly separate social worlds. No science or business policies made such interaction possible; rather, these communities were forged out of an indissoluble mixture of personal scientific relationships, business ties, and wide-ranging interests in creating new medicines and building a new field. Even though an array of public policies supported these efforts, none were as consequential as the NIH's support of basic and translational research.

4.4. Power

If the goal is to seed and develop robust regional economies based on biotechnology innovation, then there are important lessons from this pattern. First and foremost is the importance of crosscutting *networks*. Policies that emphasize the development of capacity for supporting high-tech industry (in the form of, for instance, VC funds, science parks, and specific training programs) at the expense of facilitating connections among co-located organizations are unlikely to be generative. The resources necessary to pursue biotech development were present in many locations, but only some matched those endowments with the dense networks linking ostensible competitors in a web of relationships that encouraged the formation of local communities and norms of reciprocity. Yet even the combination of network connections and capacity may not be enough absent attention to power. Analyses of the dynamics by which successful and unsuccessful biotechnology clusters emerged demonstrate that connections whose primary outcome is to cement the local dominance of a single powerful institution are unlikely to succeed unless this central player "hands off" its position to a cluster of local and interconnected young firms. Creating sufficient capacity, encouraging dense connectivity, facilitating power transitions, and maintaining a climate of openness are the key challenges that policymakers face in efforts to spark high-tech regional development. These same issues are also active in efforts to expand interdisciplinary research and training in science.

5. Policy Contention: Interdisciplinary Research and Training

Policymakers face a demanding task as they navigate between supporting novelty and innovation and strengthening replication and reproduction. Nowhere is this tension more apparent than in efforts to support and expand interdisciplinary approaches to such key substantive problems as disease, energy and climate change, sustainable development, and international security. The emphasis in science policy on question-driven interdisciplinarity (research that brings together multiple disciplinary perspectives or develops new interdisciplinary fields) is a case in point. The largely unexamined assumption in science policy is that interdisciplinarity leads to greater innovation. But is interdisciplinarity the best way to produce "transformative" research on topics that have proved intractable for single disciplines?

5.1. Institutions: Studying Emergence

A line of research by Diana Rhoten and Edward Hackett [55, 56] has investigated the effects of interdisciplinary graduate programs in comparison to more traditional discipline-based programs. Graduate students from different disciplinary backgrounds were arranged in small discussion groups (called "charrettes," after the term used in nineteenth-century French Ecoles). Among graduate students, strong disciplinary skills were a necessary background, but the creative integration of ideas did arise through interdisciplinary collaboration. The comparison between charrettes with students trained in interdisciplinary programs and charrettes with those trained in disciplinary programs and brought together for the experiment produced surprising results as advanced discipline-based students and younger interdisciplinary students produced the best projects, according to an expert panel. Rhoten and Hackett surmise that the self-selection of graduate students into interdisciplinary research accounts for some of the creative success.

For more quantitative studies of the increase in interdisciplinary scientific research, there are complex measurement issues to overcome (including, but not limited to, how to measure the lines between disciplines and the challenges of selection bias). Researchers have come up with useful indexes to analyze bibliometric data—publications and citations—that have shown an overall increase in interdisciplinarity in recent decades [57, 58]. Whether such work leads to more innovative outcomes, however, is a question that should take into account the different dimensions of interdisciplinarity.

5.2. Networks

Interdisciplinarity is both more present and successful in fields and research that is translational [59]. Work by Frickel, among others, shows that where interdisciplinary research results in a successful new academic field, the focus of that field is often social problem based, such as concerns about pollution in environmental toxicology.

Another dimension of interdisciplinarity lies in the difficulty in evaluating quality. More conventional scholars express difficulties in evaluating interdisciplinary work, which must often "prove itself" in relationship to the epistemic cultures of established disciplines [60]. Lamont's (2009) study of interdisciplinary peer review panels demonstrates that even though interdisciplinarity and objectivity are widely championed, the process and mechanics of peer review often result in reviewers favoring work that looks like their own [61]. Homophily—liking those who are similar to you—is difficult to overcome, particularly in the evaluation process; people are more likely to trust others who are similar to themselves. This kind of institutional and interpersonal inertia can lead to unanticipated consequences in trying to assess the outputs of an interdisciplinary group.

5.3. Unanticipated Consequences

Efforts to reform the peer-review system to level the competition for younger investigators and encourage higher-risk "transformative" research reverberate through individual careers, both by altering the calculus that determines success in intense competitions for grants and shaping the hiring priorities of academic organizations [12]. Even small changes to the peer-review process are likely to have large, controversial, and unforeseen effects, because blind peer review is a defining institutional feature of contemporary science, one that is tightly bound to both processes of reproduction and change and the mechanisms by which rewards are allocated.

Peer review—particularly single-blind peer review—reproduces established orders by requiring new claims to pass muster with the very people whose work defines the contemporary status quo. It is no surprise, then, that novel, interdisciplinary research proposals face steeper odds of funding. The role that status plays in scientific evaluation further exacerbates the challenge of funding novelty by ensuring that those projects most likely to be recognized as having transformative potential will emerge from labs and research teams led by investigators with successful track records [62]. Although it may be desirable to support younger investigators, doing so raises the stakes in an already high-risk game for evaluators who are themselves competing for resources under peer review. Not surprisingly, more intense competition and longer odds of success breed conservative and even rigid responses in both individuals and organizations [63].

When understood as a social system, contemporary science presents a number of paradoxes for policymakers. First and foremost, the institutional arrangements of investigator-initiated, peer-reviewed, public-science funding serve as model and guidepost even for more narrowly focused commercial endeavors [64, 65].

Those arrangements effectively create a system whose primary means of allocating resources is conservative, in the sense that it tends to reinforce the power of incumbent investigators and organizations, but whose mandate is transformative. The institutional combination of an increasingly competitive single-blind grant competition and an up-or-out tenure vote that often depends on successful grantsmanship introduces great pressure toward the selection of safer projects and topics early in scientific careers.

Those younger investigators whose prior successes, high-profile mentors and collaborators, or prestigious positions might afford them greater leeway are accorded that flexibility precisely because they have already succeeded by playing the rules of a system that they might now be expected to transform.

The flow of newcomers, hungry to make a mark on their fields, is a primary engine of novelty in scientific discovery. Nonetheless, existing institutions, power relations, and networks may mean that the most successful newcomers are also those most strongly yoked to the status quo.

The net result of equating funding of younger scientists with funding for transformative research, then, may be to make the second major grant in a career a turning point, while yielding systematically more conservative approaches on the part of junior scholars. Alternative approaches might take into account the effects of networks, for instance, by seeking out junior scientists whose early career productivity is not matched by the high-profile collaborators and mentors who provide important status signals to uncertain reviewers or grant makers. Seeking diversity in the locations and networks of researchers rather than emphasizing their career age might alleviate some of the more difficult challenges discussed earlier. We caution, however, that attending specifically to networks and locations in the case of funding for interdisciplinary work may have its own set of unanticipated outcomes.

5.4. Power

A third dimension of interdisciplinarity is related to gender and racial diversity. Rhoten and Pfirman review research that suggests that women and underrepresented minorities are more likely to engage in interdisciplinary research [66]. It may be the case that these scholars experience marginalization from more mainstream disciplines and then find a place in interdisciplinary work; in any case, the links between diversity and innovative outcomes have found support across a variety of contexts [67]. Thus inequalities in scientific institutions may have unexpected outcomes. More research needs to be done on this question, but if marginalization from mainstream scientific organizations and disciplines leads to greater diversity among interdisciplinary scholars, then this could have important implications for interdisciplinary research.

A final dimension to consider is that not all interdisciplinary research is equal. Some interdisciplinary research is conducted in well-funded centers, while other research is done in fields (such as women's studies) that struggle to find resources. Equating centers that bring together social scientists and humanities faculties with those that combine the physical and life sciences is clearly a flawed design, but how do we evaluate problem-based centers that combine physical and social scientists to consider climate change?

In sum, efforts to assess how innovative interdisciplinary research can be stimulated most effectively by science policy need to understand the key dimensions on which interdisciplinary research is carried out: knowledge context (support for problem-based research), institutional context (presence of clear processes for evaluating the research), and power (support for diversity among researchers).

6. Conclusion

By focusing on the core topics of social dynamics and allocation mechanisms through the lens of institutions, networks, and power, we provide insight into both the intended and unexpected outcomes of policy-making efforts. Our central claim is that policymakers will be well served by focusing their attention *and* resources not on individual incentives and knowledge, or on the give-and-take of interest groups, but on the concrete patterns of relationships and resource flows that lead some systems (regional economies, national ethics programs, funding practices for new fields of inquiry) to tip in one direction or the other. The challenge posed by a sociological approach to science and innovation policy is to map both the anatomy (the connections) and the physiology (the flows) of modern science in order to identify the places, practices, and participants whose positions in the system make them key passage points for efforts at change. If we conceive of science as a kinetic system and of policy as an effort to redirect, amplify, or block its energies, then the central question is always this: Where can the judicious application of resources and effort lead systems to move in favorable directions? The corollary question is: What are the larger ramifications of nudging poised systems toward particular courses? Answers to both depend on the particular features of the mandates, restrictions, challenges, and contentions that occupy (some would say bedevil) policymakers. We do not propose a one-size-fits-all solution; instead, we suggest that a sociological approach emphasizes underexamined empirical concerns with networks and power relationships as they play out in the dynamics of particular social institutions.

Scientists' resistance to (and, indeed, co-optation of) mandated ethics training reflects not only long-standing expectations about autonomy in scientific and training decisions and the powerful role of professors in universities but also the position the NIH holds at the center of an essential network for scientific life. The policy mandate was just that, but its eventual implementation and implications very much depended on networks, power, and institutionalized expectations native to academic life science in U.S. universities.

Similarly, the policy prescription created by hESC funding procedures under President Bush ran afoul of institutionalized expectations about who should make choices about scientific work (the scientists doing it, or the citizens who fund it through their tax dollars), but here reactions to those choices altered the institutional landscape of the field by creating alternative infrastructures and shifting power arrangements to favor more commercial and international interests.

While the systemic features of science help explain the course of particular policy initiatives, they also suggest why some problems offer particular challenges. Although the endowments needed to build vibrant regional life science clusters existed in nearly a dozen locations across the United States, as the biotech revolution got under way, just three of those regions became self-sustaining. In the language of network systems, all were poised, but only some tipped. The explanation for that disparity combines the structure of local networks (dense connectivity within a particular region), institutions (the organizational practices that shape how information travels through local ties), and power dynamics (the handoff from one institutional form to another). The conundrum implied by efforts to seed such regions by policy fiat, then, may stem from a focus on endowments rather than on system dynamics.

Finally, the case of policies that equate interdisciplinarity with the potential for transformative research also depends on these central features of social systems. Here, institutional context and the relative power of disciplines matter, but key challenges are driven by well-known tendencies of networks to form among like-minded individuals—and to enforce greater similarity in knowledge and approach by connected parties [68]. The very promise of interdisciplinary research—that bridging relatively homogenous disciplinary schools of thought will yield breakthrough insights—is also one of its key perils, hence the importance of institutional context, well-articulated goals, and efforts to diffuse power differentials. Moreover, the challenge of homophily suggests that interdisciplinarity is a short-term fix to a longer-term problem as, over time, success in some teams and approaches will breed longevity and thus greater similarity.

In sum, the cases we have sketched suggest the importance of adding social systems to the study of science and innovation policy. Focusing on mechanisms of reproduction and change and on the lasting consequences of resource allocation processes with an eye toward unanticipated consequences is essential to any deep understanding of science and science policy. Unanticipated consequences are often brought about by the complicated interrelationships among components of the contemporary scientific system, which turns our attention to networks, institutions, and power relationships. These central features of the social world are essential arrows in the quiver of science policymakers seeking to decide how and where to invest their efforts and resources.

6.1. Research Agenda for Science of Science Policy

To our minds, the key question for a science of science policy is relatively simple: How does one identify the points where shifting formal institutional arrangements (the primary weapon in the policymaker's arsenal) will nudge a complicated and dynamic social system in desired directions without deleterious unanticipated consequences? We suspect there are very few satisfying a priori answers to this question. Instead, our sociological approach suggests the importance of mapping key relationships, identifying sources of power, and identifying the current rules, both formal and informal, that make particular relationships wellsprings of control while defining which activities are legitimate avenues to success and what counts as failure.

In the cases discussed earlier, we saw that power hinges on the ability to fund research. The NIH and, by extension, the federal government are the key players in each of our examples. The rules of peer review and the predictable features of scientific careers in academia or the challenges of the patent system, FDA approval, and the predictable hurdles of the pharmaceutical regulatory process represent key institutions. Networks of collaboration and mentorship linking individuals and ties of funding and joint R&D connecting organizations forge groups into communities, giving force to shared expectations and bolstering existing sources of individual and collective power.

The difference between successful and co-opted ethics education policies may lie in tapping the community of connected and concerned scientists. Absent mobilization of influential individuals, new mandates are likely to be obeyed symbolically. That they are followed at all is a testament to the power wielded by the funding agencies that require them. The difference between a thriving and a stillborn biotechnology cluster resides in the connections that weld a region's scientific and organizational capacities into a community and a relational ethos that leads an area's original anchors to exert a loose hold on future connections, even as they firmly police shared values. Here, a particular form of network power allows structures to develop institutional force, but the sustainability of that configuration requires a light touch. Finally, in stem cell research, the exercise of power on the part of the federal government may have had its most lasting, and unintended, effect by nudging the early formation of networks and professional communities away from the ambit of public-sector science. With the traditional institutional center of early academic fields circumscribed, stem cell science grew in a fashion that exhibits peculiarities (conflict, fragmentation, conservativism around methods and materials) that we associate with the challenging effort to navigate contradictory rules for action and success. In every one of the instances we examined, the linkage among networks, institutions, and power is determinative, but in a unique manner in each case.

When we turn to our more prospective examination of efforts to seed transformative research by facilitating interdisciplinarity, a sociological approach emphasizing networks, power, and institutions has two key implications. First, the existing institutions and networks that shape academic careers suggest that efforts to target young investigators via standard peer-review mechanisms are likely to yield few transformations and may simply cement existing power structures, making later career-funding competitions more determinative. Second, efforts to create and maintain units at the interstices of different disciplinary standards of evaluation may be particularly dangerous for the careers of women and underrepresented minority researchers. Even though these ideas are based on cursory empirics, they suggest a way forward for efforts to examine how key institutions, networks, and power relations intermingle to create social environments with distinct dynamics of reproduction and transformation. Those processes, which we take to be exogenous to the social systems of science, account for the efficacy and consequences of policy-based efforts to steer a particular course.

This approach offers new insights into policymaking and evaluation and implies a set of near-term priorities for academic efforts to build a science of science policy. First, and most importantly, we need a clear theoretical framework for explaining how the institutions, networks, and sources of power native to science cohere in particular configurations that support distinctive social dynamics. That effort will be informed by existing theory and research, but we suspect that a particular form of empirically focused, comparative research will be necessary to its realization, which brings us to our second call. Efforts to develop a strong sociological theory of science policy require a mapping exercise or survey of mindfully chosen areas of science that should be undertaken with at least three goals in mind: (1) establishing a "state space" of institutions, relationships, and power bases, along with their common combinations in the realm of science; (2) developing a taxonomy of reproductive and transformative dynamics in social systems related to science; and (3) linking the combinations identified in goal 1 to the modal processes outlined in goal 2. We suspect that the most effective and, at least to us, interesting sociological science of science policy will theorize the link between the origins and later trajectories of social systems that will provide guidance for policymakers eager to intervene.

References

[1]   M. Weber. Science as a Vocation. In: H. Gerth, C. W. Mills (Eds.), From Max Weber: Essays in Sociology. New York: Routledge; 1918, pp. 129–158.

[2]   R. K. Merton. Priorities in Scientific Discovery: A Chapter in the Sociology of Science. American Sociological Review, 22;1957;635–659.

[3]   M. Polanyi. The Republic of Science: Its Political and Economic Theory. Minerva, 1;1962;54–73.

[4]   R. S. Burt. Structural Holes: The Social Structure of Competition. Cambridge (MA): Harvard University Press; 1992.

[5]   J. M. Podolny. A Status Based Model of Market Competition. American Journal of Sociology, 98;1993;829–872.

[6]   P. M. Blau. Exchange and Power in Social Life. New York: Transaction Publishers; 1986.

[7]   M. Weber. The Theory of Social and Economic Organization. New York: Oxford University Press; 1947.

[8]   R. Merton. The Unanticipated Consequences of Purposive Social Action. American Sociological Review, 1;1936.

[9]   J. W. Meyer, B. Rowan. Institutionalized Organizations: Formal Structure as Myth and Ceremony. American Journal of Sociology, 83;1977;340–363.

[10] P. J. DiMaggio, W. W. Powell. The Iron Cage Revisited: Institutional Isomorphism and Collective Rationality in Organizational Fields. American Sociological Review, 48;1983;147–160.

[11] J. Owen-Smith, W. W. Powell. Networks and Institutions. In: R. Greenwood (Ed.), Handbook of Organizational Institutionalism. New York: Sage Press; 2008, pp. 596–623

[12] D. Chubin, E. J. Hackett. Peerless Science: Peer Review and US Science Policy. Albany: State University of New York Press; 1990.

[13] R. K. Merton. Singletons and Multiples in Scientific Discovery—A Chapter in the Sociology of Science. Proceedings of the American Philosophical Society, 105(5);1961;470–&.

[14] J. P. Walsh, W. Cohen. Real Impediments to Academic Biomedical Research. Innovation Policy and the Economy, 8;2007.

[15] D. J. Kevles. The Baltimore Case: A Trial of Politics, Science, and Character. New York: W.W. Norton & Co.; 1998.

[16] D. Y. Wohn, D. Normile. Korean Cloning Scandal: Prosecutors Allege Elaborate Deception and Missing Funds. Science, 312;2006;980–981.

[17] G. Rowe, L. J. Frewer. Public Participation Methods: A Framework for Evaluation. Science, Technology & Human Values, 25;2000;3–29.

[18] M. S. Anderson, A. S. Horn, K. R. Risbey, E. A. Ronning, R. D. Vries, B. C. Martinson. What Do Mentoring and Training in the Responsible Conduct of Research Have to Do with Scientists' Misbehavior? Findings from a National Survey of NIH-Funded Scientists. Academic Medicine, 82;2007;853–860.

[19] R. Hollander. Ethics Education and Scientific and Engineering Research: What's Been Learned? What Should Be Done? Report of a Workshop. Washington (DC): National Academies Press; 2009.

[20] J. Evans. Playing God? Human Genetic Engineering and the Rationalization of the Public Bioethical Debate. Chicago: University of Chicago Press; 2002.

[21] S. Halpern. Lesser Harms: The Morality of Risk in Medical Research. Chicago: University of Chicago Press; 2004.

[22] L. Smith-Doerr. Learning to Reflect or Deflect? U.S. Policies and Graduate Programs' Ethics Training for Life Scientists. In: S. Frickel, K. Moore (Eds.), The New Political Sociology of Science: Institutions, Networks, and Power. Madison: University of Wisconsin Press; 2006, pp. 405–431.

[23] L. Smith-Doerr. Decoupling Policy and Practice: How Life Scientists in Three Nations Respond to Policies Requiring Ethics Education. Minerva, 46;2008;1–16.

[24] L. Smith-Doerr. Discourses of Dislike: Responses to Ethics Education Policies by Life Scientists in the UK, Italy and the US. Journal of Empirical Research in Human Research Ethics, 4;2009;49–57.

[25] M. Weber. Economy and Society. G. Roth, C. Wittich (Eds. and Transl.). Berkeley: University of California Press; 1914 (1978).

[26] C. W. Huff, L. Barnard, W. Frey. Good Computing: A Pedagogically Focused Model of Virtue in the Practice of Computing. Journal of Information, Communication and Ethics in Society, 6;2008;284–316.

[27] L. Smith-Doerr, J. Croissant. A Feminist Approach to University-Industry Relations: Integrating Theories of Gender, Knowledge and Capital. Boston (MA): Boston University unpublished manuscript; 2010.

[28] J. Thomson, J. Itskovitz-Eldor, S. Shapiro, M. Waknitz, J. Swiergiel, V. Marshall, J. Jones. Embryonic Stem Cell Lines Derived from Human Blastocysts. Science, 282;1998;1145–1147.

[29] F. Murray. The Stem-Cell Market—Patents and the Pursuit of Scientific Progress. New England Journal of Management, 356;2007;2341–2343.

[30] C. T. Scott, J. McCormick, J. Owen-Smith. And Then There Were Two: Use of hESC Lines. Nature Biotechnology, 27;2009;696–697.

[31] D. H. Guston, K. Kenniston. The Fragile Contract: University Science and the Federal Government. Cambridge (MA): MIT Press; 1994.

[32] D. L. Kleinman. Politics on the Endless Frontier: Postwar Research in the United States. Durham (NC): Duke University Press; 1995.

[33] J. Owen-Smith, J. McCormick. An International Gap in Human ES Cell Research. Nature Biotechnology, 24;2006;391–392.

[34] A. Levine. Research Policy and the Mobilization of U.S. Stem Cell Scientists. Nature Biotechnology, 24;2006;865–866.

[35] J. McCormick, J. Owen-Smith, C. Scott. Distribution of Human Embryonic Stem Cell Lines: Who, When, and Where. Cell Stem Cell, 4;2009;107–110.

[36] B. Prainsack. Negotiating Life: The Regulation of Human Cloning and Embryonic Stem Cell Research in Israel. Social Studies of Science, 36;2006;173–205.

[37] C. Fox. Cell of Cells: The Global Race to Capture and Control the Stem Cell. New York: W.W. Norton & Co.; 2007.

[38] C.-S. Lee, A. Schrank. Incubating Innovation or Cultivating Corruption: The Developmental State and the Life Sciences in Asia. Chicago: University of Chicago Press; 2008.

[39] T. Caulfield, A. Zarzeczny, J. McCormick. The Stem Cell Research Environment: A Patchwork of Patchworks. Stem Cell Reviews and Reports, 2;2009.

[40] S. Stayn. Biobanking of Blastocysts for Research to Improve Human Health: The Need for Coherent National Policy. Stanford Journal of Law, Science and Policy, 1;2009;7–18.

[41] B. Lo, L. Parham, C. Rboom, M. Cedars, E. Gates, L. Giudice, D. G. Halme, W. Hershon, A. Kriegstein, P. Kwok, M. Oberman, C. Roberts, R. Wagner. Importing Human Pluripotent Stem Cell Lines Derived at Another Institution: Tailoring Review to Ethical Concerns. Cell Stem Cell, 4;2009;115–123.

[42] The Emergence of Biotechnology: DNA to Genentech [Conference]. Philadelphia (PA): Chemical Heritage Foundation; 1997.

[43] S. B. Wright. Molecular Politics Developing American and British Regulatory Policy for Genetic Engineering, 1972–1982. Chicago: University of Chicago Press; 1994.

[44] J. Owen-Smith, M. Riccaboni, F. Pammolli, W. W. Powell. A Comparison of U.S. and European University-Industry Relations in the Life Sciences. Management Science, 48;2002;24–43.

[45] D. Fredrickson. The Recombinant DNA Controversy: A Memoir. Washington (DC): ASM Press; 2001.

[46] E. Popp-Berman. Creating the Market University: Science, the State, and the Economy, 1965–85. Sociology dissertation. Berkeley: University of California Press; 2007.

[47] R. Eisenberg. Proprietary Rights and the Norms of Science in Biotechnology Research. The Yale Law Journal, 97;1987;177–231.

[48] D. Rhoten, W. W. Powell. The Frontiers of Intellectual Property: Expanded Protection vs. New Models of Open Science. Annual Review of Law and Social Science, 3;2007.

[49] D. C. Mowery, R. R. Nelson, B. Sampat, A. Ziedonis. Ivory Tower and Industrial Innovation. Stanford (CA): Stanford University Press; 2004.

[50] J. Owen-Smith. From Separate Systems to a Hybrid Order: Accumulative Advantage Across Public and Private Science at Research One Universities. Research Policy, 32;2003;1081–1104.

[51] K. B. Whittington, J. Owen-Smith, W. W. Powell. Networks, Propinquity and Innovation in Knowledge-Intensive Industries. Administrative Science Quarterly, 54;2009;90–122.

[52] W. Powell, K. Packalen, K. Whittington. Organizational and Institutional Genesis: The Emergence of High-Tech Clusters in the Life Sciences. In: J. Padgett, W.

Powell (Eds.), The Emergence of Organizations and Markets. Princeton (NJ): Princeton University Press; forthcoming.

[53] S. Casper. How Do Technology Clusters Emerge and Become Sustainable? Social Network Formation Within the San Diego Biotechnology Cluster. Research Policy, 36;2007;438–455.

[54] J. Owen-Smith, W. W. Powell. Knowledge Networks as Channels and Conduits: The Effect of Spillovers in the Boston Biotechnology Community. Organization Science, 15;2004;5–21.

[55] E. Hackett, D. Rhoten. The Snowbird Charrette: Integrative Interdisciplinary Collaboration in Environmental Research Design. Minerva, 47;2009;407–440.

[56] D. Rhoten, E. J. Hackett, E. O'Connor. Collaborative Creation and Creative Integration: Originality, Disciplinarity and Interdisciplinarity. Thesis, 11;2009;83–109.

[57] E. Leahey. Methodological Memes and Mores: Toward a Sociology of Social Research. Annual Review of Sociology, 34;2008;33–53.

[58] A. Porter, I. Rafols. Is Science Becoming More Interdisciplinary? Measuring and Mapping Six Research Fields Over Time. Scientometrics, 81;2009;719–749.

[59] J. Jacobs, S. Frickel. Interdisciplinarity: A Critical Assessment. Annual Review of Sociology, 35;2009;43–65.

[60] V. B. Mansilla. Symptoms of Quality: Assessing Expert Interdisciplinary Work at the Frontier. Research Evaluation, 15;2006;17–29.

[61] M. Lamont. How Professors Think: Inside the Curious World of Academic Judgment. Cambridge (MA): Harvard University Press; 2009.

[62] R. Merton. Priorities in Scientific Discovery: A Chapter in the Sociology of Science. American Sociological Review, 22;1957;635–659.

[63] B. Staw, L. E. Sandelands, J. E. Dutton. Threat-Rigidity Effects in Organizational Behavior. Administrative Science Quarterly, 26;1981;501–524.

[64] J. Owen-Smith, W. W. Powell. The Expanding Role of University Patenting in the Life Sciences: Assessing the Importance of Experience and Connectivity. Research Policy, 32;2003;1695–1711.

[65] J. Owen-Smith. Dockets, Deals, and Sagas: Commensuration and the Rationalization of Experience in University Licensing. Social Studies of Science, 35;2005;69–97.

[66] D. Rhoten, S. Pfirman. Women in Interdisciplinary Science: Exploring Preferences and Consequences. Research Policy, 36;2007;56–75.

[67] S. Page. The Difference: How the Power of Diversity Creates Better Groups, Firms, Schools, and Societies. Princeton (NJ): Princeton University Press; 2007.

[68] P. V. Marsden, N. E. Friedkin. Network Studies of Social Influence. Sociological Methods and Research, 22;1993.

Notes

1. We emphasize that our focus on the three sociological mechanisms of networks, power, and institutions, and on the outcomes of unanticipated consequences, is but one sociological approach to science policy.

2. Similarly, mandated training in affirmative employment practices results in a slower pace of hiring women and minorities, whereas mentorship programs and company-wide task forces, both more positive and engaged practices, foster female and minority advancement into top management. See Frank F. Dobbin, *Inventing Equal Opportunity* (Princeton, NJ: Princeton University Press, 2009).

3. In November 2009, the NIH announced an update to the policy, which indicated that web-based-only training is not sufficient. See http://grants.nih.gov/grants/guide/notice-files/NOT-OD-10-019.html.

4. This section draws heavily on Owen-Smith's ongoing work with Mariana Craciun, Jennifer McCormick, and Christopher Thomas Scott.

5. This section draws on Powell's research with Kjersten Whittington, Kelly Packalen, and Jason Owen-Smith.

The Economics of Science and Technology Policy

Richard B. Freeman

5

1. Introduction

If you believe that long-term economic growth depends on the application of science and technology to the production of goods and services—and who in the knowledge economy does not?—then science lies at the heart of economic growth. Without increased scientific and technological knowledge, the economy would presumably end up in some static, steady state equilibrium—the economics equivalent of entropy. People would come and go, talking of Michelangelo, and the changing price of art would be the only interesting topic in economics. In his essay "Possibilities for Our Grandchildren" [1] Keynes painted such a vision of the world in the 2000s in which people had lots of time for leisure and culture but had little incentive to increase the stock of useful knowledge and apply it to create new goods and services and new ways to produce existing goods and services.

What differentiates the dynamic economy in which we live from the stasis of classical theory that Keynes painted for his grandchildren are society's investments in research and development (R&D). Investment in basic research augments the stock of useful knowledge. Investment in applied research and development turns that knowledge into innovations that raise economic well-being. Science and technology policy helps support this process and directs it to areas of social need. Economic incentives influence the career choice of students with respect to science/engineering and the decisions of firms to fund and commercialize research. Individuals, firms, and the government interact in a dynamic process that makes the whole system work and keeps Keynes' classical economic vision of the future at bay.

Normative economic theory imbeds the analysis of science policy in the same welfare-oriented framework that economists use to assess public policies and government interventions in market economies. This provides a logical framework for examining science's claim on social resources and for science of science policy.

In this chapter I consider the economics of supply and demand in the labor market for science and engineers, the way policy affects those two blades of Marshall's famous market scissors [2] to determine wages and employment of scientific-engineering workers, and some of the interactions and feedbacks in market dynamics.

2. Incentives and the Supply of Scientists and Engineers

At the heart of the economic analysis of the supply of scientists and engineers is the response of economic agents, particularly young people choosing careers, to the incentives that society gives to select scientific work over other viable alternatives. Economics does not say that incentives in the form of high salaries, good job prospects, or the sometimes lucrative prizes and prestigious awards that go to star scientists are the only factor or the main factor in decisions to work in science. Economics is about choices *on the margin*. It recognizes that persons with particular skill sets or interests may be largely unresponsive to plausible changes in incentives. If you are a ten-year-old mathematical prodigy such as the young Terence Tao, it would take massive incentives to move you into investment banking or selling used cars instead of mathematics. Similarly, if you are a musical or athletic prodigy, it would take massive incentives to induce you to solve theorems instead of starring in the entertainment or sports worlds.

Persons on the margin between science and non-science work presumably have both the ability and interests to pursue either choice and are thus likely to be sensitive to pecuniary or other social rewards in making their choice. The greater the overlap in the skill set and interest of persons between science and viable alternatives, the greater will be the elasticity of supply to incentives. For instance, students who major in the biological sciences are often conflicted between becoming doctors or bio-medical research scientists. Students interested in creating innovative high-tech businesses often view engineering and economics/business as alternative routes to that goal. As science has increasingly become a team activity and as more scientists and engineers form start-up firms to turn their ideas into useful products, the overlap in skills that make someone good in science and good in business has presumably grown. From the other side, Wall Street firms hire "quants" with skills in mathematics and physics to develop and analyze financial instruments.

There are also skills that are valuable outside of science that have little payoff in science and, conversely, skills valuable in science that have little payoff in other fields. The talent that makes someone a great actor/actress or professional wrestler is unlikely to make them productive in science or math.

And the talent that makes someone a great research scientist is unlikely to make that person a movie star or grappler in the squared circle. Because the critical skills are so different, science will lose little when a talented actor/actress chooses Hollywood or pro wrestling over Cal Tech, and conversely, Hollywood or wrestling will lose little by losing a math whiz to Cal Tech.[1]

On net, whether increased incentives for science draws persons from outside science who are more or less able than current scientists and engineers depends on the correlation of the abilities that pay off in science and those that pay off in those other fields. If the skills are positively correlated, and the person on the margin chooses science, science gains someone likely to do especially well in science while the other field loses someone who could do well in its domain. Conversely, if the two skill sets are negatively correlated, the marginal person who moves between them will increase the average ability of persons in both fields, measured in terms of the skills that matter.

Are enough young people on the margin between science and other fields so that policy interventions can substantially change the supply of scientists and engineers? Analysis of enrollments in various scientific fields, including physics, engineering, biology, and mathematics, shows that increased earnings, better scholarship and fellowship support, greater chances to attain the status of independent principal investigator, and the like, have large impacts on student decisions to enroll and graduate in science and engineering specialties [3]. In the annual survey of entering freshman conducted by UCLA's Higher Education Research Institute, students invariably report that monetary and career issues are important in choice of fields of study and careers [4].

Economists rarely question the idea that people respond to pecuniary incentives but there is a social psychology literature that warns that paying people to undertake certain actions can backfire by replacing or killing intrinsic motivation, which leads them to do less of that activity [5]. Choosing a career is not one of those activities. In the early 1970s, when the job market for PhD physicists was particularly difficult, the Physics Department of the University of Chicago invited me to give a seminar on the supply and demand for physicists. I presented a regression-based analysis that linked enrollments in physics to the lagged earnings of physicists relative to other highly educated workers and related physicist earnings to past increases in supply and changes in R&D spending [6]. The seminar chair criticized me for the naive belief that young physicists were motivated by anything other than love of science. Study physics for career reasons such as pay or job prospects? No dedicated scientist would let such mundane things affect him or her. We could have debated the merits or demerits of my regression analysis but the disagreement was settled by the graduate students and post-docs in the seminar. Troubled by their career prospects, the students booed and hissed the senior professor for failing to appreciate their concerns. This proved as well or better than any econometrics the validity of the economics approach to decisions to invest in scientific careers.

Evidence that improving pay and career prospects in science can increase the inflow of students into scientific fields notwithstanding, much U.S. policy discourse focuses on raising skills and interest in science among K–12 students to expand the supply of scientists. Improvements in teaching science, mathematics, and engineering at the K–12 level would surely benefit students and science, but targeting people years before they make their career decisions is not an efficient way to increase supply in any policy-relevant time period. Since it takes much additional education for an eager 10th grader to become a practicing scientist, someone motivated by better K–12 education would not appear on the job market for 10–15 years. Recognizing this, the National Academies of Science's 2010 Report on increasing the supply of underrepresented minorities in science made its top priority action to "increase undergraduate retention and completion through strong academic, social, and financial support" [7]. What is true for underrepresented minorities is true for all students. Many more young people enter college and university with the background and intent to pursue science and engineering than ultimately do so. Many more major in science and engineering at the bachelor's level than go on to graduate work in scientific disciplines. And many masters and PhD graduates in science and engineering who end up working outside of traditional scientific careers could be attracted into science and engineering activities with the appropriate incentives.

Considerable policy discourse also revolves around normative appeals for young people to choose science over other careers. Every few years, if not every year, leaders of the U.S. scientific community and of the high-tech business world proclaim that the country faces a shortage of scientists and engineers.[2] The economy needs more scientists and engineers. High-tech firms need more. The future of humanity needs more. Whatever the actual needs of the economy, high-tech firms, and humanity, the lesson from economics is that if the country wants additional persons in scientific disciplines, it has to "put its money where its mouth is." Students compare working as a low wage post doctorate employee with uncertain prospects of a regular job to the high pay from business, law, medicine, or investment banking. It is difficult to induce those on the margin to choose science and engineering when the economics lie in the other direction.

Past experience shows that when the United States increases incentives for investing in science and engineering, young people respond. In 1957, faced with the Sputnik challenge from the Soviet Union, the United States increased R&D spending, which greatly raised the earnings and employment prospects of scientists and engineers. It awarded large numbers of National Science Foundation (NSF) graduate research fellowships (GRFs) and National Defense Education Act fellowships to encourage entrance into scientific careers. The booming job market and generous fellowships induced large numbers of young Americans to choose science and engineering.

Fast forward to the turn of the 21st century. Despite a more than threefold increase in the number of bachelor's graduates in science and engineering, the NSF offered the same number of GRFs as it did in the 1950s. The value of the awards declined relative to other opportunities so that in 1999 the agency's Committee on Visitors concluded that "the GRF awards are no longer as attractive as they once were" [8]. The result was a drop in the proportion of science and engineering bachelor's graduates applying for the fellowships. In response, the NSF raised the stipend value of the GRFs from $15,000 in 1999 to $30,000 in 2005. In 2010 it further increased the number of awards to 2,000. Figure 5.1 shows the relation between spending on the GRF relative to gross national product and the number of GRF applicants relative to science and engineering bachelor's graduates. Statistical analysis confirms the picture in the graph of relatively high elasticities of supply to the fellowship awards [9]. In fact, the increased value of GRFs induced other fellowship-granting organizations to raise the dollar value of their graduate science fellowships, which helped induce more U.S.-born or resident students into

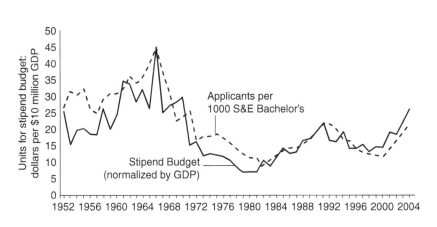

Figure 5.1.
Fraction of science and engineering bachelor's graduates applying to the GRF program compared to total GRF budget, divided by GDP.
Source: NSF-DGE various years, cumulative index of the GRF program and related data sets. Data based on the GDP from the Bureau of Economic Analysis.

graduate science and engineering. But attracting more students into science and engineering will not necessarily keep them working in the fields if the increased supply depresses career earnings and employment opportunities when they graduate.

There have been two important changes in the demographic composition of the scientific work force from the 1960s to the 2000s. The first is a large increase in the proportion of women getting higher degrees in science and engineering. In 1967, women earned 25% of bachelor's science and engineering degrees, 14% of master's level science and engineering degrees, and 8% of doctorate level engineering and science degrees [10]. Forty years later women earned 51% of science and engineering bachelor's degrees, 46% of science and engineering master's degrees, and 39% of science and engineering PhD degrees [11]. By 2008 the female share of PhDs granted was 70% in psychology and 53% in the life sciences [12]. Approximately half of applicants and winners of the NSF GRFs were women, a far cry from the minimal numbers of female applicants and awardees when the program began in the 1950s. The female share of degrees in mathematical-intensive fields also increased but seemed to plateau at about 20% in the 2000s. As a result women remained substantially underrepresented in the mathematical and computer science and architecture and engineering occupations [13].

The reasons fewer women than men are involved in mathematics-oriented activities has generated great controversy. In 2005 the president of Harvard University, Lawrence Summers, suggested that one possible explanation was that men and women differ in their mathematical abilities, possibly for some unknown innate reason. At one time men scored higher on tests of mathematical skills than women but this is no longer the case. Women have closed the gap in math test scores with men and score the same or modestly higher than men in countries that have more female-friendly cultural climates [14]. The difference between the genders is in the variation of scores around the mean. Scores for men vary more than for women so that there are relatively more men at the bottom and at the top of the distribution [15]. The relatively larger number of men with very high scores presumably contributes to the difference between the allocation of men and women between more and less mathematical fields.

In almost all science and engineering fields, including those where the female proportion of graduates is around 50% or higher, women progress less rapidly than men in academic careers. Women are as likely to receive tenure track jobs upon receipt of a PhD but are less likely to gain tenure within ten years of the doctorate [16]. Why is this?

The most important factor is the structure of academic careers, which conflicts with the normal life cycle of family formation and child bearing and rearing for women. Consider the career path in the largest scientific field, life sciences. Life scientists earn their doctorates 8.6 years after graduating college (6.9 years for those who go immediately to graduate school) and typically work at postdoctoral jobs for 3 or more years [17]. This means that they are in their early to mid-thirties when they obtain their first full-time academic job, and in their late thirties or early forties when they come up for tenure. While some women have children and spend as much time on research as they did before the child, women that have children generally devote less time to research after the birth of the child and thus are likely to produce fewer papers than male peers in the years surrounding the tenure decision. By contrast, male scientists with young children tend to work more hours than they had in the past. The result is gender differences in rates of promotion.

Another aspect of the career structure of academic science that is likely to discourage women is the tournament competition for limited slots and promotions. Academic science has many of the same attributes as golf or tennis tournaments, with competition on a reasonably clear criterion—in the case of science the production of knowledge as measured in publications and citations—that determines success in the form of promotions, research support, and so on [18]. Tournaments between people of comparable skills are an efficient way to incentivize work. However, women with the abilities to win tournaments tend to eschew such competitions in favor of more cooperative work environments. By contrast, men, including those lacking the abilities to succeed in tournaments eagerly compete in them anyway [19]. The increased importance of teamwork in science may ultimately offset the effect of the tournament job market on women but thus far it has not done so fully.

As the supply of women with science degrees keeps growing, universities and firms face pressure to alter personnel and career practices that do not mesh with the greater share of women in the science talent pool. The challenge is to find ways to make the timing of career decisions and the careers themselves more female family-friendly while maintaining the competitive pressures that drive scientific researchers.

The supply of scientists and engineers in the United States (and in most other advanced countries) has also changed greatly along one other dimension. This is in the national background of scientists and engineers. In the 1990s–2000s the number of international students and immigrant scientists and engineers from developing countries, particularly from India and China, increased substantially. Column 1 of Table 5.1 shows the great reliance of the

Table 5.1. International students are critical source of U.S. immigrants in S&E workforce, 2005

	Percentage of natural S&E workers who are foreign-born	*Percentage of foreign-born with highest degree in U.S.*
Bachelor's	5.2	64
Master's	38.6	69
Doctorate	50.9	54

Source: Degrees: NSF, Science and Engineering Indicators, 2008, chapter 2, tables 2-28, 2-30, 2-31; Post-docs: Enrollments, grad., table 2-22.

United States on foreign-born persons in natural science and engineering, particularly at the graduate levels where over half of PhDs under forty-five were born overseas.

Underlying the increase in immigrant scientists and engineers is the rapid expansion of higher education around the world. In 1970 29% of enrollments in higher education were in the United States, which together with Canada, led the world in the number enrolled relative to the number of young persons. Thereafter, European countries increased their enrollments more rapidly than did the United States, which dropped the United States to the middle of the pack. In the 1990s hugely populous China and other developing countries began expanding their higher education systems. By 2006 the U.S. share of world enrollments in higher education had fallen to 12% [20]. The growing number of science and engineering students world-wide greatly increased the potential number of immigrant scientists and engineers. Economic incentives in the form of better earnings and career opportunities in the United States than in their home country created a fairly elastic supply of science and engineering specialists to the United States, particularly from developing countries.

The attraction of American institutions of higher education for graduate study also contributed to the increased supply of foreign-born scientists and engineers. Many international students remain in the country after they graduate. The earlier they come—as undergraduates rather than graduate students, or as high school students rather than undergraduates—the more likely international students migrate to the country. Column 2 of Table 5.1 shows that huge proportions of foreign-born scientists and engineers obtained their highest degree in the United States. Policy toward international students and immigration is thus a part of science and technology policy.

Experienced researchers also respond to economic incentives. They do so in choosing the employer or sector in which they work and in the research topics on which they work. If industry or government agencies invest in a research area, scientists and engineers will shift their research to that area. The "war on cancer" induced researchers to work on medical science issues related to cancer. The National Nanotechnology Initiative spurred increased research on nanotechnology projects. Indicative of this responsiveness, when the National Institutes of Health (NIH) announced in 2009 that it was allocating $200 million to fund 200 or more special challenge grants to researchers outside of its normal grant process, the agency received over 21,000 applications. Medical scientists from one institution, the University of Minnesota Healthcare Partners, applied for 50 awards for $19.1 million in March 2009, 489 awards for $331.8 million in April 2009, and 17 awards for $21.1 million during May 1–5, 2009. NIH had to rapidly recruit over 18,000 scientists to peer review the proposals. Scientists follow the scientific and technological opportunities and their own ideas and interests but they also follow the money in deciding what to research.

Perhaps the most important change in the nature of scientific work, with huge implications for the science of science policy is the shift from a world in which most scientists worked as lone investigators, perhaps with a laboratory assistant or two, to the current world in which most scientists and engineers work in large teams. Analysis of the productivity of scientists has traditionally focused on individual productivity. Since Lotka's 1926 study of the number of scientific publications of chemists and physicists [21], analysts have documented that a few scientists contribute the most research papers, that a few papers gain the most citations, etc., so that scientific productivity follows a power law with a long fat tail. These studies fit well with a model of science in which the "stars" are the prime movers of knowledge. They suggest that policy should identify potential stars as quickly as possible and reward them with money or grants.

But over time the predominance of lone investigative work has declined. The number of persons working on scientific projects has increased greatly. In 2000 the typical paper in the sciences listed 3.5 authors, with variation among fields, compared to 1.9 authors in 1995 [22]. Scientometric evidence on patterns of co-authorship and citations highlight the links among scientists and the paper trail of their work has led to a new network analysis of the development and transmission of knowledge. Network studies fit well with a model of science, which places social interactions at the heart of scientific progress. If what matters for progress is a dense network of researchers, policy-makers should spread resources more widely.

The changing nature of scientific work raises important questions that readily fit with economic analysis. What incentives lead scientists to collaborate

with others? How does the allocation of credit in team-based production affect the career path of scientists, particularly younger persons just beginning
their research lives? What determines the productivity of teams of scientists?
What is the optimal composition of a team? How does the formation of postdoctoral associations and unions to protect the interests of younger researchers affect their pecuniary and non-pecuniary work conditions? What kinds
of work relations will emerge in the new world of team science? Economists
concerned with science have not yet focused on these questions but they surely
will.

3. Demand for Scientists and Engineers

Institutions of higher education hire scientists and engineers to do research,
usually on grants that the scientists and engineers raise themselves, and/or to
teach and mentor the next generation of scientists and engineers. In the United
States, universities conduct the bulk of basic research, much of which is government funded. In Germany and some other countries, government funds more
basic research at research institutes independent of universities.

Industry hires scientists and engineers to design and develop new commercial products or processes based on scientific advances or to help implement or spread those products or processes in ways that increase profits. Table
5.2 shows that in the United States and in most other advanced countries,
private industry undertakes the preponderance of R&D spending and thus
hires most research scientists and engineers. In 2008, business funded 67% of
U.S. R&D and conducted 73% of R&D, the difference resulting from substantial government support for industrial research [23].

Much like industry, the government hires scientists and engineers for
mission-oriented projects to further specific goals. Sixty-one percent of total
government R&D is for defense, 21% for health, and 6% for space, compared
to 6% for general science. Still through mission-oriented R&D as well as support of general science, the federal government funded 57% of U.S. basic
research in 2008.

In addition to funding research, government affects R&D through the
patent protection that it gives to new discoveries or inventions. Patents give
the inventor or discoverer monopoly rights over the new knowledge for the
period of the patent. Economists analyze patents in terms of the trade-off
between the static inefficiency from the temporary monopoly and the dynamic efficiency from the incentive that patents give to knowledge creation
[24, 25]. In the absence of patents the only way firms could keep others from
poaching their trade secrets would be through industrial secrecy. They would

Table 5.2. Gross expenditures on R&D by performing sector, for selected countries: Most recent year (percent)

Country	Business	Government	Higher education	Private nonprofit
United States (2007)	71.9	10.7	13.3	4.2
Japan (2007)	77.9	7.8	12.6	1.7
China (2007)	72.3	19.2	8.5	0.0
Germany (2007)	69.9	13.9	16.2	0.0
France (2007)	63.2	16.5	19.2	1.1
South Korea (2007)	76.2	11.7	10.7	1.4
United Kingdom (2007)	64.1	9.2	24.5	2.1
Russian Federation (2007)	64.2	29.1	6.3	0.3
Canada (2008)	56.1	9.6	33.8	0.5
Italy (2006)	48.8	17.2	30.3	3.7

Note: Top 10 R&D performing countries.

Source: Organisation for Economic Co-operation and Development, Main Science and Technology Indicators (2009/1).

only research areas that could be so protected, and thus would do less research than if they could have legal protection through a patent. Another disadvantage of industrial secrecy is that it can in principle last forever, which would deprive others of the knowledge and opportunity to improve on the invention. But patents do not protect all knowledge associated with R&D. To prevent researchers with leading-edge knowledge from taking this knowledge to a competitor, many firms require employees to sign non-compete agreements. These are legal documents in which the employees agree that they will not undertake similar work elsewhere for some period of time. State law governs the enforcement of non-compete agreements. Some states such as Massachusetts enforce these agreements. Others such as California have made them invalid. This has consequences for the location and nature of inventors' activities [26].

In 1980 Congress decided that universities receiving federal research grants were too slow in commercializing inventions or discoveries from those grants. To encourage universities to be more pro-active, Congress enacted the Bayh-Dole Act, which allowed them to file for patent protection on findings from government-funded research. This was part and parcel of a general movement in the 1980s and 1990s to strengthen patent protection. While the overall effort has received mixed reviews from economists [24], the Bayh-Dole Act is widely viewed as successful in getting university researchers to try to move their discoveries more rapidly into commercial use [27].

Another way to induce private actors to undertake R&D and make the knowledge public is to run a prize competition which gives large monetary prizes to those who succeed in making the relevant discovery. As an example of such a prize system, the X-prize Foundation offered $10 million prizes in the 2000s for inventors who achieved goals that it viewed as having "the potential to benefit humanity" such as a spacecraft, lunar explorer, or a more efficient automobile (http://www.xprize.org). Some analysts suggest that prizes should also be used to spur pharmaceutical companies to develop drugs for rare diseases or diseases in developing countries where incomes are too low to justify a profit-making firm seeking to cure the disease [28].

Economists also study how firms respond to tax write-offs for R&D. Whenever the government tax advantages a particular activity, firms have incentives not only to increase that activity but also to re-label other activities to fit under the tax break. This creates a problem in estimating the impact of changes in taxes on actual R&D. But the problem is manageable. In 2000, Bronwyn Hall and John Van Reenen reviewed studies of R&D tax credits in many countries and concluded that firms did indeed respond by undertaking more real research to the R&D tax credits [29]. There is thus evidence of demand responsiveness to policy-induced incentives comparable to the evidence of supply responsiveness.

Economic analysis of the demand for R&D highlights the ways in which investment in knowledge differs from investment in tangible capital goods. Knowledge has the properties of a public good, in that once it is made public, there is no way to exclude firms or researchers from using it (beyond the patent system) and that one person's use does not deplete it for others [30]. To the contrary, the more people that use a body of knowledge the more likely someone will improve on it.

The information created by R&D distinguishes investments in research from investments in tangible physical capital in an important way. As a firm or principal investigator learns from initial research whether a particular research path is or is not promising, there is the *option* of deciding whether or not to pursue that path further. Many firms such as those in the pharmaceutical industry divide R&D projects formally into stages[3] that reflect this aspect of research. These firms do not fund the entire project on the basis of its having a positive expected net present value at the outset. If the project goes well, the firm proceeds. If the project goes poorly, it pulls the plug on the project and saves money. This is similar to an option in finance, where the investor buys the right to buy or sell some item in the future when the investor will have better knowledge of its value. Potentially risky projects with an expected negative net present value today may turn out to be profitable through the lens of an option. Since the value of options rises with variance in potential re-

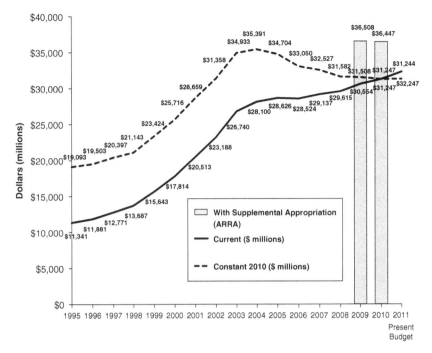

Figure 5.2.
The volatility of the NIH budget in the great doubling and in the ARRA stimulus.

Source: FASEB, 2010.

turns, the option perspective leads firms and principal investigators to undertake riskier potentially transformative research than they would otherwise do. Although few firms explicitly base R&D decisions on the mathematics of option valuation [31], evidence that returns to R&D are highly skewed [32, 33], with the bulk of returns coming from relatively few projects, has the hallmark of option behavior.

Research and development spending can also be viewed from the perspective of *portfolio* analysis, which stresses the value of diversification in investing in different assets or projects to reduce risk. Measuring risk by the variance of returns, the formula for the summation of variances shows that undertaking different projects that have low positive correlated returns or better yet negatively correlated returns reduces the total risk. Since R&D is risky and firms/researchers/government program officers are presumably risk averse, the economics recommendation is that decision makers do better to form portfolios of projects rather than put all their money into the most promising one.

4. The Dangers of Volatile R&D Spending

In the macro-economy, private investment is the "squeaky wheel" that produces recessions while government spending is the stabilizer that dampens private sector fluctuations. In R&D the opposite is true. Government spending is the volatile component while private industry spending is the stabilizer. In the United States the ratio of government-funded R&D to gross domestic product has varied substantially over time as policy priorities changed. The ratio rose in the late 1950s and early 1960s as the government responded to Sputnik. It dropped in the late 1960s when the government cut back defense and space programs, it stabilized in the late 1970s as the government increased R&D for energy in response to the 1970s oil price shock, and then it fell in the late 1980s when the government cut defense-related and energy-related R&D. Federal spending increased sharply for bio-medical sciences after President Clinton and Congress agreed in 1997 to double the nominal budget of the National Institute of Health over the next five years. President Bush completed the doubling in 2003 but then stabilized the budget so that real NIH spending fell over the remainder of his term as president. This effectively negated the expansionary impact of the doubling. Three years into the post-doubling squeeze of NIH, the biomedical research community was in an uproar over the harm that the decline in real spending was having. According to Whitehead Institute founder Robert Weinberg, "The marvelous engine of American biomedical research that was constructed during the last half of the 20th century is being taken apart, piece by piece" [34]. Elias Zerhouni, Bush's director of NIH, expressed alarm at the effect of the cutbacks on the careers of entering bio-medical scientists: "Without effective national policies to recruit young scientists to the field, and support their research over the long term, in 10 to 15 years, we'll have more scientists older than 65 than those younger than 35. This is not a sustainable trend in biomedical research and must be addressed aggressively" [35].

The NIH experience highlights two problems with volatile government R&D spending. The first is that large spending increases are likely to increase the costs and reduce the productivity of research compared to more gradual increases in spending. Rapid buildups in R&D produce larger increases in costs than gradual buildups because it takes time for people and resources to meet the new demand, and because costs tend to rise non-linearly in the short run. This means less output for the research dollar. The second problem is that rapid increases must level off, and when they do, this invariably leaves some people and projects caught in the pipeline. During the doubling period many more scientists applied for lucrative grants (that supply responsiveness again), but the number of applications rose even more in the aftermath as researchers who feared that their careers would end without further support applied several times for the scarce funds. The NIH, which is the single largest employer of biomedical researchers in the United States, with more than 1,000 principal investigators and 6,000 to 7,000 researchers, cut employment of principal investigators by 9% in the post-doubling period.

The costs of the volatile R&D spending are mindful of the costs of volatile capital spending in the classic business cycle accelerator model of investment. In the accelerator model, an increase in demand for output induces firms to seek more capital stock to meet the new demand. This increases investment spending. When firms reach the desired level of capital stock, they stop investing, save to replace decaying capital. The equivalent of demand for output in research is federal R&D spending. The equivalent of investment spending is the creation of jobs for new researchers. As Zerhouni correctly observed, it is the young people who build their skills as graduate students or post docs during the acceleration phase of spending and bear much of the cost of the deceleration.

Following the onset of the Wall Street implosion and ensuing recession, President Obama's American Recovery and Reinvestment Act (ARRA) stimulus package included $20.5 billion in additional research funding. The stimulus to science was initially set at $14.0 billion, but in the conference committee reconciling the House and Senate versions of the bill, Senator Spector of Pennsylvania added $6.5 billion for the NIH. Figure 5.2 shows the pattern of change in NIH spending from 1995 through 2010 and the proposed 2011 budget. The burst of ARRA money for research followed by a huge post-2010 cutback has the potential to create a problem comparable to that which followed the doubling of NIH spending from 1998 to 2003. But having learned from the NIH doubling experience, agencies, universities, and principal investigators have sought ways to smooth the spending of funds and buffer the drop off in spending when ARRA ends. Knowing that this burst of spending is temporary will at the minimum prevent the shock that occurred when the NIH doubling ended.

If ever there was a science policy problem where economics can help policy makers, it is in finding ways to avoid the "falling off the cliff" scenario at the end of a burst of spending.

5. Conclusion: How Much Should the Public Support R&D?

How should a taxpayer evaluate the billions of dollars that the U.S. government spends on R&D directly or indirectly by awarding patents or tax credits or subsidies for private research and development activities?

The economics answer is to examine the rate of return to R&D spending. Many economic studies of R&D use production functions to estimate the impact of R&D on outcomes and to assess its rate of return. Because it is difficult to trace the effects of basic research on output these studies focus on private rates of return to firm-based R&D. They typically relate a firm's sales or value added to labor, physical capital, and an estimate of its "knowledge capital" based on its R&D expenditures and an assumed rate of depreciation of the R&D created knowledge. Firms that invest in R&D have higher output [36], which translates into a reasonably high rate of return to the investment. Estimates that look for spillovers from one organization's R&D to others, which are not captured in its sales or profits, suggest even higher social rates of return.

The production function methodology is an incomplete analysis of the social payoff to science. As noted, it does not assess the value of the basic research. It does not address the impact of the increased spread of scientific and economic competence around the world on the payoff from research. In a global world, where knowledge travels rapidly and where multinationals locate production in low wage countries, the "stickiness" of knowledge to the locale that undertakes the research has greater salience than when the United States and other advanced countries had a near monopoly in high-tech areas. Multinationals are concerned with their return to R&D, not to whether the return benefits the country in which they do the R&D or any other particular locality.

Putting these issues aside, economic analysis of R&D still provides at best only crude guidance to the payoff from future research programs. The reason is that R&D has, by its very nature, highly uncertain outcomes. Research is a voyage into the unknown, so that even well-determined estimates of returns from past spending may not be indicative of future returns. But the uncertainty does not vitiate what economics can contribute to the science of science policy. Studies of the supply of persons to scientific activities and of the factors that influence R&D spending have implications for the effectiveness of policy tools and the way they operate by changing incentives. The economic analysis also lays out ways for policy makers to think about how much and in what ways to support scientific research directed toward social goals. Ideally, scientific investigation that proceeds sequentially yields a distribution of future outcomes with a long positive "tail," which can help policy makers pattern research support to reflect the option value of the research. And, as befits any research-based topic, it highlights important areas in which further research can advance the goal of making science policy more scientific.

References

[1]   Lorenzo Pecchi and Gustavo Piga, eds. *Revisiting Keynes: Economic Possibilities for Our Grandchildren* (Boston: MIT Press, 2008) contains the original article and the thoughts of modern economists.

[2]   A. Marshall. Principles of Economics (published 1890): Book Five: General Relations of Demand, Supply and Value. Marxist Internet Archives. Available at: www.marxists.org/reference/subject/economics/marshall/bk5ch03.htm.

[3]   Richard B. Freeman. *The Market for College Trained Manpower* (Cambridge, MA: Harvard University Press, 1971).

[4]   UCLA, Higher Education Research Institute. Freshman Survey. Available at: www.heri.ucla.edu/cirpoverview.php.

[5]   Alfie Kohn. *Punished by Rewards: The Trouble with Gold Stars, Incentive Plans, A's, Praise, and Other Bribes* (Boston: Houghton, Mifflin and Company, 1993).

[6]   Richard B. Freeman. Supply and Salary Adjustments to the Changing Science Manpower Market: Physics, 1948–1973. *The American Economic Review* 65(1975): 27–39.

[7]   National Academy of Sciences, National Academy of Engineering, and Institute of Medicine Committee on Underrepresented Groups and the Expansion of the Science and Engineering Workforce Pipeline; Committee on Science, Engineering, and Public Policy; Policy and Global Affairs; Expanding Underrepresented Minority Participation: America's Science and Technology Talent at the Crossroads. National Academies Press, 2010, p. 9.

[8]   Committee of Visitors. Report of the committee of visitors, National Science Foundation, Graduate Research Fellowship Program, June 17–18, 1999.

[9]   Richard B. Freeman, Tanwin Chang, and Hanley Chiang. Supporting "the Best and Brightest" in Science and Engineering: NSF Graduate Research Fellowships. In Richard Freeman and Daniel Goroff, *Science and Engineering Careers in the United States* (Chicago: University of Chicago Press, 2010).

[10] U.S. National Science Foundation. Science and Engineering Degrees: 1966–2006, NSF-08-321, October 2008, table 3.

[11] U.S. Bureau of the Census. Statistical Abstract 2010, table 788.

[12] U.S. National Science Foundation. Doctorate Recipients from U.S. Universities: Summary Report 2007–08 Special Report, NSF 10-309, December 2009, table 7.

[13] U.S. Bureau of the Census Statistical Abstract 2010 Table 603. Employed Civilians by Occupation, Sex, Race, and Hispanic Origin, 2008.

[14] Janet S. Hyde and Janet E. Mertz. Gender, Culture, and Mathematics Performance. *PNAS* 106(22)(June 2, 2009): 8801–8807; Luigi Guiso, Ferdinando Monte, Paola Sapienza, and Luigi Zingales. Culture, Gender and Math. *Science* 320(5880) (May 30, 2008): 1164–1165.

[15] Stephen Machin and Tuomas Pekkarinen. Global Sex Differences in Test Score Variability. *Science* 322(5906)(November 28, 2008): 1331–1332.

[16] Donna K. Ginther, Walter T. Schaffer, Joshua Schnell, Beth Masimore, Faye Liu, Laurel L. Haak, and Raynard S. Kington. Diversity in Academic Biomedicine: An Evaluation of Education and Career Outcomes with Implications for Policy, September 22, 2009. Available at SSRN: http://ssrn.com/abstract=1677993. Also see Donna Ginther and Shulamit Khan, *Science and Engineering Careers in the United States*. Ed. Richard B. Freeman and Daniel F. Goroff (Chicago: University of Chicago Press for NBER Science Engineering Workforce Project, 2009).

[17] National Science Foundation, Doctorate Recipients from U.S. Universities: Summary Report 2007–08 Special Report, NSF 10-309, December 2009. Available at: www.nsf.gov/statistics/nsf10309/pdf/tab18.pdf.

[18] Richard Freeman, Eric Weinstein, Elizabeth Marincola, Janet Rosenbaum, and Frank Solomon. CAREERS: Competition and Careers in Biosciences. *Science* 294(2001): 2293–2294.

[19] Muriel Niederle and Lisa Vesterlund. Do Women Shy Away from Competition? Do Men Compete Too Much? *Quarterly Journal of Economics* 122(2007): 1067–1101. Also Explaining the Gender Gap in Math Test Scores: The Role of Competition. *Journal of Economic Perspectives* 24(2)(Spring 2010): 129–144.

[20] UNESCO on-line data files, as calculated by author.

[21] A. J. Lotka. The Frequency Distribution of Scientific Productivity. *Journal of the Washington Academy of Science* 16(1926): 317–323.

[22] Stefan Wuchty, Benjamin F. Jones, and Brian Uzzi. The Increasing Dominance of Teams in Production of Knowledge. *Science* 316(5827)(May 18, 2007): 1036–1039.

[23] M. Boroush. *New NSF Estimates Indicate That U.S. R&D Spending Continued to Grow in 2008* (Washington, DC: National Science Foundation, 2010). Also National Science Board. Science and Engineering Indicators 2010, National Science Foundation, NSB 10-01, 2010, appendix table 4-4.

[24] A. Jaffe and J. Lerner. *Innovation and Its Discontents: How Our Broken Patent System Is Endangering Innovation and Progress and What to Do About It* (Princeton, NJ: Princeton University Press, 2002).

[25] A. Jaffe and M. Trajtenberg. *Patents, Citations, and Innovations: A Window on the Knowledge Economy* (Cambridge, MA: MIT Press, 2002).

[26] Marx Matt, Deborah Strumsky, and Lee Fleming. Mobility, Skills, and the Michigan Non-Compete Experiment. *Management Science* 55(6)(June 2009): 875–889.

[27] Stephen A. Merrill and Anne-Marie Mazza, eds. Committee on Management of University Intellectual Property: Managing University Intellectual Property in the Public Interest Lessons from a Generation of Experience, Research, and Dialogue, National Research Council.

[28] Michael Kremer. Patent Buyouts: A Mechanism for Encouraging Innovation. *Quarterly Journal of Economics* 1137(1998): 113; also see www.cato.org/pubs/regulation/regv23n2/kremer.pdf.

[29] B. Hall and J. Van Reenen. How Effective Are Fiscal Incentives for R&D? A Review of the Evidence. *Research Policy* 29(2000): 449–469.

[30] Paula Stephan. Economics of Science. Available at: http://dimetic.dime-eu.org/dimetic_files/Economics.of_.Science.August24.07.pdf.

[31] M. Hartmann and A. Hassan. Application of Real Options Analysis for Pharmaceutical R&D Project Valuation—Empirical Results from a Survey. *Research Policy* 35(2006): 343–354.

[32] D. Hartoff, F. M. Scherer, and K. Vopel. Exploring the Tail of the Patent Value Distribution. In O. Granstrand, ed., *Economics, Law, and Intellectual Property: Seeking Strategies for Research* (Boston/Dordrecht/London: Kluwer Academic Publishing, 2003).

[33] F. M. Scherer and D. Hartoff. Technology Policy for a World of Skew-Distributed Outcomes. *Research Policy* (29)(2000): 559–566.

[34] Robert Weinberg, cited in *Cell*, July 2006

[35] D. Faust. Why Consecutive Years of Flat Funding of the NIH Is Putting a Generation of Science at Risk. Senate Committee on Health, Education, Labor and Pensions, Washington DC, March 11, 2008, cites the Zerhouni quote.

[36] Bronwin J. Mairesse Hall and P. Mohnen. NBER Working Paper No. 15622, December 2009.

Notes

1. In October 2010, the Nova Public Broadcasting System television highlighted a microbiologist, Rachel Collins, who combined science with wrestling. Outside of her laboratory she was MisChif, champion of the Shimmer female wrestling promotion, www.pbs.org/wgbh/nova/secretlife/scientists/rachel-collins/show/mschif/.

2. To the extent that the job market for scientists and engineers clears quickly, the meaning of shortages may simply reflect the desire of employers to hire more scientists and engineers at lower wages. If wages are high and rising, it takes some years for supply to respond, but economics are loathe to call the normal adjustment process a shortage. In 1987 the NSF publicized projections of great shortages of scientists and engineers that turned out to be based more on a desire to increase the supply of scientists so large companies could hire them cheaply than on any realistic analysis of market conditions. Analysts within NSF knew about the weaknesses of the projections but the then director Erich Block ignored their concerns and cited the study in arguments on education, immigration, and employment policy. When this misuse of analysis in science policy was discovered in 1992, *Science and Nature* editorialized against it and the NSF Director Neal Lane, who took office after the event apologized for the NSF. See Eric Weinstein, How Government, Universities, and Industry Create Domestic Labor Shortages of Scientists and High-Tech Workers, www.nber.org/~peat/PapersFolder/Papers/SG/NSF.html.

3. The usual division is among drug discovery, in which the firm looks at numerous compounds that may have medicinal value, preclinical trials with animals, and three phases of clinical trials undertaken to obtain Food and Drug Administration (FDA) approval of drugs.

6

A Situated Cognition View of Innovation with Implications for Innovation Policy

John S. Gero

1. Introduction

Herbert Simon, in his 1968 Karl Compton Taylor lectures at the Massachusetts Institute of Technology [1], introduced the notion that there should be a science of those things that humans generated in addition to the science of those things that occurred naturally. He called this the *Sciences of the Artificial.* The science of innovation and innovation policy falls squarely into Simon's purview of the artificial. Like all sciences, the science of such artificial constructs as innovation and innovation policy must commence with the recognition that there are phenomena to be observed and studied and about which testable hypotheses need to be generated and tested. If such hypotheses survive testing and are shown to have adequate predictive capacities, then they may be elevated to the status of theories. Scientific research into innovation and innovation policy is still at an early stage where there is not yet full agreement on what all the phenomena are, there is not an adequate set of testable hypotheses, and the theories are still being developed rather than the outgrowth of tested hypotheses [2, 3]. This is not unusual in immature sciences.

This chapter presents the view that one of the reasons for the current state is a lack of a sufficiently wide ambit in our understanding of the various phenomena that go to make up innovation and not simply immaturity.

As is usual in immature fields, there is a lack of an agreed ontology for the field, and as a consequence there is a lack of agreement on the terminology used to describe all the phenomena. The terms "creativity" and "innovation" are often conflated, and this causes confusion. In this chapter I will distinguish them as follows: creativity is a process that produces novel, unexpected, and useful ideas, often simply called "creative ideas," which may be multiple forms ranging from intellectual property in research papers and patents to prototypes [4–9], while innovation is the process that turns creative ideas into products or processes [10, 11]. Innovation is the realization or embodiment of creative ideas. This separation of the phenomena of creativity and innovation is important. It allows us to deal with each of them separately, both in terms of studying them and in terms of how they are dealt with in organizations. Both idea generation and idea realization may occur in various domains and across various life-cycle stages [12, 13]. In all cases, they involve a producer and one or more adopters of the creative idea and the producer and adopters of the embodiment of the creative idea—the innovation. The producer of the creative idea can be in the same organization as its adopter but need not be. The producer of the embodiment is rarely in the same organization as its adopters, that is, consumers. Where necessary to disambiguate the adopter of the creative idea from the adopter of innovation, we will call the former the "innovator."

This chapter presents the argument that one phenomenon that has not been adequately accounted for in many approaches to innovation and hence innovation policy is the changing understanding of the producers and adopters of the creative idea and of its resulting innovation and the interaction of the creative idea and the innovation with the understanding of the adopters. This can be captured by taking a cognitive view of the processes involved. By cognitive view we mean a mental view. In order to develop this we need to have a brief introduction to an area of cognitive science called "situated cognition."

2. Situated Cognition

Situated cognition [14] is a set of concepts that includes that what you think the world is about affects what it is about for you, that is, any system operates within its own worldview, and that worldview affects its understanding of its interactions with its environment [14–16]. When we say a person or group of people is "situated" [17], we mean that they have a worldview that is based on their experience (rather than using the artificial intelligence meaning that it is embodied in an environment). Situated cognition involves three basic ideas: situations, constructive memory, and interaction.

2.1. Situations

From this cognitive perspective situations are mental constructs that structure and, hence, give meaning to what is observed and perceived based on a worldview. This implies that the meanings of things are not in them but in the observer. Such meanings are personal and social constructions based on experience. If we call everything around an observer the environment, then an observer, based on her or his situation, takes selective input from the environment and constructs meanings about the environment. This indicates that different observers in the same environment but with different situations will construct different meanings about the environment. We are familiar with this behavior. Take as an example the payment of substantial bonuses to individuals in the banking and finance industry as the environment. For those individuals the worldview from their situation leads them to perceive that the bonuses are justifiable compensation for the risks they have taken and the benefits they have brought to the company. For many in the general public the worldview from their situation leads them to perceive that these bonuses are unwarrantedly large.

Further, the same observer in the same environment at a later time when his or her situation has changed may construct a different meaning for the same environment. We are also familiar with behavior. Take as an example the reading of a research paper. Sometimes, during the initial reading of the paper, we might think that the paper has nothing to offer. However, a later reading will change our view of it. The paper hasn't changed, but we have changed our situation in between the first and last reading.

Take the case where you have just been dismissed from your job on the same day your spouse has called to say that your child has been found to have stolen items from school and that the credit card company has sent a letter reducing your credit limit. You may well think the world is out to get you. As you are walking down the street you notice a person walking toward you but before they reach you they cross the road, even though there is no crossing there. You may well think, "Even that person doesn't like me." Now take the case where your boss has called you in to say that you will be one of the few in your division to be awarded a bonus this year on the same day your spouse has called to say that your child has just made letter grade at school and that the credit card company has sent a letter waiving a disputed charge. As you are walking down the street you notice a person walking toward you but before they reach you they cross the road, even though there is no crossing there. You may well not even consciously think about that person. What is happening here is that the observed external world is the same but the meanings given to what was observed depend on the situation of the observer.

Slightly more formally, we can state that situations may be thought of as the set of concepts and their relationships that embody the ontology of the world under consideration. This ontology includes the value systems associated with the concepts that build expectations about the behavior of the world and are used to take decisions in and about that world [18]. Changing situations changes the value system of the world. Situations can change in one of three ways to produce a change in a value system:

- concepts can be added or deleted;
- relationships between existing concepts can be added, deleted, or modified in strength; or,
- concepts can be substituted either for a subset of existing concepts or for all existing concepts.

2.2. Constructive Memory

In 1896 Dewey published a seminal work on human thinking, which languished for a while and was only rediscovered relatively recently. In that work he introduced the concept that today is called "constructive memory." This concept is best exemplified by a quote from Dewey, via Clancey [14]: "Sequences of acts are composed such that subsequent experiences categorize and hence give meaning to what was experienced before."

Bartlett [19] demonstrated that human memory was not like a filing system full of cards with data on them that could be accessed by knowing an index for the card (which is very much like the memory of a computer). Rather than being simply a storage location, memory was a process that constructed a memory when there was the need to have a memory, and when there was no sensate experience and no need for that memory, then that memory did not exist.

> Remembering is not the re-excitation of innumerable fixed, lifeless and fragmentary traces. It is a . . . reconstruction, or construction, built out of the relation of our *attitude* towards a whole active mass of organised past reactions or experience, and to a little outstanding detail which commonly appears in image or in language form. [19]

The implication of this is that memory is not laid down and fixed at the time of the original sensate experience but is somehow a function of what comes later as well. It may be viewed as follows. Sensate experience is stored as an experience. Memories are constructed initially from that experience in response to demands for a memory of that experience, but the construction of the memory includes the situation pertaining at the time of the demand for the memory. The effect of this is that the memory is not just a function of the original experience, but it is also a function of what has happened since the original experience and of the situation that prevails when the demand for the memory is made. Each memory, after it has been constructed, is added to the experience so that the experience is augmented by memories of it. These memories require processing of the experience as opposed to factual recall of aspects of the experience. These we will call "fact memories" rather than just "memories." New memories of the experience are constructed as a function of

Figure 6.1.
(a) and (b)
Individual images.
(c) The two images
from (a) and (b)
juxtaposed—note
that the white image
of a wine glass
emerges from their
juxtaposition.

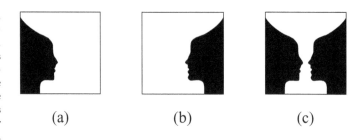

(a)   (b)   (c)

the original experience, the previous memories of it, and the current situation. New memories can be viewed as new interpretations of the augmented experience.

Emergence occurs when properties are observed that are not directly derivable from the elemental properties of a system [20]. Emergence may be seen as one example of constructive memory, in that it can be viewed as new interpretations of the experience.

This conception fits well with Gombrich's view of emergence as seen in the works of creative people: "In searching for a new solution Leonardo (da Vinci) projected new meanings into the forms he saw in his old discarded sketches" [21].

Take the three images in Figure 6.1. Parts (a) and (b) show two images. Part (c) shows the two images next to each other and a third image, the white wine glass shape, emerges as a consequence of the juxtaposition of the two original images but is not part of either of them.

2.3. Interaction

The third plank of situated cognition is the notion of interaction: changes in situations and changes in memory are a consequence of interactions between adopters and producers, between producers and the creative ideas they produce, between adopters and the creative ideas they turn into innovations, and, finally, between consumers as adopters of innovations as products.

We can observe the effects of interaction changing our view of the world in our daily lives. Imagine the following scenario. You are at the movies with a friend and while watching the movie you think to yourself, "This is the worst movie I have ever seen," and you try and look at your watch in the dark to ascertain how much longer you have to suffer. However, as you are exiting the cinema, your friend says, "What an amazing movie! Did you grasp the symbolism in the . . . ? Did you see how the camera shot Hitchcockian angles?" Your friend goes on to extol the virtues of the movie in strong terms. It is likely that you will go home thinking that you had a different experience than the one you sensed at the time of watching the movie itself and will tell the people at home, "I just saw this amazing movie. Superficially it has nothing to offer, but the symbolism . . ." Because of the interaction subsequent to your sensate experience during the movie, your situation—your view of the world—has changed.

3. Innovation as Understood from Situated Cognition

The central hypothesis of this chapter is that innovation is a process that changes the value systems of both producers and adopters.[1] The values are encapsulated in the situation that producers and adopters construct using their individual or collective views of the world they interact with.

We can categorize creative ideas and innovations as artifacts that have been intentionally produced. In order to talk about such artifacts in a consistent manner, independent of their form and domain, it is useful to describe them and their production using an ontology. One ontology for intentionally produced artifacts, which we will now just call artifacts, is the function-behavior-structure (FBS) ontology [5, 22]. We will use this ontology both to describe artifacts and to locate value systems associated with artifacts.

The FBS ontology provides all the constructs needed to represent the properties of an artifact. We will initially use examples from the design of physical artifacts, as they are easier to comprehend than conceptual artifacts, but these concepts apply equally to virtual artifacts, such as processes, strategies, and instructions.

- *Function* (F) of an artifact is its teleology ("what it is for"). An example is the function "to control access," which humans generally ascribe to the behavior of a door.
- *Behavior* (B) of an artifact is the attributes that can be derived from its structure ("what it does"). An example of a behavior of a physical artifact is "weight," which can be derived directly from the product's structure properties of material and geometry.
- *Structure* (S) of an artifact is its components and their relationships ("what it consists of"). For physical artifacts, it comprises geometry, topology, and material. For conceptual artifacts, it can comprise concepts and their connections.

Humans construct relationships between function, behavior, and structure through experience and through the development of causal models based on both reasoning about and interactions with the artifact. Function is ascribed to behavior by establishing a teleological connection between the human's goals and the measurable effects of the artifact. Behavior is causally related to structure, that is, it can be derived from structure using physical laws, heuristics, or experience. This may require knowledge about external effects and their interaction with the artifact's structure. There is no direct relationship between function and structure.

The FBS ontology does not distinguish between different embodiments of an artifact. All artifacts can be captured as function, behavior, and structure, whether or not they are embodied in a symbolic computational environment, a symbolic language environment, or in the physical world. This makes the FBS ontology an appropriate basis for describing artifacts at any stage in their life cycle.

Value systems can be defined in terms of artifact properties that relate to the notion of usefulness for adopters in the life cycle of an artifact. In the FBS view of the world, this includes function, as it captures the usefulness of artifacts by definition. It also includes behavior as a measure for the potential of an artifact to achieve the function. Structure is not a part of a value system because it is not related to usefulness in a strict sense. However, structure can be viewed as an implicit value system, since its design is driven by intended function and behavior.

Value systems are encapsulated in situations that may be different for every adopter. Situations are the carriers of the value systems. As such, they produce expectations that guide interpretations. One way to comprehend this is to conceive of the world as being composed of three kinds of subworlds: the world external to us—the "external world," the world internal to us—the "internal world," and within the internal world is a world of expectations that are the designs of the artifacts we are generating—the "expected world."

The external world contains symbolic or physically embodied value systems made available for interpretation. The value systems may be explicit or implicit. Explicit value systems include function or behavior. Implicit value systems are externally embodied structures that afford certain behavior and function.

The interpreted world provides an environment for analytic and associative activities, related to current and previous value systems. It uses interpretation and memory processes, both of which are represented in Figure 6.2, using "push-pull" arrows to account for their dynamic character as an interaction of data-push and expectation-pull [23]. As a result, interpretations and memories can change over time, which can then affect subsequent interpretations and memories. It is in this dynamic world where implicit value systems may become explicit, that is, where structure, once interpreted, is turned into behavior that then may have functions attributed to it.

The expected world (within the interpreted world) forms goals through focusing on parts of the interpreted value systems and predicts the effects of actions to modify the (explicit or implicit) value systems in the external world.

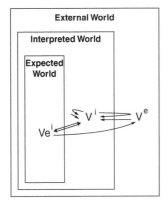

Figure 6.2.
Value systems (V) encapsulated in a situation (interpreted and expected worlds), interacting with externally embodied value systems.

Source: After Gero and Kannengiesser 2004.

V^e = Externally embodied value system
V^i = Interpreted value system
Ve^i = Expected value system
⟶ = Action
⇄ = Interpretation/constructive memory
⟺ = Focusing

The situation changes as a result of interactions between the three worlds (and "push-pull" interactions within the interpreted world). In turn, changes in the situation set up expectations that drive both interpretations and what situations can be constructed in the future. This means that the same external world with different situations produces different interpreted worlds and then different expected worlds. As the situation changes, the encapsulated value systems change accordingly.

4. Inducing Change of Value Systems

How are changes of value systems brought about? Given that value systems are encapsulated in a situation, this question is not the same as: How can we produce artifacts with novel functions or behaviors? Exploring how value systems can be changed requires an understanding of the interactions between producers and adopters that can affect situations. These interactions can be viewed as part of a two-way communication process in which producers aim to influence adopters [24], and adopters provide direct or indirect feedback to producers.

4.1. Changing Adopter Situations

There are three ways of inducing change in adopter situations:

1. *Social influence*: This is based on presenting explicit value systems (V^e) that the adopter accepts without much self-reasoning. Examples

include product marketing, peer pressure (which may be part of a "viral marketing" strategy), and product tests or recommendations from trusted authorities (e.g., newspapers, consumer groups and industry associations).

2. *Affordance*: This is an adopter's interpretation process that makes implicit value systems (V^e) explicit in the way intended or unintended by the producer. This process can be characterized as entailing a small amount of interaction between data-push and expectation-pull in this process. In other words, the data presented are consistent with the adopter's grounded expectations (or conventions) [25]. Hence, affordance is very much correlated with the notion of sustaining changes. For example, a mobile phone of reduced physical dimensions affords "better portability," sustaining the adopter's existing needs.

3. *Emergence*: This comprises interpretation and constructive memory processes with more significant amounts of interaction between the adopter's expectations and the (explicit or implicit) value system (V^e). It can be viewed as a form of "unintended" innovation, based on mechanisms such as analogical reasoning. An example of an emergent innovation is Scotch tape, whose initial function, "to mend books," was transformed by the end user into a number of different functions, such as "to wrap packages" and "to curl hair" [26]. Other examples of emergent innovations, according to Redström [27], include the record player (originally a sound reproduction device, turned into a musical instrument by DJs) and the skateboard (originally a children's scooter, but the handles accidentally fell off and children experimented with it).

These three types of change apply both to the adopters of creative ideas, the innovators, and the adopters of innovative artifacts, although most commonly they are associated with the latter.

4.2. Changing Producer and Innovator Situations

In general, it is advantageous for producers and innovators to monitor and analyze changes in adopters' value systems. Original producers use this information to refine their creative ideas. Innovators use this to refine their innovations. Current and future competitors use the same information to identify the key technologies and to assess their own capabilities for entering the market with similar innovations but improved characteristics. In addition, producers may generate new creative ideas based on their analyses of innovators' value systems. Innovators may generate new innovations based on the same creative ideas depending on their analyses of adopters' value systems. These ideas may target existing markets or the creation of new markets.

What is common in all of these cases is that the producers' and innovators' value systems can change based on changes in their situations. There are three ways of inducing change in innovator situations:

1. *Direct feedback*: This may be available through questionnaires, customer support, complaint forms, or other feedback provided by adopters. This feedback represents explicit value systems (V^e) and can be viewed as a direct form of communication from adopters to producers. Participatory design methodologies integrate explicit user feedback in the process of designing, aiming to identify opportunities for improvement and novel ideas in the early stages of innovation.

2. *Observations*: This can be seen as a form of indirect feedback, based on studying the intentional use of an innovation by adopters. A good example is Scotch tape, mentioned earlier. Here, the various modes of use invented by the adopters (wrapping packages, curling hair, etc.) were observed (and interpreted as functions) by the innovators. They then refined their product by creating a range of product variations adapted to the specific functions: "As a result, 3M (the company of the producers) came out with a hair-setting Scotch Tape, a medical Scotch Tape used for binding splints, a reflective Scotch Tape for roads, and so on" [28]. This new range of products can be seen as a consequence of changes in adopters' value systems followed by changes in the innovators' value systems.

3. *Emergence*: This generates value systems that are novel with respect to producers, innovators, and adopters. They result from the producers' or innovators' interpretation and constructive memory processes and their interactions with the adopters' value systems. For example, when Sony introduced the Walkman, it explicitly changed the size of portable music devices by eliminating the loudspeaker and replacing it with earbuds. However, in doing so it produced an emergent value: listening to music became a private rather than a public activity and consequentially spawned an entire industry based on the private listening of music. This flowed onto other forms of private listening artifacts.

The products resulting from the changes in the producers' and/or innovators' value systems can again lead to innovation, by subsequently changing the adopters' value systems. This shows that innovation involves a set of interactions between producers, innovators, and adopters, which can be viewed as a process of reflective conversation [26].

5. Effects of Changes of Value Systems

Schumpeter, in his seminal book *Capitalism, Socialism and Democracy* [29], described innovation as a form of "creative destruction," where the innovation destroys the existing product or process through displacement. This matches our cognitive notion of changing situations and its value system through concept substitution. However, an innovation has potentially three forms of acting on the existing order: augmentation, partial substitution, or displacement through total substitution (see Figure 6.3). Only the latter matches Schumpeter's "creative destruction" (see Figure 6.3(d)).

We can observe such behavior as innovations occur. The case shown in Figure 6.3(b) is common, where new values are added to existing ones. This can be seen, for example, when new features are added to products and then those features become the norm not only for new consumers but also for existing consumers, who now see the product they currently own as incomplete. An example was the addition of a global positioning system (GPS) capability to cell phones. This innovation had the effect of devaluing existing phones that did not have that capability. This is one way in which innovation generates market growth. The case shown in Figure 6.3(c) is common in mature markets, where one feature substitutes for an existing feature, often with the same functionality. This has a similar effect as adding a feature, in that it changes the expectations of both new and existing consumers. Voice dialing replacing finger-based dialing on phones is an example of such a substitution. However, transformative innovations are those where one entire set of values is displaced by a new set (see Figure 6.3(d)). A totally new situation then exists, one that does not simply grow a market but creates new markets. The introduction of the laptop computer is one such example of this. Prior to its introduction, there was no market to be addressed, however, its introduction completely replaced the notion of moving desktop computers around and opened

Figure 6.3.
(a) Original situation S_o. (b) New situation, S_n, that augments existing situation. (c) New situation that substitutes part of existing situation and hence destroys part of it. (d) New situation that substitutes previous situation completely and hence destroys it.

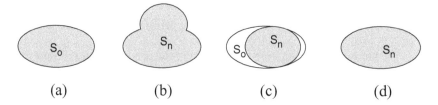

(a)   (b)   (c)   (d)

up a completely new set of values associated with computers, values that had not existed before.

6. Studying Innovation and Innovation Policy

The cognitive view described here cannot be modeled using formal causal models; phenomena are a consequence of individual or group acts for which we do not have casual models. Presented here were the social effects of individual cognitive behavior. There is an emerging field that deals with this, called "computational sociology," or "computational social science." Computational social science models social interactions and simulates the resulting social behavior through the use of computational agents rather than equation-based methods, utilizing a multi-agent system [30–40]. It has the capacity to produce phenomena that are the consequence of social interaction rather than based on causal models.

Computational social science provides the means by which we can model the processes of the production of creative ideas, the interaction between these ideas and their take-up by innovators, the interaction between innovators and adopters, the interaction between the adopters and the innovations they are adopting, between the innovators and the consumption by adopters of their innovations and the interaction between the producers of the creative ideas and their consumption in innovations. We are in a position to study and test this cognitive approach to innovation and to innovation policy [41–44]. Much of phenomenological behavior, as a consequence of social interactions, is emergent. Innovation and innovation policy can be studied as a driver of this emergent behavior. It can also be studied initially as an emergent phenomenon itself, as a consequence of multiple small effects whose drivers can only be viewed at a macro level.

The science of innovation policy requires both theoretical models and empirical data on which to found and test those theoretical models. Generally, models of innovation and innovation policy are presented qualitatively and are often untestable [10, 45–48]. A situated cognition-based, multi-agent system has the capacity to be a workbench to test innovation policies.

6.1. A Workbench to Test Innovation Policies

Innovation policies can be presented as multiple, variable inputs to a large-scale, interacting social system of creators of ideas, innovators who take up those ideas to generate products, and adopters of those products. In addition to these, there may be other actors in the system, such as research funding bodies, who interact with creators of ideas, venture capitalists who interact with innovators, development funding bodies who interact with innovators, marketers who interact with innovators and adopters, and retailers who interact with innovators and adopters.

A situated cognition, multi-agent, computational system, where agents represent the different classes of actors in the chain of innovation, from creators of ideas and their funders to adopters, can be designed and implemented that has innovation policy as exogenous inputs and emergent behavior as endogenous inputs. In this system each class of actor has a set of agents whose behavior is programmed but changeable, so that different behavioral hypotheses can be tested to determine their effects on innovation and innovation capability. Each agent has the capacity to observe some of the other agents and, hence, to indirectly interact with them. This produces social interactions that can result in emergent behavior (i.e., behavior that is not programmed). Viral marketing is an example of an emergent behavior.

A workbench based on this situated cognition, multi-agent computational system can have all of its exogenous inputs specified, and then it runs a simulation of the policy represented by those inputs based on various assumptions about the behaviors of the various classes of actors in the system. The agents change their situations as the simulation proceeds and as they develop more knowledge about the behavior of the other agents. Exogenous inputs to such a simulation would include such variables as funding agency policies, availability of venture capital, research and development (R&D) tax policies, and so on. Endogenous inputs to an agent would include such variables as the behavior of other members of its class and the strength of the social ties of that class. Different ranges for the values of the inputs can be used to run a set of simulations to observe the systemic behavioral effect of that policy variable.

The workbench can be built at any level of granularity modeling for which data either exist or can be reasonably estimated. The system can be further disaggregated, and by focusing on the innovator, it can be used to study innovation processes. Multi-agent systems of this kind can be readily scaled up so that social systems involving thousands and even tens of thousands of agents are computationally tractable.

Such a workbench provides a tool to determine the phenomenological behavior of the changes in the value systems of creators, innovators, and adopters driven by an innovation policy and, hence, to test the innovation policy itself [49].

References

[1] H. A. Simon. Sciences of the Artificial. Boston (MA): MIT Press; 1969.

[2] I. Feller. Science of Science and Innovation Policy: The Emerging Community of Practice. In this volume.

[3] J. Thomas, S. A. Mohrman. A Vision of Data and Analytics for the Science of Science Policy. In this volume.

[4] M. Boden. The Creative Mind: Myths and Mechanisms. 2nd ed. London, New York: Routledge; 2003.

[5] J. S. Gero. Design Prototypes: A Knowledge Representation Schema for Design. AI Magazine, 11;1990;26–36.

[6] J. S. Gero, M. L. Maher. Modeling Creativity and Knowledge-Based Design. Hillside (NJ): Lawrence Erlbaum; 1993.

[7] M. A. Runco. Creativity: Theories and Themes: Research, Development and Practice. New York: Academic Press; 2006.

[8] M. K. Sawyer. Explaining Creativity: The Science of Human Innovation. New York: Oxford University Press; 2006.

[9] R. J. Sternberg. The Handbook of Creativity. New York: Cambridge University Press; 1998.

[10] D. Archibugi, J. Howells, J. Michie. Innovation Systems and Policy in a Global Economy. New York: Cambridge University Press; 1999.

[11] C. Edquist. Systems of Innovation: Technologies, Institutions and Organizations. London: Pinter Publishers; 1997.

[12] L. B. Archer. Technological Innovation: A Methodology. London: Royal Academy of Art; 1970.

[13] N. Roozenburg, J. Eekels. Product Design: Fundamentals and Methods. Hoboken (NJ): Wiley; 1995.

[14] W. Clancey. Situated Cognition: On Human Knowledge and Computer Representations. Cambridge: Cambridge University Press; 1997.

[15] J. Dewey. The Reflex Arc Concept in Psychology. Psychological Review, 3;1896; reprinted in 1981;357–370.

[16] J. S. Gero. Towards the Foundations of a Model of Design Thinking. DARPA Project BAA07-21, 2008.

[17] G. J. Smith, J. S. Gero. What Does an Artificial Design Agent Mean by Being "Situated"? Design Studies, 26;2005;535–561.

[18] J. S. Gero, U. Kannengiesser. Understanding Innovation as a Change of Value Systems. In: R. Tan, G. Gao, N. Leon (Eds.), Growth and Development of Computer-Aided Innovation. Berlin: Springer; 2009, pp. 249–257.

[19] F. C. Bartlett. Remembering: A Study in Experimental and Social Psychology. New York: Cambridge University Press; 1932/1977.

[20] D. Chalmers. Strong and Weak Emergence. In: P. Davies, P. Clayton (Eds.), The Re-Emergence of Emergence. New York: Oxford University Press; 2006.

[21] E. Gombrich. Studies in the Art of the Renaissance. New York: Phaidon; 1966.

[22] J. S. Gero, U. Kannengiesser. The Situated Function-Behaviour-Structure Framework. Design Studies, 25;2004;373–391.

[23] J. S. Gero. Recent Design Science Research: Constructive Memory in Design Thinking. Architectural Science Review, 42;1999;3–5.

[24] N. Crilly, D. Good, D. Matravers, P. J. Clarkson. Design as Communication: Exploring the Validity and Utility of Relating Intention to Interpretation. Design Studies, 29;2008;425–457.

[25] D. Brown, L. Blessing. The Relationship Between Function and Affordance. Paper No. DETC2005-85017. ASME 2005 Design Theory and Methodology Conference, Long Beach, California, 2005.

[26] D. A. Schön. Reflective Practitioner: How Professionals Think in Action. New York: Basic Books; 1983.

[27] J. Redström. RE: Definitions of Use. Design Studies, 29;2008;410–423.

[28] D. A. Schön, J. Bennett. Reflective Conversation with Materials. In: Bringing Design to Software. New York: ACM; 1996; pp. 171–189.

[29] J. A. Schumpeter. Capitalism, Socialism and Democracy. New York: Harper; 1942.

[30] C. Castelfranchi. The Theory of Social Functions: Challenges for Computational Social Science and Multi-agent Learning. Cognitive Systems Research, 2; 2001;5–38.

[31] J. Casti. The Computer as Laboratory: Toward a Theory of Complex Adaptive Systems. Complexity, 4;1999;12–14.

[32] J. M. Epstein. Generative Social Science: Studies in Agent-Based Computational Modeling. Princeton (NJ): Princeton University Press; 2007.

[33] J. M. Epstein, R. Axtell. Growing Artificial Societies: Social Science from the Bottom Up. Washington (DC): Brookings Institute Press; 1996.

[34] G. N. Gilbert, R. Conte. Artificial Societies: The Computer Simulation of Social Life. London: UCL Press; 1995.

[35] G. N. Gilbert, J. Doran. Simulating Societies: The Computer Simulation of Social Phenomena. London: UCL Press; 1994.

[36] R. Hegselmann, U. Mueller, K. G. Troitzsch. Modelling and Simulation in the Social Sciences from the Philosophy of Science Point of View. Boston (MA): Kluwer Academic Publishers; 1996.

[37] M. W. Macy, R. Willer. From Factors to Actors: Computational Sociology and Agent-Based Modeling. Annual Review of Sociology, 28;2002;143–166.

[38] H. J. Miller, E. S. Page. Complex Adaptive Systems: An Introduction to Computational Models of Social Life. Princeton (NJ): Princeton University Press; 2007.

[39] R. Sosa, J. S. Gero. Creative Social Systems. In: D. Ventura, M. L. Maher, S. Colton (Eds.), Creative Intelligent Systems. Menlo Park (CA): AAAI Press, AAAI Spring Symposium; 2008, pp. 90–94.

[40] R. Sosa, J. S. Gero. Diffusion of Creative Design: Gatekeeping Effects. International Journal of Architectural Computing, 2;2004;518–531.

[41] J. S. Gero, A. Gomez. Exploring Knowledge Transfer in a Society of Designers. In: M. Noell Bergendahl, M. Grimheden, L. Leifer, P. Skogstad, P. Badke-Schaub (Eds.), Design Information and Knowledge. Stanford (CA): Design Society; 2009, pp. 99–110.

[42] R. Sosa, J. S. Gero. Innovation in Design: Computational Simulations. In: A. Samuel, W. Lewis (Eds.), ICED'05: Engineering Design and The Global Economy, CD Paper 529.61. Institution of Engineers, Australia, 2005.

[43] R. Sosa, J. S. Gero. Computational Explorations of Compatibility and Innovation. In: N. Leon-Rovira (Ed.), Trends in Computer Aided Innovation. New York: Springer; 2007, pp. 13–22.

[44] R. Sosa, J. S. Gero. Social Structures That Promote Change in a Complex World: The Complementary Roles of Strangers and Acquaintances in Innovation. Futures, 40;2008;577–585.

[45] H. Dubberly. Toward a Model of Innovation. Interactions, XV;2008;28–36.

[46] A. Akintoye, M. Beck. Policy, Finance & Management for Public-Private Partnerships (Innovation in the Built Environment). Oxford, Ames (IA): Wiley-Blackwell; 2008.

[47] L. M. Branscomb, J. H. Keller. Investing in Innovation: Creating a Research and Innovation Policy That Works. Boston (MA): MIT Press; 1999.

[48] P. Llerena, M. Mireille. Innovation Policy in a Knowledge-Based Economy: Theory and Practice. New York: Springer; 2005.

[49] J. R. Holland. Emergence. New York: Basic Books; 1999.

Note

1. Much of this, as well as the next section, is drawn from Gero and Kannengiesser, 2009.

7

Technically Focused Policy Analysis
M. Granger Morgan

1. Introduction

Harvey Brooks [1] was careful to always draw a distinction between policy for science and science for policy. This chapter is about what Brooks called science for policy, the analysis of policy issues in which the technical details really matter.

Of course, there are many problems that are *about* technology. These are problems for which a competent policy analyst can do a fine study without deep technical understanding. Suppose, for example, that the government of India wanted to make greater use of existing direct broadcast satellites to provide adult education services in rural areas. In this case, an analyst need not know anything about the details of how the satellites, the data downlinks, or the TV sets work. He or she only needs to know what the system costs, who it takes to run it, and what sorts of services it can provide. In contrast, suppose that the International Telecommunications Union was planning to convene a meeting of the World Radiocommunication Conference in order to reallocate parking orbits for geostationary satellites along with the downlink frequencies they use in the Asian region. Clearly, to prepare for such a meeting, the government of India would need analysis that is based on a deep understanding of the technologies that are involved, including the likely future cost and performance of high-power microwave amplifiers, the relative cost and advantages and disadvantages of placing gain on the ground *versus* placing it on the spacecraft, likely future launch alternatives, and a host of similar topics. It is this latter class of technical-focused policy analysis that is the focus of this chapter.

2. Typical Analytical Strategies

While many of the tools needed to perform technical-focused policy analysis are similar to those of all policy analysis, an important difference is that this form of analysis involves problems in which, if one is to avoid reaching dumb or silly answers, it is necessary for the analyst to get "inside the black box" [2] and consider the details of the technical systems that are being considered. A first step in any such analysis is to determine whether the technical details actually *do* matter and if so how much detail should be included. As Quade [3] has noted, "Good policy analysis should seek to establish the boundaries of the issue under investigation where thought and analysis show them to be and not where off-the-cuff decisions or convention . . . would have them."

Tools for technical-focused policy analysis have evolved gradually over a period of many decades. Good analysts choose from a large repertoire of analytical tools and methods. Often they start by building or adopting a static or dynamic model that describes the operation of the physical and social system they are analyzing. Such models may take many different forms, ranging from simple formulations based on conservation of mass and energy to closed-form dynamic models of physical processes such as air pollution transformation and dispersion, to accounting tools such as input-output models that are linked to environmental loadings to perform life cycle analysis (EIO/LCA), or agent-based models in which the performance of the system is an emergent property of many interacting simple rules or influences. Analysts should strive to keep the analysis as simple as possible to address the needs of the problem at hand, but no simpler [4]. Since technical people and organizations become easily enamored with model building, this is often simpler said than done!

Having developed an appropriate characterization of the relevant physical and social system, most analyses then move on to develop a formal characterization of the preferences of decision makers and apply those in some form of normative assessment, such as cost-effectiveness, benefit-cost, or probabilistic decision analysis, using either single or multiple attributes to perform an evaluation and comparison of different policy options. This stage of the analysis is typically not very different than that of any form of quantitative policy analysis.

Performing good policy analysis is as much an art as it is a science [4]. Success requires a deep understanding of the limitations as well as the strengths of the various tools and methods that are available and both a willingness and an ability to choose strategies and methods that fit the problem at hand. Unfortunately, too often this does not happen. Many analysts command a small set of tools and bring them to bear on whatever problem comes their way. As Abraham Maslow [5] has noted, "When the only tool you have is a hammer, every problem begins to resemble a nail."

3. Development of the Tools for Analysis

Some of the earliest tools and methods in quantitative policy analysis are those of *operations research*. These grew out of British and American efforts to improve targeting of anti-aircraft fire and aerial bombing, and to locate and destroy enemy submarines during the Second World War [6]. These methods were further refined in the postwar period by groups such as the RAND Corporation, first for defense applications and subsequently for a range of civil applications, such as dispatching fire and police services [7]. At Harvard [8] and Stanford [9], the closely related ideas of optimal statistical decision theory, or *decision analysis*, were refined and applied to a range of policy problems, largely for private firms but also occasionally to topics of public policy [10].

Methods of *technology assessment*, developed in an effort to anticipate how specific technologies might evolve and what consequences might result, were also developed at about that same time. Early examples include the work of academics such as Cornell's Ray Bowers [11], the National Academy of Sciences (NAS) Committee on Science and Astronautics [12], and practitioners such as Roy Amara and Joe Coates.

Conventional tools of engineering analysis, including such simple but powerful ideas as mass and energy balance, [13] as well as more complex strategies as simulation modeling, also became common. However, with the exception of analysts working in the decision-analytic tradition, most of the work in quantitative policy analysis through the 1980s involved deterministic analyses in which best estimates (or sometimes upper bounds) were used. When two analyses reached different conclusions, it was often impossible to know if they were saying different things or simply producing results that both lay within an unstated range of uncertainties.

The language and ideas of micro-economics have become the *lingua franca* of much work in policy analysis, with ideas such as marginal cost and consumer surplus now widely employed. Several tools originally developed in economics are now part of the standard analytical repertoire of those who practice quantitative policy analysis. *Benefit-cost analysis* is perhaps the most obvious example [14, 15]. Recent years have also seen the application of other ideas, such as the use of *options* [16, 17] originally developed in the corporate finance community.

For more than a century, the characterization and treatment of uncertainty had been an integral part of experimental science. As Carl Sagan [18] noted, "Every time a scientific paper presents a bit of data, it's accompanied by an error bar—a quiet but instant reminder that no knowledge is complete or perfect." As growing numbers of people, whose original training was in experimental science, entered the field of policy analysis, this culture was gradually transferred [4]. For example, as late as the 1970s, most analyses performed for the U.S. Environmental Protection Agency (EPA) contained little or no formal treatment of uncertainty. Today, virtually all such analysis contains at least some quantitative discussion and formal treatment of uncertainty.

Bottom-up *life-cycle analysis* (LCA) has become an increasingly popular tool [19]. To overcome the limits that such an analysis can encounter when the boundaries of analysis are drawn too narrowly, an economy-wide approach known as EIO/LCA has been developed [20]. This approach uses an input-output table of the entire economy (the EIO part) to which has been linked databases on energy uses and environmental emissions. EIO/LCA inherently yields only approximate answers, but because it looks across the full economy, it can sometimes identify large impacts that have been overlooked by conventional LCA.

Practitioners in technically based policy analysis have been slow to incorporate ideas from modern behavioral decision science [21, 22], although examples are becoming more common [23, 24]. Similarly, applications of methods from Bayesian inference are still relatively rare but are growing more common [25–27]. Most technically focused policy analysis does a relatively poor job of incorporating considerations of interest group politics and the political environment within which policy recommendations must be implemented [28]. Presumably this is because most such analysts have little or no background in these areas. Improving this situation presents a clear challenge for those engaged in educating future generations of technically focused policy analysts.

4. Who Performs Technically Based Policy Analysis?

Institutions that perform high-quality, technically based policy analysis can be classified into five groups:

1. private-sector firms
2. consulting firms and think tanks
3. mission-oriented government agencies
4. analysis groups whose specific mission is to support government
5. university academic and research programs

A few large corporations have a tradition of in-house development and use of technically based policy analysis. More often companies commission such analysis from consulting firms. This has been especially true in areas such as the application of decision analysis in firms' strategic planning [9, 29].

Think tanks, including Federally Funded Research and Development Centers (FFRDCs) such as RAND, MITRE, and IDA, have been a primary source of analysis for federal agencies, especially the Department of Defense

(DOD). Analyses done in most nonprofit think tanks, such as Resources for the Future (RFF) or the Brookings Institution, tend to be heavily economics based and to involve only modest technical content. However, in some areas, such as environmental regulation, space, or telecommunications policy, some of these organizations have developed considerable technical expertise.

Some mission-oriented federal agencies, such as the Department of Energy (DOE), the EPA, and the DOD, have developed considerable in-house expertise to perform technically based policy analysis, both for their own use and to inform broader policy discourse. Such capability is much less common in state governments.

Government agencies often turn to consulting firms for a specific analysis they need. They will often use think tanks, or the National Research Council (NRC) when the analysis they need is more general in nature. Many think tanks are capable of doing sophisticated modeling and other forms of quantitative policy analysis. In contrast, the NRC rarely does heavy-duty analysis but is much more likely to synthesize and evaluate work of this kind that is already available.

Three organizations created specifically to provide analyses for government deserve mention: the Office of Technology Assessment (OTA) of the U.S. Congress; the Congressional Research Service (CRS); and the General Accountability Office (GAO).

The OTA was established in 1972 to provide independent, technically focused policy analysis for Congress. After struggling for a few years to find a working model, it became a very successful bipartisan analysis group under the leadership of Jack Gibbons [30]. However, Congress chose to defund it in 1995, after the Republican sweep of both Houses. Over time, the CRS has begun to build more in-depth technical analytical capability and perform assessments that are quite substantive. As an experiment, beginning in 2002, Senator Bingaman's office has explored using the GAO for technology assessment. A small number of such studies have been produced [31, 32]. There have been several other efforts both to refund the OTA or to create other institutional arrangements to fill what many see as a gap in analytical capability for Congress [30, 33].

5. Educating Practitioners for Technically Based Policy Analysis

Most of the first generation of practitioners in technically based policy analysis received their education in conventional fields of science or engineering and then acquired their policy analytic skills on their own. Since the 1970s that has changed, as several major university programs have created master's and PhD programs that prepare students with technical backgrounds for careers in the area of technology and policy. Both the Sloan Foundation and the National Science Foundation (NSF) helped seed a number of these programs. Today, there are well-established programs at Berkeley, Carnegie Mellon, the Massachusetts Institute of Technology (MIT), and Stanford and emerging programs at several other institutions, including the University of Maryland and the State University of New York (SUNY) at Stony Brook.

Operating an educational program in science, technology, and policy requires constant attention to maintain an unstable equilibrium [34]. Without continuous attention there is a tendency for such programs to either evolve into programs in the social studies of science and technology or to lose their policy focus and become some form of specialized technical program. The former happened at Cornell, the latter at Washington University in St. Louis. The American Association for the Advancement of Science (AAAS) maintains an online directory of graduate programs in science, engineering, and public policy [35]. Note that programs that combine substantial technical education with the development of skills in modern quantitative policy analysis are clearly a minority among the many programs that are listed.

6. Does Analysis Matter?

Kingdon [36] has articulated a model of the policy process that involves three parallel streams of processes involving problems, policies, and politics. The first, as well as the second, although to a slightly lesser degree, is the realm of technically based policy analysis. Analysts identify issues that they believe are important problems and perform analysis that clarifies the nature of the problem and suggests possible solutions. Policy entrepreneurs then work to spread and promote such policy strategies and solutions. When occasionally the broader political agenda shifts so that the three streams align at the same moment, a "policy window" is opened. If, at that moment, good solutions, buttressed by good analysis, are available, then analysis can have a significant impact on policy. This was the case, for example, in the decision to adopt an emissions trading approach to the control of sulfur dioxide. Air pollution experts had analyzed the sources, transport, and deposition of sulfur air pollution for many years. In collaboration, economists at CalTech, RFF, and elsewhere had developed ideas about tradable emission permits. When the clean-air rewrite occurred in a political environment that was not friendly to conventional command and control regulation, policy entrepreneurs on the Hill, at the Council of Economic Advisers, and elsewhere saw an opportunity to promote a market-based solution, and they were successful [37, 38].

The importance of the broader political agenda is well illustrated by Professor Jon Peha's account to me of how his work on communication for first responders came to have impact:

> I wrote several papers on how the "fragmented" U.S. policy for public safety communications meant far too much money was being spent on systems that failed unnecessarily often. Once this issue hit the agenda, my papers became an important part of the discussion, as I had quantified the problems with systems that few dared to question, and the problems turned out to be huge. I suggested some alternatives based on this. While I'd like to claim that I succeeded in putting this on the agenda, or that my ideas drifted in Brownian motion until hitting a policymaker, I can't. My work bumped into the national agenda for two reasons, neither of which had anything to do with me or with research. First, Hurricanes Katrina (and Rita and others) reminded people that public safety communications matters, and it's important to appear to be doing something about it. Second, the former CEO of Nextel started pushing a specific plan to build new systems, so policymakers had to have an opinion on whether his proposal was good or bad, and what the alternatives might be. I think that's why people noticed my work, and it began to matter. These issues got some attention whenever people spoke about September 11, but it wasn't sustained. I can't know, but I suspect that if Katrina had hit ten years later, my work might have gone unnoticed outside academic circles for ten additional years. But once the work got noticed, it spread very quickly.

Sometimes analysis done at just the right moment can have a major impact on an ongoing policy debate. This was the case, for example, when Lave, Hendrickson, and McMichael [39] demonstrated that recycling the lead-acid batteries of electric cars would result in more lead released to the environment than if those same cars were fueled with leaded gasoline at the same time that California was debating requiring the adoption of electric vehicles.

However, the more common way in which analysis has an impact on policy is through a slow process of diffusion. Someone does a piece of analysis that yields a result. Other analysts get interested and do related work. Slowly, over time, a consensus builds, so that finally, when a decision maker addresses the issue, he or she gets much the same advice from most experts when asked. Sometimes this process can be *very* slow. For example, it took over half a century between the time that Ronald Coase and Leo Hezlett first showed the advantages of allocating radio frequency spectrum via auctions and the time the Federal Communications Commission (FCC) finally adopted the idea in the 1990s [40, 41].

This process can be disrupted by political manipulation designed to over-emphasize uncertainty in the minds of nonexperts or even distort and misrepresent the science [42, 45]. The current widespread public confusion over whether climate change is "real," in the face of many NRC and IPCC assessments, is a clear example of the power that money spent by groups, such as the Global Climate Coalition, can have on confusing and delaying action on an important issue. But just as the Indiana House failed to change physical reality when in 1897 it passed House Bill #246 by a vote of 67 to 0 to simplify the value of π to 3.2, so too simply passing laws that say "make it so" or otherwise ignoring physical reality will not make real problems in technology and public policy disappear. The Indiana Senate tabled the "pi bill" after talking with a knowledgeable mathematician [43].

There is no way to avoid the fact that ideology, short-term political interests, or simple ignorance or misunderstanding of the natural world or of engineered systems will, from time to time, lead to silly and ultimately unrealistic policy outcomes. While it is certainly an extreme example, the former Soviet Union is not the only society that has fallen, or will fall, prey to misguided policies of the sort promoted by Trofim Denisovich Lysenko [44].

The objective of practitioners of careful and balanced technically focused policy analysis is to ensure that whenever possible such outcomes are avoided and, when they are not, to work to ensure that sooner or later policy prescriptions based on a realistic understanding of the natural and technical world prevail.

References

[1]   H. Brooks. The Scientific Adviser. In: R. Gilpin, C. Wright (Eds.), Scientists and National Policy Making. New York: Columbia University Press; 1964.

[2]   N. Rosenberg. Inside the Black Box: Technology and Economics. New York: Cambridge University Press; 1982.

[3]   E. S. Quade. Analysis for Public Decisions. New York: Elsevier; 1975.

[4]   M. G. Morgan, M. Henrion, M. Small. Uncertainty: A Guide to Dealing with Uncertainty in Quantitative Risk and Policy Analysis. New York: Cambridge University Press; 1990.

[5]   A. Maslow as quoted at www.abraham-maslow.com/m_motivation/Maslow_Quotes.asp. Accessed October 30, 2010.

[6]   J. D. C. Little. Philip M. Morse and the Beginnings. Operations Research, 50; 2002;146–148.

[7]   E. J. Ignall, P. Kolesar, A. J. Swersey, W. E. Walker, E. H. Blum, G. Carter, H. Bishop. Improving the Deployment of New York City Fire Companies. Interfaces, 5;1975; 48–61.

[8]   H. Raiffa, R. Schlaifer. Applied Statistical Decision Theory. Boston (MA): MIT Press; 1968.

[9]   R. A. Howard, J. E. Matheson. Readings in Decision Analysis. Menlo Park (CA): SRI International; 1977.

[10] R. A. Howard, J. E. Matheson, D. W. North. The Decision to Seed Hurricanes. Science, 176;1972;1191–1202.

[11] R. Bowers, J. Frey. Technology Assessment and Microwave Diodes. Scientific American, 226;1972;13–21.

[12] H. Brooks, R. Bowers. Technology: Process of Assessment and Choice. In: A. H. Teich (Ed.), Technology and Man's Future. New York: St. Martins Press; 1977, p. 275.

[13] M. G. Morgan, F. C. McMichael. A Characterization and Critical Discussion of Models and Their Use in Environmental Policy. Policy Sciences, 13;1981; 345–370.

[14] L. B. Lave. Benefit-Cost Analysis: Do the Benefits Exceed the Costs? In: R. Hahn (Ed.), Risks, Costs, and Lives Saved: Getting Better Results from Regulation. New York: Oxford University Press; 1996, pp. 104–134.

[15] E. J. Mishan. Elements of Cost-Benefit Analysis. London: George Allen and Unwin; 1972.

[16] R. de Neufville, S. Scholtes. Flexibilities in Design. Boston (MA): MIT Press; in press.

[17] D. Patiño-Echeverri, B. Morel, J. Apt, C. Chen. Should a Coal-Fired Power Plant Be Replaced or Retrofitted? Environmental Science & Technology, 41;2007; 7980–7986.

[18] C. Sagan. Demon-Haunted World: Science as a Candle in the Dark. New York: Random House; 1995.

[19] R. E. Miller, P. D. Blair. Input-Output Analysis: Foundations and Extensions. Englewood Cliffs (NJ): Prentice Hall; 1985.

[20] C. T. Hendrickson, L. B. Lave, H. S. Matthews. Environmental Life Cycle Assessment of Goods and Services: An Input-Output Approach. Washington (DC): Resources for the Future; 2006.

[21] D. Kahneman, P. Slovi, A. Tversky. Under Uncertainty: Heuristics and Biases. Cambridge: Cambridge University Press; 1982.

[22] M. G. Morgan, B. Fischhoff, A. Bostrom, C. Atman. Risk Communication: A Mental Models Approach. New York: Cambridge University Press; 2002.

[23] M. E. Paté-Cornell, L. M. Lakats, D. M. Murphy, D. M. Gaba. Anesthesia Patient Risk: A Quantitative Approach to Organizational Factors and Risk Management Options. Risk Analysis, 17;1997;511–523.

[24] E. Paté-Cornell, P. S. Fischbeck. PRA as a Management Tool: Organizational Factors and Risk-Based Priorities for the Maintenance of the Tiles of the Space Shuttle Orbiter. Reliability Engineering & System Safety, 40;1993;239–257.

[25] M. J. Small. Methods for Assessing Uncertainty in Fundamental Assumptions and Associated Models for Cancer Risk Assessment. Risk Analysis, 28;2008; 1289–1308.

[26] N. A. Stiber, M. J. Small, M. Pantazidou. Site-Specific Updating and Aggregation of Bayesian Belief Network Models for Multiple Experts. Risk Analysis, 24;2004;1529–1538.

[27] L. Wasserman. Bayesian Model Selection and Model Averaging. Journal of Mathematical Psychology, 44;2000;92–107.

[28] J. L. Pressman, A. Wildavsky. Implementation: How Great Expectations in Washington Are Dashed in Oakland; or, Why It's Amazing That Federal Programs Work at All, This Being a Saga of the Economic Development Administration as Told by Two Sympathetic Observers Who Seek to Build Morals on a Foundation of Ruined Hopes. Berkeley: University of California Press; 1973.

[29] Lumina Systems. See www.lumina.com/ana/usesofanalytica.htm. Accessed October 30, 2010.

[30] M. G. Morgan, J. Peha. Science and Technology Advice to the Congress. Washington (DC): RFF Press; 2003.

[31] G.A.O. Technology Assessment: Protecting Structures and Improving Communications During Wildland Fires. In: GAO-05-380. Washington (DC): G.A.O.; 2005.

[32] G.A.O. Technology Assessment: Using Biometrics for Border Security. In: GAO-03-147. Washington (DC); 2002.

[33] G. J. Knezo. Technology Assessment in Congress: History and Legislative Options. CRS Report RS21586, updated May 20, 2005, 6pp, at www.dtic.mil/cgi-bin/GetTRDoc?Location=U2&doc=GetTRDoc.pdf&AD=ADA465379. Accessed October 30, 2010.

[34] M. G. Morgan. Technology and Policy. In: D. Grasso and M. B. Burkins (Eds.), Engineering Education for the 21st Century: A Holistic Approach to Meet Complex Challenges. New York: Springer; 2010, p. 299.

[35] American Association for the Advancement of Science. Guide to Graduate Education in Science, Engineering and Public Policy, on-line guide at www.aaas.org/spp/sepp/. Accessed October 30, 2010.

[36] J. W. Kingdon. Agendas: Alternative and Public Policies. New York: Little, Brown and Company; 1995.

[37] R. W. Hahn, R. G. Noll. Designing a Market for Tradable Emissions Permits. In: W. Magat (Ed.), Reform of Environmental Regulation. Cambridge (MA): Ballinger; 1982, p. 190.

[38] R. W. Hahn. Economic Prescriptions for Environmental Problems: How the Patient Followed the Doctor's Orders. The Journal of Economic Perspectives, 3; 1989;95–114.

[39] L. B. Lave, C. T. Hendrickson, F. C. McMichael. Environmental Implications of Electric Cars. Science, 268;1995;993–995.

[40] R. H. Coase. Comment on Thomas W. Hazlett: Assigning Property Rights to Radio Spectrum Users: Why Did FCC License Auctions Take 67 Years? Journal of Law and Economics, 41;1998;577–580.

[41] T. W. Hazlett. Assigning Property Rights to Radio Spectrum Users: Why Did FCC License Auctions Take 67 Years? Journal of Law and Economics, 41;1998; 529–576.

[42] C. Mooney. The Republican War on Science. New York: Basic Books; 2006.

[43] Purdue Ag. Econ., Indiana Local Government Information Website, specifics on the Pi Bill are available at www.agecon.purdue.edu/crd/Localgov/Second%20Level % 20pages/Indiana_Pi_Story.htm, undated. Accessed October 30, 2010.

[44] D. Joravsky. The Lysenko Affair. Chicago: University of Chicago Press; 1986.

[45] N. Oreskes, E. M. Conway. Merchants of Doubt: How a Handful of Scientists Obscured the Truth on Issues from Tobacco Smoke to Global Warming. New York: Bloomsbury Press; 2010.

Science of Science and Innovation Policy

The Emerging Community of Practice

Irwin Feller

8

1. Introduction

The more highly lauded advances in scientific knowledge and derived innovations are presented as essential to long-term economic growth and competitiveness [1], the higher the level of attention paid by the federal government to its policies and programs that nurture the U.S. scientific enterprise. This heightened attention underlies the recent consensus that a new or an improved "science" of science policy involving the construction of new theories, models, data, and methods of analysis is needed to assist federal government policymakers in crafting better-informed decisions.

The starting point for any discussion of the new social science of science policy, of course, is Dr. Marburger's 2005 Science editorial, "Wanted: Better Benchmarks," and related presentations [2, 3]. These statements have simultaneously crystalized and given political saliency to long-standing concern among both policy-making and research communities that U.S. science policy was meandering along well-trod paths that obscured as much as they revealed changing external environments. They also are credited with catalyzing recent federal initiatives, such as the ongoing activities of the National Science and Technology Council (NSTC) Committee on Science and new federal agency programmatic initiatives, most notably the National Science Foundation's (NSF) Science of Science and Innovation Policy (SciSIP) program [4, 5]. As evidenced by the Office of Management and Budget's (OMB) August 4, 2009, memorandum to executive departments and agencies to "develop 'science of science' policy tools that can improve management of their research and development portfolios and better assess the impact of their science and technology investments," the momentum generated by these initiatives has continued across the transition from the George W. Bush to the Barack Obama administrations. These statements have served to frame the opening research agenda for the new science of science policy on questions of resource allocation and priority setting.

Both top-down and bottom-up influences connected to demand-side and supply-side influences may be observed in shaping the market for new models and evidence. The most visible of contemporary top-down, demand-side influences flows from what has been termed the new public management paradigm [6]. This paradigm is manifested both in legislative enactments, such as the 1991 Government Performance and Results Act, and in executive branch emphasis on effective and efficient public-sector management practices, as represented during the Bush administration by the OMB's articulation and implementation of a performance assessment and rating tool (PART) and more recent directives by the OMB in the Obama administration calling for an "Increased Emphasis on Program Evaluations" [7]. The provisions of the 2009 American Recovery and Reinvestment Act (ARRA), requiring documentation that the stimulus support provided to federal science agencies has been a job creation technique, reflect a similar imperative. Coupled with the call currently echoed across all levels of government for evidence-based decision making, these policies impose increased demands on public-sector organizations across all functional areas, including science, to set measurable goals and to document—typically in quantitative form—performance set against these goals. Institutional frameworks, network and behavioral models of science and engineering workforce organization, and cognitive models of discover processes are also of keen interest to policymakers who seek predictable outcomes for effort invested.

A bottom-up, supply-side influence has been the development over recent decades of increasingly powerful and sophisticated analytical and computational techniques for collecting, distilling, and presenting large(r) quantities of data related to various aspects of scientific activity. The development of these techniques presents new opportunities, or is promoted as such, to address old questions in new ways more consonant with a contemporary emphasis on quantitative forms of evidence.

Both performers and users are voicing concern, however, that existing frameworks and data sets are increasingly inadequate to capture the current dynamics of the functioning of the U.S. science (technology and innovation) systems. Historically, there have been important contributions to the science of science policy that are grounded in works, for example: Solow and Abramowitz, who documented the importance of productivity change or whatever residual factors other than growth in inputs and capital-deepening accounting accounted for secular growth in per capita output; Arrow and Nelson, who set out a theoretical framework of the economics of invention; and Mansfield and Griliches, who did their pioneer empirical studies of the social savings of technological innovation and the diffusion of innovation [8–15].

Yet even among those whose work continues to enlarge and enrich these traditions, there is a sense that new models are needed—models that rely on both quantitative and qualitative analysis. Given recognition of the existence of a "well developed body of social science knowledge that could be readily applied to the study of science and innovation," as stated in the NSTC Committee on Science's 2008 report, *The Science of Science Policy: A Federal Research Roadmap*, there are grand expectations for the new science of science policy. Important questions include: What is lacking in or missing from the current stock of knowledge or evidence (and implicitly for whom and for what purposes)? Phrased differently, in the context of the theories, models, and data that currently influence discourse on post–World War II U.S. science policy, although not necessarily determining observed policy decisions or outcomes [16, 17], what are the knowns that need to be revised or discarded in light of changing events or conditions or the unknowns that need to be identified and subjected to critical examination, thus permitting their effective and efficient manipulation by policymakers, and where should the focus be? For example, should it be on priority setting among fields or domains of science, on project and proposal criteria, on incentive and funding mechanisms, or on the interrelationships among these and other determinants of the performance of U.S. science? Relatedly, what role, if any, is there for general models that venture to synthesize findings from a plethora of diverse research studies, each expertly crafted but limited in scope and/or embodying a delimited disciplinary or methodological approach?

The questions posed presume a synthesis or at least a cross-fertilization of bodies of research that traditionally are relegated to intellectual silos. In light of what previous studies have termed the "uncertain connections" between the generation of new knowledge (in the form of theories, models, and data) and the use of this knowledge by policymakers [18], critical questions arise: What needs to be done to build a community of practice among researchers and between researchers and policymakers to foster productive use of the new knowledge emerging from new investments in a science of science policy? Is it a matter primarily of generating better theories, data, and tools, or is it instead the need to develop fundamentally different ways of communicating new findings to satisfy policymakers' needs? Indeed, this latter question needs to be extended to the community of science of science policy researchers itself, as it has tended to organize into self-contained clusters, taking limited notice of work conducted by others, and then not always in a reaffirming tone

[19]. Alternatively, is building a community of practice mainly a matter of increasing the influence of policymakers on the research agenda so that more rather than less policy-relevant questions are asked, even if the former cannot be answered with the precision or in the time frames congenial to academic research? Finally, though, are there limits to how closely knit this community of practice can be, and if so, what are these limits? That there are constraints is manifestly obvious from ongoing debates on the funding of global climate change, alternative energy resources, stem cell research, and cyber, food, and national security. Whether they can be loosened by better science remains to be determined.

The purpose of this chapter, therefore, is neither to champion the recent initiatives nor call attention to earlier landmark studies to echo refrains about there being nothing new under the sun. Instead, the purpose of this chapter is to: (1) scope out what a new science of science policy might or should look like; (2) outline the types of findings that might reasonably be expected to flow from it; and (3) describe the challenges that lie before it in attempting to build the community of practice among researchers and between policymakers and researchers, as described in Dr. Marburger's chapter in this book. Of necessity, the approach and coverage presented here in addressing these questions are selective. Several approaches that are not delved into here are finely and expertly mapped in previous chapters in this book. Among the more obvious contributions that are omitted from this chapter are the history of U.S. science and innovation policy, landmark accounts of the workings of the U.S. science advisory apparatus, and literature that addresses the origin, disciplinary content, and impact of science policy as a discrete field of research [20–24]. Also, space restriction requires a scant coverage of the relationships between "science policy" and "innovation policy," even as public support for science continues largely to be shaped by assessments of its prospective utilitarian benefits. Fred Gault's chapter that follows focuses mainly on the science of innovation policy.

2. What Is the New Science of Science Policy?
2.1. Defining the Landscape
Two aspects of recent formulations of a science of science policy warrant especial attention. First, and foremost, is the very use of the word "science." This word choice suggests that what is being sought is something above and beyond, or at least different, from "research on research" or counterpart formulations (e.g., economics of technological change; sociology of science; program evaluation; scientometrics) previously used to categorize academic

inquiry and reflexive practitioner insights or memoirs into these matters. Setting the goal of creating a (new) science, or using the word to describe the content of new initiatives, introduces nettlesome epistemic and methodological questions that extend beyond recurrent tugs of war among different social science disciplines—economics, political science, sociology, history of science—or between the social sciences in aggregate and physical, life, and engineering sciences. Rather, the questions relate to what is meant by a science, and the degree to which employment of putatively scientific approaches can produce sufficient consensus about theories, models, and data leading policymakers to believe that they are better informed and, more importantly, that they can employ the new knowledge to make better decisions, however measured or assessed.

Second is the bounded set of decisions—at least in the initial formulations—for which new knowledge is being sought, namely, questions or policy choices relating to the allocation of resources. For example, more scientific approaches are sought to determine how much should be spent on science and technology year after year, and how these expenditures should be allocated among the various fields of science. This orientation has both ex-ante and ex-post elements. Ex-ante, it is designed to improve decisions relating to federal investments or expenditures; ex-post, it is to evaluate performance or the returns from prior investments in policies, programs, and projects. The sequencing of decisions is implicitly spliced together via feedback loops from evidence of performance to determination of future investments.

Immediately apparent in this formulation of the decisions of interest is that it takes into account only one side of Brooks's dichotomy that has served as the organizing framework for much of the discourse on post–World War II U.S. science and technology policy—policy for science/and science in policy [25]. This truncated formulation leads to subsuming or omitting coverage of many other long-standing issues in the larger discourse on U.S. science policy, such as how social values affect the determination of research priorities [26], how the governance of science affects research performance [27, 28], or the broader and more diverse set of analytical, empirical, and normative issues subsumed under the rubric social studies of science.

Differences in the framing of research and policy questions and the use of techniques and data sets across the disciplines that have produced the bulk of the research literature on science policy issues are well known. For this reason, a repeated emphasis in the launching of new initiatives to build a science of science policy is that multiple disciplinary perspectives are needed, with an added nudge in the direction on interdisciplinary research. Acceptance of these propositions, though, still leaves unexamined what is meant by a science. Science, or, more precisely, modes of scientific inquiry, can mean different things and take on different forms, even within a single discipline.

Galison [29] observes, "Like Gaul, the practice of twentieth-century physics is divided into 3 parts": experiment, theory, and instrumentation. Further, Galison asserts, "Each subculture has its own rhythms of change, each has its own standards of demonstration, and each is embedded differently in the wider culture of institutions, practices, inventions, and ideas." This postulate has relevance here, for it identifies the existence of creative tension among bona fide, credentialed scientists within a single, well-defined field. Parallel distinctions among theorists, experimentalists, and tool developers have likewise been noted in the biological sciences [30]. Similar differences exist within and across the social and behavioral science fields that are seen as the foundation stones for building a new science of science policy.

Customarily, modes of scientific inquiry are treated as complementary, reinforcing, and synergistic—the linkages among the works of Kepler, Brahe, and Newton being an oft-cited example here. Theory leads to new predictions that in turn induce new efforts at data collection; the design and construction of new techniques to collect, manipulate, or distill these data in turn lead, albeit indirectly and over time, to experiments to test whether or not the predictions are correct. Recent policy interest in prizes as spurs to scientific and technological discoveries that in part draw intellectual nurturance from recent work on tournament models of competition in R&D may be viewed as one such contemporary example [31, 32]. In a reverse manner, illustrated by the intellectual linkages over time between Machlup's [33] and Foray's [34] conceptualizations and measurements of the "knowledge" input in the "knowledge economy, assemblage of new data by existing or new techniques can make visible new patterns that elaborate upon or modify maintained theories, thereby inducing a search for new explanations.

The working, albeit implicit, assumption of ongoing initiatives to build the new science is that these complementarities and synergies exist, and that whatever tensions (or disequilibria) in the state of knowledge among modes as each advances along its self-defined path are productive. In Rosenberg's [35] phrase, such tensions serve as focusing devices and inducement mechanisms across modes of inquiry, identifying and prioritizing research agendas and providing "goods"—models, frameworks, data, tools, and techniques—that can be exchanged across what Galison has termed trading zones.

Modes of inquiry, however, also may move at different rates of change. In the process, they may be or become isolated from one another and thus produce findings incompatible with or inconsistent with each another, at least at specific points in time. Tools for assembling, sifting, and presenting data with weak theoretical foundations ("measurement without theory" is Koopmans's telling phrase [36]) or used in ways that confound or extend beyond their appropriate use (as has been suggested for bibliometrics in van Leeuwen [37]) can produce the semblance of quantitative precision much valued in this era of evidence-based decision making. The tools may yield widely erroneous predictions, however, lacking sound foundations such that the measures or methods used are not used correctly. For example, consider the Limits to Growth "computer that cried wolf" imbroglio on the environmental policy of the 1970s [38]. Poorly conceived or generated data likewise may serve as policy snares, as illustrated by recent debates on U.S. comparative production of scientists and engineering, thereby entrapping decision making in arcane but nettlesome disputes about the reliability and validity of findings while decisions need to be made.

Moreover, data, indicators, or metrics, however sophisticated the means by which they are compiled, constructed, or presented, may be consistent with multiple implicit or explicit but competing a priori theories. Lack of a solid theoretical grounding lends itself to a cabinet filled with policy prescriptions: some may be beneficial, some may be harmless nostrums (but beneficial to the vendors), and some may interfere with or negatively interact with other more beneficial approaches.

The contemporary penchant for innovation scorecards and global rankings of universities, for example, seems to fit the setting described by Koopmans as follows: "The various choices as to what to 'look for,' what economic phenomena to observe, and what measures to define and compute are made with a minimum of assistance from theoretical conceptions or hypothesis regarding the nature of the economic processes by which the variables studied are generated" [36]. Among the theoretically or historically grounded adjustments needed to make sense of, and correctly interpret, the trunkful of performance indicators, metrics, or scorecards currently being offered to policymakers are accounting for differences in initial settings, accounting for differences between relative and absolute changes, avoidance of extrapolating nonlinear trends or those having self-limiting factors, and the use of measurement systems that vary across nations.

Recently, concerns have been voiced that an imbalance exists among the progress of different modes of scientific inquiry, especially the apparent current lead of measurement over theory. In particular, developments in data processing and distillation are seen as outpacing improved understanding of underlying frameworks. Thus according to the 2007 National Research Council (NRC) report, "A Strategy for Assessing Science," "Science policy seems to be in particular need of improved basic understanding of the apparently uncertain paths of scientific progress as a basis for making wise, more efficient investments. Without this improved understanding, extensive investments into collecting and analyzing data on scientific outputs are unlikely to provide valid predictors of some of the most important kinds of scientific progress" [31].

These comments are not presented as a paean to theory, however. Countervailing concerns arise when theory is constructed about assumptions deemed unduly simple or naive, is tested by methods that involve the use of surrogates or proxies for data that have not been collected or cannot be accessed because of administrative rules, or employs technically sophisticated methods whose inner workings are either not visible or comprehensible, except to its adepts. As noted by Sachs, "Theory . . . can be a great enemy of honest observations and thought, . . . especially when it forgets that it is theory or model and hardens into unstated, perhaps unconscious dogma or assumptions" [39]. None of these issues is new in considering internal methodological debates within specific fields of science. They are perennials in the social science disciplines upon which the new science of science and innovation is to be built [40], and they feature prominently in debates about economic theory, centering about the Friedman proposition that the test of a theory is not whether or not its assumptions are realistic but whether or not it leads to correct predictions.

Concerns about the integration of theory (or models), data, and measurement are evident among both researchers and policymakers. Leamer's [41] call for taking the "con" out of econometrics, for example, has a contemporary application to science policy in Salter and Martin's [42] expression of concern about the "simplistic and often unrealistic assumption" built into econometric models of publicly funded basic research. Indeed, even as policymakers call for new models, they express a degree of skepticism about them, hesitant at times to accept findings produced by arcane methodologies that they do not understand or well briefed by staffs to understand that findings are, or can be, highly sensitive to numerous specification and estimation procedures.

Calling attention to these issues highlights latent tensions in the development of a new science of science policy. As much as progress along each mode of inquiry is to be sought and welcomed when it occurs, it is their integration, in a consistent and coordinated manner, that is most needed, especially in fruitfully connecting advances in knowledge with improved decision making. Unbalanced or disconnected scientific advance carries with it the risk of sipping rather than drinking deeply from newly located springs of knowledge.

2.2. Data-Based Science Policy

The subject of greatest agreement in recent efforts to build a science of science policy is the need for improved data. As in any field of science, accurate data are needed to describe the current state of the world, thereby intimating whether this state meets societal needs or expectations. Debates about data accuracy are often at the forefront of the determination of whether or not there is a need for government action—recall the 1960 debates about the definition and magnitude of U.S. poverty or contemporary debates about climate change—as well as the size of scope of the proposed policies. Data quality obviously influences the predictive accuracy of findings from estimation models and techniques, however sophisticated.

In each of these dimensions, improvements and advances in data collection are foundational components of the development of a new science. Here are three specific examples. First, the size and significance of alleged "shortages" in the U.S. production of scientists and engineers has been a recurrent problem in setting U.S. science and education policies. Disputes about the accuracy of these estimates in the 1980s ensnared the NSF in a pipeline study imbroglio [43]; more recently, the dire statements about such shortages in "rising above the gathering storm" have been called into question [44]. Second, U.S. national statistics on industrial research and development (R&D) are based on outdated definitions and relationships, a problem compounded by the lack of information about respondents, and how they report survey data [45]. Third, for all the recent attention paid to U.S. performance in innovation, systematic data for the United States comparable, say, to the European Community Innovation Survey do not exist. For the second and third examples, the NSF's newly designed 2008 Business R&D and Innovation Survey is an important step forward toward addressing these data needs. It is only part of what needs to be done though. In particular, with respect to adequate data on innovation, the United States is playing catch-up, even as the sources and characteristics of innovation are becoming increasingly fungible [46].

2.3. Science as Experimentation

The concept of science as experimentation is largely absent: there is little evidence of the purposeful (theory-based) design of alternative states of being that can be used to compare the effects of an intervention (a policy or a program) under controlled conditions. Experimentation can serve as an important and a useful approach, especially in those situations, as described by Machlup, where "conflicting hypotheses are equally good explanations of the same set of events, and only one of them, at best, may actually turn out to be correct" [33]. An orientation toward experimentation also accords with the "science policy" part of the science for science policy paradigm, for policies, as Wildavsky has observed, are not eternal truths; rather, they should be considered as "hypotheses subject to modification and replacement by better ones until these in turn are discarded" [47].

Perspective again is needed as to what is meant by an experimental bent. It is generally recognized that randomized experiments cannot be constructed for many science policies and programs; thus it is misleading to establish this approach as the only basis for credible evidence regarding policy effectiveness or program performance. Quasi-experimental design, in contrast, pervades the methodological and empirical literature on evaluations of R&D programs [48–50], with creative, indeed heroic, efforts being made by researchers to construct comparison groups or counterfactual situations in order to isolate the effects of a program [51]. But this evaluative work tends to be retrospective, often requiring ad hoc, imperfect research designs, further constrained by cost, lack of timeliness, and administrative barriers to data.

The analytical task here is to determine which science policy decisions are amenable to experimentation. The result is likely to be something more than holding up randomized experiments as the minimum standard and thus rejecting essentially out of hand experimentation as infeasible for science and innovation programs but something less than Rivlin's proposal for "systematic experimentation," in which a new method or model was "tried in enough places to establish its capacity to make a difference and the conditions under which it works best" [52]. Jaffe's [53] proposal for using a regression-discontinuity design to assess the effects of research awards on scholarly performance is an example of what is possible.

2.4. Allocation Paradigms

The initial framing of the agenda for a new science of science policy as a set of ex-ante and ex-post allocation decisions lends itself to using economic concepts as a heuristic for reviewing existing economic frameworks for federal government support of science. In particular, when juxtaposed with the aforementioned catalogue of theories, models, methods, and data relating to criteria for investing in science and effectively linking scientific advance and innovation, the review highlights both the overlap and the gaps between general economic theories underlying public support for science and the criteria-based approaches employed in making specific decisions.

There are readily identifiable macroeconomics and microeconomic dimensions to the science allocation questions. Intermediate between the two, deriving its policy urgency from a set of macroeconomic measures but its rationale, program design, and details from microeconomic variables and relationships, is a third dimension centering about national strategies for choosing between mission-oriented and technology-oriented funded R&D [54–56].

The macroeconomic perspective stems from the body of research associated with the work of Solow and Abramowitz of the 1950s and the subsequent growth accounting work of Denison, Jorgensen, Baumol, Romer, and others, indicating that a sizable portion of the observed growth in output per capita could not be explained in input growth or capital deepening alone but, rather, was attributed to improvements in "technical change," productivity growth, or what came to be termed the "residual." This line of research continues on today in the form of increasingly sophisticated work rooted in endogenous growth theory [57, 58, 59].

The macroeconomic perspective tends to lead to attention on the share of GDP allocated to R&D, its apportionment between the public and private sectors, among different fields of science and technology, and across different public-sector functional fields and industrial sectors. It is the approach typically found in American Association for the Advancement of Science (AAAS) annual volumes on federal R&D expenditures, in NSF Science & Engineering Indicators reports, and in federal budget documents.

The macroeconomic dimension's major connection to policy is through recurrent debates about the optimal ratio of R&D to GDP to achieve desired rates of long-term economic growth or, alternatively, the level necessary to retain or achieve international economic competitiveness and associated macroeconomic objectives. The association made between R&D and macroeconomic objectives provides a theoretical and an empirical underpinning for the European Union's 2000 Lisbon Strategy and the targets set in the Seventh Framework Programme (2007–2013) of having member states reach a goal of national investments of at least 3 percent of GDP. Likewise, for the United States, the connection provides the foundation for the Obama administration's recently announced goal as part of its Strategy for American Innovation of "more than 3 percent" of GDP in "public and private research and development."

In terms of its relevance for and contribution to a science of science policy, the major shortcoming of this approach is that it provides only a skeletal structure to frame answers to the question of how much but none of the exterior facing or internal furnishings to complete the building of a national science edifice. The approach is only loosely connected to the criteria or priority-setting literature noted earlier, for example, about which fields of science to support or how much for each. Moreover, even accepting that utilitarianism is the basis for the social contract legitimizing sector support of basic research [60], the macroeconomic approach gives short shrift to the contributions that such research may make to other societal goals. As with the Kennedy era race to the moon, or the views of the NRC Committee on Particle Physics in the 21st Century, that there is an "intrinsic value" to research on "elementary particle physics as part of the broader scientific and technological enterprise" [61], the achievement of a scientific or technological goal may itself have intrinsic value, worthy of national support.

The microeconomic dimension centers about the need for, or appropriateness of, government support of nonmission-oriented research, especially basic research, and of the development or promotion of "domestic" or civilian technologies. Here, beginning mainstream analysis is identified with the works of Nelson [62] and Arrow [13] and their attention to (market failure) deviations—indivisibilities, inappropriability, and uncertainty—from the (Pareto-) efficient allocation of resources held to exist in competitive equilibrium characteristics. Thus, according to Arrow, "we expect a free-enterprise economy to under-invest in invention and research (as compared with an ideal) because it is risky, because the product can be appropriated only to a limited extent, and because of increasing returns in use. This under-investment will be greater for more basic research" [13]. Mansfield and others' [63] estimates of divergences between private and social returns from industrial innovation and Jaffe's [64] explication of the role of knowledge spillovers from private-sector R&D benefits also came to be viewed as additional theoretical and empirical support for the contention that (competitive) private-sector markets tend to underinvest in scientific research.

In the context of the widespread acceptance across both major political parties and the general, if intermittently, uneven upward trend since the 1950s in budgetary support for basic research across most federal agencies under both Democratic and Republican administrations and Congresses, U.S. science policy may be said to have accepted the Nelson–Arrow framework. Indeed, this framework has become so commonplace in the economic justification for public support of basic research that it is easy to overlook the intellectual and political transformation that it represented when first articulated. Historically, from America's founding days, when colonies offered prizes and premiums for specific technological achievements, through the early national period, where public funds were provided for exploratory surveys of coastlines and internal expeditions, the U.S. government has always supported various forms of mission-oriented R&D [65, 66]. What was slower in coming, albeit not for lack of efforts, was support for research not directly connected to specific missions or problems [67].

Far less agreement exists, however, about the application of the market failure framework to technology policy. Here, the disagreements are of two major types: first, the counterpoise of the government failure model to the market failure model; and, second, the continuing challenge of developing industry-specific and technology-specific algorithms to operationally distinguish between the two cases.

The government failure model as applied to R&D, briefly stated, is that the public sector tends to invest too much and in the wrong places, as well as to crowd out private-sector activities. Several case histories of the failure of federal government-supported technology development and commercialization programs, encapsulated in Cohen and Noll's observation that, "The history of the federal commercialization programs . . . is hardly a success story" [68], provide empirical support for this proposition. The government failure model became the intellectual mountain from which the recent Bush administration's OMB could hurl down thunderbolts that opposed or quashed existing and proposed domestic technology programs, such as the National Institute of Standards and Technology's Advanced Technology Program. Federally funded R&D projects were seen as "stepping beyond the legitimate purposes of government to compete with—or unnecessarily subsidize—commercial ventures," to inflate "the cost of research by bidding up the price of human and capital resources," and "by directly benefiting corporations that could fund their own R&D projects without federal assistance" [69].

Debates about market failure and government failure at times have become either-or propositions, providing a blanket endorsement or rejection of specific policies or programs. Thus Stiglitz noted, "The popularity of the market-failure approach has caused many programs to be justified in terms of market failures. But this may simply be rhetoric. There is often a significant difference between the stated objective of a program to remedy some market failure and the design of the program" [70]. Relatedly, Wolf has observed: "The choice between markets and governments is not a choice between perfection and imperfection, but between degrees and types of imperfection, between degrees and types of failure" [71].

In this contested analytical environment, the challenge, or opportunity, for a science of science policy is to provide the credible evidence that enables policymakers to make the nuanced decisions that will take into consideration both types of failure yet will lead to the efficient and productive uses of public funds. This is not a simple matter. One may agree, for example, with a diagnosis that innovation market failure and underinvestment in technology "implies the need to establish a long-term institutional framework for the support of basic research, generic-enabling research, and commercialization" [56], but a follow-on prescription, sage though it may be, that "The extent to which support should be directed to each (industrial or technological area) will vary with the sources of sectoral innovation market failure," leaves policymakers at the starting line. If there is any area of research where new theories, models, and evidence hold the potential for improving federal science policy, then it is here.

3. What Can or Should Be Expected from a Science of Science Policy?

Can one predict scientific advancement, at least in ways amenable to and useful for priority setting? In key respects, this is the central question contained in the initial formulation of the call for better benchmarks so that the decisions of policymakers produce a more efficient, productive, higher rate of return from federal (and state) government investments in basic and applied research among fields of science. The search for criteria to guide federal investments in science indeed is one of the cornerstones upon which the post–World War II emergence of science policy as a distinct field has been constructed [72]. The search has yielded multiple solutions, albeit most consisting of variations on a few themes. For example, a concordance aligning Weinberg's internal and external criteria [73, 74], the OMB's more recent articulation of quality, relevance, and performance [75], and the National Academies' emphasis on leadership in the most promising areas of science and technology [76] would likely show much overlap, little overt contradiction, and mainly the layering of additional criteria, so much so that the task shifts from specifying criteria to assigning relative weights among them.

However, if there is any single leitmotif to contemporary attempts to answer this question, it is that scientific advance, as well as the uses made of such advances, is characterized by high degrees of uncertainty. Thus

> History . . . shows us how often basic research in science and engineering leads to
> outcomes that were unexpected or took many years or even decades to emerge. . . .
> The measures of the practical outcomes of basic research usually must be retro-

spective and historical and . . . the unpredictable nature of practical outcomes is an inherent and unalterable feature of basic research [76].

A more recent NRC study reaches essentially the same conclusion:

No theory of scientific progress exists, or is on the horizon, that allows prediction of the future development of new scientific ideas or specifies how the different types of scientific progress influence each other—although they clearly are interdependent. . . . Only in hindsight does the development of various experimental claims and theoretical generalizations appear to have the coherence that creates a linear, inexorable path [31].

Even the OMB's articulation of a set of R&D investment criteria, which contain a heavy emphasis on quantitative performance measures, reflects considerable appreciation for the uncertainties surrounding returns from federal investments in basic research:

Agencies should define appropriate output and outcome measures for all R&D programs, but agencies should not expect fundamental basic research to be able to identify outcomes and measure performance in the same way that applied research or development are able to do. Highlighting the results of basic research is important, but it should not come at the expense of risk-taking and innovation [77].

Each of the several techniques that have been developed in recent years (including foresight modeling, bibliometrics, data mining, web scraping, and road mapping) may be viewed as search techniques for improving predictive accuracy. Depending on how they are used in specific decision settings, the use of such structured decision-making techniques or various indicators or metrics may complement or substitute for expert judgment the scientific community's hallmark approach. But, however used, they still leave open the possibilities of Type I and Type II errors: incorrectly rejecting or giving low priority to a field or theory (e.g., oncongenes) or incorrectly assigning and investing in a field or theory that proves fallow (e.g., cold fusion) [78–82].

Further downstream, even if one assumes a new workable model or set of algorithms that yields more accurate predictions about future trends in scientific discovery, this would still leave open the question of the degree of consensus about the findings emerging from such investments. Disagreements are frequent about the importance as well as the correctness of specific findings [83, 84].

Questioning of specific findings of course is the normal state of normal science. Indeed, this questioning is why review articles and meta-analyses of the impacts of any number of science and technology policies and programs need to be written [85–87]. Rather, even within fields bound tightly together by paradigms and theories that clearly differentiate them from other fields, an entire approach to a specific subject—underlying assumptions, model specification, data sources, estimation, or experimentation procedures—can produce competing "schools of thought," such that findings emerging from one school are not incorporated, indeed, challenged and rejected, by the other. For example, "salt water" (MIT; Harvard) and "fresh water" (Minnesota; Chicago; Rochester) approaches to economic growth differ considerably, leading to quite different messages about economic policy, especially innovation policy [88].

A potentially even more serious problem arises when a professionally, highly lauded, and operationally important theory or approach leads to untoward outcomes, as contended in accounts of the collapse of Long-Term Capital Management's reliance on the Black-Sholes–Merton risk model and more recently in accounts attributing the 2007–2008 financial debacles to dependence on the efficient capital market thesis [89, 90]. Given changing environmental conditions or systemic rather than partial equilibrium dislocations (or, alternatively, extreme and thus assumed or low probability or ignored values of the parameters explicit or implicit in the model's formulation), the collective, vetted, and putatively evidence-based judgment or predictions of even the best and the brightest may be wrong.

Similar issues arise in attempting to predict the contribution of scientific advance to innovation. Viewed broadly, research on innovation, especially that portion that segues into evaluating existing federal R&D/technology development programs rather than on science, per se, is the mainstay of contemporary research on science and innovation policy. There is no lack of models of innovation-diffusion processes or of evidence of various forms on the effects of past and current federal (and state) government diffusion-innovation programs. If anything, the plethora of such models and analytical perspectives may be at issue, both for researchers and policymakers. The large number of variables that are held to shape a nation's innovative capacity and performance, such as science policy, technology policy, capital market arrangements with their valleys of death, intellectual property rights regimes, and education policy, to list but a few of the major identified components, multiplied by the number of competing theories and dissimilar empirical findings, is itself a challenge. And that challenge is magnified, at least for policymakers, if, as is frequently the case, competing models, with attendant competing or inconsistent policy prescriptions, vie for attention.

Perspective is needed in interpreting these comments, which are not intended to dismiss or discount the potential value of new theories and models of scientific discovery but, rather, to suggest that expectations that new theories or proffers of quantitative evidence will lead to unequivocal or uncontested policy recommendations about scientific priorities should be modest. Advances in the direction of better predictive models are likely to be of the low-frequency, high-impact type. A corollary to this conclusion is that efforts to predict the direction and magnitude of such advances by new data and forecasting techniques alone so as to be better positioned to make decisions about how much and in what directions to fund basic research are a stretch. The use of these techniques also may be dysfunctional, inducing heavy-traffic and bandwagon effects in the direction of "hot" research projects and thereby increasing the quantity of wasted effort and resources if the road mapped leads to a cul-de-sac.

These comments, though, are not intended to provide a free ride for expert judgment as a priority-setting mechanism. A stream of empirical research and participant observation, as described in Feller [91], has pointed to the influence of variables such as small group dynamics, the forms in which criteria are presented, and the content of instructions provided by funding agencies on panel agencies. Indeed, if anything, to the extent that agnosticism about the likelihood of advances in developing new predictive theories of science serves to buttress existing reliance on expert judgment selection mechanisms, the greater the need will be for critical scrutiny of the inner workings of these mechanisms.

4. Building a Community of Practice

Research-based consideration of the impact of knowledge on policy is essential if the science of science policy is to connect to, much less actually influence, policy. As with the criteria for scientific choice question, this is not a new issue. A corpus of insightful previous work on "knowledge utilization," encompassing but extending well beyond science policy, is readily accessible, if only looked for and consulted.

In brief, among the contemporary issues relevant to embryonic efforts to have a science of science policy actually contribute to policymaking are the following:

1. To date, the search for a new science of science and innovation has primarily been an executive branch activity, originating with the OMB and the Office of Science and Technology Policy, which likely accounts for the emphasis on efficiency and effectiveness. Congressional interest

in or willingness to accept findings from a science directed so heavily toward these objectives is problematic, especially given the well-known decentralization among several committees and subcommittees in both the House and the Senate regarding authorizations and appropriations for federal expenditures for R&D.

Considerations of distributive politics involving efficiency-equity trade-offs pervade congressional considerations of federal investments in science and innovation, as obviously for other budget categories as well. These trade-offs were evident in congressional debates over competitive, merit-based allocations and geographic quota-funding formulae surrounding the establishment of the NSF [92]. They are evident in many overt and nuanced forms, such as decisions relating to the establishment of National Institutes of Health (NIH) centers [93] and the irresistible allure and presence in authorizations and appropriations of earmarks, set-asides, and sheltered competitions that benefit specific states, institutions, or performers, and selective funding of agencies or programs whose distributive effects match the interests of member constituencies [94–97]. As suggested by Department of Energy (DOE) secretary Steven Chu, difficulties in getting Congress to agree to his proposals to curtail DOE R&D funding for cars that run on hydrogen fuel cells over the opposition of firms and universities engaged in such research, the de facto earmarking of almost all federally funded highway research, and the increasing number of states deemed eligible over time to benefit from sheltered NSF and NIH research competitions, iron triangle arrangements among program participants (or their lobbying organizations), congressional (sub) committees, and entrepreneurial program managers also make it difficult to terminate, shrink, or keep from expanding science and innovation programs inconsistent with allocative efficiency criteria [98, 99].

2. A special policy-oriented conundrum arises from the visibility and support provided for science in the Obama administration's stabilization and growth policies. It is that answers have already been provided from many of the allocation questions about which the new science is designed to provide new models and more reliable evidence. Among these are the economic basis for the 3 percent R&D/GDP goal, the implied connections between science and innovation, and the "evidence" base upon which recent budgetary decisions, such as the doubling of the R&D budgets of the NSF, the DOE's Office of

Science, and the National Institutes of Standard and Technology, have been made.

3. Distinctions made by Weiss [100, 101] between knowledge creep and decision accretion and between the instrumental and enlightenment effects of research-based knowledge, the former involving use of findings with respect to specific decisions and the latter involving a longer time, often a circuitous influence on the way policy decisions are framed and possibly answered, offer important perspectives here in analyzing researcher–policymaker connections. Scientific advance is typically a process of knowledge creep, with new findings adding to, modifying, and possibly requiring the rejection of earlier findings, but themselves having to undergo a process of vetting in open environments potentially rich in competing theories, models, and data. Decision making, at least as it pertains to the allocation questions subsumed in the initial research agenda for a science of science policy, is not a one-time, either-or, irreversible action. Rather, it is that the accumulation of a set of decisions over time produces an "enterprise" or a "policy" that takes on the patina of a purposively designed system.

5. Conclusion

Understanding how such processes work is especially important for ongoing efforts to build or, more precisely, widen, deepen, and strengthen a community of practice among policymakers, researchers, and others. To return from a different vantage point to this introduction's opening theme, that the call for a science of science policy reflects an assessment by some set of federal government decision makers that the extant body of research does not provide them with the answers or evidence they need to make decisions, it seems obvious to observe that the research agenda of those seeking to advance the science of science policy needs to relate to some degree to the questions/decisions of policymakers. To say this is not to suggest that the relationship is unidirectional or that it should be hierarchical. A focus on policy relevance does not imply that research agenda needs to be specifically problem focused. As represented by critiques of the requirements of the ARRA, that each grant recipient provide quarterly data on the number of jobs created or retained as a result of the stimulus money [102], it can also include suggesting to policymakers that they may be asking the wrong questions or asking them in ways that induce policies or behaviors that are counterproductive to the ends being pursued [27, 103].

The flip side of this interaction is that there may be policy questions of such complexity that it would be chimerical to expect new insights or algorithms from a science of science policy effectively to substitute for muddling through or informed judgments. Not all important questions can be answered (to the satisfaction of those seeking an answer) within specific time frames; not all lines of inquiry may prove (equally) productive. Setting realistic, if at times modulated, goals about what a line of inquiry can accomplish has benefits for both users and performers. For the former, it lessens the prospects of buyer's remorse and perhaps contributes to increased recognition, appreciation, and utilization of the advances in knowledge that are in fact realized. For the latter, it reduces pressures to torque research agendas to meet short-term demands for "results" or to overstate the power or significance of research findings.

References

[1]   Executive Office of the President. A Strategy for American Innovation: Driving Towards Sustainable Growth and Quality Jobs. Washington (DC): National Economic Council; 2009.

[2]   J. H. Marburger. The Science of Science and Innovation Policy. In: Science, Technology and Innovation in a Changing World: Responding to Policy Needs. Paris: OECD; 2007, pp. 27–32.

[3]   J. H. Marburger. Wanted: Better Benchmarks. Science, 308;2005;1087.

[4]   National Science Foundation. Social, Behavioral and Economic Sciences— Science of Science and Innovation Policy: A Prospectus. Available at www.nsf .gov/sbe/scisip/scisip_prospectus.pdf.

[5]   J. Lane. Assessing the Impact of Science Funding. Science, 324;2009;1273–1275.

[6]   D. F. Kettl. The Global Revolution in Public Management: Driving Themes, Missing Links. Journal of Policy Analysis and Management, 16;1997;446–462.

[7]   P. Orsag. Increased Emphasis on Program Evaluations. Washington (DC): Office of Management and Budget; 2009.

[8]   M. Abramovitz. Resource and Output Trends in the United States Since 1870. American Economic Review, 46;1956;5–23.

[9]   R. M. Solow. Technical Change and the Aggregate Production Function. Review of Economics and Statistics, 39;1957;312–320.

[10] Z. Griliches. Research Costs and Social Returns: Hybrid Corn and Related Innovations. Journal of Political Economy, 66;1958;419–431.

[11] Z. Griliches. Issues in Assessing the Contribution of Research and Development to Productivity Growth. Bell Journal of Economics, 10;1979;92–116.

[12] Z. Griliches. Hybrid Corn: An Exploration in the Economics of Technological Change. Econometrica, 25;1957;501–522.

[13] K. Arrow. Economic Welfare and the Allocation of Resources for Invention. In: R. Nelson (Ed.), The Rate and Direction of Inventive Activity: Economic and

Social Factors. Princeton (NJ): National Bureau of Economic Research; 1962, pp. 609–624.

[14] Z. Griliches. Hybrid Corn and the Economics of Innovation. Science, 132;1960; 275–280.

[15] E. Mansfield. Technical Change and the Rate of Imitation. Econometrica, 29;1961; 741–766.

[16] D. B. Audretsch, B. Bozeman, K. Combs, M. Feldman, A. Link, D. Siegel, P. Stephan, G. Tassey, C. Wessner. The Economics of Science and Technology. Journal of Technology, 27;2002.

[17] M. Callon. Four Models of the Dynamics of Science. In: S. Jasanoff, G. Markle, J. Petersen, T. Pinch (Eds.), Handbook of Science and Technology Studies. Thousand Oaks (CA): Sage Publications; 1995, pp. 29–64.

[18] National Academy of Sciences. Knowledge and Policy: The Uncertain Connection. Washington (DC): National Academy Press; 1978.

[19] A. Teich, I. Feller. Toward a Community of Practice. In: Report on the AAAS-NSF SciSIP Grantee Workshop. Washington (DC): American Association for the Advancement of Science; 2009, pp. 4–19.

[20] M. Brown. Federal Advisory Committees in the United States: A Survey of the Political and Administrative Landscape. In: J. Lentsch, P. Weingart (Eds.), Scientific Advice to Policy Making. Leverkusen Opladen, Germany: Budrich Publishers; 2009, pp. 17–39.

[21] A. Bromley. The President's Scientists. New Haven (CT): Yale University Press; 1994.

[22] R. Pielke, R. Klein. The Rise and Fall of the Science Advisor to the President of the United States. Minerva, 47;2009;7–29.

[23] H. Sapolsky. Science Policy. In: F. Greenstein, N. Polsby (Eds.), Policies and Policymaking: Handbook of Political Science, vol. 6. Reading (MA): Addison-Wesley; 1975, pp. 79–110.

[24] B. Smith. American Science Policy Since World War II. Washington (DC): Brookings Institution; 1990.

[25] H. Brooks. The Government of Science. In: R. Gilpin, C. Wright (Eds.), Scientists and National Policy Making. Cambridge (MA): MIT Press; 1968, pp. 73–97.

[26] B. Bozeman, D. Sarewitz. Public Values and Public Failure in U.S. Science Policy. Science and Public Policy, 32;2005;119–136.

[27] P. Aghion, P. David, D. Foray. Can We Link Policy Practice with Research on "STIG Systems"? Toward Connecting the Analysis of Science, Technology and Innovation Policy with Realistic Programs for Economic Development and Growth. In: D. Foray (Ed.), The New Economics of Technology Policy. Cheltenham, UK: Edward Elgar Publishing; 2009, pp. 46–71.

[28] R. Whitley. Changing Governance of the Public Sciences. In: R. Whitley, J. Glaser (Eds.), The Changing Governance of the Sciences. Dordrecht, Netherlands: Springer; 2008, pp. 3–27.

[29] P. Galison. Trading Zone: Coordinating Action and Belief. In: M. Biagioli (Ed.), The Science Studies Reader. New York, London: Routledge; 1999, pp. 137–160.

[30] O. Harman, M. Dietrich. Rebels, Mavericks, and Heretics in Biology. New Haven (CT): Yale University Press; 2008.

[31] I. Feller, P. Stern. A Strategy for Assessing Science. Washington (DC): National Academies; 2007.

[32] Innovation Inducement Prizes at the National Science Foundation. Washington (DC): National Academy Press; 2007.

[33] F. Machlup. The Production and Distribution of Knowledge in the United States. Princeton (NJ): Princeton University Press; 1962.

[34] D. Foray. The Economics of Knowledge. Cambridge (MA): MIT Press; 2004.

[35] N. Rosenberg. The Direction of Technological Change: Inducement Mechanisms and Focusing Devices. Economic Development and Cultural Change, 18;1969; 1–24.

[36] T. C. Koopmans. Measurement Without Theory. The Review of Economics and Statistics, 29;1947;161–172.

[37] T. N. van Leeuwen. Modelling of Bibliometric Approaches and Importance of Output Verification in Research Performance Assessment. Research Evaluation, 16;2007;93–105.

[38] W. D. Nordhaus, R. N. Stavins, M. L. Weitzman. Lethal Model 2: The Limits to Growth Revisited. Washington (DC): Brookings Institution; 1992, pp. 1–59.

[39] O. Sachs. Scotoma: Forgetting and Neglecting in Science. In: R. B. Silver (Ed.), Hidden Histories of Science. New York: A New York Review Book; 1995, pp. 141–187.

[40] J. Rule. Theory and Progress in Social Science. Cambridge: Cambridge University Press; 1997.

[41] E. E. Leamer. Let's Take the Con Out of Econometrics. The American Economic Review, 73;1983;31–43.

[42] A. J. Salter, B. R. Martin. The Economic Benefits of Publicly Funded Basic Research: A Critical Review. Research Policy, 30;2001;509–532.

[43] D. Greenberg. Science, Money and Politics. Chicago: University of Chicago Press; 2001.

[44] M. Teitelbaum. Testimony Before the Subcommittee on Technology and Innovation. Washington (DC): Committee on Science and Technology, U.S. House of Representatives; 2007.

[45] L. Brown, T. Plewes, M. Gerstein. Measuring Research and Development Expenditures in the U.S. Economy. Washington (DC): National Academy Press; 2005.

[46] E. von Hippel. Adapting Policy to User-Centered Innovation. In: D. Foray (Ed.), The New Economics of Technology Policy. Cheltenham, UK: Edward Elgar Publishing; 2009, pp. 327–336.

[47] A. Wildavsky. Speaking Truth to Power. Boston (MA): Little, Brown, and Company; 1979.

[48] B. Bozeman, J. Melkers. Evaluating R&D Impacts: Methods and Practice. Boston (MA): Kluwer Academic Publishers; 1993.

[49] A. Link. Evaluating Public Sector Research and Development. Westport (CT): Praeger; 1996.

[50] R. Ruegg, I. Feller. A Toolkit for Evaluating Public R&D Investment. Gaithersburg (MD): National Institutes of Standards and Technology; 2003.

[51] R. S. Jarmin. Evaluating the Impact of Manufacturing Extension on Productivity Growth. Journal of Policy Analysis and Management, 18;1999;99–119.

[52] A. Rivlin. Systematic Thinking for Social Action. Washington (DC): Brookings Institution; 1971.

[53] A. Jaffe. Building Programme Evaluation into the Design of Public Research-Support Programmes. Oxford Review of Economic Policy, 18;2002;22–34.

[54] H. Ergas. The Importance of Technology Policy. In: P. Dasgupta, P. Stoneman (Eds.), Economic Policy and Technological Performance. Cambridge: Cambridge University Press; 1987, pp. 51–96.

[55] D. C. Mowery. Economic Theory and Government Technology Policy. Policy Sciences, 16;1983;27–43.

[56] S. Martin, J. T. Scott. The Nature of Innovation Market Failure and the Design of Public Support for Private Innovation. Research Policy, 29;2000;437–447.

[57] P. Aghion, P. Howitt. Endogenous Growth Theory. Cambridge (MA): MIT Press; 1999.

[58] P. M. Romer. Increasing Returns and Long-Run Growth. Journal of Political Economy, 94;1986;1002–1037.

[59] P. M. Romer. Endogenous Technological Change. Journal of Political Economy, 98;1990;S71.

[60] D. Guston, K. Kenniston. Introduction: The Social Contract for Science. In: D. Guston, K. Kenniston (Eds.), The Fragile Contract. Cambridge (MA): MIT Press; 1994, pp. 1–41.

[61] Revealing the Hidden Nature of Space and Time. Washington (DC): National Academy Press; 2006.

[62] R. R. Nelson. The Simple Economics of Basic Scientific Research. The Journal of Political Economy, 67;1959;297–306.

[63] E. Mansfield, J. Rapoport, A. Romeo, S. Wagner, G. Beardsley. Social and Private Rates of Return from Industrial Innovations. The Quarterly Journal of Economics, 91;1977;221–240.

[64] A. Jaffe. Economic Analysis of Research Spillovers: Implications for the Advanced Technology Program. Gaithersburg (MD): National Institutes of Standards and Technology; 1996.

[65] H. DuPree. Science in the Federal Government. New York: Harper Torchbooks; 1957.

[66] J. Hughes. The Governmental Habit. New York: Basic Books; 1977.

[67] D. Hart. Forged Consensus. Princeton (NJ): Princeton University Press; 1998.

[68] L. Cohen, R. Noll. The Technology Pork Barrel. Washington (DC): Brookings Institution; 1991.

[69] Executive Office of the President. The President's Management Agenda, Fiscal Year 2002. Washington (DC): Office of Management and Budget; 2001.

[70] J. Stiglitz. Economics of the Public Sector. 2nd ed. New York: Brookings Institution; 1988.

[71] J. C. Wolf. Government or Markets. Cambridge (MA): MIT Press; 1990.

[72] E. Shils. Criteria for Scientific Development: Public Policy and National Goals. Cambridge (MA): MIT Press; 1968.

[73] A. M. Weinberg. Criteria for Scientific Choice. Minerva, 1;1963;159–171.

[74] A. M. Weinberg. Criteria for Scientific Choice II: The Two Cultures. Minerva, 3;1964;3–14.

[75] Office of Management and Budget. R&D Investment Criteria. Washington, DC, 2002.

[76] Evaluating Federal Research Programs. Washington (DC): National Academy Press; 1999.

[77] D. Brown. Program Assessment Rating Tool Guidance No. 2008-01. Washington (DC): Office of Management and Budget; 2008, p. 76.

[78] I. B. Cohen. Revolution in Science. Cambridge (MA): Harvard University Press; 1985.

[79] I. Feller, G. Gamota. Science Measures as Accurate and Relevant Forms of Evidence. Minerva, 45;2007;17–30.

[80] E. Hook. Background to Prematurity and Resistance to "Discovery." Berkeley: University of California Press; 2002.

[81] D. Kelves. Pursuing the Unpopular: A History of Viruses, Courage and Cancer. In: R. B. Silver (Ed.), Hidden Histories of Science. New York: A New York Review Book; 1995, pp. 69–112.

[82] A. Kohn. False Prophets. Oxford: Basil Blackwell; 1986.

[83] S. Cole. Making Science. Cambridge (MA): Harvard University Press; 1992.

[84] T. Folger. Is Quantum Mechanics Tried, True, Wildly Successful, and Wrong? Science, 324;2009;1512–1513.

[85] P. A. David, B. H. Hall, A. A. Toole. Is Public R&D a Complement or Substitute for Private R&D? A Review of the Econometric Evidence. Research Policy, 29; 2000;497–529.

[86] L. Georghiou, D. Roessner. Evaluating Technology Programs: Tools and Methods. Research Policy, 29;2000;657–678.

[87] B. Hall, J. Van Reenen. How Effective Are Fiscal Incentives for R&D? A Review of the Evidence. Research Policy, 29;2000;449–469.

[88] D. Marsh. Knowledge and the Wealth of Nations. New York: Norton & Company; 2006.

[89] J. Fox. The Myth of the Rational Market. New York: Harper Business Books; 2009.

[90] P. Krugman. How Did Economists Get It So Wrong. New York Times Magazine Section. September 2, 2009, pp. 26ff.

[91] I. Feller. Mapping the Frontiers of Evaluation of Public-Sector RD Programs. Science and Public Policy, 34;2007;681–690.

[92] D. Kleinman. Politics on the Endless Frontier. Durham (NC), London: Duke University Press; 1995.

[93] F. Manning, M. McGeary, R. Estabrook. Extramural Centers: Criteria for Initiation and Evaluation. Washington (DC): National Academy Press; 2004.

[94] J. M. de Figueiredo, Brian S. Silverman. Academic Earmarks and the Returns to Lobbying. Journal of Law and Economics, 49;2006;597–625.

[95] D. Hegde, D. C. Mowery. Research Funding: Politics and Funding in the U.S. Public Biomedical R&D System. Science, 322;2008;1797–1798.

[96] A. Payne. Earmarks and EPSCoR. In: D. Guston, D. Sarewitz (Eds.), Shaping Science and Technology Policy: The Next Generation of Research. Madison: University of Wisconsin Press; 2006, pp. 149–172.

[97] J. D. Savage. Funding Science in America. Cambridge: Cambridge University Press; 1999.

[98] S. Power. Chu Opposes Hydrogen Car, but Lawmakers Give Green Light. Wall Street Journal, July 28, 2009.

[99] Y. Wu. NSF's Experimental Program to Stimulate Competitive Research (EPSCoR): Subsidizing Academic Research or State Budgets? Journal of Policy Analysis and Management, 28;2009;479–495.

[100] C. Weiss. Research for Policy's Sake: The Enlightenment Function of Social Science Research. Policy Analysis, 3;1977;531–545.

[101] C. Weiss. Knowledge Creep and Decision Accretion. Science Communication, 1;1980;381–404.

[102] D. Goldston. Mean What You Say. Nature, 458;2009.

[103] I. Feller. A Policy-Shaped Research Agenda on the Economics of Science and Technology. In: D. Foray (Ed.), The New Economics of Technology Policy. Cheltenham, UK: Edward Elgar Publishing; 2009, pp. 99–112.

9 Developing a Science of Innovation Policy Internationally

Fred Gault

1. Introduction

This chapter moves the discussion of the book from the science of science policy to the science of innovation policy. This connects the work on the understanding of the science system to the need for work on delivering value to the market in the form of new goods and services and contributing to economic growth and social welfare.

As innovation deals with the market, firms become principal players in the discussion, along with education and research institutions and government. However, the consideration of the role of government is expanded beyond its support for science. The discussion now deals with the provision of the framework conditions within which systems of innovation function, the provision of incentives to innovate, and the development of components of what could be an innovation policy, or strategy. The extent to which governments coordinate the components of innovation policy is also relevant and will be addressed, but coordination raises issues of governance, which is a broader topic, especially in a federal system. The aim of this chapter is to pose a set of problems to be examined as part of a new social science of innovation policy.

As with the science of science policy,[1] the science of innovation policy is a field of interdisciplinary research that is expected to provide a scientifically rigorous and quantitative basis for the assessment, by practitioners and researchers, of the impacts of innovation policy, as well as a better understanding of its dynamics. It involves a community of practice able to develop theoretical and empirical models of the activity of innovation, leading to better-informed approaches to policymaking in the area of innovation. This is a significant challenge given that innovation systems are global, complex, dynamic, and nonlinear in their response to policy interventions. Innovation policy is also complex, but the benefit of better understanding of how policy works is an increased likelihood of anticipating the economic and social impacts of policy interventions once the policy is implemented. As all countries are part of systems of innovation, with some functioning better than others, this is not an interventionist agenda. It is a start on the path to understanding how new products come to market and what the outcomes and impacts are as they diffuse throughout the economy and from country to country.

This analysis of innovation policy owes much to John Marburger, who also contributes to this volume. He put the case for a science of science and innovation policy at the Organization for Economic Cooperation and Development (OECD) Blue Sky II Form in 2006 (Marburger, 2007). Since then, the National Science Foundation (NSF), under the program direction of Kaye Husbands Fealing and her successor, Julia Lane, has managed three solicitations on the subject of the Science of Science and Innovation Policy (SciSIP). An American Association for the Advancement of Science (AAAS)–NSF workshop[2] of SciSIP grant holders was held in March 2009 to assess progress and to start to build a community of practice around SciSIP as an emerging discipline.

It is an opportune time to consider the subject, as the world is recovering from a financial crisis that is rooted in innovation in financial services. New debt-based products were brought to market, diffused widely, lost value, and forced governments to act in "innovative" ways to save the financial system from collapse. Innovation can result in economic decline as well as economic growth, and the immediate question this poses is: What is the minimum set of conditions that has to be in place to prevent a recurrence of such a situation?

Another contribution to this discussion was *The Science of Science Policy: A Federal Research Roadmap* (NSTC, 2008), "Report to the Sub-Committee on Social, Behavioural, and Economic Sciences," of the National Science and Technology Council (NSTC). It set out a science of science policy road map that included three themes: understanding science and innovation; investing in science and innovation; and, using the science of science policy to address national priorities. This is an important document in the context of the activities of the U.S. federal government and for the evolution of innovation policy. A second document laid out the direction of *Social, Behavioural and Economic Research in the Federal Context* (NSTC, 2009). In NSTC (2009), innovation and creativity are linked together throughout and, after a discussion of the "complex ecosystem of innovation," the following observation was made:

> Efforts to unravel the ecosystem are essential for understanding how innovation systems work. These efforts will lead to better monitoring of educational outcomes,

financial returns to R&D and the innovation life-cycle, as well as better ways of monitoring and evaluating the outcomes of our nation's public and private R&D efforts. One component of this effort is the development of an interagency "science of science policy" task group that is preparing a report on this emerging science, with a focus on innovation. (NSTC, 2009: 24)

Both documents are clear on the importance of understanding how the innovation system functions. However, they focus on a "science of science policy" rather than on the "science of science and innovation policy." There is also little on the science of policy, as the documents are more concentrated on science policy as managed by the U.S. federal government.

This chapter supports Marburger's call for cross-disciplinary work on understanding how innovation policy works or does not work. Of course, this presupposes that there is a language of discourse and well-understood objectives for innovation policy against which to judge its effectiveness. Marburger provided one of such objectives when he observed the following:

In Congress, multiple committees and subcommittees authorize and appropriate funds in an intense advocacy environment from which politics is rarely excluded. Organizing this chaos would be easier if we had "big models" of the sort economists use to intimidate their adversaries. More seriously, the entire process would benefit from the level of scholarly activity that exists today in economic policy. (Marburger, 2007: 30)

In what follows, goals for an innovation policy are considered before offering an agenda for the development of a science of innovation policy. Next is a review of what innovation is in order to establish a language of discourse, to confirm that the activity of innovation can be measured, and to introduce policy components that could play a role in innovation policy. That list is not complete, and others might formulate it differently, but it allows the question to be asked about the best way to coordinate some or all of the components as part of creating an innovation policy. This leads to a discussion of policy implementation, evaluation and policy learning, and the role of international organizations in this. Finally, there is a link back to the subject of the book, the science of science policy, before drawing some conclusions.

2. Why Innovation Policy?

One answer to the question of why there should be an innovation policy was provided by U.S. President Barack Obama in his innovation strategy,[3] which was released in September 2009. The broad objective for such a strategy was given as sustainable growth and quality jobs (Executive Office of the President, 2009) and the means of getting there were catalyzing breakthroughs for national priorities, promoting competitive markets that spur productive entrepreneurship, and, investing in the building blocks of American innovation. The policy was released as countries were recovering from the financial crisis of 2008–2009 and were beginning to ask how they were going to pay for the bailouts of banks, and other private institutions, and the provision of stimulus packages to keep economies going. Growth and jobs are exactly what is needed in such a situation, and it is even better if the growth is sustainable and the jobs are of high quality. There are other reasons for introducing an innovation strategy.

Tom Friedman (2006) has chronicled the major economic and social changes of the last twenty years and their implications for innovation. New markets have opened and technologies have converged to provide powerful mobile telecommunications and online applications. These market opportunities in Brazil, China, Eastern Europe, and India have also made the global marketplace more competitive, and the pressure is on the industrialized countries to produce new and attractive goods and services to gain a greater share of the new markets and to learn how to manage value chains that span the globe. While the pressure is on business to get out there and compete, the people who have the knowledge to make this happen are retiring, and the clear message from the demographic distribution is that a significant part of the experienced labor force will be gone over the next few years. That demographic trend provides another opportunity for new or improved health care technologies and practices to deal with an aging population.

With market opportunities increasing and the number of experienced workers decreasing, there is a need for not only economic growth but for increased productivity growth to deliver the economic growth needed to pay for social services over the next decade with fewer people.

While there are market opportunities and the need to care for citizens, there also are global issues such as climate change and poverty. Climate change is affecting supply and demand for energy, food, and water, and changes in eating habits and the coupling of energy and food through biofuels are having a global impact as well. Poverty is linked to the return of diseases long thought to be under control and to conflict. Dealing with global poverty is a national security issue that innovation can help address. Innovation can also help deal with climate change and save the planet. The outcome, for the developed countries, is a need for innovation, whether it is a part of a policy or not, to deliver sustainable productivity growth while making the planet a better place for the next generations.

This was the basis for innovation strategy in 2006. Then there followed innovation in financial services and the recession of 2008–2009. Innovation can be bad as well as good, and it is important to be able to talk about it, and to measure it, and then to develop a better understanding of how it works. As that understanding grows, there can be a parallel growth of understanding how policy influences innovation and its outcomes. This is the beginning of a science of innovation policy.

3. An Agenda for a Science of Innovation Policy

If innovation is important to the well-being of society, as a by-product of the economic growth it can drive, then policy to promote innovation is important to businesses, governments, and people. If innovation policy is important, then understanding how innovation policy works is imperative. That is why a social science of innovation policy (SoIP) matters, and in a rapidly changing global and complex world, the matter is of some urgency.

At the lowest level of this new subject is innovation, the putting of new or improved goods or services on the market as part of value creation. There are many disciplines involved in understanding how products get to market and then how they are sold. Examples are economics and the theory of the firm, the sociology of markets, and the psychology of consumers, and that is before the natural science and engineering disciplines are brought in to explain the new product development and the networks needed for distribution. The point is that there are many areas of expertise surrounding the activity of innovation. Systems theorists describe the actors involved in some aspect of innovation as part of a system that could be local (a cluster), national, or global, or a mixture of all of these.

When the activity of innovation is viewed as part of a system, there are the system boundaries to consider, such as education of the labor force, regulations, predisposition to risk, and health care. Some take generations to change and are seen as static by analysts working with time scales of a decade or less, while others can change within a decade, such as moving from high tariffs to freer trade, or the provision of universal health care. In electronic commerce, the change can be more rapid, with implications for gambling and gaming. The time scales are important, as are the ways in which changes to the various framework conditions can interact with one another. A regulation forbidding certain types of research, and product development, may, for example, result in the products, and the social value, being produced elsewhere.

Policies to promote aspects of innovation are dealing with a complex environment, with different framework conditions changing, or being changed, over different time scales, and then there is the activity of innovation itself, taking place within this multidimensional box. It is not surprising that feedback loops in the system give rise to nonlinearities that make policy intervention less than intuitive, at least to a systems theorist. How, then, should a science of innovation policy begin?

A first step in developing a science of innovation policy is developing a taxonomy of the possible components of innovation policies, separating them into areas for direct or indirect policy intervention, and the framework conditions that help the system work. A second task is the understanding of the coordination of some of the components by various levels of government and across different institutions. This is an issue of governance. Third, there is the question of how well the system of components and coordination mechanisms will work when they are implemented. That raises political science questions about institutions, standards, and interactions, sociological questions about communities of practice and the learning capacity of groups, institutions, and regions, and economic questions about growth, employment, and priorities for resource allocation. Those intent on including all of the social, behavioral, and economic sciences could find questions that can be addressed by the disciplines of geography, cultural anthropology, or criminology.

Understanding how an innovation policy works, once it is implemented, is of more than academic interest, as the insights can be used to evaluate and improve parts or all of the policy. Evaluation in this chapter is more than an audit conducted by accountants who want to know if the objectives of the project were followed and that the resources were allocated effectively and efficiently. In this case the evaluation has to include the social and economic impacts of the activity, and it requires some time for the outcomes and the impacts to be seen. As an example, a tax policy to promote research and development (R&D) could be seen to be producing progressively more participating firms in the years following its introduction. A broader analysis of the distribution of the number of firms according to the value of R&D performed might find that new participants were dominated by firms that were small performers of R&D that were taking the opportunity to reclassify existing work as R&D in order to claim the benefit. This would give rise to a different debate about the success and the impact of the policy than one based on just counting participating firms.

The learning that results from evaluation has direct benefits for the economy and the society. The importance of institutional learning in innovation policy, and in the science of innovation policy, must involve an increased role for the social, behavioral, and economic sciences as they have the machinery to deal with the human and institutional learning and interactions that are part of the innovation process. This does not diminish the importance of the natural sciences and engineering, but it does call for more interdisciplinary activity. Another shift in focus that can be expected in a science of innovation policy is from basic science and the commercialization of new knowledge to the turning of existing knowledge into value in an effective way.

Part of the new subject of SoIP is the use of a common language to support discourse, and there is a key role for statistical indicators of the activity of innovation, the linkages of the actors, the outcomes, and the social and economic impacts of the activities and linkages. These indicators are needed to monitor and to evaluate policies that affect innovation, including the framework conditions, the more direct interventions, and the means of coordinating policy activities.

Developing the science of innovation policy is an international challenge, as all businesses in all countries are engaged in some form of innovation and are supported or constrained by national and international framework conditions. The NSF is supporting work on the subject, the European Union (EU) 7th Framework Program could be used to advance such work, and a recent study commissioned by the European Commission, DG Research, reports on policy mixes for R&D in Europe (Nauwelaers, 2009). While the policy mixes report does not deal explicitly with innovation, it does get close to the questions that must be answered, or at least addressed, by a science of innovation policy. In Africa, the African Union (AU) is considering establishing an African Observatory for Science, Technology, and Innovation, which could support work on the science of innovation policy in Africa, could be a repository for indicators and innovation policies of AU member states and others, and could be a source of information and analysis.

A final item on the agenda is the place of time and dynamics. Marburger called for the "big models" of the sort economists use to intimidate their adversaries. The science of innovation policy needs models that can take into consideration the boundary conditions imposed by frameworks created by the government, history, and culture, and by physical constraints, and that allow the modeling of the dynamic effects of the innovation activities in the system. Once such models exist, supported by data, they provide a basis for hypothesis testing and policy learning. They could also support a scenario analysis as part of policy learning.

4. Language, Measurement, and Policy Components

4.1. Language and International Organizations

Innovation is a global activity and delegates to committees of the OECD have been discussing innovation, its place in policy, and the need to measure it and its impacts for more than twenty years. In the 1990s, participants in the working groups of Eurostat, the European statistical office, joined in the discussion as part of managing the EU Community Innovation Survey (CIS). While the policy imperatives change from day to day, the need to measure and understand the activity of innovation remains. Over the years of discussion, a common vocabulary and grammar have emerged that facilitates the discussion, and it has been codified in manuals on three separate occasions (OECD, 1992; OECD/Eurostat, 1997, 2005).

The manual that provides guidance on the collection and interpretation of innovation data is called the Oslo Manual, now in its third edition (OECD/Eurostat, 2005). The Oslo Manual provides the operational definition of innovation that is used in surveys in the European Union in most OECD countries, and in other parts of the world. The basic definition of innovation is the following:

> An innovation is the implementation of a new, or significantly improved product (good or service), or process, a new marketing method, or a new organization method in business practices, workplace organization or external relations. (OECD/Eurostat, 2005: 46)

Innovation is connected to the market through the "implementation":

> A common feature of an innovation is that it must have been implemented. A new or improved product is implemented when it is introduced on the market. New processes, marketing methods or organizational methods are implemented when they are brought into actual use in the firm's operations. (OECD/Eurostat, 2005: 47)

The Oslo Manual also adopts a systems approach for classifying actors and their activities, linkages, outcomes, and impacts of the activity of innovation. The actors are governments, businesses, and higher education and research institutes. Examples of innovation activities that may, or may not, lead to the activity of innovation are research and development, capital investment, training, and acquisition of intellectual property. Linkages deal with information or knowledge flow and can be two-way or one-way. Examples are contracts, collaboration arrangements, service agreements, and consultations. The outcomes may be a greater market share, higher skill levels for the production staff, and fewer staff. The longer-term impacts are illustrated by the way the mobile phone has changed the way people live and do business.

The Oslo Manual is the result of a consensus process, and the last revision took three years under the guidance of the OECD Working Party of National Experts on Science and Technology Indicators (NESTI). At the end of that process, member countries agreed to accept the text, and it became the language of discourse until the next revision. The process is not limited to OECD member countries and the European Union. NESTI observers have included Chile, China, Israel, and the Russian Federation. International organizations also participate, including the African Union (AU) New Partnership for Africa's Development (NEPAD) Office of Science and Technology, the Latin American Ibero-American Network on Science and Technology Indicators (RICYT), and the United Nations Educational, Scientific, and Cultural Organization (UNESCO) Institute of Statistics (UIS).

4.2. Measurement

As part of the international attempt to understand innovation, the European Union runs the Community Innovation Survey in its twenty-seven member states, and quite a few non-European Union OECD countries have also done innovation surveys close to the CIS model. In addition, the AU NEPAD Office of Science and Technology is in the process of supporting surveys in nineteen African countries, based on the Oslo Manual (Gault, 2010).

Most recently, the United States has revised its survey of R&D to launch in 2009 a Business R&D and Innovation Survey (BRDIS), run by the Census Bureau on behalf of the NSF (U.S. Census Bureau, 2008). It will provide the first comprehensive official statistics on innovation in the United States. Based on the 2009 responses, questions were modified and new questions were added to the survey that was sent out in 2010.

The point here is that there are many countries, all using the same concepts and definitions, from the same Oslo Manual, measuring the activity of innovation. In the case of the CIS, the measurement has been going on for seventeen years.

One of the more robust findings of innovation surveys, in most OECD countries (OECD, 2009d), is that more firms innovate than do R&D, so a large population of firms will get the knowledge that they transform into value by means other than their own R&D. The surveys also show that universities and government laboratories are low on the list of information sources of knowledge for innovation. Clients, suppliers, and competitors are high on the list.

There are many other findings from innovation surveys, which suggest ways in which governments could support innovation more effectively and help small firms grow. An example is the Small Business Innovation Research (SBIR) program in the United States (Wessner, 2008). One of the reasons for supporting the growth of small firms is that larger firms have a higher propensity to do R&D. This means that support for growth is indirect support for increasing the activity of R&D.

However, this is a chapter on the science of innovation policy, not on innovation policy, nor on innovation. Now that a language of discourse has been established, and it has been demonstrated that the activity of innovation can be measured, and the language used to interpret the results, the next stage is to look at what makes up an innovation policy.

4.3. Policy Components

A strategy, or policy, for innovation can consist of one or many policy components. In Table 9.1, potential components of innovation strategies are grouped under six headings: Markets; People; Innovation Activities; Public Institutions; International Engagement. Not all of the components turn up in all strategies, but the objective is to present them and raise questions about how policies can advance the objectives of the components.

The policy components in Table 9.1 are elaborated on in the Appendix at the end of this chapter, and earlier versions are found in Gault (2010). They have a wide range of applicability, as some are appropriate to the developed countries and others can be used in developing counties. They could be classified differently as health care, or education, or could be provided by the private sector as well as the public sector or through a public-private partnership. Developing the typology, or typologies, is a question for practitioners of the science of innovation policy. Table 9.1 is just a beginning.

Once there is a language for international and national discourse and confirmation that the concepts used in the discourse can be measured in ways that produce robust and reproducible findings, the policy components that contribute to the outcomes can be classified, and they too can be topics of discussion. What is missing is consideration of how the policy components are linked together as part of one, or more than one, innovation policy. That is the subject of the science of innovation policy and of the next section.

5. Building an Innovation Policy: Coordinating the Components

Innovation policies consist of a set of components managed, or coordinated, by government(s). They range from a single intervention managed by one

Table 9.1.   Possible components of an innovation policy

Component activities

1. Markets

1.1	Brand recognition
1.2	Lead market
1.3	Competitive engagement
1.4	Financial services

2. People

2.1	Labor force
2.2	Demographics and demand for innovation
2.3	Migration

3. Innovation activities

3.1	Technology and practices
3.2	User innovation
3.3	User-driven innovation
3.4	Demand-driven innovation
3.5	Open innovation

4. Public institutions

4.1	Infrastructure
4.2	Procurement
4.3	Priority setting
4.4	Standard setting
4.5	Public finance
4.6	Government departments (including granting councils and knowledge transfer activities)
4.7	Education, training, and research
4.8	Health
4.9	Monitoring and evaluation

5. International engagement

5.1	Big science
5.2	International cooperation and development
5.3	Global challenges

department, such as a tax credit for expenditure on information and communication technology (ICT) networks, to a wide range of initiatives, drawn from the components in the previous section, that will require a "whole of government" approach.

As all countries differ in their history, culture, and innovation systems, there is no single answer to how many components there should be in an innovation policy and how those components should be coordinated and at what level. As the literature of a science of innovation policy develops, there may appear some guidance on how innovation policy works in countries of different sizes and government structures.

5.1. Levels of Coordination

If the leaders of the country believe that the global challenges discussed in this chapter's Introduction have to be addressed, as well as the domestic issues, such as competing in a global economy with an aging and a diminishing labor force, then the policy will be coordinated at the highest level. In a parliamentary government, the lead would be the prime minister and the committee would be the cabinet, or a selection of cabinet ministers.

If the concern is with industry, and its ability to compete, then the coordination could be given to the minister responsible for industry. Similarly, if the issue is the need for a better-educated and trained population engaged in lifelong learning, then the coordination could be left to the minister of education, if there is one. Whether there is or is not such a department, consideration should be given to coordination between national, regional or state, and urban administrations.

If the issues are seen to be sectoral, such as helping the service sector to be more competitive, then the coordination could be done at the subdepartment level within a ministry.

The coordination mechanism will depend on the form of government (federal or central), the nature of the population (culturally homogeneous or multicultural), the size of the population (large or small), the nature of the policy intervention (bottom-up or top-down), and on the culture and the history of the country. For example, it is easier to manage policy if the senior managers went to the same institutions of education, hold the same values, and move naturally from business to government to research institutions and to nonprofit organizations in the course of their careers. Whether this is a fundamental advantage is another question for the practitioners of innovation policy. There is also the issue of governance and how the coordination works in, for example, a country with a federal government requiring cooperation at the federal, state, and municipal levels to achieve policy objectives.

5.2. Engaging the Stakeholders

Innovation is about bringing products to market. Innovation policies have little hope of succeeding if industry leaders, industry associations, and representatives of civil society are not part of the discussion. As people are key to all strategies, leaders in education and training should be involved, as well as the government leaders promoting the policy.

This suggests that, in addition to well-thought-out coordination, there should be a role for a council of stakeholders to contribute to the formulation of the policy and to its implementation. Such a council is not a science or research council, or a science and technology council. It should be an innovation council, as the issues are developing new products and processes to compete locally and globally and to give rise to sustained growth through improved productivity. These are very concrete goals, which are of more immediate concern in the aftermath of the 2008–2009 recession, than the important but longer-term issue of supporting the formal generation of knowledge through the performance of R&D. Most industrial innovators in most OECD countries do not do R&D.

The coordination and the components coordinated will reflect the governance structure, history, and culture. Federal governments will act differently from central governments, as will multicultural countries from the more homogeneous. That is why there is no single innovation policy. However, as President Obama has demonstrated, there are innovation strategies that have policy components and coordination mechanisms. The question now is what happens when they are implemented and then how they are improved.

6. Implementation, Evaluation, and Learning

Implementing a policy requires the machinery of government to function. Tax policies are relatively easy, as there is a tax system in place and it is a matter of adding yet another investment tax credit to an existing list and then administering it. Putting in place a voucher scheme to encourage small and medium-sized enterprises (SMEs) to purchase advice, knowledge, training, or technical assistance from public institutions may require new organizational structures and education of the clients for the scheme.

Whatever the means of implementation, there must be ongoing monitoring and then evaluation to confirm that the policy is meeting its objectives. The monitoring can include statistical indicators that confirm that the propensity to innovate in SMEs in, for example, logistics services is going up, or case studies to find out why the percentage of revenues due to the introduction of new services over the last three years is not going up in SMEs in logistics services, even though the propensity to innovate is. Or, there can be a combination of both statistical measures and case studies. The analysis of the outcomes and impacts of the policy being administered may cross national boundaries.

Once there are reports of the evaluations and evidence from the statistical indicators, the coordinating function and the council of stakeholders can review the situation and if need be revise the policy, or its means of implementation, to move closer to achieving the policy objectives. This might involve a consultation process with the industry and groups affected by the policy outcomes. Whatever the process, it should result in institutional learning and better policy. As some of those affected by the policy may be abroad, this can become an international discussion.

6.1. The International Dimension

This review of how innovation policies are developed took place at a time when the OECD was working on an innovation strategy for delivery in May 2010 (OECD, 2009a) and the European Union was reviewing the state of its work on an innovation strategy that began in 2006 (CEC, 2009). In the African Union, and NEPAD, there is work on innovation strategies.

To add to the understanding of innovation policy, and its coordination and implementation, international organizations conduct studies of innovation policy at the invitation of countries. An example is the OECD review of South Africa (OECD, 2007). UNESCO works closely with the African Union on science, technology, and innovation policy, and at least eighteen countries have requested UNESCO (Division for Science Policies and Sustainable Development) assistance with the review or formulation of science and technology policies. The NEPAD Office of Science and Technology is supporting work on surveys of innovation in nineteen countries with a view to developing innovation indicators, published in 2010 in a new African Innovation Outlook.

The World Bank supports case studies and runs forums at which findings are disseminated. In the proceedings of the 2007 forum, the comment was made that "most of the knowledge that any country will need if it is to grow and prosper will be produced by others. As a result, the capacity to identify, find, acquire, adapt, and adopt this existing knowledge must be an indispensable component of any country's STI capacity building strategy" (Watkins and Ehst, 2008). This is the same problem faced by the firm in any country that innovates but does not do R&D.

While there is international work on innovation strategies, country reviews to help both developed and developing countries deal with their innovation systems and policies, and forums for discussing innovation systems, policies, and capacity building, there is no systematic analysis of which innovation policy components work well in which circumstances, how policy components are coordinated, how stakeholders are brought into policy development, and how policies are implemented, evaluated, and revised. Both the analysis and the increased understanding that will result are challenges for a science of innovation policy.

6.2. Learning

Those implementing an innovation policy can learn from monitoring, case studies, and evaluation. However, innovation and innovation policy are complex, and that makes analysis, learning, and better understanding difficult, but it provides even stronger motivation for a science of innovation policy. Learning also results, as in any science, in an accumulation of knowledge codified in publications and held tacitly by a community of practice. As the science of innovation policy evolves, unexpected uses will be found for that knowledge that will be a benefit of developing a science of innovation policy.

Because of its complexity, the analytical approach to innovation has been one of systems analysis where the actors engage in activities, there are linkages among the actors, and there are outcomes and impacts of the activities and linkages. The problem is that the linkages provide feedback loops that result in nonlinear responses to policy interventions. The system is also dynamic, as the 2008–2009 financial crisis demonstrated as financial systems failed. Systems *can* fail.

This gets back to the suggestion by Marburger, that part of a science of innovation policy is the development of models that can deal with a complex, dynamic, global, and nonlinear innovation system and that can be used for scenario analysis and learning. This also provides a bridge to the science of science policy, which is the actual topic of this book.

The science of science policy could benefit from a systems approach dealing with the actors, such as government department and funding bodies, universities and research organizations, and the framework conditions that influence them, such as immigration policy, support for K–12 education, and incentives for "restoring American leadership in fundamental research" (Executive Office of the President, 2009). The science of science policy necessarily has a longer time horizon than a science of innovation policy, but the two are linked as the new knowledge created by science is converted to market value by the process of innovation. In addition, as practitioners in each discipline move from the academy to government and industry, the capacity to absorb the concepts and to participate in the debates will grow.

7. Conclusion

This chapter deals with three subjects: innovation, innovation policy, and, the science of innovation policy. Each of these subjects requires different tools, and knowledge, but there are common elements, such as the language needed to talk about them and the statistical measurements needed to monitor them and to support evaluation.

A case has been presented for the development of a science of innovation policy. It draws on the experience in countries and in international organizations. The argument for the case includes the benefits that will follow from a better understanding of policy components and their coordination and from the policy learning that will result from the evaluation of implemented innovation policies or strategies.

The chapter may seem out of place in a book on the science of science policy, but the science of science policy and the science of innovation policy are strongly coupled, and practitioners can share common approaches to analysis, especially the application of systems theory to policy problems. The science systems and the innovation systems include complexity, global effects, dynamics, and the nonlinearity to policy intervention that will follow from the feedback loops resulting from the inclusion of linkages between the actors in the system. While the two sets of systems interact, the inclusion of markets, value chains, trade regulation, and other market-related framework conditions argues for a separate approach to the science of innovation policy from the science of science policy. As an example, including dynamics in the science of innovation policy could lead to an understanding of where the economic systems work and, more importantly, where they fail.

In a world where economic systems fail, with devastating consequences, a science of innovation policy is not an academic exercise—it is a survival mechanism.

Appendix: Components of an Innovation Policy

This Appendix provides a set of components that could be used in an innovation policy. How they are used, and many have been used, depends on how they are coordinated and on the way(s) in which the policy is implemented. The set is by no means exhaustive, and it should be understood that different ways of coordinating the components and implementing a policy can lead to quite different outcomes, even if the components are the same. An earlier discussion of these components is given in Gault (2010).

A1. Markets

A1.1. Brand Recognition

Presenting the country as the best place on earth to live and work, supported by a first-class infrastructure, to do R&D, to innovate, to manage trade, and to enjoy a high quality of life, in a safe and an attractive environment, is a goal. A country that can establish and maintain such a brand can attract the highly qualified people, foreign, direct, and portfolio investment, and can retain the inward flow during times of economic and social turmoil. Being the best place to be also has implications for the education, training, and development of the people who support the infrastructure and provide the nontradable services (LO, 2008).

A1.2. Lead Market

A highly educated population with intellectual curiosity could be a lead market for technologies and for applications that use the technologies. Lead markets are attractive to leading-edge producers of goods and services, but there is a danger, pointed out by Christensen, of listening only to the most advanced customers (Christensen, 1997, 2008). Governments, through procurement and support for trade, can contribute to the lead market.

The European Union has launched a lead market initiative (LMI), which is an important innovation policy (Gault, 2010: 87). It focuses on six markets: eHealth; sustainable construction; technical textiles for intelligent personal protective clothing and equipment; bio-based products; recycling; and, renewable energy.

A1.3. Competitive Engagement

One of the reasons the country is the best place to do business, create knowledge, and live is that it supports an outward-looking approach to business. This includes the capacity to participate in and manage global value chains and a culture that supports the learning of languages and international involvement. The goal is to be an effective player on the international stage. This requires outward-looking people with the skills needed to play in the international arena, and it has implications for education and training and for cultural institutions.

A1.4. Financial Services

Firms require finance to start up, to do research to produce new products, and to bring the new products to market. While banks and other financial institutions can support established firms, there is a need for intelligent and patient angel investors and venture capital firms that understand the sector, the market, and the risk of trying to bring new products to the market.

A2. People

A2.1. Labor Force

People are part of the means of production, and in a global economy trading in knowledge products, the workers have to be well educated, self-directed, and able to engage in lifelong learning. As part of global engagement, some experience in their career gained from outside of the country can be considered an asset. These requirements have implications for education policy and reform, training and development policy in public and private institutions, and migration policies that encourage the mobility of the highly qualified (OECD, 2008a).

However, the labor force is not just made up of the highly qualified. There are many more people who are part of the economy and society who produce goods and services, both tradable and nontradable. Their approach to these tasks is part of making the country the best place in which to live. Education and training policies must take account of the needs of the entire workforce.

A2.2. Demographics and Demand for Innovation

People are a source of opportunities for an innovation strategy. In most of the industrialized countries, the population is aging. This is a technical and an organizational opportunity to care for an aging population and to gain new and marketable knowledge from this activity. Also, people embody knowledge, and as their departure from the workplace accelerates, there is a need to capture and retain the knowledge that is being lost. This is an opportunity for nontechnological innovation using the techniques of, for example, knowledge management.

A2.3. Migration

With globalization, the highly qualified are becoming more mobile, and OECD countries are the net beneficiaries of this (OECD, 2008a). This has implications for innovation policies, as the highly qualified contribute to the creation and diffusion of knowledge (Auriol, 2007). From the perspective of the sending countries, there are issues about using the diaspora (Kuznetsov, 2006) as a source of knowledge and of remittances. When it comes to the impact of mobility on innovation, there is little or no evidence (OECD, 2008a), and this is one of the statistical challenges for innovation policy. There is also a question of how mobility policies fit into innovation policies and the extent to which intervention in these two areas is coordinated.

A3. Innovation Activities

A3.1. Technologies and Practices

Firms can innovate by adopting technologies new to the firm. Governments can provide incentives to do this, especially if there is a national view of which technologies to support. In the German high-tech strategy (BMBF, 2006), seventeen technologies and practices are advanced.

A3.2. User Innovation

The ICTs and, to a growing extent biotechnologies, are modular platform technologies that provide a basis for innovation on the platform. The platforms also make it easier to modify the technologies to suit user needs and to create knowledge in the process. This user innovation has always been present in the economy (von Hippel, 1988), but now it is easier (Dyson, 2007), and it raises questions about how the intellectual property created by the activity is managed (Gault and von Hippel, 2009; von Hippel, 2005). Consumers can also engage in user innovation by modifying a product to serve their needs and then presenting a firm with the prototype or blueprints to produce the product commercially.

A3.3. User-Driven Innovation

User-driven innovation describes the exchange of information between a user of a product and the producer, with a view to improving the product. It does not involve the transfer of prototypes or blueprints.

A3.4. Demand-Driven Innovation

Demand-driven innovation deals with private and public procurement that provides incentives for responding firms to innovate. This can be done by requiring challenging specifications of products or the use of advanced technologies or practices in the production and delivery of products (see Section A4.2).

A3.5. Open Innovation

While ICT platforms encourage user-initiated innovation, they also enable the flow of knowledge across the boundaries of countries and institutions, resulting in more "open" innovation (Chesbrough, 2003; OECD, 2008b). This takes various forms, of which the open source approach in software development is one, but there is also the drawing of new ideas and technologies into the firm and the outsourcing of activities. The walls of the firm are porous, but a consequence of this is the requirement for people to be able to work with the international networks that are readily available in addition to more local networks where participants can meet face-to-face. The expanded use of networks means that knowledge is not just stored in people or embodied in machines and practices, but it is also stored in the network. People can do more things, and more things better, because of the network capital that they can draw upon and contribute to. Enhancing network capital is a goal for an innovation strategy. Measuring it is another matter.

A4. Public Institutions

Public institutions set priorities, educate and develop the workforce, manage the public health care system and health research, and set policies that govern mobility. These activities can influence innovation, and in doing all of these things, public-sector institutions can engage in the same innovation activities as those that go on in the private sector. Here the activities of public institutions that could form part of an innovation policy are presented.

A4.1. Infrastructure

Technology and practices provide the infrastructure that supports the economy and the society. The infrastructure includes the ICT networks and well-managed roads, ports, and logistic services. Technologies and practices are also integral parts of the education, health, and financial services infrastructure. A first-class infrastructure is an important element of an innovation strategy. While the components of the infrastructure may be in place in OECD countries, no policymaker would argue that the infrastructure works as well as it should, or does not need reform.

A4.2. Procurement

Governments at all levels, education and research institutions, and health institutions have enormous purchasing power that can be used to influence the path of technologies and practices, and it is not just the purchasing power but the leadership. A well-established example is the case of numerically controlled machine tools (Mansfield, 1968). These tools were developed by the Massachusetts Institute of Technology on a contract from the U.S. Air Force and appeared in 1951. They were then commercialized by the industry and introduced in 1955.

The procurement process allows public institutions to be lead users and to provide critical feedback to the suppliers. Extreme examples of this arise in the case of large scientific establishments that are pushing the frontiers of the possible and need computing and measurement speeds, analytical capacity, and materials that do not exist in the commercial world. Solving the scientific and engineering problems produces knowledge that can be commercialized.

In a global world, with freer trade, it is more difficult to use procurement to develop the domestic market, but the role of procurement in innovation policy is a key issue that has been neglected (Elder and Georghiou, 2007). However, it is part of the EU lead market initiative.

A4.3. Priority Setting
Expertise in ICT networks, biotechnology, nanotechnology, new materials, energy sources, and other technologies and applications requires highly qualified but scarce human resources, and this raises a question as to whether an innovation strategy should involve priority setting in order to make the most of the knowledge available in the country. As sectors differ significantly in their requirements, this has to be taken into account.

A4.4. Standard Setting
Standards are integral to innovation policy and to trade policy. They can be set by international organizations, such as the International Organization for Standardization (ISO), a specific example being the ISO/TC 229 work on nano-technology standards, or they can evolve from use and become de facto industry standards. They can deal with technologies and also with how research is done, an example being bioethics and related standards of practice. The European Commission summarizes its position as follows: "The global promotion of EU norms and standards and innovative initiatives can give a decisive first mover advantage to European companies in the spirit of the lead market initiative" (CEC, 2006). Standard setting is part of the EU lead market initiative.

A4.5. Public Finance
If new firms are to be created, and survive and grow, then they need financing at various stages of their development, from angel investors and venture capitalists, and support from development banks and the established banking system. The public sector provides a regulatory environment that maintains confidence in the system and allows it to provide the services needed, both national and international. It may also provide development banks to fill the gaps not covered by the private sector and export development banks to support firms in the export of their goods and services.

In addition, departments of finance can stimulate innovation, and its components, through tax policy, such as R&D tax credits and capital consumption allowances adjusted to encourage capital investment in particular technologies. There are those who would argue that innovation policy is tax policy (Licht, 2008).

A4.6. Government Departments, Including Granting Councils

Departments of government spend significant amounts on targeted support programs, such as the U.S. Small Business Innovation Research Program (SBIR) or the Canadian Industrial Research Assistance Program (IRAP[4]). They also provide direct support for R&D through grants, contracts, and contributions and through mission-related research and collaboration with researchers from business and higher education.

Government departments can also promote dialogue with society on issues that can affect markets for new products, such as genetically modified foods, working conditions in countries from which products are imported, or the regulation of financial service industry products. Such dialogues can also encourage the culture of innovation.

A4.7. Education, Training, and Research

The institutions, public and private, are challenged to produce numerate and literate people capable of assessing the risks resulting from innovative activity, and the rewards. How this is done raises issues of reform of the institutions providing the education and training. However, monitoring the place of education in the innovation system has raised questions about what is being measured and what the consequences might be of producing a misleading set of indicators (Hawkins, et al., 2007).

Knowledge is another product of institutions of education and research, and the issue is how this knowledge is protected through the use of intellectual property instruments and then how it is commercialized. The same question arises with government laboratories.

A4.8. Health

Health institutions have opportunities to be innovative in providing health services, and some of this responds to the impact of private-sector innovation. An example of private-sector innovation is the provision of standardized foods containing trans-fatty acids and sugar, leading to obesity and type 2 diabetes, and putting pressure on the scarce resources of the health care system. This is similar to the financial service example used earlier where private-sector innovation resulted in unexpected outcomes, which placed a demand on public resources. The difference is the time scale—the first was measured in months, the second in years.

Health institutions do research as well as provide services, and there is the broader issue of justifying the expenditure on research in public institutions in the health sector (Bernstein, et al., 2007).

A5. International Engagement

A5.1. Big Science

A specific form of international engagement is active participation in large experimental facilities such as the European Organization for Nuclear Research (CERN) and the International Thermonuclear Energy Reactor (ITER). From the innovation policy perspective, the interest is in commercializing the knowledge that results from pushing technology to its limit. An example is the contribution to medical imaging made by work on elementary particle detectors. There is also the World Wide Web, which came out of CERN and which provides a platform for many unexpected commercial applications. Scientific organizations also provide postdoctoral training and develop the very highly qualified workforce.

A5.2. International Cooperation and Development

Scientific cooperation among member states is an objective of the European Union, and Germany and Japan cooperate with developing countries as a way of addressing global challenges. There are scientific benefits, but the cooperation also builds knowledge of different markets and opens opportunities for commercial activity.

Germany and Japan are collaborating with developing countries as part of their approach to innovation policy. In Germany, cooperation will support collaboration with research groups and innovative industry clusters with German research groups and competence networks. Germany is also supporting the Heiligendamm-L'Aquila Process (HAP) involving dialogue between the outreach group from the key emerging economies, the O5 (Brazil, China, India, Mexico, and South Africa), and the G8 to address the promotion and protection of innovation and ways to increase energy efficiency (BMBF, 2008). Japan's strategic promotion of science and technology (S&T) diplomacy is designed to strengthen S&T cooperation with developing countries as part of resolving global issues, using Japan's advanced S&T. The global issues include the environment, energy, natural disaster prevention, infectious disease control, and food security.

An OECD and a UNESCO workshop on innovation for development in January 2009 concluded that innovation should be inserted into the Poverty Reduction Strategy Papers.[5] It also stressed the need for more knowledge about innovation in developing countries that could be produced through case studies or country reviews of innovation policy in developing countries, similar to those conducted by the OECD. The findings of the workshop are summarized in the UNESCO 2009 report.

An incentive for including work with developing countries as part of an innovation policy is the reduction of the inequities that are potential causes of conflict and disease, which can spread rapidly, and starvation. Innovation through collaboration can also foster a culture of innovation in the developing countries, leading to economic growth and related benefits. Collier (2007) points out that growth, as an objective, is not universally accepted in the development community unless it is qualified with terms such as "sustainable" or "pro-poor" but argues: "The problem of the bottom billion has not been that they have had the wrong *type* of growth, it is that they have not had *any* growth" (emphases added). Innovation strategies in developed countries and cooperation agreements have a role to play.

In April 2009, the OECD workshop "Innovating Out of Poverty" stressed the importance of recognizing agriculture as a knowledge-intensive sector and the key role for science, technology, and innovation contributing to this. The workshop chair, Calestous Juma, provided a list of challenges for world leaders, which is now being disseminated (OECD, 2009d).

A5.3. Global Challenges

Challenges that affect all countries, including developing countries, can be addressed through innovation. These include climate change, sustainable energy, food and water security, and population health, as the world deals with the present pandemic and prepares for the next. Green innovation (OECD, 2009a) ensures that green activities are part of innovation, innovation policy, and human resource development, and that they are part of the price signal.

References

Auriol, L. 2007. The International Mobility of Doctorate Holders: First Results and Methodological Advances. In *Science, Technology and Innovation Indicators in a Changing World: Responding to Policy Needs*, eds. Anthony Arundel, Alessandra Colecchia, and Fred Gault, 193–212. Paris: OECD.

Bernstein, A., V. Hicks, P. Boorbey, T. Campbell, L. McAuley, and I. D. Graham. 2007. A Framework to Measure the Impacts of Investments in Health Research. In *Science, Technology and Innovation Indicators in a Changing World: Responding to Policy Needs*, eds. Anthony Arundel, Alessandra Colecchia, and Fred Gault, 231–250. Paris: OECD.

BMBF. 2006. *The High-Tech Strategy for Germany*. Bonn, Berlin: BMBF.

BMBF. 2008. *Strengthening Germany's Role in the Global Knowledge Society: Strategy of the Federal Government for the Internationalization of Science and Research*. Bonn, Berlin: BMBF.

CEC. 2006. *Putting Knowledge into Practice: A Broad-Based Innovation Strategy for the EU*. Brussels: COM, 502, final.

CEC. 2009. *Renewing Community Innovation Policy in a Changing World*. Brussels: COM, 442, final.

Chesbrough, H. 2003. *Open Innovation: The New Imperative for Creating and Profiting from Technology*. Boston: Harvard University Press.

Christensen, C. M. 1997. *The Innovators Dilemma: When New Technologies Cause Great Firms to Fail*. Boston: Harvard University Press.

Christensen, C. M. 2008. Forward: Reflections on Disruption. In *The Innovator's Guide to Growth: Putting Disruptive Innovation to Work*, eds. S. D. Anthony, M. W. Johnson, J. V. Sinfield, and E. J. Altman, vii–xiv. Boston: Harvard Business Press.

Collier, P. 2007. *The Bottom Billion: Why the Poorest Countries Are Failing and What Can Be Done About It*. Oxford: Oxford University Press.

Dyson, F. 2007. Our Biotech Future. *The New York Review of Books*, LIV (12): 4–8.

Elder, J., and L. Georghiou. 2007. Public Procurement and Innovation—Resurrecting the Demand Side. *Research Policy* 36: 949–963.

Executive Office of the President. 2009. *A Strategy for American Innovation: Driving Towards Sustainable Growth and Quality Jobs*. Washington, DC: Executive Office of the President/National Economic Council/Office of Science and Technology Policy.

Friedman, Thomas, L. 2006. *The World Is Flat: A Brief History of the Twenty-First Century*, 2nd ed. New York: Farrar, Straus and Giroux.

Gault, F. 2010. *Innovation Strategies for a Global Economy: Development, Implementation, Measurement, and Management*. Cheltenham, UK: Edward Elgar Publishing.

Gault, F., and E. von Hippel. 2009. *The Prevalence of User Innovation and Free Innovation Transfers: Implications for Statistical Indicators and Innovation Policy*. Cambridge, MA: MIT Sloan School of Management Working Paper no. 4722-09.

Hawkins, R. W., C. H. Langford, and K. S. Sidhu. 2007. University Research in an "Innovation Society." In *Science, Technology and Innovation Indicators in a Changing World: Responding to Policy Needs*, eds. Anthony Arundel, Alessandra Colecchia, and Fred Gault, 171–192. Paris: OECD.

Kuznetsov, Y. 2006. *Diaspora Networks and the International Migration of Skills: How Countries Can Draw on Their Talent Abroad*. Washington, DC: World Bank Institute Development Studies.

Licht, G. 2008. Nachgefragt: Innovationsverhalten von KMU Steuerpolitik ist Innovationspolitick. *ZEWnews* (July/August): 3.

LO. 2008. *Employee-Driven Innovation*. Copenhagen: LO, the Danish Confederation of Trade Unions.

Mansfield, E. 1968. *The Economics of Technological Change*. New York: W.W. Norton & Company.

Marburger, J. 2007. The Science of Science and Innovation Policy. In *Science, Technology and Innovation Indicators in a Changing World: Responding to Policy Needs*, eds. Anthony Arundel, Alessandra Colecchia, and Fred Gault, 27–32. Paris: OECD.

National Academy of Sciences. 2008. *An Assessment of the SBIR Program*. Edited by C. W. Wessner. Washington, DC: National Academies Press.

National Science and Technology Council (NSTC). 2008. *The Science of Science Policy: A Federal Research Roadmap*. Report on the Science of Science Policy to the Sub-Committee on Social, Behavioural and Economic Sciences, Committee on Science, National Science and Technology Council. Washington, DC: NSTC.

National Science and Technology Council (NSTC). 2009. *Social, Behavioural and Economic Research in the Federal Context*. Sub-Committee on Social, Behavioural and Economic Sciences. Washington, DC: NSTC.

Nauwelaers, C. 2009. *Policy Mixes for R&D in Europe*. Maastricht, the Netherlands: UNU-MERIT. Available at: www.ec.europa.eu/research/policymx.

OECD. 1992. *OECD Proposed Guidelines for Collecting and Interpreting Technological Innovation Data—Oslo Manual*. Paris: OECD.

OECD. 2007. *OECD Reviews of Innovation Policy: South Africa*. Paris: OECD.

OECD. 2008a. *The Global Competition for Talent: Mobility of the Highly Skilled*. Paris: OECD.

OECD. 2008b. *Open Innovation in Global Networks*. Paris: OECD.

OECD. 2009a. *2009 Interim Report of the OECD Innovation Strategy: An Agenda for Policy Action on Innovation*. Paris: OECD.

OECD. 2009b. *Green Growth: Overcoming the Crisis and Beyond*. Paris: OECD.

OECD. 2009c. *Growing Prosperity, Agriculture, Economic Renewal, and Development: Outcome Document for the Experts Meeting on "Innovating out of Poverty."* Paris: OECD.

OECD. 2009d. *Innovation in Firms: A Microeconomic Perspective*. Paris: OECD.

OECD/Eurostat. 1997. *Proposed Guidelines for Collecting and Interpreting Technological Innovation Data—Oslo Manual*. Paris: OECD.

OECD/Eurostat. 2005. *Guidelines for Collecting and Interpreting Innovation Data—Oslo Manual*. Paris and Luxembourg: OECD/Eurostat.

UNESCO. 2009. *Innovation for Development: Converting Knowledge to Value. Summary Report, Paris 28 to 30 January 2009*. Paris: UNESCO.

U.S. Census Bureau. 2008. *2008 Business R&D and Innovation Survey*. Washington, DC: U.S. Census Bureau. Available at: www.bhs.econ.census.gov/BHS/BRDIS/.

von Hippel, E. 1988. *The Sources of Innovation*. New York: Oxford University Press.

von Hippel, E. 2005. *Democratizing Innovation*. Cambridge, MA: MIT Press.

Watkins, A., and M. Ehst. 2008. *Science, Technology, and Innovation: Capacity Building for Sustainable Growth and Poverty Reduction*. Washington, DC: World Bank.

Wessner, Charles W., ed. 2008. *An Assessment of the SBIR Program*. Washington DC: The National Academies Press.

Notes

1. There is a description of SOSP given at www.scienceofsciencepolicy.net/blogs/sosp/pages/sospabout.aspx.

2. The details of the AAAS workshop are available at www.aaas.org/spp/SciSIP/.

3. In the text, the word strategy and policy are used interchangeably.

4. Information on the IRAP program is available at www.nrc-cnrc.gc.ca/eng/ibp/irap/about/index.html.

5. The Poverty Reduction Strategy Papers are described at www.imf.org/external/NP/prsp/prsp.asp.

Empirical Science Policy— Measurement and Data Issues
Editors' Overview

PART TWO

Policymakers typically want empirical information for several reasons. They would like to understand the impact of previous investments. They would like to be able to have some understanding of the likely impact of future investments. And they would like to be able to characterize their existing investment portfolios. The four chapters in this part describe various aspects of the current state of empirical science policy and provide related, but distinct, visions of the future.

In most policy areas, such as health, labor, or education policy, researchers have access to both survey and administrative data for analysis. These data typically provide some connection between investment decisions and outcomes at the appropriate behavioral unit of analysis. That is not the case in science policy. There are several major data challenges before science policy research achieves the same level of sophistication as these other fields: the information within administrative systems must be reoriented to connect investments with outcomes, and there must be a broader and deeper collection of information on both inputs and outputs, particularly on the scientific workforce. Finally, a deeper challenge, one not faced by other policy fields, must be addressed, namely, how to describe the scientific enterprise in general and scientific advances in particular.

The lack of data in science policy has not gone unnoticed. Indeed, the Office of Management and Budget (OMB) and the Office of Science and Technology Policy (OSTP) have asked federal agencies to "develop outcome-oriented goals for their science and technology activities, establish procedures and time lines for evaluating the performance of these activities, and target investments toward high-performing programs. Agencies have been told to develop "science of science policy" tools that can improve the management of their research and development (R&D) portfolios and better assess the impact of their science and technology investments: "In order to facilitate these efforts, Federal agencies, in cooperation with the Office of [sic] Science and

Technology Policy and the Office of Management and Budget, should develop data sets to better document Federal science and technology investments and to make these data open to the public in accessible, useful formats."[1]

Science policy practitioners have been aware for some time now that the current data infrastructure is inadequate. The National Science and Technology Committee's Interagency Working Group on the science of science policy identified lack of data as a critical gap in the implementation of evidence-based science policy. In a workshop designed to roll out the road map for federal investments, ten options were identified for measuring and tracking federal funding—participants overwhelmingly agreed upon three.

> Nearly 94 percent of the participants were in favor of establishing a universal portal for data set sharing (federal and nonfederal) that captures information about federal funding. Ninety-two percent agreed that a shared research environment, which would allow for data sets capturing information about federal funding to be integrated and analyzed by researchers, was a high priority. Eighty-nine percent of the participants agreed that federal funding agencies should standardize their administrative records systems for initial awards as well as annual and final reports. These three options were also ranked as the number one priority by the greatest percentage of participants.[2]

The lack of data on the impact of science investments became very clear to decision makers upon the passage of the 2009 American Recovery and Reinvestment Act. Most of the estimates that were used for estimating the impact of science investments came from the Bureau of Economic Analysis' RIMS II model, which is derived from a 1992 input-output model of spending flows. This approach functionally equates the impact of science to the impact of building a football stadium or an airport: the impact is derived from the demand side, and depends on the amount of spending on bricks and mortar and workers.[3] We rely on such outdated models for several reasons. The first is that U.S. scientific data infrastructure is oriented toward program administration rather than empirical analysis. The result is that seventeen science agencies have seventeen different data silos, with different identifiers, different reporting structures, and different sets of metrics. The second is that the focus of data collection is on awards, which are not the appropriate unit of behavioral analysis. Awards are the intervention of interest; the activities of the scientists who receive the awards need to be followed. A third reason is that the current data infrastructure does not allow science investments to be coupled with scientific and economic outcomes. In particular, Grants.gov provides a unified portal to find and apply for federal government grants, but goes no farther. Research.gov and science.gov provide information about research and development results associated with specific grants, and a consortium of federal agencies provides R&D summaries at www.osti.gov/fedrnd/. Another obvious challenge is the fact that the reporting system is manual (with obvious quality implications) and relies on principal investigators to make reports during the active period of the award, despite the fact that the impact of science investments often results many years after the award has ended. Finally, despite the fact that science agencies believe that their impact includes both workforce and social impacts, there is no systematic tracking of the students supported by federal funds, and the broader impact of science investments is similarly rarely documented.[4] A previous effort to collect R&D information on federal awards, RADIUS,[5] was discontinued in 2006.

Albert Einstein reputedly said that not everything that can be counted counts, and not everything that counts can be counted. Yet metrics of inputs, outputs, outcomes, and linkages between them comprise a central contribution of the empirical part of science and innovation policy. Adam B. Jaffe's chapter addresses several aspects concerning data choices, modeling, and extrapolation of causal inference. It particularly highlights the empirical limitations and pitfalls in processes designed to measure causal linkages between government funding and education inputs to outcomes such as knowledge generation, productivity, and social welfare (see Figure 10.1 in his chapter). The chapter is structured as one would construct an empirical paper, (1) initially focusing on objectives of the analysis, estimation methodologies, and data collection procedures, (2) troubleshooting estimation challenges, such as endogeneity, multicollinearity, and omitted variable bias, (3) distilling important findings, particularly returns to R&D, including spillover effects, returns to intangible assets, lag effects, and the dynamics of transcending to a long-run equilibrium over time, and (4) assessing the lessons learned regarding returns of specific government programs and the implications of international interactions of inputs in the global sphere of knowledge generation and diffusion.

In a tightly packed chapter, Jaffe gives particularly clear direction to empirical researchers. As an expert in the use of patent data, he provides several orthogonal interpretations of the meaning of rising patent citations. Patent data are often used to proxy contributions of prior knowledge in the technological innovation process. However, this widely used measurement can lead to findings that are misdirected. For example, high levels of patenting in a region could be caused by cross-fertilization of R&D activities between firms or by some underlying activity or institution in the region beyond any firm's control. The unobservables (and thus unmeasurables) are the underlying phenomena that we need to understand, but their impact could be falsely attributed to control levers that policymakers exercise.

Jaffe gives several methodological approaches that mitigate this empirical issue. Interestingly, he suggests that randomized trials could be a useful evaluative tool for science and technology policy. However, he suggests that there are other methods that are not as politically charged. Even in the selection of empirical techniques, institutional influences matter.

Measurement of rates of returns to intangible assets has long been a necessary, intriguing, and frustrating process. Jaffe's chapter emphasizes the importance of measuring differences between the private and social returns of R&D. Jaffe argues that one means of getting a better estimation of these returns is to obtain measurements at different levels of aggregation—local, state, federal, and global. He posits that higher rates of return should be observed at increasing levels of aggregation. However, yet again, measurement difficulties confound this process. This remains a ripe area for research, particularly since national income accounts do not reflect adequately returns to intangible assets.

Jaffe distills a large literature on science policy outcomes into a few important lessons learned from recent federal funding decisions regarding the National Science Foundation (NSF) and the National Institutes of Health (NIH), and the impact of the R&D tax credit on technological innovation. Two key summary points emerge. First, empirical research on the impact of science and innovation policies should attempt to measure additionality effects—a comparison of the difference between what has occurred and what would have occurred had the policy not been implemented. Second, it is critically important that researchers understand underlying processes and institutions underpinning policies and eventual outcomes. Without this knowledge, causal linkages between inputs and outcomes are tenuous.

As E. J. Reedy, Michael S. Teitelbaum, and Robert E. Litan point out in their chapter, our current infrastructure does not do a very good job of capturing key information about the appropriate unit of analysis to study the impact of science investments: the people who do science. The most granular unit is comprised of individuals (clearly, individuals can and do form clusters as project teams, scientific subfields, and scientific disciplines). A credible data infrastructure should capture the full universe of individuals funded by federal science agencies, not just principal investigators and co-principal investigators but also others such as graduate and undergraduate students, postdoctoral fellows, lab technicians, and science administrators. The increasing globalization of science means that it is important to capture not only domestic scientists but also immigrants (and emigrants). However, as the authors point out, insufficient empirical data are available to provide this evidence. On the supply side, the NSF's Division of Science Resource Statistics captures cross-sectional information on doctoral students on almost the universe of U.S. doctoral recipients in the Survey of Earned Doctorates and follows a sample longitudinally in the Survey of Doctoral Recipients. In addition, a field of degree question has been added to the American Community Survey. But limited data exist on post-doctoral students and on the mobility and outcomes of the global science, technology, engineering, and mathematics (STEM) workforce. As the authors indicate, insufficient empirical data are available to provide evidence on the global workforce. Surprisingly, science agencies only collect data on principal investigators and do not systematically collect data on students involved in federal grants during the duration of the award. Consequently, outcomes such as the co-founding of Google by former graduate student Sergey Brin are uncovered serendipitously rather than systematically.

The capture of inputs is only part of the requirement of a data infrastructure. The infrastructure must also capture information about multiple outcomes, one of the most important being advances in science. These advances need to be identified and described in terms of scientific portfolios measured along multiple dimensions: scientific structure, geography, award size, diversity, and broader impact. At a high level, policymakers typically want to know about the clusters of research topics that have been funded, the emerging scientific areas, the geographic, demographic, and disciplinary distributions of research investments, and the disciplinary distribution of research investments, including multidisciplinary collaboration, and the riskiness of the portfolio. It is also necessary for the most fundamental practice of science policy: for proposal review and recommendation purposes, programs need to identify the appropriate reviewers and panelists to ensure the best possible peer review of proposals. However, the rapidly changing nature of science has made it extremely difficult to characterize portfolios.

The current approach has taken two paths. One is a largely manual categorization of incoming proposals, which names scientific topics or disciplines and then groups proposals in a fashion that makes sense to the people who have to use the information for a specific purpose. This approach is tedious and error prone. The other is to use bibliometric tools to describe publications and citations based on the disciplinary categories of journals. However, the time lags are such that the characterization is of the outcomes of investments made long ago, and the most widely available data sets are proprietary.

A major focus of science investment is also economic outcomes. Lynne Zucker and Michael Darby point out how much work has already been done in creating data sets of economic outcomes. In addition to the discussion in Jaffe's chapter, a large-scale National Bureau of Economic Research (NBER) patent database already exists; this has been expanded by creating a standard social network patent database at the individual inventor and aggregate levels.[6] Similarly, a large-scale database of Initial Public Offerings (IPOs) already exists.[7] And, Zucker and Darby themselves have already done pioneering research[8] in creating an integrated database that can trace the links from government investment in R&D through the path of knowledge creation, its transmission and codification, and ultimately, in many cases, to commercial uses yielding a better standard of living and better jobs. Their project integrates and complements key databases on science and innovation by using a system of unique identification numbers (IDs) for firms and other organizations and for individual scientists and engineers as they appear as principal investigators, authors, dissertation writers or advisors, inventors, and/or firm officers, directors, and key employees. This set of identifiers is critical, because the most productive scientists—the "star innovators"—wear many hats simultaneously. The database integrates data on government grants, journal articles, dissertations, patents, venture capital, initial public offerings, and other firm data. It links to major public databases via widely used financial market identifiers. The database has three tiers: a public graphics-based site primarily oriented toward policymakers and the media, a public site providing access to researchers for downloads and database queries limited to the public constituent databases or aggregates derived from the licensed commercial databases, and on-site access at the NBER.

As Jim Thomas and Susan Albers Mohrman note in their chapter, new cyber-infrastructure capabilities mean that we have new ways of capturing the universe of information on the ways in which scientists create and transmit knowledge. Some researchers have expended substantial effort creating and visualizing data sets linking research inputs with output.[9] Others exploit the new cyber-enabled ways of capturing data on the way in which scholars communicate. The MESUR project, www.mesur.org, has created a set of relational and semantic Web databases from over 1 billion usage events and over 10 billion semantic statements to combine usage, citation, and bibliographic data that go well beyond the current bibliometric approaches.

Reedy, Teitelbaum, and Litan do note that there has been progress. Sections 1102 and 1201 of the 2007 America COMPETES Act require data studies and examination of public laws and initiatives for promoting national innovation. The NSF's Division of Science Resources Statistics has restructured its major R&D Survey—the Business Research and Development and Innovation Survey (BRDIS)—to try to capture information on firms' R&D investments and measures of innovation outputs in the United States. In addition, the Bureau of Economic Analysis (BEA) is experimenting with R&D "satellite accounts" to be added to the national accounts. Yet, as they point out, there is much more to be done, not the least building a data infrastructure that builds more strongly on the U.S. federal tax system and the statistical system built on it (such as the U.S. Census Bureau and the BEA). This system is a major and an underutilized resource to measure the economic outcomes of science investments. It could be the source of much useful information, such as detailed financial data for the population of businesses, whether employer owned or not or whether publicly owned or not, the effect of the R&D tax credit use, the links between scientific investments and firm start-ups, and the subsequent earnings and employment trajectories of former graduate and undergraduate students.

As these authors note, however, it is also important to understand how science gets translated into innovation. As such, their chapter goes beyond an examination of the traditional data sources of science policy to emphasize the importance of capturing data on the individuals key to that transition—entrepreneurs. The goal is to utilize existing administrative data from federal agencies and their grantee institutions and match them with existing research databases on economic, scientific, and social outcomes. Those data could, in principle, be matched in an automated (not a manual) fashion, with many data sets identified in this chapter upon which to draw.

As should be clear, the empirical basis for building a science of science policy is not strong. Thomas and Mohrman's chapter provides an important vision for the future. They point out the complexity of the data system needed for the different aspects of science policy. Because there are many different sources of data, and many types of users, it is critical to build a data infrastructure that is open and accessible to the broader research community as well as to science policy practitioners and science agencies. Failure to do so will result in an analysis that is neither generalizable nor replicable and, hence, not scientific. In addition, the data set will not be utilized to the maximum extent possible and will not be developed and enhanced as scientific advances are made. These authors also emphasize the overarching importance of making sense of data, as they note "human judgment applied to the synthesis of information about contextually determined purpose and constraints." The challenge is daunting, but the authors note that the science of science policy community has the advantage of being able to follow the example of other policy communities and to take advantage of the enormous number of tools available.

The news is not all bad. Substantial existing investments could be quickly leveraged to advance the empirical basis of science policy. Federal agencies already collect data on federal investments at the award, individual, and institutional levels for the purposes of managing awards. Academic institutions collect data on all individuals working on projects in their financial and human resources systems. As Zucker and Darby note, academic researchers have collected large bodies of data on such scientific and innovation outcomes as citations, patents, business start-ups and IPOs. Substantial investment has been made in visualization and other tools that convey complex information about science to a lay audience. The federal science agencies have begun to exploit these investments to build a broader platform with the STAR METRICS[10] Consortium. This consortium is anticipated to be a broad partnership of federal science and technology funding agencies based on a shared vision for developing data infrastructures and products to support evidence-based analyses of science and technology returns on investment, as well as to inform policy-making. This new approach addresses many of the major data challenges identified in this overview and discussed in each chapter. It is focused on reorienting information within administrative systems to connect investments with outcomes, and it collects broader and deeper information on both inputs and outputs, particularly on the scientific workforce. By following many of the suggestions made in the four chapters, the infrastructure can be enhanced to allow the community at large to describe the scientific enterprise in general and scientific advances in particular. In practical terms, these chapters have identified a number of key steps necessary to advance the empirical foundations of the science of science policy. These include the following:

1. Support the important fragmented efforts that are all labor intensive and that require both the extensive reporting on the part of scientists and extensive data cleaning on the part of the data developer.
2. Identify the incentives necessary to develop a bottom-up approach whereby the science of science policy community of researchers will voluntarily contribute data.
3. Support the storage and data resources needed for research in the science of science policy in a variety of ways.
4. Promote open access. Accessible data are central to the replicability of analysis and central to good science.

5. Support the development and deployment of next-generation tools for information management and analysis that provide the foundation for basic research in the science of science policy.

Notes

1. M-09-27, Memorandum for the Heads of Executive Departments and Agencies, August 4, 2009.

2. Science of Science Policy Workshop Report, http://scienceofsciencepolicy.net/media/p/528.aspx.

3. Julia Lane, "Assessing the Impact of Science Funding," *Science*, vol. 324, no. 5932 (June 5, 2009): 1273–1275. DOI: 10.1126/science.1175335.

4. Special Issue, *Social Epistemology on the U.S. National Science Foundation's Broader Impacts Criterion*, vol. 23, nos. 3 and 4 (2010).

5. The Rand Database for Research and Development in the United States.

6. Lee Fleming, "A Social Network Database of Patent Co-Authorship to Investigate Collaborative Innovation and Its Economic Impact," NSF Award 830287.

7. Martin Kenney, "The Initial Public Offering Database," NSF Award 0915257.

8. Lynne Zucker and Michael Darby, "Linking Government R&D Investment, Science, Technology, Firms and Employment: Science & Technology Agents of Revolution (Star) Database," NSF Award 083983.

9. K. Borner, "Recommendations for Evaluating Large, Interdisciplinary Research Initiatives," *Trans-NCI Evaluation Special Interest Group* (March 12, 2008).

10. Science and Technology in America's Reinvestment—Measuring the Effects of Research on Innovation, Competitiveness, and Science.

Analysis of Public Research, Industrial R&D, and Commercial Innovation

Measurement Issues Underlying the Science of Science Policy

Adam B. Jaffe

10

1. Introduction

The "Science of Science Policy" should be grounded in the quantitative analysis of the processes of innovation and technical change. Modern economic analysis of these issues is usually traced to the 1950s. The path-breaking work of Abramovitz [1] and Solow [2] showed that there was a large "residual" of aggregate productivity growth that could not be explained by capital accumulation, making the subject of technical change hugely important to both a positive understanding of the process of economic growth and to a normative analysis of public policy. At about the same time, Griliches's [3, 4] pioneering work on hybrid corn showed that it was possible to measure important aspects of the process of technological change quantitatively, and to evaluate the contribution of government investments to these processes. In 1962, the National Bureau of Economic Research (NBER) published *The Rate and Direction of Inventive Activity*, the proceedings of a conference on the economics of technical change that defined the research agenda of the subfield for decades.

These pioneering efforts launched a new stream of research in which economists and other social scientists have undertaken to measure and quantify the determinants and effects of innovation and technical change. The best overall summary of the issues raised by the science of science policy remains Griliches's 1979 article, "Issues in Assessing the Contribution of Research and Development to Productivity Growth" [5]. This paper is to the economics of innovation what Keynes's *General Theory* is to macroeconomics—virtually all of the important ideas that people talk about even today were there in some form.[1]

An important public policy context for these efforts was created by the Government Performance and Results Act of 1993 (GPRA), which requires all government agencies to report on the outputs and outcomes of their programs. There has been much discussion since the passage of the GPRA as to the difficulty of quantifying the arguably intangible outputs and outcomes of science and technology programs. I have argued elsewhere that, indeed, measurement of these effects raises subtle and difficult issues that must be attended to using appropriate statistical techniques as well as by using multiple and diverse quantitative metrics [7]. In this chapter I discuss these issues and approaches as they apply to the challenges of the science of science policy.

2. Background

Richard Freeman's chapter in this volume provides an overview of the contributions of economics to the science of science policy. One of these is "evidence-based statistical models" for undertaking the benefit-cost analysis of government programs. Such models require systematic measurement and quantitative analysis of the relationships between and among government programs and the multiple aspects of the innovation process. The first step in thinking about measurement issues is to understand the general relationships among the phenomena of interest. Figure 10.1 presents a highly simplified schematic of the interplay among government policy, public and private organizations involved in innovation and technical change, and the consequences of those activities.[2]

Each box captures an important category of actors in or consequences of
Figure 10.1.   the process. The green arrows indicate flows of resources, the red arrows out-
Schematic overview
of innovation
system.

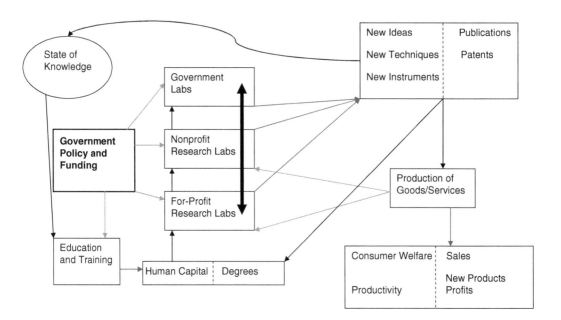

comes or consequences, and the blue arrows outputs of one aspect of the process that feed back to serve as inputs to another set of actors. Boxes divided by a dotted line indicate economic concepts or constructs on the left of the dotted line, and proxies or measurements that might be taken as representing those concepts are on the right side of the dotted line.

Many of the details of this figure could have been presented somewhat differently, and many additional details could reasonably be added. But two basic and important points will emerge from any reasonable characterization of the system. First, causality is very difficult to pin down, as everything depends on more or less everything else. Second, a lot of the important inputs and outputs are either unobservable or measured only with considerable error. These are big problems for quantitative inference. In a sense, all of the more specific problems of the science of science policy are merely distinct manifestations of these two fundamental problems. One could argue that these profound limitations make it hopeless to draw meaningful conclusions, but policy decisions have to be made. As emphasized by John Marburger in his chapter in this volume, better decisions will be made if we have a better understanding of these phenomena.

In this chapter I address some of the most important manifestations of these fundamental issues in the science of science policy, including:

1. the ultimate objectives in devising metrics of innovation;
2. the role of proxies;
3. endogeneity, unobservables, and selection bias;
4. private versus social rates of return and spillovers;
5. the cumulative nature of innovation and other dynamic effects;
6. the role of government and the special needs of data to support program assessment;
7. the United States as part of a global innovation system; and
8. the danger of a little knowledge.

3. The Objectives of Measurement

The first objective in devising metrics is to undertake social science research into the sources and mechanisms by which society produces new technology, and the economic and social consequences when it does so. This requires measures of the inputs, both human and material, to the process of technology development. For both human and material inputs, these include stocks (human capital and accumulated knowledge, equipment) and flows (hours of scientist/engineer work, chemicals). In order to understand the mechanisms, measures of intermediate products are also needed, such as new knowledge that is produced by research and is in turn an input into the development of new products or processes. Next we need measures of the output of the technology development process, that is, new ways of doing things or new products. Finally, to use the language of the GPRA, we also need measures of outcomes of the innovation process, that is, the benefits that society derives from having new technologies in use. These include various concepts of productivity, and also more specialized measures of benefits, such as reduced morbidity and mortality in the case of medical technologies.

A second, more specific objective is the assessment and evaluation of public policies. I address this in more detail later, but the primary data need of assessment that goes beyond those identified in the previous paragraph is data on individuals, firms, and other institutions tracking their involvement (or lack thereof) with the programs that are to be evaluated.

Finally, we collect innovation metrics in part for the purpose of spotting trends that may signal changes in the system or emerging issues that may require attention. For the most part, the data elements already identified (inputs, intermediate and final outputs, and outcomes) are the same data that one would want to monitor for emerging trends.

4. The Role of Proxies

All social scientists engage in various degrees of looking under the lamppost for the watches they dropped in the street, because the light is better there. The only alternative is to build more lampposts, but we will never cover the whole territory. So metrics will always be, at best, imperfect. There are some generic strategies to deal with this imperfection. The most obvious is to use multiple metrics, preferably chosen so that there is reason to believe that the errors in the different metrics are uncorrelated with each other [9]. Another strategy is to examine the phenomena we care about at multiple levels of aggregation, or to use "long differences" or other averaging methods to mitigate the variance due to measurement error. These approaches rely, to varying degrees, on assumptions that the measurement error is unsystematic and hence subject to reduction through averaging. These assumptions may not always hold and are difficult to test.

The characteristics that make for "good" proxies include:

1. a high signal/noise ratio;
2. errors that are unbiased and uncorrelated with other phenomena of interest;
3. linearity (or another known functional relationship) between the proxy and the underlying phenomenon;

4. stability over time in the relationship between the proxy and the underlying concept;

5. stability across settings (institutional, geographic) in the relationship between the proxy and the underlying concept (or variation that is itself subject to proxy);

6. low susceptibility to manipulation; and

7. subject to consistent measurement at different levels of aggregation (geographic and institutional).

The difficulty of assessing the quality of proxies is easily illustrated by the case of citations or references to earlier patents that appear in patent documents. The number of citations made by the average patent granted in the United States has been rising steadily for several decades. If such citations were to be taken as a proxy for the contribution of previous technological developments to the development of new ones, then the rising patent rate could be interpreted as an increased "fecundity" of the existing knowledge base in generating new developments. But alternative interpretations of the observed trend include the following:

1. The number of patents in the preexisting base has been rising, so they are not each becoming more fecund, there are just more of them.

2. Knowledge is diffusing faster than it used to, so a larger fraction of the preexisting knowledge base is known and available to the typical inventor at any moment in time.

3. The search capabilities of the patent office have improved, so even if the inventors don't know any more than they used to, the examiners are finding more citations to include.

4. Patent practices have changed, so that the average patent embodies a larger "chunk" of new knowledge, leading on average to more citations made per patent but not more per unit of new knowledge.

A conceptually related set of issues arises from the fact that at a given moment in time, U.S. patents make on average more citations to earlier work than do the patents of other jurisdictions around the world. The core challenge, then, is the extent to which the change in the metric is an artifact of the process that generates the proxy, or whether it reflects differences in the underlying phenomenon of interest. This can never be resolved absolutely, and typically even partial resolution requires identifying assumptions that may not be testable.[3]

5. Endogeneity

As shown in Figure 10.1, everything is related to everything else, and typically through more than one mechanism. This makes the core task identified earlier—understanding the sources of innovation and the mechanisms by which it is brought forth—very hard. Conclusions about causation can only be drawn conditionally on identifying assumptions, meaning that there is an element of untestable belief behind virtually any conclusion that is drawn. A couple of examples illustrate this point.

In earlier work I showed that firms that perform research and development (R&D) in technological areas in which a lot of R&D is performed by other firms enjoy higher R&D productivity ("measured" in terms of patents and productivity improvements), all else being equal [11]. This has been interpreted as evidence of "spillovers" of knowledge benefiting firms' technological neighbors. But conceptually it could also be evidence that certain regions of technology space are more fruitful at a moment in time; firms are attracted to such regions, so we observe a higher level of R&D activity in such regions, and firms' R&D is more productive precisely because the area is fruitful. (The standard jargon is that variations in "technological opportunity" explain both variations in R&D intensity and in R&D productivity.) Hence the positive correlation between firms' R&D productivity and the amount of R&D in their neighborhood is not causal but simply a result of the endogeneity of the locus of R&D activity itself. My work dealt with this possibility by including in the regression analysis control variables for location in technology space. The identifying assumption that is necessary to maintain the "spillover" interpretation is that these controls—which were essentially arbitrary in the level of detail at which they captured location—were adequate to capture the variations in research productivity associated with the choice of research topic. In this event, the observed relationship of productivity to the R&D of other firms is over and above the technological opportunity effect and hence attributable to spillovers. Subsequent work using a number of different models and approaches, and different data sets, has confirmed the spillover phenomenon, suggesting that it is real. But there is no decisive test as to whether controls for technological opportunity are adequate, so endogeneity can never be ruled out definitively.

The second example is the widely observed phenomenon that the private internal rate of return to R&D investment appears to be considerably higher than the private internal rate of return to investment in fixed capital. Now, there are a number of "real" reasons this might be true. One is that it's riskier (although if the risk is diversifiable it would not justify a risk premium). Another is information asymmetries, thus the market does not reach the equilibrium that would erase the difference in the rates of return to the two forms of investment. Yet another is measurement problems with R&D and its return, in particular the problem that investment in equipment that is used for R&D is not properly tracked in the data. In addition, there is an important endogeneity problem: all kinds of unobservable attributes of firms produce unobservable variations in the likely productivity of R&D. We observe firms that do a lot of R&D earning high profits, all else being equal, but this may be because both the level of R&D and profitability are being driven by these unobservable variations.[4]

Partial solutions to this problem come in roughly three forms. The most commonly used is structural modeling, in which the determinants of endogenous variables are themselves brought within the model. Assumptions about functional forms and exclusion restrictions "identify" statistically the causal relationships of interest, purified of any effect of reverse causality or left-out variables. Of course, these identifying assumptions are difficult to test. Occasionally, people are very clever and come up with instruments whose exogeneity really cannot be questioned (such as Vietnam-era draft lottery numbers). More commonly, instruments are either based on dubious exclusion restrictions, or they are uncorrelated with the phenomena of interest, making them useless.[5]

A second approach is to try to eliminate the effect of unobservables by identifying "control groups" that differ with respect to some endogenous variable but that, we believe, are similar with respect to the important characteristics, even though we cannot actually observe the characteristics. One version of this approach includes "fixed effects" and "difference" models, in which we assume that the important unobservables are constant over time for a given firm or individual. Another version is "matched pairs," in which the behavior or performance of individuals with an observable characteristic of interest is compared to the behavior or performance of randomly selected individuals who are identical to the first in all observable respects.

Finally, in some circumstances, it may be possible to reproduce experiment-like conditions so that variables of interest can be thought of as uncorrelated with left-out variables. Randomized trials have not been used to evaluate science and technology policy, but they are considered acceptable in other public policy assessment arenas, such as job training and health insurance. As discussed in more detail later in this chapter, however, despite having advocated randomized trials for science/technology programs in my 1998 book chapter, I have more recently come to the view that approaches that fall under the "structural modeling" rubric can tell us everything we might hope to learn from randomized trials, with far less political pain.

As already suggested, solutions to this problem are at best partial, in the sense that they will always depend, on some level, on untestable identifying assumptions. But if these assumptions are plausible, and if results tend to be confirmed with different approaches that rely on *different* assumptions, then we gradually accumulate understanding.

6. Private Versus Social Rates of Return and Spillovers

The gap between the social and private rates of return to investment in knowledge and technology is the primary reason innovation is a topic of policy concern. Yet measurement of this gap, and of spillovers, is very difficult.

It is important to distinguish the forms of spillovers related to innovation: "technological" or "knowledge" spillovers, and "pecuniary" or "rent" spillovers [12]. Knowledge spillovers correspond to the phenomenon that one firm that is doing research on a topic generates knowledge that another firm may use to reduce the cost or increase the success rate of its research. Knowledge spillovers act as a technological externality, meaning that the total cost to society of producing new knowledge is reduced. Rent spillovers correspond to the likelihood that a firm's economic exploitation of new knowledge that it has created is likely to leak some of the economic benefits to its customers (in the form of consumers' surplus that the firm does not capture) or its competitors (if they copy the innovation and earn profits as a result). Rent spillovers act as a pecuniary externality, meaning that the benefit to the spillover recipient is offset by losses to the spillover generator; society as a whole does not gain. Knowledge spillovers are important to endogenous growth models, because they are a source of increasing returns in society as a whole. Pecuniary spillovers do not generate increasing returns, but they are still important from a policy perspective, because they still generate a gap between the private and social returns to investment and hence suggest socially suboptimal investment rates in the absence of policy intervention.

There are three categories of approaches to measuring spillovers. One is to look for correlations, as discussed earlier [11]. If the economic success of one agent or group of agents is correlated with the actions of some other agent or group of agents, then we may be willing to infer that spillover from the latter's actions to the former's success is the explanation for the correlation. Second, we can look for proxies for the spillover flow itself, such as citations. Ideally, we combine these two approaches and show that patterns of citations or some other proxy for the flow of spillovers are consistent with patterns of spillovers inferred from correlations between different agents' actions and performance.

Finally, we can infer spillovers by measuring rates of return at different levels of aggregation. As we move from measuring impacts at the level of individual firms to industries and to society as a whole, or from cities to states to countries and to the whole world, we should be "capturing" an ever-larger fraction of the spillovers being generated by some act of knowledge creation. This means that if spillovers are important, we should observe higher rates of return (however measured) as we increase the level of aggregation at which the measurement occurs. Systematic exploitation of this phenomenon is hindered by the frequent difficulty of measuring the rates of return in comparable ways at different levels of aggregation.

7. Dynamics and the Cumulative Nature of Knowledge

There tend to be long and variable lags between when inputs are brought to bear, when outputs are produced, and when outcomes are realized. This makes empirical research difficult and makes it hard to understand relationships. Longer time series are the only way that these questions can really be answered.

For many purposes in understanding the innovation process, stocks of knowledge—the accumulated quantity of previous inputs or intermediate products—are often as important as current flows. To estimate stocks, one must account for depreciation or obsolescence of past investments. The appropriate depreciation rate depends on whether one is thinking about private or public knowledge stocks. From a private perspective, if Firm B finds an alternative to one of Firm A's products, then this makes Firm A's knowledge regarding the product obsolete. But from a public perspective, Firm A's "obsolete" knowledge may still be productive. Finally, stocks, such as human capital, move around over time. If we do not have good information on these movements, then it may be impossible to keep track of the relevant quantities for a given institution or region.

8. Assessment of Government Programs

Measuring the impact of government programs on innovation or knowledge creation raises all of the problems discussed earlier. In addition, several other issues are created by the attempt to identify the impact of government intervention in the economy.

First, one needs to ask whether a given public program is increasing knowledge (or some other "real" objective) or merely increasing an indicator of it. When public policy rewards certain behavior, firms or individuals will find ways to report that they are doing more of the rewarded activity, whether their real behavior has changed or not. There is, for example, a large literature on the extent to which the R&D tax credit actually increases R&D, as distinct from just increasing reported R&D [13].

Second, one needs to take account of the endogenous responses of the economy that mitigate or offset the direct effects of government intervention. After all, economic systems tend to be in some sense in equilibrium; when disturbed, they will tend back toward that equilibrium. If, for example, tax incentives do succeed in increasing the amount of actual spending on R&D, then this will tend to bid up the price of R&D inputs, so that the increase in real R&D activity will be somewhat less than the increase in R&D spending, at least in the short run.[6]

Third, when the government supports a research project or the research program of a firm, and that project or firm is observed to be successful, then there remains the question whether that success was in some way fostered by the government, or whether the government is simply good at guessing who is going to be successful regardless of support. To know if policy is fostering success, one needs some kind of counterfactual to the historical observation or a baseline against which to compare. Government research agencies provide a host of information on the performance of their grantees; in some cases this information is intended explicitly to respond to the GPRA mandates to measure outputs and outcomes. These publications have lots of good and interesting information, but none of them presents this information relative to an explicit counterfactual. As a result, one cannot know the extent to which government-supported research would have come forth otherwise. The reports assume that the results would not have occurred but for government support, and that is probably true to a significant extent. But to answer science of science policy questions related to the *relative* productivity of different government investments, one needs to measure the impact relative to the "but for" scenario. To do so requires an understanding of how government interacts with the system it tries to effect, and modeling and statistics to account for that interaction.

The scientific "gold standard" for determining the effect of a government program relative to what would otherwise have occurred is to perform randomized experiments. In principle, just as we give some people a drug and some a placebo to determine if the drug really works, we could randomly fund some otherwise-qualified grant applicants and not fund others, and then measure the difference in performance in the funded and unfunded groups. Needless to say, this would be politically difficult to implement. An alternative, which is almost as good, is to compare applicants who are funded to those who were denied funding based on the agency's own selection criteria. We expect, of course, that those who were funded were *ex ante* more likely to succeed than those who were not; that's why they were funded. If, however, we retain information on the rankings or scores assigned to all of the applicants (successful and unsuccessful), then that information can be used to control statistically for the expected or *ex ante* difference in performance of the two groups, and thereby extract the effect of the government funding.[7]

Fourth, one needs to distinguish between average and marginal effects. Put aside for the moment the problem of measurement relative to a counterfactual, and assume that if there were no National Institutes of Health (NIH), and never had been, then the state of medical care in the United States would be much weaker and society would be much worse off than it is. Assuming this is true, however, it doesn't flow logically that doubling the NIH budget would double the results, or even necessarily increase our state of knowledge significantly. That kind of question was never really posed before the NIH budget was doubled in the late 1990s. Similarly, the current discussion of big increases in spending on research related to energy and climate change neither examines what the effects will be on the margin nor what the new long-run equilibrium will be.[8]

Finally, it is necessary to distinguish net returns from gross returns. Although it is easy to look at major technology programs such as the National Aeronautics and Space Administration (NASA) or the Internet and say that there have been large social benefits, it is also clear that the investments have also been large in many cases. Big benefits imply a high social return only if those benefits are big *relative to* the expenditure. Often, that comparison is simply not made.

9. The United States as Part of the Global Innovation System
The role of innovation and new technology in the global economic system is very much in the news. Consider the following developments:

- China is greatly increasing PhD production.
- The number of foreign PhDs in U.S. schools is dropping.
- Foreign firms continue to open research facilities in the United States.
- U.S. firms continue to open R&D facilities in other countries such as China.

For each phenomenon, it is possible to tell a good story about why it is good for U.S. citizens, and equally possible to tell a story about why it is bad for the United States. Which story is correct depends on the relative significance of spillovers, on the one hand, and international economic competition, on the other. It would be nice to know whether any of these phenomena should be encouraged or discouraged to maximize benefits to the United States, but there is insufficient evidence. In particular, we know very little about what happens to foreigners who get PhDs in the United States, or about the flow of people into and out of foreign-owned R&D facilities, either here or abroad. Research is necessary in order to minimize the chances of neomercantilist policy responses to these phenomena.

10. A Little Knowledge Is a Dangerous Thing

A careful analysis of the impact of National Science Foundation (NSF) funding of economics research used a "differences in differences" approach to see whether people who got funding increased their publishing relative to their historical base more than people who applied for funding and were denied [14]. The results suggested that NSF funding did increase publication for people early in their career, but not for more senior researchers. The paper was never published, but it was used to question the value of NSF funding. This is definitely a cautionary tale. No matter how carefully science policy research is undertaken and the results qualified, results may be misused. I am sympathetic to those who would therefore prefer not to ask the awkward questions. But I would insist that we must do so. If we don't, then there will never be a science of science policy.

11. Conclusion

The current emphasis on and interest in the science of science policy offers the prospect of major progress on our fundamental understanding of the processes of technical change, and for systematic analysis of public policies relating to science and technology. This progress will require a cooperative effort between the public agencies that make science and technology policy and the research community. The agencies will need to provide the data and research infrastructure, and the research community will need to focus its attention on the research questions that are important for public policy.

One data and infrastructure need that has been emphasized by many researchers relates to data on scientists and engineers. The chapter in this volume by Zucker and Darby emphasizes the role of star scientists in the technological innovation process, and the chapter by Reedy, Teitelbaum, and Litan the role of a technically trained workforce and technology entrepreneurs. With respect to all of these questions related to individuals' contributions to the process of technological change, empirical quantification is limited by the disjointed and incomplete nature of our data on the training of scientific and technical workers, the career trajectories of scientists and engineers, and their funding by government agencies. This is a solvable problem that requires only appropriate resources and coordination among the agencies that touch the development of scientists and engineers at various points in their careers.

Another area that is ripe for major progress is the quantitative assessment of government-support programs for science and technology. The econometric/statistical technology for the comparative evaluation of these programs to yield appropriate measures of marginal rates of return exists. In order for systematic progress to be made in this area, what is needed is increased attention to these issues by researchers, and the systematic retention of data by the agencies on all applicants (successful and unsuccessful), and their evaluation within the funding process. These data then need to be made available to outside researchers (with confidentiality protections, as necessary) so that repeated, reproducible analyses can be undertaken.

Advancement of our understanding of important social phenomena is a long-term project. We have learned much since the quantitative importance of technological change was brought forward by Abramovitz, Solow, and Griliches. The science of science policy has now received support from both Republican and Democratic administrations. It is to be hoped that this represents the initial stage of a sustained, multiyear effort to improve the quantitative basis for systematic policymaking.

References

[1] M. Abramovitz. Resource and Output Trends in the United States Since 1870. American Economic Review, 46;1956.

[2] R. Solow. Technical Change and the Aggregate Production Function. Review of Economics and Statistics, 39;1957;312–320.

[3] Z. Griliches. Hybrid Corn: An Exploration in the Economics of Technological Change. Econometrics, 25;1957;501–522.

[4] Z. Griliches. Research Costs and Social Returns: Hybrid Corn and Related Innovations. Journal of Political Economy, 66;1958;419–431.

[5] Z. Griliches. Issues in Assessing the Contribution of Research and Development to Productivity Growth. Bell Journal of Economics, 1979;92–116.

[6]   S. Kuznets. Problems of Definition and Measurement. In: R. Nelson (Ed.), The Rate and Direction of Inventive Activity. Princeton (NJ): Princeton University Press; 1962, pp. 19–52.

[7]   A. Jaffe. Measurement Issues. In: L. B. a. J. Keller (Ed.), Investing in Innovation: Creating a Research and Innovation Policy That Works. Cambridge (MA): MIT Press; 1998, pp. 64–84.

[8]   A. Pakes, Z. Griliches. Patents and R&D at the Firm Level: A First Look. In: Z. Griliches (Ed.), R&D, Patents and Productivity. Chicago: University of Chicago Press; 1984, pp. 55–72

[9]   Z. Griliches. Economic Data Issues. In: M. I. a. Z. Griliches (Ed.), Handbook of Econometrics. North Holland (Amsterdam); 1986, pp. 1466–1514.

[10] A. Jaffe, M. Trajtenberg. Patents, Citations and Innovations: A Window on the Knowledge Economy. Cambridge (MA): MIT Press; 2002.

[11] A. Jaffe. Technological Opportunity and Spillovers of R&S: Evidence from Firms' Patents, Profits and Market Value. American Economic Review, 76;1986;984–1001.

[12] A. Jaffe. The Importance of "Spillovers" in the Policy Mission of the Advanced Technology Program. Journal of Technology Transfer, 23;1998;1–19.

[13] B. Hall, J. V. Reenen. How Effective Are Fiscal Incentives for R&D? A New Review of the Evidence. Research Policy, 29;2000;449–469.

[14] A. Arora, A. Gambardella. The Impact Of NSF Support for Basic Research in Economics. Pittsburgh (PA): Heinz School of Public Policy Working Paper, Carnegie Mellon University; 1996.

Notes

1. For an earlier overview, less complete from today's perspective but still fascinating, see reference [6] above.

2. Figure 10.1 is a lineal descendant of the "knowledge production function" model presented in reference [8], greatly enriched by much discussion in the ensuing literature.

3. For a systematic framework for thinking about these issues, specifically with respect to patent citations, see reference [10] above.

4. Note that this problem also infects estimates of the *social* rate of return to R&D, but only to the extent that the social rate of return is correlated with the private rate of return. It does not undermine the evidence of a large *gap* between the private and social rates of return, since profit-maximizing firms are not responding to this gap.

5. I once had the brilliant idea to use dummies for which an accounting firm was used to certify a firm's annual financial statement as an instrument for measurement error in R&D. It probably was exogenous—but also, as it turned out, uncorrelated with measured R&D.

6. Powell, Owen-Smith, and Smith-Doerr emphasize in Chapter 4 in this volume that the response of private institutions to any specific public policy will depend in

important ways on ethical, power, and social relationships, in addition to the incentive effects discussed here.

7. In the program evaluation literature, this technique is called "regression discontinuity." For a discussion of its application to government research support programs, see reference [10] above.

8. Kei Koizumi, in Chapter 14 of this volume, discusses in detail the limitations of the historical data available to federal agencies for budgeting purposes and the lack of information on marginal returns to federal investments.

11

The Current State of Data on the Science and Engineering Workforce, Entrepreneurship, and Innovation in the United States

E. J. Reedy, Michael S. Teitelbaum, and Robert E. Litan

1. Introduction

The ideas that come from the scientists and engineers in our economy, and the businesses that bring these innovations to market, are responsible for a significant portion of the economic growth we experience. Policymakers seem to agree that increases in our science and engineering workforce and growth in the rate and/or scale of entrepreneurship would be in our nation's long-term best interest.

However, it is more difficult than it may appear to measure the achievement of these objectives. Historically, progress in science and engineering has been measured largely by its inputs, such as the amount of dollars devoted to research and development (R&D) or the number of engineers educated at our universities. Outputs, such as the number of new inventions or new businesses started each year, may be more difficult to measure, but they also give us a better sense of our economic impact in these arenas. Given the significant resources devoted to science and engineering, more attention to this type of metric is long overdue.

In this chapter, we provide an overview of the data available in three key areas when considering potential outcome measures in the science of science policy: growth in our science and engineering workforce, the innovations that our country produces, and the entrepreneurial businesses that commercialize them. Ultimately, we will argue that most policymakers would prefer to make investments in science and engineering that can be tracked through their life cycle—from intangible aspects of research and development to the actual scientists, entrepreneurs, and businesses that bring new products and services to society (typically through a for-profit commercialization). We will focus on government-produced data, describing currently available information as well as improvements that are under way before highlighting the gaps that remain and warrant attention.

One of the primary challenges in this area is the limitations of our current statistical systems. At best, the system does an imperfect job of linking inputs to outputs. Aggregate data, in particular, are no longer adequate. As Zucker and Darby point out in their chapter, future data must, at the micro level, track both inputs and outputs in a timely manner in order for the data to be useful to policymakers and other parties interested in the future of science-related innovation and entrepreneurship.

2. Scientists and Engineers

We need not rehearse at length here the importance of scientists and engineers for U.S. policy and business. For more than a century, and especially since World War II, the U.S. economy has benefited from a science and engineering workforce that is both substantial in size and exceptional in quality. Over the past few decades, U.S. scientists and engineers have pioneered much of the basic and applied research that has produced a flowering of fundamental knowledge in the life sciences, the physical sciences, mathematics, health and medicine, agriculture, and the technologies of everyday life that we all take for granted. U.S. scientists and engineers also have produced major advances in world health, security, communication, and overall global prosperity.

Many may be surprised to learn that the "science and engineering workforce," even broadly defined, constitutes a relatively small fraction of overall U.S. employment (a proportion that holds true for other countries as well, regardless of their levels of economic development). The most recent statistics regarding education indicate that there are approximately 12.4 million people in the United States whose highest degree is in a science and engineering (S&E) field. The actual number of jobs in this country that require a science and engineering background, however, is far lower. The data indicate that only between 4.3 and 5.8 million people are employed in S&E occupations.[1]

We agree that the size of this workforce is an important metric—and one that we explore in much greater detail later. But there are two crucial points that are neglected in much of the conversation about scientists and engineers. First, it is not so much the number or quantity of such individuals that matters but their quality. Continued U.S. leadership in innovation requires that our scientists and engineers lead the world in creativity and productivity, regardless of the growing number of workers labeled "scientists and engineers" in such countries as China and India, each of which has a population three to four times the size of the United States.

Second, the sustainability of the national science and engineering workforce should also be a key policy goal. This requires the proper matching of scientific and engineering skills to research needs as well as large companies and entrepreneurial endeavors. Given continuing technological change and the lengthy education required for science and engineering careers, this matching process is likely to become ever more complicated over time. Data about both the supply and demand sides of this important part of the labor force will play a critical role in how successful this matching turns out to be.

2.1. Data Overview and Definitions

A clear and universal definition of the phenomenon being measured is essential to the creation of successful metrics. In the domain of scientists and engineers, we find some ambiguity in the terms. While some data sources define individuals as scientists because of their educational backgrounds, others tie the definition to their occupations. These are very different concepts, because many people trained as scientists and engineers do not ultimately take jobs that are considered to be part of the science workforce. And conversely, there are people in science and engineering careers who may have educational backgrounds in other fields (or multiple fields). The data presented earlier reveal the wide disparity between the two measurements: while educational measures suggest that there are 12.4 million scientists and engineers in the United States, occupation measures indicate that there are only between 4.3 and 5.8 million science and engineering jobs.

Next we consider the data and metrics used for the measurement of the science and engineering workforce, both by educational background and occupation.

Educational Measures.   Discussions of the adequacy of America's scientific and engineering workforce often begin with the K–12 education system. Although the terms "scientist" and "engineer" are not widely used in K–12 education, many of the initial statistics relating to the scientific and engineering pipeline are collected for these grades under the rubrics of science, technology, engineering, and mathematics (STEM) education. These statistics most commonly come from standardized testing assessments in the classroom—such as those compiled by the National Center for Education Statistics (NCES) or the National Science Foundation (NSF) (and, indeed, NSF data are often based on NCES data)—or from entrance exams for higher education. Under both the Bush and the Obama administrations, the reporting of student data has become more uniform, but much of the data and compilation is still controlled at the state or local level.

While data concerning K–12 education offer a sense of the pipeline for future scientists and engineers, the data related to postsecondary education are the primary educational measures of our success in this area. Reports typically present information on the numbers of individuals who have earned their highest degrees in the science and engineering fields. These data provide very relevant information regarding individuals' training, but defining the S&E workforce with these criteria may obscure important facts. Most importantly, information about degrees may not be relevant to an individual's current employment. Under the education definition, those with PhDs in biology or master's degrees in engineering would be defined as part of the S&E workforce, even if they were employed as executives or salespeople in any industry. Furthermore, degrees attained do not provide any indication of years that passed since the degree was received. A person with a degree in a science or engineering field that is out of date would be counted as a member of the S&E workforce alongside a recent graduate, but the outdated degree holder may not be capable of work at the same level of sophistication.

Occupational Measures.   As a result of the limitations of these educational definitions of the science and engineering workforce, occupational definitions of the workforce are more common. These data classify individuals as part of the S&E workforce if their occupations fall into specific classifications. Using the comprehensive list of U.S. occupations provided in the Standard Occupational Classification (SOC) system,[2] the NSF's Scientists and Engineers Statistical Data System (SESTAT) distinguishes between "Science and Engineering Occupations" and "Non-Science and Engineering Occupations." For both S&E and non-S&E occupations, the major occupational categories are further disaggregated into subcategories. The major categories of S&E occupations include computer and mathematical scientists, life scientists, physical scientists, social scientists, and engineers. Postsecondary teachers in these S&E fields also are included.

To expand on the aforementioned example, a company executive with a degree in biology or engineering, even in an industry such as pharmaceuticals, would be defined under the occupational system as "outside the science and engineering workforce." In contrast, people working in an occupation listed under "computer and mathematical scientists" would be classified as part of the S&E workforce, regardless of their educational backgrounds. Individuals with degrees in physics and chemistry, then, can be in the same category as those with degrees in philosophy or history.

These occupational definitions provide greater clarity regarding the job-related activities of those in the S&E workforce and move beyond the limitations of education measures, which may be less relevant to workforce status. Table 11.1 summarizes the survey data available for use in identifying and understanding the science and engineering workforce, from both educational and occupational perspectives.

Data Assessment and Suggestions for Future Work.   While the two types of data described earlier offer useful (but quite different) measures of the size of the S&E workforce, more sophisticated data collection and analysis would allow us to learn much more about this workforce. Next, we outline the areas for future work by the statistical agencies and the research community.

Longitudinal Educational Data.   Existing longitudinal student data are sparse and limit analysis of the educational system. A few states have instituted longitudinal data collection systems and research programs to analyze these data, but even those states that have had longitudinal tracking systems in place for some time lack longer-term data on student outcomes, such as occupations or incomes. Recent funding included in the American Recovery and Reinvestment Act of 2009 may help address this problem, since the legislation funds the creation of statewide longitudinal data systems to track the progress of individual students over time.

Bridges Between Education and Workforce Data.   Linking education and workforce data would result in a much more robust understanding of the current state of the S&E workforce, the future pipeline of science and engineering workers, and the drivers of growth in this domain. Early bridges are beginning to be constructed that will allow for the two distinct data systems to be linked, but much more progress is required in order to truly understand the impact of our education policies on the workforce.

Education/Occupation Disparities.   The disparity between educational measures of the size of the S&E workforce (14 to 21 million people) and occupational measures (4 to 7 million jobs) suggests that there is a significant population of those with science and engineering degrees who are not in jobs classified as S&E positions. This discrepancy suggests two possible—and equally plausible—interpretations.

Table 11.1. Workforce data

Data Collecting Agency	Series name	Description	Notes
U.S. Department of Education, National Center for Education Statistics	Integrated Postsecondary Education Data System (IPEDS)	Institutional survey of enrollments, program completions, graduation rates, faculty and staff, finances, institutional prices, and student financial aid	System of interrelated surveys conducted annually of every college, university, and technical and vocational institution that participates in federal student financial aid programs
National Science Foundation	National Survey of College Graduates (NSCG)	Survey of recipients of bachelor's or master's degrees in science or engineering fields	Years surveyed: 1993, 1995, 1997, 1999, 2001, 2003, 2006
	National Survey of Recent College Graduates (NSRCG)	Survey of recipients of bachelor's or master's degrees in science or engineering fields from U.S. institutions between July 1, 1996, and June 30, 1998	Years surveyed: 1993, 1995, 1997, 1999, 2001, 2003, 2006
	Survey of Doctoral Recipients (SDR)	Survey of doctoral degree recipients from U.S. institutions in science or engineering fields	Years surveyed: 1993, 1995, 1997, 1999, 2001, 2003, 2006
	Scientists and Engineers Statistical Data System (SESTAT)	Integrated data from NSCG, NSRCG, and SDR	Years surveyed: 1993, 1995, 1997, 1999, 2003, 2006
Bureau of Labor Statistics	Current Population Survey (conducted by the Bureau of the Census for the Bureau of Labor Statistics)	Monthly national survey of 60,000 households, representing approximately 110,000 individuals	
	Current Employment Statistics Survey	Monthly national sample survey of 150,000 businesses and government agencies, representing approximately 390,000 work sites	Source of official monthly estimates of employment and unemployment

1. The S&E categorization system is failing to include jobs in the S&E workforce that actually require S&E education. Occupations that are classified as outside of science and engineering may require greater scientific capabilities than the categorizations assume. In this case, we have a measurement problem, and there may not be a true mismatch between individuals' educational backgrounds and their careers. Currently available data simply may not be providing insight into the extent to which those with S&E degrees make use of this education outside of the traditional S&E occupations.

2. Those with S&E educational backgrounds are taking jobs—either out of choice or necessity—outside of S&E fields. In this case, further investigation is necessary to determine if these individuals prefer such careers, or if external forces pushed them to careers outside the field. An analysis of these possible external forces would be especially interesting, as these are the areas in which policy changes may be effective.

The National Science Foundation, the agency that collects these data, is aware of these ambiguities and, therefore, advises caution in interpreting the data. The NSF is currently working with the Joint Program in Statistical Methodology[3] to clarify what respondents to surveys about the scientific content of their work actually think these questions mean.[4]

Measurement of Postdoctoral Researchers.   The measurement and classification of postdoctoral researchers in the S&E workforce poses a particular challenge, as these individuals serve dual roles. First, they are trainees, obtaining highly sophisticated education beyond the doctoral level. Second, these individuals also are research workers, funded by research grants to conduct bench-level research. While postdoctoral positions are commonly seen as temporary stepping-stones to permanent academic research positions, there is a lack of research describing the postdoctoral career trajectory or quantifying the size of this population and its trends over time. The data we do have suggest that the number of STEM postdoctoral researchers has increased rapidly.

- 22,900 U.S. citizens and permanent resident visas are occupied in academic post-doc positions (Survey of Doctorate Recipients [SDR] estimate).
- 26,600 persons on temporary visas are in academic post-doc positions (General Social Survey [GSS] estimate).
- 13,000 U.S.-educated persons are occupied in post-doc positions not covered by GSS (SDR estimate).

- 26,500 post-docs are on temporary visas and in positions not covered by GSS (estimate derived by assuming that the proportion of temporary visa post-docs in other sectors and other parts of academia is the same as in the portion covered by GSS).

The bulk of this growth has been among temporary visa holders, primarily researchers from universities outside of the United States who are admitted to the country on temporary visas. Post-docs are also heavily concentrated in biomedical fields.[5]

Labor Market Analysis.   More research concerning the labor market for doctoral-level scientists and engineers in the aggregate also would contribute to a more comprehensive understanding of the S&E workforce overall. The doctoral degree has long been seen as a research degree designed for those wishing to pursue research in academe, yet the majority of recent doctoral graduates find employment outside of traditional academe tenure-track positions.[6] Researchers consider pay levels and trends in order to assess the supply and demand and have found that the supply of doctoral graduates in most (though not all) fields of science and mathematics is ample, if not excessive. Pay levels for doctoral graduates in most (though, again, not all) fields of science and engineering are relatively low in relation to other occupations requiring many years of education beyond the bachelor's degree and in relation to the investments of time and money required to earn the degree. This investment, of course, is substantial. In some fields—especially in the largest, the biomedical sciences—the length of time to the PhD has become very long (between seven and eight years, on average), and even then most recent doctoral graduates find that they must undertake a further postdoctoral research period of between two and five years in order to be competitive in the labor market. The opportunity costs of foregone earnings during this extended period of student and quasi-student status are quite large.

Analysis of Temporary Visa Holders.   A sizable portion of the growth in the number of STEM researchers in recent years has come from abroad. Many of these researchers come to work or study in the United States on H-1B or other temporary visas. The H-1B visa was established legislatively in 1990 in response to employer claims of shortages of "high-tech" workers. The annual number of H-1B visas issued is substantial, on the order of 100,000 or more in recent years. Since the visas are valid for multiple years, the stock of H-1B visa holders residing in the United States is considerably larger than the annual flow.

H-1B visas are now one of the more controversial aspects of U.S. immigration policy. While this subject is outside the domain of this chapter, it is important to note that there are little concrete data on these visa holders to inform our understanding of this population of workers often in S&E fields. The most well-informed estimate cited by researchers comes from B. Lindsay Lowell. Lowell estimates that the H-1B population doubled between 1998 and 2001, and that it reached more than 500,000 workers by 2005.[7] This is a nontrivial number relative to the workforce with STEM occupations, estimated by the NSF to be about 5 million.

In addition to the H-1B population, numerous other visa categories are used to bring scientists and engineers from abroad to the United States. These include:

- F-1—a student visa that allows recipients to work up to twenty hours a week during school and full-time during vacations;
- J-1—an exchange visitor visa that is often used for postdoctoral researchers employed as research assistants;
- L-1 and L-2—a visa for intra-company transferees and their spouses that allows them to work;
- O-1—visas for people "of extraordinary ability"; while the population on this visa is quite small, these individuals are permitted to work and may contribute significantly to the S&E fields;
- TN—a visa for Canadian/Mexican nationals that allows them to provide professional services; and
- E-3—a two-year visa for Australian nationals (with similar criteria to H-1B visas) that can be extended indefinitely.

Data concerning each of these populations are quite weak, and there is little information regarding the number of scientists and engineers holding these temporary visas. Better data would inform a debate that is now largely based on advocacy and anecdote.

3. Entrepreneurs

Scientists and engineers may be the foundation of the innovation in this country, but it is the entrepreneur who helps achieve societal returns from the scientists' knowledge creation. It is the entrepreneur's role as the primary vehicle for the commercialization of new scientific knowledge—and as an engine for economic growth in our economy—that brings entrepreneurship into the domain of science policy. Scientists and engineers develop new knowledge, but it is often an entrepreneur who recognizes the value of the knowledge for the general public and brings the new product or process to the market. Sometimes a scientist or an engineer *can also* become an entrepreneur, but often not. Policies at the intersection of science and entrepreneurship include all those that support new business creation and growth: support for small business innovation research, R&D tax credits, and university technology transfer programs, among many others. Given the importance of entrepreneurship in disseminating new knowledge, a discussion of the outcome measures in the science of science policy must also include metrics that provide for a greater understanding of entrepreneurship.

3.1. Data Overview and Definitions

The challenges involved in determining the size of the scientist and engineer population pale in comparison to the obstacles involved in measuring entrepreneurship for research purposes. The first challenge may be the inherent dynamism and turbulence of new firms, as well as their (almost by definition) small size. New firms are continually born, and young firms often die. Fast growth and acquisitions further complicate an already chaotic environment. Furthermore, new businesses start very small and generally at a very local level, often with just one person working in his or her home. Figure 11.1 presents the

Figure 11.1.
Stylized description of current data coverage.
Source: *Understanding Business Dynamics: An Integrated Data System for America's Future.*
See http://books.nap.edu/openbook.php?isbn=0309104920.

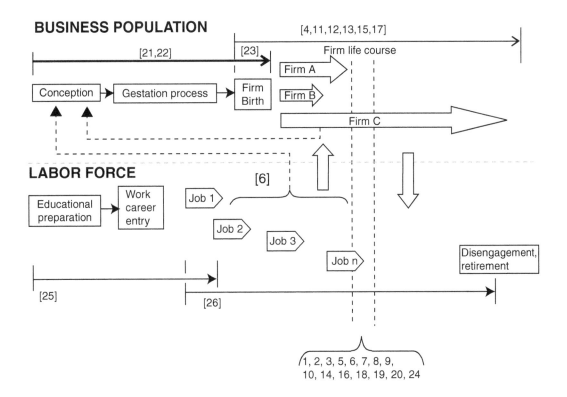

complicated and dynamic careers of entrepreneurs and the courses of their businesses.

Unfortunately, national statistical agencies are best equipped to collect data at the very other end of the business spectrum—at the level of the largest, most stable firms in the economy. The dynamism, volatility, and small scale of entrepreneurship make it very difficult for national statistical agencies to measure the phenomenon. Nonetheless, most agencies have significantly improved their data infrastructures and time series data in recent years.

Definitions pose additional challenges for researchers in this arena. While the word "entrepreneur" refers to an individual, many definitions and metrics focus on the entrepreneur's business. Data sets focused on the individual typically define entrepreneurship based on the individual's employment status or work activities; those focused on the firm often define entrepreneurship based on the age of the firm or the firm's size. We next review the data sets in each of these areas.

Individual-level Data. Data sets that capture information about entrepreneurship often define an entrepreneur as someone who is self-employed, the owner of a business, or an individual who forms a start-up enterprise. This definition almost always implies at least a component of management *and* ownership, and thus does not include "intrapreneurs," employees who are responsible for entrepreneurial ventures within larger companies.

For many years, self-employment statistics were the only internationally comparative measures of entrepreneurship, and data showing demographic trends in entrepreneurship over time are still limited to self-employment measures, typically collected through population surveys. Limiting the definition of entrepreneurship to self-employment, however, is too narrow. This definition excludes those who may have been self-employed when they started new businesses but have since graduated to other legal forms and even employ others. More recent data collection efforts have defined entrepreneurship around business ownership and the employment of other individuals, and more work along these lines is expected.[8] Table 11.2 presents information concerning the data sets that can be used for determining the size of the entrepreneur population and understanding its characteristics, using the employment status of the owner to define entrepreneurship.

Firm-level Data. While individual-level measures of entrepreneurship consider the entrepreneur and his or her business as a single entity, firm-level measures accommodate the more complicated relationship between entrepreneurs

Table 11.2. Individual-level entrepreneurship data

Data Collecting Agency	Series name	Description	Notes
Bureau of Labor Statistics	Current Population Survey (conducted by the Bureau of the Census for the Bureau of Labor Statistics)	Monthly national survey of 60,000 households representing approximately 110,000 individuals	Provides employment status data (including self-employment) that may be used to define entrepreneurship. The Kauffman Index of Entrepreneurial Activity is calculated from these monthly files.
Census Bureau	Survey of Business Owners (SBO)	Survey of self-employer and employer business populations completed every five years, with 2.4 million responses expected in 2007	Years surveyed: 1982, 1987, and 1992. Related surveys were collected as the Survey of Minority-Owned Business Enterprises, Survey of Women-Owned Businesses, and Characteristics of Business Owners in 1997, 2002, and 2007.
	Integrated Longitudinal Business Database (LBD)	Research database that integrates self-employment records into the Longitudinal Business Database data set of all employer business establishments from 1975 to 2005	
	Longitudinal Employer-Household Dynamics (LEHD)	Database that links employer and worker records in a longitudinal file	Provides a variety of public-use data products along with research data set
	Self-Employment Dynamics Database	Research database with expected public tabulations that will track sole proprietors each year from 1994 onward as an extension of the LEHD and ILBD projects	Currently in development
National Science Foundation	National Survey of College Graduates (NSCG), National Survey of Recent College Graduates (NSRCG), Survey of Doctoral Recipients (SDR)	Most of these surveys include a self-employment measure, with some years including other concepts such as involvement in a start-up board	
Federal Reserve Board	Survey of Consumer Finance	Triennial survey that gathers information on wealth in business ownership	2010 survey will expand the information collected on this population

and the businesses they create. Entrepreneurs create new organizations, but these entities may eventually become independent from their founders, with new owners and new employees who were not present at the business's birth.

Firm-level definitions typically focus on the age of the business or the size of the business (measured by the number of employees). In the past, statistical agencies and others often equated entrepreneurship with small business. While new firms almost always start out small, it is important to note that most people would not consider all small businesses to be entrepreneurial, either because of their lifestyle goals or specific industries. Additionally, the definition of "small business" often includes fairly large firms. The Small Business Administration (SBA), for example, considers all firms with less than 500 employees to be "small" in all but a few industries. More recently, U.S. statistical agencies have been making greater efforts to track the age of firms as well as their size.

Another challenge in collecting firm-level data is the treatment of new branches of existing firms. Most national statistical offices remain most comfortable reporting establishment-level data, or data that treats all business locations as the same, regardless of whether they are independent business locations or report to a larger company. While trends in firm-level and establishment-level data sets are often similar, significant differences can occur over time, and these would be obscured if the data were not disaggregated by firms and establishments.

Finally, most available firm-level data are collected too infrequently, making it very difficult to observe trends over time. Many U.S. businesses are only contacted by the U.S. Census Bureau every five years as a part of the Economic Census. Other U.S. statistical agencies, notably the Bureau of Labor Statistics (BLS) and the Internal Revenue Service (IRS), have more frequent and comprehensive firm-level data, but privacy considerations and administrative requirements impede the sharing of such data among all of the relevant agencies.[9]

Table 11.3 presents the data sets with firm-level data for the study of entrepreneurship.

3.2. Data Assessment and Suggestions for Future Work

While entrepreneurship data need considerable work, and we next outline a wide range of specific areas for improvement, it is important to acknowledge the significant progress that has been made in this domain in recent years. Several agencies have made changes that have enhanced the data available to researchers; we present some changes made by the Census Bureau, the NSF, and the BLS.

Table 11.3. Firm-level entrepreneurship data

Data Collecting Agency	Series name	Description	Notes
Bureau of Labor Statistics	Business Employment Dynamics	Quarterly administrative data derived from the Quarterly Census of Employment and Wages	1992 forward, with shortest delay in publication of establishment-level data
Census Bureau	Longitudinal Business Database (LBD)	Longitudinal research data set available in the Census Research Data Centers, which track employer businesses	Annually since 1976
	Economic Census	Survey conducted every five years, in years ending in 2 and 7	
	Annual Survey of Manufacturers	Survey of manufacturing establishments with one or more paid employees; conducted annually, except for years ending in 2 and 7	A similar survey of the services industry is now in development.
	Business Dynamics Statistics	Public database derived from the LBD that follows cohorts of establishments since 1977	Tracks the annual changes in employment for growing and shrinking businesses at the establishment level
National Science Foundation	R&D Expenditures at Universities and Colleges	Institutional survey conducted annually since fiscal year 1972	The proposed expansions would cover commercialization and technology transfer, including start-up businesses created.
	Micro-business Innovation Survey	Approved new survey of businesses with five or fewer employees	Currently in development
Federal Reserve Board	Survey on Small Business Finance	Owner characteristics, firm size, use of financial services, and the income and balance sheets for businesses with less than 500 employees	2003, 1998, 1993, and 1987; canceled in 2007

Census Bureau.   The Census Bureau has endeavored to improve firm-level measures of entrepreneurship through changes in its longitudinal research database (LRD). The LRD started initially as a research product that linked together business records over time to permit the analysis of business dynamics, going back to 1977. Unfortunately, there are significant time gaps, as these data rely disproportionately on the Economic Census, which is completed once every five years. However, the recent publication of the Business Dynamics Series offers helpful summary-level tables on business dynamics at the state, industry, and business cohort levels.

National Science Foundation.   The NSF's entrepreneurship surveys also have changed remarkably. Significant time and effort were spent on the Business R&D and Innovation Survey (BRDIS), which will soon provide a wealth of additional details on the types of R&D and innovation activities in firms in the United States. While the tabular data from this survey will be informative, the most important information for the science of science policy will result from linking other business data to this survey in a meaningful way, allowing researchers to track outcomes from reported R&D and innovation activities. Analyses of these data could be enhanced if the Census Bureau (which collects the BRDIS for the NSF) expanded researcher access to all of its data.

In addition to BRDIS, the NSF will implement a new survey on innovation in micro-businesses in 2011. This program to measure innovation in firms smaller than five employees is now in its infancy and very little information about it is currently available. The new NSF survey may, however, expand available data in ways that could be replicated at other national statistical offices and lead to real advancements in the science underlying both entrepreneurship and innovation, a topic we will turn to shortly.

The NSF also has attempted to redesign its Survey of Research and Development Expenditures at Universities and Colleges[10] to include the addition of a new module on commercialization and technology transfer. This change is important and reflects the increased role of universities in economic development. While this module did not receive final Office of Management and Budget (OMB) approval for the 2009 fielding of the survey, it is hoped that work on the module will continue.

Bureau of Labor Statistics.   The notable change at the BLS in recent years has been the introduction of very timely establishment openings and closings data as a part of their Business Employment Dynamics (BED) program. With only a nine-month delay, BED is the earliest indicator available on national- and state-level trends in business expansions and contractions.

The efforts by these agencies and others—including the IRS, which has made improvements to its data infrastructure and continued to clarify its institutional research and statistical mission—could prove pivotal to future analyses of entrepreneurship. We next outline other areas for improvement.

Longitudinal Data. As in the case of metrics for scientists and engineers, meaningful metrics for entrepreneurship are enhanced by the use of longitudinal data that track individuals throughout their educations and careers. Collecting this type of longitudinal data is challenging, especially for a population like entrepreneurs who make frequent changes, moving into and out of self-employment or other entrepreneurial activity (and then back again).

Various agencies nonetheless are making improvements in longitudinal data collection. For the first time, the Census Bureau's Longitudinal Employer-Household Dynamics (LEHD)[11] program and its Integrated Longitudinal Business database are creating a statistical backbone that will begin to provide longitudinal data on businesses, workers, and the self-employed. These efforts have not been fully funded in the past, but prospects for full funding in the coming years are promising and should be pursued. In addition to the current efforts of the BLS, the agency has added a series of entrepreneurship questions to round twenty-four of the National Longitudinal Youth Survey.[12]

Entrepreneurship Education and Training Data. Entrepreneurship education is becoming more frequent at the primary, secondary, and tertiary levels, and science and engineering programs, in particular, have started to include these programs in their curricula. Entrepreneurship training and education courses for those already in the workforce also have become common. Unfortunately, no data are currently collected on entrepreneurship education and training, and there is, therefore, no means of quantifying the investments and outcomes of these activities. While the federal statistical agencies are unlikely to become a primary source of data on this subject, data from other sources are necessary in order to evaluate the effectiveness of particular programs or the interventions more generally.

Immigrant Entrepreneurship Data. The lack of information regarding immigrant scientists and engineers is mirrored by a dearth of data concerning immigrant entrepreneurs. Anecdotal evidence suggests, however, that some categories of immigrants are important drivers of economic growth as scientists and engineers and as entrepreneurs.

Analysis of Entrepreneurial Teams. Research suggests that many new businesses are started by teams of individuals working together rather than by a single entrepreneur. Data sets that focus on individuals rather than on firms could be greatly improved by mechanisms that allow for the study of entrepreneurial teams as they start new companies. This topic is especially important for analyses of businesses that started as a result of technology transfer, as there is great interest in the relative contributions of both scientific and nonscientific personnel.

Measurement of the Services Industry. It is widely acknowledged that the economic statistical infrastructure in the United States is designed to measure the economy as it was in the 1950s. As a result, the services industry—which represents the majority of the U.S. economy—has been neglected far too long, and current efforts to improve this situation are very welcome—even if they are long overdue. The Census Bureau is currently developing a survey for the services industry, similar to its existing Annual Survey of Manufacturers. It is not yet clear if the broader improvements related to services measurement will eliminate a majority of the noise in the data that currently exist or if additional improvements will be needed.

Regional and Local Entrepreneurship Data. Economic development is largely a local activity in the United States, yet limited data are available on entrepreneurship at the local and regional levels due to a combination of legal and practical roadblocks. Confidentiality concerns are primary, as specific firms become easier to identify in the smaller pool of local businesses. Administrative records are increasingly used for local and regional work, but their narrow conceptual reach limits analysis. While the statistical agencies have made some strides in prioritizing regional-level data, this role has not been codified in many agency missions, directives, or funding priorities.[13] It is not yet clear if the statistical agencies will undertake major revisions to existing surveys to improve local and regional data collection. This effort would certainly increase the relevancy and accuracy of the data collected—and enhance the statistical offices' base of support.

Business Financing Data. There is a dearth of data on the very important topic of how businesses are financed. The Federal Reserve cancelled the Survey of Small Business Finance in 2007, and current data collection in this domain is now limited to a few questions on the Census Bureau's Survey of Business Owners. As anecdotal evidence suggests that the recent recession has had a significant impact on business financing, and that these changes are affecting commercialization and business growth, data collection in this area is now only more important. While the Federal Reserve may resume its survey at some point, a more lasting impact may be achieved if a different statistical agency assumes this responsibility.

Data Synchronization. Greater data synchronization across statistical agencies would allow for the agencies to understand better where differences exist in their data, identifying more gaps in measurement and opportunities for streamlining collection.

Timely Data. The BLS's BED program, which is built from records gathered from states as a part of the Quarterly Census of Employment and Wages,[14] has increasingly become a source for timely data on changes in establishments, including births and deaths.[15] The BED could introduce other imputation methods to speed the release of establishment closure data (something already under consideration). Additionally, if there were an appetite for additional survey-based data on new and emerging firms, then the BED would seem a logical home for a program to collect such data. Surveys in this area could cover topics already referenced, such as training, support, and networks.[16]

4. Innovation

While the previous sections of this chapter primarily focused on measurement of people and businesses, the following section brings the discussion to its most fundamental level: innovation. Innovation has been defined as "The design, invention, development, and implementation of new or altered products, services, processes, systems, organizational structures, or business models for the purpose of creating new value for customers and financial returns for the firm." It is innovation that drives our economy's future growth and the improvements in living standards we have experienced. The benefits of innovation are often considered at the micro level in the incremental advances we see in products or processes, but much of the real evidence for the importance of innovation can be seen at the macro level. Studies demonstrating returns to productivity beyond that accounted for by traditional measures of capital investments in labor and equipment reveal that it is innovation that moves our economy forward.[17]

4.1. Data Overview and Definitions

Innovation is typically measured in two distinct ways: in terms of the inputs in the process, and in terms of the outputs that result. We next describe the data sources for each of these methods.

Inputs.   Innovation inputs include various types of investments, from physical capital (e.g., research facilities) to human effort (e.g., scientific research). Table 11.4 presents information regarding three data sets that can be used to measure the inputs of innovation.

Outputs.   Innovation outputs, in contrast, include the creation of IP, disclosures of inventions, and new products or services that are brought to market. Patents are the most common measure of innovation, but analyses of

Table 11.4.   Innovation input data

Data Collecting Agency	*Series name*	*Description*	*Notes*
Bureau of Economic Analysis	Proposed NIPA R&D and Innovation Satellite Accounts (with Census, BLS, National Science Foundation, and other agencies contributing data)	Tracks investments in specific innovation input activities to allow recognition of longer-term returns of these investments	Calculations currently track software investments in the core GDP accounts
National Science Foundation	R&D Expenditures at Universities and Colleges	Institutional survey conducted annually since fiscal year 1972	
	Business R&D and Innovation Survey	Firm-level survey of five main topic areas, including: financial measures of R&D activity; company R&D activity funded by others; R&D employment; R&D management and strategy; and intellectual property, technology transfer, and innovation	Redesign of R&D Survey transition occurred for fiscal year 2008 data
	Micro-business Innovation Survey	Approved new survey of businesses with five or fewer employees	

Table 11.5.   Innovation output data

Agency	Series name	Type of statistics collected	Other important notes
Patent and Trademark Office	Patent Grant Bibliographic Data	Weekly update includes bibliographic text of each patent granted	Provides underlying micro-data that are linked by researchers into the National Bureau of Economic Research Patent Database and other similar products
	Patent Application Bibliographic Data	Weekly update includes bibliographic text of each patent application	
National Science Foundation	Business R&D and Innovation Survey	From 2008, will include introduction of new products and services to the market	

patents issued typically use them as a proxy for more technical and scientific innovation activities. Patents are limited, in that not all innovations can be patented, having instead to be treated as trade secrets or other types of IP or process improvements. Within university settings, common metrics include disclosures of inventive activity, start-ups created, and licenses generated. Europe has led the way in measuring outputs of innovation as introductions of new products or services to the market. And from the macroeconomic perspective, innovation is often measured as the increase in total factor productivity. Table 11.5 details three sources that can be used to measure outputs from innovation.

4.2. Data Assessment and Suggestions for Future Work

BRDIS Data.   The BRDIS, discussed earlier, is the flagship statistical effort to measure innovation inputs and outputs in the United States. The collection of data for calendar year 2008, using the redesigned BRDIS, according to reports from the NSF, went smoothly and achieved high response rates. This success no doubt testifies to the extraordinary effort that the NSF invested in the redesign. These new data will allow for expanded measures of R&D, as well as new output measures, such as the introduction of new products and services to the market. Many of these concepts are drawn from the Community Innovation Survey (CIS), which U.S. statistical agencies had been reluctant to adopt in the past. Full analyses of these data will likely be publicly available in late 2010 or early 2011. The results of this product will get us to the early stages of knowing what new publications and research will be possible using this data. Particular attention should be given to possible industry-level or subnational disaggregations, as well as longitudinal analyses.

Micro-business Innovation Survey.   Expanding upon the BRDIS, efforts are now under way to develop a "micro-business" innovation survey that would contribute to a greater understanding of innovation in both developed and developing companies. Although most small businesses are not innovative and make little investment in innovation inputs, a nontrivial portion is making significant investments that may result in disruptive innovations, new industries, and other sources of economic change. Data from this type of survey may lead to a more robust understanding of innovation and how new, innovative companies grow in this country.

The current CIS framework excludes small businesses and new businesses from its measurement of innovation. This decision may be appropriate, given the conceptual framing of many of the survey's key questions. However, the NSF appears to be recognizing that there are some significant potential benefits to exploring a new set of questions to look at emergent forms of innovation in small businesses. The United States has an opportunity to take a leading role among national statistical agencies in finding a conceptual framework that can be replicated internationally and to create a global picture of innovation and entrepreneurship.

R&D Measurement.   The Bureau of Economic Analysis (BEA) is the co-ordinating body and would-be producer of proposed statistics on improved investment measures of R&D and innovation at the macro level. Most importantly, the BEA is driving many of the improvements already discussed to NSF surveys, both directly and indirectly. The BEA uses "satellite accounts" to experiment with measures that are consistent with GDP but not yet official. The agency began tracking R&D in a satellite account in 2006 and plans to incorporate R&D measures into core GDP calculations in 2013. The BEA also continues to explore potential new satellite accounts that may include other intangible asset investments such as those in IP, licensing of IP, and some measures of human capital.[18] These additional accounts may be implemented in the same time frame as the R&D account, but a one- or two-year delay is probable. The BEA's impressive effort in this area will need continued budgetary support over a lengthy project time line.

Patent Data.   Patent statistics have become a core part of science and policy debates regarding innovation. These data are not only very relevant to innovation but also are easily accessible, as patent data must, by law, be made public in a nonanonymous record. Furthermore, patent applications require documentation of prior patents relevant to the current patent, as well as information on researchers involved and other rich contextual information, offering researchers a wealth of data for analysis.

While the depth and breadth of patent data have drawn many academics to study these data, it must be noted that the data are incomplete. Many innovations cannot be or are never patented. Other types of intellectual property (IP) registrations, such as trademarks and copyrights, may be less rich, but they can be used to expand measures of innovation in nonpatentable arenas. Work with these data has begun at the OECD and the U.S. Patent and Trademark Office but will need to be fleshed out in the coming years.

5. Conclusion

The national statistical offices play a critical—if an unappreciated—role in defining the statistical information that is available for research on S&E workforce development, entrepreneurship, and innovation, among many other topics. The science of science policy has brought together these three areas, as well as many other previously distinct policy debates, and has revealed their common data needs. Ultimately, policymakers need data that will allow researchers to track science investments throughout their life cycle—starting with their beginnings in R&D, documenting the scientists, entrepreneurs, and businesses that bring the new ideas to the market, and determining the outcomes, from a variety of perspectives. It is our hope that the summary offered here, and the discussion of areas for future work, will push statistical agencies further in this direction.

This chapter has focused almost exclusively on the importance of high-quality data for academic research and for policy decision making. But it is important to note that these data serve other purposes as well. Businesses, too, are affected directly by the government's statistical infrastructure. Both large and small businesses rely upon data from the statistical agencies to plan future products or service offerings. Robust, relevant, and current data will allow both businesses and government to make more informed decisions.

Notes

1. See http://www.nsf.gov/statistics/seind10/c3/c3h.htm.

2. The Standard Occupational Classification (SOC) system was developed by an interagency committee of the U.S. government, chaired by the Office of Management and Budget, and it is used by all federal agencies in the interest of data comparability.

3. A graduate student training program located at the University of Maryland and co-sponsored by the University of Michigan and Westat. See http://www.jpsm .umd.edu/jpsm/.

4. Nirmala Kannankutty, Science Resources Studies, National Science Foundation, personal communication, September 21, 2009.

5. See http://www.nsf.gov/statistics/seind10/c3/c3h.htm.

6. See http://www.nsf.gov/statistics/seind10/c3/tt03-18.xls.

7. B. Lindsay Lowell, "Temporary Visa for Highly Skilled Jobs: A Brief Overview of the Specialty Worker H-1B Visa," presentation at a Policy Briefing on Temporary Worker Programs, Institute for the Study of International Migration, Georgetown University, March 28, 2008. See http://isim.georgetown.edu/Event%20Summaries& Speeches/Sloan/Lowell,%20TWPBriefing%20H1Bs%203-28-08.pdf.

8. Nadim Ahmad and Anders Hoffmann, "A Framework for Addressing and Measuring Entrepreneurship," OECD Statistics Working Paper No. 2, January 2008, available at SSRN, http://ssrn.com/abstract=1090374.

9. See http://www.nap.edu/catalog.php?record_id=11738.

10. See http://www.reginfo.gov/public/do/PRAViewICR?ref_nbr=200905-3145-002.

11. LEHD combines federal and state administrative data on employers and employees with core Census Bureau censuses and surveys. These data have been used in recent years to provide very rich employment dynamics data, but transitions into and out of self-employment were not included.

12. See http://www.kauffman.org/Blogs/DataMaven/May-2009/Call-for-Comment— BLS-Proposes-Major-Improvements.aspx.

13. The Bureau of Economic Analysis is a recent exception to this rule, having publicly committed to implementing regional components for future data series.

14. These concepts were conceptualized in a series of papers from the BLS.

15. See http://www.bls.gov/news.release/pdf/cewbd.pdf.

16. For more information see R. L. Clayton, J. A. Elvery, A. Sadeghi, J. R. Spletzer, and D. M. Talan, "Proposal for Improvement: Quarterly Census of Employment and Wages and the Business Employment Dynamics," Online Proceedings of the 2008 Kauffman Symposium on Entrepreneurship and Innovation Data, http://www.kauffman .org/research-and-policy/data/2008data.aspx

17. See multiple studies from Jorgenson at http://www.economics.harvard.edu/ faculty/jorgenson/bibliography_jorgenson; Carol A. Corrado, Daniel E. Sichel, and Charles R. Hulten, "Intangible Capital and Economic Growth," FEDS Working Paper No. 2006-24, June 2006, available at SSRN, http://ssrn.com/abstract=943769; Tony Clayton, Mariela Dal Borgo, and Jonathan Haskel, "Innovation Index Based on

Knowledge Capital Investment: Definition and Results for the UK Market Sector," Institute for the Study of Labor (IZA) Discussion Papers 4021, 2009, available at http://ideas.repec.org/p/iza/izadps/dp4021.html.

18. See http://www.kauffman.org/uploadedFiles/ResearchAndPolicy/EntrepreneurshipData/2008data/innovation-measurement.pdf.

12 Legacy and New Databases for Linking Innovation to Impact

Lynne Zucker and Michael Darby

1. Introduction

Three of the foundations of an evidence-based platform for the science of science policy include robust and accessible databases that are designed to permit rapid analyses, strong models identifying critical points or levers that policy changes can directly affect, and evidence on a range of innovation and impact measures. The greater the generality of the levers or critical points identified, the more likely that there will be prior relevant evidence to guide new policy initiatives.

Legacy databases generally cover established industry. We will review major examples of legacy databases in Table 12.1, many created by government agencies as a way of documenting their routine activities, such as the U.S. Patent and Trademark Office. Emerging industries are less well covered by the government sources, or other databases drawing heavily upon government data, since it may take five to ten years or more for data on them to be collected systematically by government agencies. It may often be difficult to define these industries clearly enough early on [1]. Emerging industries are especially important to understand because the flow from science to industry is generally most visible and crucial to success of firms entering the new technology, and because metamorphic or radical industry change takes place through the emergence and success of new firms operating close to the knowledge frontier [2–4]. Investors, the companies that serve them, and others, from recruiters to vendors, recognize the importance of emerging industries, and so it is not surprising that the gap in public databases on emerging industries has encouraged the development of a robust commercial database business. We review selected examples of databases on emerging industries in Table 12.2.

Many of the existing databases have a strong implicit or explicit model that underlies their construction. To sell over time, a commercial vendor has had to demonstrate a strategic advantage gained from using their database; the underlying model and specific strategy/policy levers are often left implicit.

Table 12.1. Selected science and technology databases: U.S and/or international, panel or cross-section

Database name	Name/archive	Web link	Access	Start	End	Format	Unit	Examples of variables
Computer Retrieval of Information on Scientific Projects	NIH-CRISP	http://crisp.cit.nih.gov/	Public	1972	2006	Search driven	Various	Grants, funded organizations, principal investigators
County Business Patterns	U.S. Census Bureau	http://www.census.gov/econ/cbp/index.html	Public	1977	2008	CSV and others	County/state	Total number of establishments, employment, annual payroll, NAICS or SIC classification
DARPA Budget	DARPA	http://www.darpa.mil/budget.html	Public	2000	2009	PDF	Programs—R&D	Year, program #, estimated fund
Defense Budget Materials	Department of Defense	http://www.defenselink.mil/comptroller/defbudget/fy2007/index.html	Public	1998	2009	Microsoft Excel PDF	Programs	Year, program, R&D
Deloitte Recap	Deloitte Recap	http://www.recap.com/	Commercial	N/A	N/A	N/A	Company	Products, alliances, clinical trials, patents
Dialog S&T Content	Dialog LLC	http://www.dialog.com/products/guide/science.shtml	Commercial	N/A	N/A	N/A	Various	Patents (international), trademarks, S&T breakthroughs, company profiles
DOE Patents	Department of Energy: Office of Scientific and Technical Information	http://www.osti.gov/doepatents/index.jsp	Public	N/A	N/A	Search driven	Patents	Patent #, abstract, patent application #

(continued)

Table 12.1. *(Continued)*

Database name	Name/archive	Web link	Access	Start	End	Format	Unit	Examples of variables
Google Scholar	Google Scholar	http://scholar.google.com/	Public	c. 1925	2009	Search driven	Individual publication citing work	Scholarly publications (articles, books, working papers, theses, with citations by other scholarly publications
Historical Cross-Country Technology Adoption (HCCTA) Data Set	NBER	http://www.nber.org/hccta/	Public	1788	1999	CVS Microsoft Excel	Country (year, technologies, GDP, education, etc.)	Year, country, technology adopted, education, GDP
ISI Highly Cited	Thomson/ Reuters ISI	http://isihighlycited.com/	Public	2001	2006	Search driven	Published research articles	Name, year, ISI science category, country, employment history
ISI Web of Knowledge	Thomson/ Reuters	http://apps.isiknowledge. com/	Restricted	1900	2009	Search driven	Published research articles	Authors, year, ISI science category, addresses
Kauffman Firm Survey	NORC - Enclave	http://sites.kauffman.org/ kfs/	Public	2004	2008	SAS SPSS STATA	Company	New businesses; 3-wave on FICA, legal status, # of employees, patents
Kauffman Index of Entrepreneurial Activity	Kauffman Foundation	http://www.kauffman.org/ research-and-policy/ kauffman-index-of -entrepreneurial-activity. aspx	Public	1996	2008	Microsoft Excel	Various	Entrepreneurs age & gender, industry, region
Knowledge Express	Knowledge Express	http://www.knowledgeex- press.com/	Commercial	N/A	N/A	N/A	Various	Drugs, agreements, corporate profiles, pipelines

Longitudinal Business Database	ISR - Michigan Census Research Data Center	http://www.isr.umich.edu/src/mcrdc/data.html	Restricted	1976	2001	N/A	Company	U.S. business establishments
Micro Data on Patents and Trademarks	European Policy for Intellectual Property	http://www.epip.eu/datacentre.php	Non-commercial public	1975	2008	STATA	Various	European Patent Office & U.S. granted patents, applicants names and addresses, matching to AMADEUS, U.S. trademarks
National Science Foundation Surveys of Public Attitudes Toward and Understanding of Science and Technology, 1979–2001	ICPSR	http://dx.doi.org/10.3886/ICPSR04029	Restricted	1971	2001	Text SAS SPSS	Individual	Attitudes, knowledge, policy opinions on biotech
NBER-RPI Scientific Papers Database	NBER	http://www.nber.org/RPI-sci-pap/	Restricted	1981	1999	CSV SAS STATA	Research articles published	Scientific publications, citations, Top 110 U.S. universities and Top 200 U.S. R&D firms
NIH Data Book	NIH—Report	http://www.report.nih.gov/nihdatabook/Default.aspx #15	Public	N/A	2010	Microsoft Power-Point Excel	Various	Research grants, institutions, success rates, principal investigators

(*Continued*)

Table 12.1. (*Continued*)

Database name	Name/archive	Web link	Access	Start	End	Format	Unit	Examples of variables
NIST-TIP Advanced Technology Program, ATP Business Reporting Surveys	NORC—Enclave	http://www.norc.org/DataEnclave/Datasets/NIST-TIP/NIST-TIP+Overview.htm	Restricted	2000	2004	N/A	Company	New companies funded by ATP: Variables not disclosed
NIST-TIP Advanced Technology Program, ATP Joint Venture Survey	NORC—Enclave	http://www.norc.org/DataEnclave/Datasets/NIST-TIP/NIST-TIP+Overview.htm	Restricted	N/A	N/A	N/A	JV project	Joint venture projects funded by ATP: Variables not disclosed
NSF Science and Engineering Statistics Database	NSF	http://www.nsf.gov/statistics/	Public	1951	2010	Excel PDF	Various (country, state, Organization)	Funding by agency, field, budget, function, state; university grants & R&D spending, firm R&D spending
NSF Survey of Federal Funds for Research and Development	NSF-WebCASPAR	http://webcaspar.nsf.gov/	Public	1951	2008	SAS Transport CSV	Federal agency	Agency, Year, Amount, Field, Character of work
Panel Study of Entrepreneurial Dynamics	ISR	http://www.psed.isr.umich.edu/psed/data	Public	1998	2006	SAS SPSS	Individual	Venture firms/longitudinal survey: product, perceived success, problems
Patent Lens	Patent Lens	http://www.patentlens.net/daisy/patentlens/patentlens.html	Public	N/A	N/A	Search Driven	Patent	Technology, patent #, country

Name	Source	URL	Access	Year	Year	Format	Regions/organizations	Variables
RaDIUS—RAND Database of Research & Development in the U.S.	Closed [Dr. Della-Piana at cdellapi@nsf.gov]	https://radius.rand.org/	Restricted	N/A	N/A	Search Driven	Regions/organizations	Number of Federal R&D Grants, amount of R&D Funding
RDDS Search	DARPA	http://www.dtic.mil/descriptivesum/	Public	2000	2010	Search Driven	Programs—R&D	Year, organization, cost, description
Research Portfolio On-line Reporting Tool	NIH Report	http://report.nih.gov/index.aspx	Public	2005	2010	Search driven	Various	Budget, funded organizations, categorical spending
S&E State Profiles	NSF	http://www.nsf.gov/statistics/states/	Public	1995	2007	Microsoft Excel, PDF	U.S. states	Year, # of PhDs, # of PhD awarding institutions, R&D spending
Science and Technology Pocket Data Book	NSF	http://www.nsf.gov/statistics/databook/	Public	1994	2000	PDF	Country	National R&D funding patterns, education in S&T, international R&D spending
Science and Technology-Based Economic Development Programs [United States]: A Study of Evaluation Efforts, 1996	ICPSR	http://dx.doi.org/10.3886/ICPSR02591	Restricted	1996	1996	SPSS	Programs/state	Organizational information, evaluation activities, etc.
SDC Platinum	Thomson/Reuters SDC	http://thomsonreuters.com/products_services/financial/financial_products/deal_making/investment_banking/sdc	Commercial	1985	2010	N/A	Transactions	New issues, M&A, poison pills, etc. [firm, year, etc.]

(Continued)

Table 12.1. *(Continued)*

Database name	Name/archive	Web link	Access	Start	End	Format	Unit	Examples of variables
Small Business Administration TECH-Net	Small Business Administration	http://tech-net.sba.gov/tech-net/public/dsp_search.cfm	Public	1983 (1998 STTR)	2010	Search Driven	SBIR (SME alone) or STTR (SME + university) Grant	Recipient firm info, abstract, funding, expected results for both; research partner also information for STTR
SOI Tax Stats—Corporation Tax Statistics	IRS	http://www.irs.gov/taxstats/bustaxstats/article/0,,id=97145,00.html	Public	1980	2002	Microsoft Excel	Industry sectors	# of businesses, total receipts, net income, form of business
Survey of Earned Doctorates	NSF	http://www.nsf.gov/statistics/srvydoctorates/	Public-Org. Restricted-Individuals	1966	2006	N/A	Organization Individual	Doctorates, field, sex, ethnicity, country of origin, years taken, etc.]
U.S. Patent Citations Data File	NBER	http://www.nber.org/patents/	Public	1963	1999	SAS CSV	Patent	All utility patents, citations, broad match to Compustat, S&T areas
U.S. Patent Full-Text and Full-Page Image Databases	USPTO	http://patft.uspto.gov/	Public	1790	2010	Text Graphic images	Patent	Patent number, category, year, claims

Table 12.2. Selected science and technology databases: Emerging technologies

Database name	Name/archive	Web link	Access	Start	End	Format	Unit	Examples of variables
BIOPHARMA	BIOPHARMA	http://www.biopharma.com/	Commercial	1934	2009	Search Driven	Product/Company	Price, technology used
BioScan	Closed	On floppy disk	Commercial	1982	2001	Search Driven	Company	Products, alliances, history
GenBank*	NCBI/NLM/NIH	http://www.ncbi.nlm.nih.gov/sites/entrez?db=nucleotide	Public	1969	2009	Search Driven	Research article - published	Year, author, journal name, location (submitting author), nucleotide sequences linked to DNA, protein sequences & structure
GenETHX	Georgetown UNRSBL	http://bioethics.georgetown.edu/databases/GenETHX/gene.htm	Public	N/A	2009	Search Driven	Documents	Year, abstract, source
Key Biotech Indicators in OECD Member /Non-Member Countries	OECD	http://www.oecd.org/document/30/0,3343,en_2649_34537_40146462_1_1_1,00.html	Public	Varies	Varies	Text	Country	# of companies, R&D expenditures, patents, public R&D expenditures
Environment, Health and Safety Research	Wilson Center for Scholars	http://www.nanotechproject.org/inventories/ehs/search/	Public	1972	2008	Search Driven	Research Project	Abstract, principal investigator, funding source, country
ETHXWeb	Georgetown U–NRSBL	http://bioethics.georgetown.edu/databases/ETHXWeb/basice.htm	Public	N/A	2009	Search Driven	Documents	Year, abstract, source

(Continued)

Table 12.2. *(Continued)*

Database name	Name/archive	Web link	Access	Start	End	Format	Unit	Examples of variables
Inventory of Agrifood Nanotechnology	Wilson Center for Scholars	http://www.nanotechpro-ject.org/inventories/agrifood/	Public	2000	2005	Microsoft Access	Research Project	Abstract, principal investigator, technique, sector
nano EHS Virtual Journal	ICON/Rice University	http://icon.rice.edu/virtualjournal.cfm	Public	1962	2010	Search Driven	Research article - published	Environment, health & safety (EHS) impact of nanotech
Nano Particle Library	NIOSH–NIL	http://nanoparticlelibrary.net/index.asp	Public	N/A	2010	Search Driven	Research article - published	Interactive report generator. Abstract, author, element, structure, exposure pathway, risk exposure group
Nano Particle Library	NIOSH–NIL	http://nanoparticlelibrary.net/index.asp	Public	N/A	2010	Search Driven	Research article	Abstract, author, element, structure
Nanobank—Documenting Nanoscience & Technology	NanoBank.org	http://www.nanobank.org/	Public to non-profits	1976	2006	N/A	Country/Organization/Individual	Articles, patents, grants, linked by organization IDs, geographic IDs, year; authors, inventors & PIs, title, abstract
NanoEthicsBank	NanoEthics-Bank	http://ethics.iit.edu/NanoEthicsBank/index.php	Public	1986	2008	Search Driven	Document	Research articles, gov't. reports, technical standards [year, author, abstract, URL, etc.]

Name	ID	URL	Access			Type	Content	Fields
Nanomedicine Publications	Nanomedicine Research	http://www.nano-biology.net/literature.php	Public	N/A	2010	Search Driven	Research article - published	Year, author, abstract, journal name
Nanotechnology Database	Nanotechnology Database	http://www.wtec.org/loyola/nanobase/oldwelcome4.htm	Public	N/A	N/A	Search Driven	Organization	Type, contact info
Publication Search	IOM–SAFENANO	http://www.safenano.org/AdvancedSearch.aspx	Public	N/A	2010	Search Driven	Documents	Year, abstract, source
Virtual Journal of Nanoscale Science & Technology	VJNano	http://www.vjnano.org/	Public	2000	2010	Search Driven	Research article published	Year, author, title, location of each author, abstract, category of nano-science, links to article if subscriber
Virtual Journal of Biological Physics Research	VJBioPhysRes	http://vjbio.aip.org/bio/	Public	2000	2010	Search Driven	Research article published	Year, author, title, location of each author, abstract, category of nano-science, links to article if subscriber
Virtual Journal of Quantum Information	VJQuantInfo	http://vjquantuminfo.aip.org/quantuminfo/	Public	2001	2010	Search Driven	Research article published	Year, author, title, location of each author, abstract, category of nano-science, links to article if subscriber
Virtual Journal of Ultrafast Science	VJUltrafast	http://vjultrafast.aip.org/ultrafast/	Public	2001	2010	Search Driven	Research article published	Year, author, title, location of each author, abstract, category of nano-science, links to article if subscriber

In contrast, to receive competitive funding, university-built databases are more likely to have an explicit model, including both research and policy impacts, before funding is received. We take strategy (commercial) and policy (nonprofit) as two sides of the same coin requiring the identification of critical points or levers to make a significant difference in innovation and in desired outcomes, and strong priors based on earlier empirical evidence on the causal path from lever to innovation and outcome.

As we will consider in more detail in the next section, if the model of innovation and impacts selected is static, then some of the potential policy levers will disappear. For example, the flow of knowledge from discovering scientists and their institutions to other scientists/institutions often enables entry into a new technology area, so policy levers associated with this transfer may often be critical ones. Most databases, however, fail to measure this important set of links. The model underlying the database guides the kinds of data included and the connections made within the data elements. Jaffe's points in this book about the need to study the innovation system as an integrated set of processes and structures support the importance of an explicit model underlying a database. Since many of the databases are driven by the administrative needs of a large government agency, data in one database may be mission defined and not integrated with other data to form a more comprehensive and flexible data system. One of the databases currently under construction, the STAR database, has as its major goal the integration of these and other data and goes a long way to fulfilling Jaffe's outline. The STAR database, with its crosscutting IDs for organizations and persons, will provide a rich data source for network analysis and studies of regional technology clusters.

2. Models of Innovation and Impacts as Database Guides

The main challenge for a robust evidence-based platform for science policy is to capture and link innovation to impacts related to it. No one database can do it all, but with links to impacts even a relatively narrowly focused database can be very valuable. The standard model focuses on innovations close to the commercialization process, following Griliches [5] in relying primarily on patent data [6–8]. This approach has developed excellent public databases focused on the patent-related aspects of the innovation process, and more recently on impacts for public firms [9]. Innovations in basic science have also been estimated in economic growth equations [10], and science explored in other ways as well (see Paula Stephan's excellent review [11]). These studies taken as a whole have become standard setting for later work that builds on these shoulders of giants. These standard models are less helpful, however, when change is radical and fast moving, as it often is for basic science-driven paradigm shifts with strong new enabling technology, such as new tools—gene sequencers, scanning probe microscopes, and atomic force microscopes—in biotechnology and nanotechnology, respectively [12, 13]. (For an early example of an invention of a method of inventing that is not tool driven, see Griliches [14].)

When innovation is radical, archetypically when driven by breakthrough discoveries in basic science, the change in the underlying knowledge base is a jump process, where science can cumulatively develop for variable lengths of time before a breakthrough occurs [15]. Science and technology advances during the cumulative period will be reasonably linear, but there will often be a clear discontinuity when the breakthrough occurs, followed by explosive growth—in the science itself, in the birth of new firms, in the growth of new jobs, and in new university centers, institutes, and academic departments. Depending on the degree of discontinuity with prior knowledge and the breadth of the breakthrough, replacement of old industry with new follows [4], given appropriability and opportunity [16].

To explain science-driven change, a new model of knowledge flow and capture by the scientists making breakthrough discoveries in science occur has been developed. This model has also been extended to explain the subsequent impact of these star scientists on the formation and success of new firms and the resulting metamorphic industry change. We briefly summarize it here.

The importance and visibility of the flow of knowledge from science to industry are primarily due to the importance of the de facto intellectual property rights inhering in the *natural excludability* of highly tacit and initially scarce knowledge that accompanies most breakthroughs [3, 17]. This occurs when the discovery—especially an "invention of a method of discovery" [14]—is sufficiently costly to transfer due to its complexity or tacitness [18–21] that the information can effectively be used only by employing those scientists in whom it is embodied.

De facto rights are not generally part of case law or professional canons but, rather, form automatic natural barriers to knowledge transmission, often reinforcing social boundaries around the new knowledge as well. *Natural excludability* enables the effective capture of rights by the discovering scientist; secrecy may extend and reinforce these rights. Holding constant the value of the knowledge, natural excludability significantly slows the diffusion of knowledge through knowledge capture by the discovering scientist. Even after the discoveries begin to be more widely known, the amount of background tacit knowledge required to use them successfully often bars those not directly working with a discovering scientist from entering the research or application area [22], and may extinguish the area completely if those who can transmit leave it before doing so [23]. To apply the knowledge codified in a patent often requires the participation of the discovering scientist, such that successful university patent licensing requires participation of the inventing scientist 71 percent of the time (reported in Jensen and Thursby [24] and Thursby and Thursby [25]).

Technological opportunity and appropriability—the principal factors that drive technical progress for industries [16, 26]—are also the two necessary elements that created extraordinary value for our stars' intellectual human capital during the formative period in two emerging technologies that we have studied in detail, biotechnology and nanotechnology. When the new techniques have diffused widely, access to stars is less essential, but once the technology has been commercialized in specific locales, internal dynamics of agglomeration tend to keep it there [27–30].

There is no inevitability about the virtuous circles that drive this process, and thus few countries have the conditions under which these processes operate unfettered, and some areas within countries are also better able to take advantage of these opportunities [31–35]. Much work remains to be done to specify these conditions in a more general and fundamental way, but we lay out here the key elements, based on our understanding, that have made the U.S. system work so well.

Figure 12.1.
Flows of break-through knowledge and finance in the U.S. National Innovation System.

Figure 12.1 provides a schematic of the U.S. national innovation system. As with any evolutionary survivor, it works well not because of any particular feature but because of the way many parts work together—including redun-

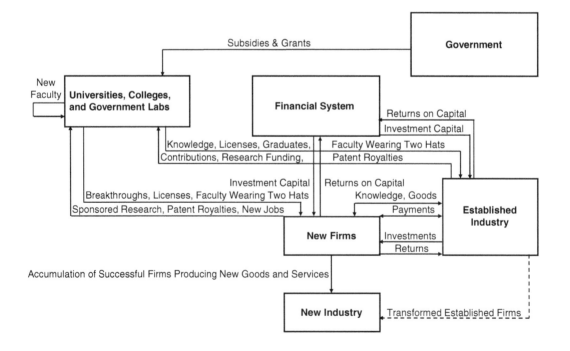

dant means of accomplishing a given end. First, we should note that besides its background role in establishing and enforcing the rules of the game, the government sector is not really necessary for innovation in the form of gradual within-industry improvement of processes (inching up or perfective technological progress), nor are universities and government laboratories, except for their general educational function for the workforce. Innovation could, and often does, occur entirely within the private sector, typically being internally financed in established firms or via venture capital and ultimately public offerings for new firms. Indeed, the majority of firms in most industries at any given time achieve only perfective technological progress, gradually improving the way things are done, entirely through internal industrial efforts [2, 4].

Metamorphic progress, which drives very rapid growth in a few companies in a few industries, may also occur within existing firms or as a result of an invention made by an individual or a small group already employed in industry that starts up a new firm. The federal government's ongoing investment in basic research at the great research universities does, however, lead sometimes to exploitable opportunities that can only be grasped and brought to success by great, discovering scientists until the ideas have been codified and diffused. The star scientists are needed because others lack the necessary competency.

This brings us to the two important 1980 institutional changes: the Bayh-Dole Act and the U.S. Supreme Court ruling upholding the patenting of living organisms and parts created by genetic engineering. The latter ruling simplified the protection of biotechnology inventions, particularly in the pharmaceutical industry, and made it easier to obtain venture capital and then public financing of firms not expected to show a profit for ten to fifteen years if they were successful. The Bayh-Dole Act established that federal contractors had the right and duty to patent inventions and to exploit them commercially or license others to do so. Furthermore, the inventors were to receive at least 20 percent of the resulting royalties. Currently, the market rate for university inventors averages between 40 and 50 percent, with wide variability across campuses [36].

The Bayh-Dole Act was meant to ensure that inventions in the space program would be exploited instead of put into the public domain, where no firm had an incentive to invest in reducing them to practice. The universities supported the act's passage because it greatly reduced their cost of patenting federally supported inventions by eliminating the need for case-by-case applications and lobbying for waivers required to do so. Because it established a national policy of patenting results as in the public interest, it legitimated a practice that many academics frowned upon, reducing the burden on academic scientists whose inventions were patented. It also provided the inventors with a financial incentive to try to find a firm that would license their invention or start one themselves if need be.

The coincidence between the Bayh-Dole Act and the biotechnology revolution provided the seedbed for development of the high-science firm built around a cadre of university scientists. The pioneers of this new institutional form transformed the pharmaceutical industry and its methods of drug discovery. Similar firms have since driven applications in fields as diverse as lasers and nanotechnology. Licensing the university patents is often used to nail down the preliminary property rights required to obtain venture financing. The cost of licensing is likely to be reasonable, as there are generally no takers other than the one recruited or founded by the inventor(s). The new firm or new laboratory of an established firm might be located within the vicinity of the star's university laboratory or might lie on the commuting route, thereby facilitating extra hours of work. Because even tenured professors have a role between independent contractors and full-time employees, they are generally free to sell or use their three summer months and a reasonable amount of school year time. Reasonable is often undefined, but one or even two weekdays and one or two weekend days would typically be tolerated by a university in the case of a productive professor who is seen at the university frequently, goes to lunch with departmental colleagues, and meets his or her classes. Work done on company property and recorded in notarized laboratory notebooks is patented by the firm typically without additional compensation to the university.

Thus a star scientist can keep his or her position at the university and all of the associated research support and access yet can actively participate as a principal in a new firm formed to exploit a line of work begun on campus. The majority of the returns—if there were any, the costs of research often being prodigious—accrue to the founders and investors in the firm, including a number of graduate students who can become millionaires by investing sweat capital and receiving part of their pay as shares or stock options. Most star scientists do not follow this path, but many do. This is the story of the American biotech industry, and it seems to be the template for many applications of nanotechnology. Stars have multiple motives and do not have to choose one, since the actions implied by each are largely congruent.

Following the rapid growth period after a breakthrough, either there is a slowdown or the next major innovation takes place, with the associated jump process related to it. The jump process itself is often initially driven by a few scientists, most often highly creative and productive scientists we have termed star scientists. The sharp discontinuity of a breakthrough is mirrored in the larger size of stock price jumps experienced by star-guided firms as the outcomes of their research programs are learned [15].

3. What Existing S&T Databases Deliver

Databases on the micro level, not aggregated to current S&T areas or industries, and enabled to track both science and its commercial application, are needed to explore the jump processes of scientific breakthroughs and their impacts. But as we can see in Table 12.1, databases are typically integrated only across a scientific (bibliometric) domain or a commercial domain, and even within these domains the integration is often limited to a very small number of different substantive areas. While we can characterize some of the databases as innovation or outcome oriented, the problem we face is that many of the major data elements, such as patents, are used in some research as inputs to the innovation process, and in other research as outputs. It is this kind of relationship among data elements, among others, that led to the development of the virtuous circles model in Figure 12.1.

A wide range of U.S. and international panel or cross-sectional databases is summarized in Table 12.1. One of the better-linked databases, the National Bureau of Economic Research (NBER) U.S. Patent Citations Data File (public), links Compustat data on stock-exchange-listed U.S. companies with U.S. patents. This link provides a connection between patents, considered to be both an output of the innovation system and an input into commercialization, with extensive financial outcome data. The SDC Platinum™ (commercial) focuses on financial market transactions, that is, on the financial outcomes of scientific discoveries and inventions that survive to receive financial market funding, from venture capital to one of the major stock exchanges. It links the companies across a variety of different types of transactions, including venture capital financing, merger and acquisition, and joint ventures and alliances. Thomson Reuters also maintains two citation-oriented bibliographic databases to track the scientific literature and its citation process over time. One is ISI (Institute for Scientific Information) Highly Cited, a public database that covers the top scientists defined by citation counts; the other is ISI Web of Knowledge (commercial); neither database is integrated with SDC data, despite the fact that all three are owned by the same parent company.

Within databases in Table 12.1, links to other parts of the innovation system are rare to nonexistent. Only occasionally are the data in a form that encourages linking with outside data sources, with an exemplar again the NBER links with U.S. patents and the Compustat-using source IDs as well as internal links within their database. This work is standard setting, and we all benefit tremendously from these labors that began early when little was in electronic form.

If the data were linked among the data sets in Table 12.1, then, where possible, we would have a database enabled to answer the basic policy questions about interrelation among resources put into science and innovation and the impacts of these systems. Without this integration, which requires considerable resources to accomplish and cooperation across many separate entities, policymakers—and individual research projects—do and redo this integration to address specific policy-relevant (and theory-driven) questions.

Because of the mixed public and commercial origin of these databases, with many of the impact-related databases commercially produced, the resulting merged databases often contain limited-use data that are bound by the licensing agreement of the specific commercial vendor. Making aggregated subsets available will in some cases be allowed, but that is of marginal utility to the policymaker and researcher when the question changes and a new underlying data set must be constructed from the micro level. Thus the obstacles are not readily resolved to enable more sharing in the scientific community of the fruits of individual scientific labor, nor are we very close to having an integrated database of the type we need to drive policy, one that can readily and flexibly assess the science and innovation system in relation to its impacts.

In this section, we have raised some questions about what we see as major blocks to further development of truly useful and available databases. First is access, since many of the databases are restricted or expensive to license, blocking out many researchers and policymakers. They are also very expensive to create and maintain, such that unless they serve an agency mission, they may disappear at some point when budgets are cut. Development of databases takes an enormous amount of resources and effort, limiting the size that may automatically limit the data included in it. The kind of integrated data structure pictured in Figure 12.1, then, is very difficult to reach in any truly comprehensive fashion, given the way that funds are allocated to those investigators constructing the databases. The method (or methods) of integration needs to be shared and built in, preferably published to the Web. A federally supported data infrastructure would resolve many of these problems by creating standards, providing access to researchers, and supporting the infrastructure over the long run.

4. Emerging Technologies Databases

Why include emerging technologies? Emerging technologies are typically subsets of general science and technology databases, rolled in with broader areas and not identified separately. For standard models, rolling emerging technologies into overall data reflects the understanding that similar processes operate throughout. However, the jump processes involved in major breakthroughs, as we discussed earlier, we believe involve different processes, or at least have some processes that are significantly more important in the emerging area than in established areas that would be obscured or blurred when not identified separately. Identification in the overall databases is preferred, since it readily allows comparisons between the standard model and the accelerated model typical of breakthroughs with strong enabling technologies. In practice, probably in part because of the overall effort involved in collecting data and in determining reasonable boundaries of a new technology, databases typically contain one emerging technology.

Isolating technologies by considering single technology areas or by using measures that are seldom or never used for established technology areas makes comparisons across emerging industries as well as comparisons to established industries difficult and in some cases impossible. How can we increase comparability? In building the STAR database, we tackled some of these issues. First, one has to sacrifice some precision, some better measures, to make one area comparable to another. While we think discoveries rather than citations to articles is a better measure of the kind and amount of knowledge held by a scientist about a breakthrough, we can't find a way to make the discoveries in nanotechnology comparable to biotechnology, let alone compare across multiple high-technology areas.

Also, data on a new technology area are often highly perishable, as they get overwritten as the industry develops. So it is extraordinarily important to gather the information early and often, but it isn't possible to do this kind of intensive data collection across all industries, or even for too large a subset. This leads to one-off databases that can't be replicated in other science/industry areas.

Table 12.2 provides some examples of databases focused on emerging technologies; we overrepresent the nanotechnology area because there are so many public websites available. Many of these will probably be ephemeral and disappear when their funding ends or when faculty responsible for their creation go on to other topics. In biotechnology, most of the websites and published directories disappeared over time, even commercial ones. Industry data fared especially poorly in being retained; the European Union (EU) Biotechnology Archive has been unable to collect copies of many of the databases it knew had been created. Other data might have been lost as costs of maintaining and updating increased dramatically. For example, GenBank is now maintained and updated by the National Library of Medicine's National Center for Biotechnology Information, moving from a commercial product of Intelligenetics. GenBank was initially created at Los Alamos in a National Science Foundation (NSF)-funded research project.

With emerging industries especially, as the data become more micro level, new information is revealed about the organization of its commercialization.

Using ISI Thomson Reuters data, we can see that subunits of a company, as well as locations, become revealed as we move from the enterprise level to the local establishment, as shown in Table 12.3. Data at the establishment level are particularly revealing of the range of industries and related products in which the company is operating. It is possible to examine local concentration around particular subtechnologies if you cumulate across companies, producing finer data than available from most other sources. For public companies, some of these data are reasonably available, but for start-ups and other privately held companies, there is often considerable less information, providing especially important data about breakthrough areas of technology where the range of applications isn't well known.

The detailed data illustrated in Table 12.3 raise a number of challenges for the researcher and for potential policy uses of the data. To begin with, it suggests a more micro level of analysis that both provides more understanding of the underlying technology and its nuances and provides a challenge to our standard ways of classifying industry, and, to some extent, also of classifying firms. Taxonomic assignment to an industry won't be very satisfying to the research once these micro-level results are in, since such assignment will gloss over many of the nuances of industry location, including multi-industry relevance that will make standard analysis difficult.

At the same time, databases that provide important micro-level detail add to our knowledge and understanding of the innovation process and its outcomes, serving as a detector of subareas, of diversification, and of technology localization, drawing from the examples in Table 12.3. Perhaps it will be important to fund analyses at a number of levels of aggregation, and across a wide assembly of measures.

5. Accessible Policy Guidance from Graphic Links Between S&T and Impacts

Some with much Washington, D.C., experience suggest that data are viewed as the plural of anecdote. Much policy is based on individual cases that are vivid, and also may involve in-person testimony to Congress. It is difficult to envision replacing this system with a complex database that requires programmer interface and running regressions. A series of graphs or other visual tools will make more sense in a hectic environment where information coming in needs to be very clear, direct, and transparent.

How much is a graph worth? It may be priceless when communicating with policy audiences and the general public, because it holds one's attention better than the same concepts and results expressed in words. Some can be

Table 12.3. Enterprise and establishment lists built from legacy databases: Ten selected examples of name and location variations

Enterprise preferred name: CHIRON CORPORATION

Establishment name in record	City	State	Country
CHIRON CORP.	EMERYVILLE	CA	USA
Chiron Inc.	La Jolla	CA	USA
Chiron Viagene	San Diego	CA	USA
Chiron Vaccines	Emeryville	CA	USA
Chiron Vaccines	Siena		ITALY
CHIRON BEHRING	MARBURG		GERMANY
CHIRON DIAGNOST.	CERGY		FRANCE
CHIRON DIAGNOST.	ALAMEDA	CA	USA
CHIRON GRP.	WASHINGTON	DC	USA
CHIRON MIMOTOPES PTY. LTD.	CLAYTON		AUSTRALIA

Enterprise preferred name: GENENTECH INC.

Establishment name in record	City	State	Country
GENENTECH	SAN FRANCISCO	CA	USA
GENENTECH	SAN FRANCISCO	CA	USA
GENENTECH	Atlanta	GA	USA
Genentech Pharmaceut. Inc.	San Francisco	CA	USA
Dep't. Mol. Oncol. Genentech Inc.	San Francisco	CA	USA
GENENTECH FDN. GROWTH & DEV.	CHARLOTTESVILLE	VA	USA
Genentech Inc. Labs	San Francisco	CA	USA
GENENTECH CORP.	SAN FRANCISCO	CA	USA
Biostat Genentech Inc.	San Francisco	CA	USA
Genentech BioOncol. Inc.	San Francisco	CA	USA

Enterprise preferred name: INTEL CORPORATION

Establishment name in record	City	State	Country
INTEL	PALO ALTO	CA	USA
Intel Israel	Haifa		Israel
Intel Res.	Berkeley	CA	USA
Intel Corp.	Austin	TX	USA
INTEL CORP.	SANTA CLARA	CA	USA
Intel Corp.	Cambridge		England
Intel Prod. Shanghai Ltd.	Shanghai		Peoples R. China
Intel Technol. Philippines Inc.	Cavite		Philippines
Intel Technol. Sdn. Bhd.	George town		Malaysia
Intel Co.	Hillsboro	OR	Ireland

Enterprise preferred name: SONY CORPORATION

Establishment name in record	City	State	Country
SONY CO. LTD.	TOKYO		JAPAN
SONY ELECTR. INC.	San Jose	CA	USA
Sony Elect.	San Jose	CA	USA
SONY RES. CTR.	YOKOHAMA		JAPAN
Sony Comp. Entertainment	Tokyo		Japan
Sony Semicond. Corp.	San Antonio	TX	USA
SONY Int. Europe GmbH	Stuttgart		Germany
Sony Mus. Entertainment Inc.	New York	NY	USA
Sony Pictures Imageworks	Culver City	CA	USA
SONY BROADCASTING PROD. CO.	TEANECK	NJ	USA

especially effective summaries of the main points. We present three figures here to illustrate our point and encourage you to visit the ICON Rice website (http://icon.rice.edu/centersand inst/icon/report.cfm) for an excellent example of a Web-based tool that can quickly produce graphs of different relations among the key elements of research articles on nano environment, health, and safety.

Evidence of the special role that star scientists play in shaping the formation and transformation of biotechnology-using industries, independently from their potentially separable research discoveries, is shown in Figure 12.2 (adapted from Zucker, Darby, and Armstrong [37]).

This figure illustrates the finding that star articles are a much stronger indicator of firm success than are popular alternatives, such as all firm articles coauthored with top research university faculty members or venture capital funding. Audretsch and Stephan had analyzed the locational patterns of university scientists appearing in the prospectuses of biotechnology firms going public in March 1990 and November 1992, many of whom overlapped with our set of stars [38]. In recent work we show that firms with deeper star involvement do go public significantly more quickly than other biotech firms,

Figure 12.2.
Success of U.S. biotech firms by ties to star scientists, links to top-112 research-university faculty, and venture-capital funding levels.
Source: L. Zucker and M. Darby (2007), p. 452.

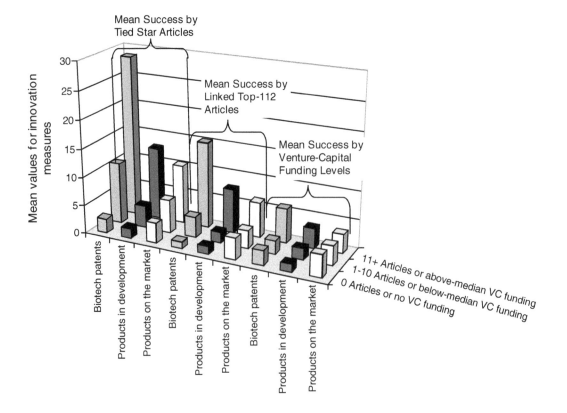

implying that the characteristics described by Audretsch and Stephan differed systematically from the entire population of firms running the risk of going public [34].

Figure 12.3 compares cumulative active star years (stars in light color) and firm entry (circles in black) in the United States and in the world for biology, chemistry, and medicine (taken from Zucker and Darby 2006).

Figure 12.3.
Biology/chemistry/medicine star scientists and firm entry, U.S. regions and top-25 science and technology countries, 1981–2004.
Source: L. Zucker and M. Darby (2006).

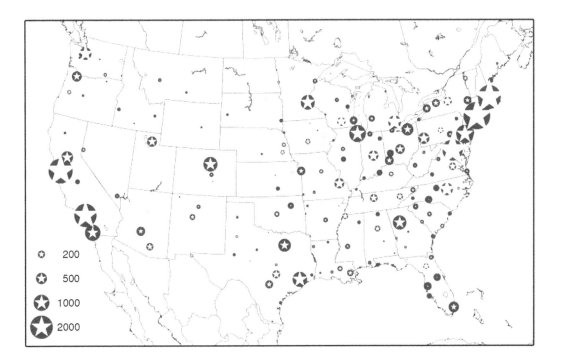

Note the correspondence between the cumulative active stars and cumulative firm entry. The size of the stars and circles indicate the numbers of each, but note the change in scale in moving from the upper to lower panel of Figure 12.3.

It is important to emphasize the general results as well: the number of star scientists and engineers active in a region or country has positive (with one exception) and generally significant effects on the probability of a firm entering in all six science and technology areas. These effects are numerically substantial, as illustrated in Figure 12.4 (taken from Zucker and Darby [39]). These results are even stronger if the analysis is restricted to the first third of the stars who met a higher ISI hurdle than required of later selectees.

In conclusion, there are a large number of science policy relevant databases, most Web deployed and many public. These riches are diminished by failing to identify critical points or levers that might make a significant difference in innovation and desired outcomes. It is rare to have both innovation and outcome data in the same database, and when both are available, they are seldom linked in ways that would be useful as a base for empirically based policy. There are more databases built around the standard model of innovation processes and impacts, though emerging areas in science and technology are becoming better represented.

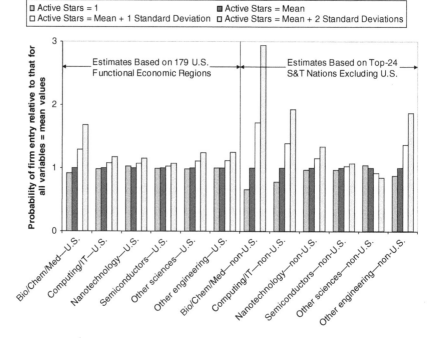

Figure 12.4.
Star scientists and engineers increase the probability of firm entry into new technologies: Relative probabilities with different numbers of active stars, all other variables = mean values.
Source: L. Zucker and M. Darby (2006).

Micro-level data can often be quite valuable, especially for emerging industries, increasing significantly the amount of data available, and can also allow internal linking more often, especially if links to external data sources are also included. Graphical illustration of key aspects of science and technology impacts, with wider policy audience, leads to a more empirically guided policy. Looking forward, policy decisions will improve with better-grounded information on which to make a decision. It decisively moves away from the one-case approach. While improving information on which decisions are made, database-derived visual results in no way presume a particular outcome. Rather, different parts of the information, say, emphasizing scientific productivity more than its commercial output, will certainly be weighted differentially by different stakeholders. In this way, those who prepare and present the information don't unduly influence decisions but simply provide a better context for making excellent decisions that will have a positive and beneficial result in science and technology.

Acknowledgments

We acknowledge outstanding research assistance by Nahoko Kameo. This research has been supported by grants from the Ewing Marion Kauffman Foundation and the National Science Foundation (Grant SES-0830983). Certain data included herein are derived from the *High Impact Papers, Science Citation Index Expanded, U.S. State Indicators,* and *U.S. University Indicators* of the Institute for Scientific Information®, Inc. (ISI®), Philadelphia, Pennsylvania, © Copyright Institute for Scientific Information,® Inc., 2000–2004. All rights reserved. This chapter is a part of the NBER's research program in productivity. The views expressed herein are those of the authors and not necessarily those of their funders, employers, or the National Bureau of Economic Research.

References

[1]   M. Delapierre, B. Madeuf, A. Savoy. NTBFs—The French Case. Research Policy, 6;1998;989–1003.

[2]   A. Harberger. A Vision of the Growth Process. American Economic Review, 88; 1998;1–32.

[3]   L. Zucker, M. Darby. Star Scientists and Institutional Transformation: Patterns of Invention and Innovation in the Formation of the Biotechnology Industry. Proceedings of the National Academy of Sciences, 93;1996;12709–12716.

[4]   M. Darby, L. Zucker. Growing by Leaps and Inches: Creative Destruction, Real Cost Reduction, and Inching Up. Economic Inquiry, 2003;1–19.

[5]   Z. Griliches. Patent Statistics as Economic Indicators: A Survey. Journal of Eco-
      nomic Literature, 28;1990;1661–1707.

[6]   A. Jaffe. Real Effects of Academic Research. American Economic Review, 79;1989;
      957–970.

[7]   A. Jaffe, M. Trajtenberg, R. Henderson. Geographic Localization of Knowledge
      Spillovers as Evidenced by Patent Citations. Quarterly Journal of Economics,
      63;1993;577–598.

[8]   R. Henderson, A. Jaffe, M. Trajtenberg. Universities as a Source of Commercial
      Technology: A Detailed Analysis of University Patenting 1965–1988. Review of
      Economics and Statistics, 80;1998;119–127.

[9]   B. Hall, A. Jaffe, M. Trajtenberg. Market Value and Patent Citations. Rand Jour-
      nal of Economics, 36;2005;16–38.

[10] J. Adams. Fundamental Stocks of Knowledge and Productivity Growth. Journal
      of Political Economy, 98;1990;673–702.

[11] P. Stephan. The Economics of Science. Journal of Economic Literature, 34;1996;
      1199–1235.

[12] M. Darby, L. Zucker. Grilichesian Breakthroughs: Inventions of Methods of In-
      venting in Nanotechnology and Biotechnology. Annales d'Economie et Statis-
      tique, 79/80;2005;143–164.

[13] D. Baird. Thing Knowledge: A Philosophy of Scientific Instruments. Berkeley:
      University of California Press; 2004.

[14] Z. Griliches. Hybrid Corn: An Exploration in the Economics of Technological
      Change. Econometrics, 25;1957;501–522.

[15] M. Darby, Q. Liu, L. Zucker. High Stakes in High Technology: High-Tech Market
      Values as Options. Economic Inquiry, 42;2004;351–369.

[16] A. Klevorick, R. Levin, R. Nelson, S. Winter. On the Sources and Significance of
      Interindustry Differences in Technological Opportunities. Research Policy, 24;
      1995;185–205.

[17] L. Zucker, M. Darby. De facto and Deeded Intellectual Property Rights. Annales
      d'Economie et Statistique. Forthcoming.

[18] R. Nelson, S. Winter. An Evolutionary Theory of Economic Change. Cambridge
      (MA): Harvard University Press; 1982.

[19] N. Rosenberg. Inside the Black Box: Technology and Economics. Cambridge:
      Cambridge University Press; 1982.

[20] K. Arrow. Economic Welfare and the Allocation of Resources for Invention. In:
      R. R. Nelson (Ed.), The Rate and Direction of Inventive Activity: Economic and
      Social Factors. Princeton (NJ): Princeton University Press; 1962, pp. 609–626.

[21] K. Arrow. The Limits of Organization. New York: W.W. Norton; 1974.

[22] H. Garfinkel. Studies in Ethnomethodology. Englewood Cliffs (NJ): Prentice
      Hall; 1967.

[23] D. MacKenzie, G. Spinardi. Tacit Knowledge, Weapons Design, and the Unin-
      vention of Nuclear Weapons. American Journal of Sociology, 101;1995;44–99.

[24] R. Jensen, M. Thursby. Proofs and Prototypes for Sale: The Tale of University
      Licensing. American Economic Review, 91;2001;240–250.

[25] J. Thursby, M. Thursby. Who Is Selling the Ivory Tower? Sources of Growth in University Licensing. Management Science, 48;2002;90–104.

[26] R. Nelson, E. Wolff. Factors Behind Cross-Industry Differences in Technical Progress. New York: New York University; 1992.

[27] G. Grossman, E. Helpman. Innovation and Growth in the Global Economy. Cambridge (MA): MIT Press; 1991.

[28] A. Marshall. Principles of Economics. 8th ed. London: Macmillan; 1920.

[29] D. Audretsch, M. Feldman. R&D Spillovers and the Geography of Innovation and Production. American Economic Review, 86;1996;630–640.

[30] K. Head, J. Ries, D. Swenson. Agglomeration Benefits and Location Choice: Evidence from Japanese Manufacturing Investment in the United States, NBER Working Paper. Cambridge (MA): NBER; 1994.

[31] P. Cooke. Regional Innovation Systems, Clusters, and the Knowledge Economy. Industrial and Corporate Change, 10;2001;945–974.

[32] P. Cooke. Globalisation of Bioregions: The Rise of Knowledge Capability, Receptivity & Diversity. Cardiff, Wales: Centre for Advanced Studies; 2004.

[33] P. Cooke. Rational Drug Design, the Knowledge Value Chain and Bioscience Megacentres. Cambridge Journal of Economics, 29;2005;325–341.

[34] M. Darby, L. Zucker. Real Effects of Knowledge Capital on Going Public and Market Valuation. In: N. Lamoreaux, K. Sokoloff (Eds.), Financing Innovation in the United States, 1870 to the Present. Cambridge (MA): MIT Press; 2007, pp. 433–467.

[35] R. Nelson, N. Rosenberg. Technical Innovation and National Systems. In: R. R. Nelson (Ed.), National Innovation Systems: A Comparative Analysis. Oxford: Oxford University Press; 1993.

[36] S. Lach, M. Schankerman. Incentives and Invention in Universities. Rand Journal of Economics, 29;2008;403–433.

[37] L. Zucker, M. Darby, J. Armstrong. Commercializing Knowledge: University Science, Knowledge Capture, and Firm Performance in Biotechnology. Management Science, 48;2002;138–153.

[38] D. Audretsch, P. Stephan. Company-Scientist Locational Links: The Case of Biotechnology. American Economic Review, 86;1996;641–652.

[39] L. Zucker, M. Darby. Movement of Star Scientists and Engineers and High-Tech Firm Entry, NBER Working Paper. Cambridge (MA): NBER; 2006.

13

A Vision of Data and Analytics for the Science of Science Policy

Jim Thomas and Susan Albers Mohrman

1. Introduction

This chapter will examine and provide examples of the kinds of data and analytical capabilities that should underpin the science of science policy (SOSP). We view policy as a purposeful intervention into a complex global science and innovation system. The quality of policy decisions is defined as their effectiveness in achieving the purposes they are intended to achieve. Data and analytical capabilities must be capable of illuminating the dynamics of the science system within its broader context to yield knowledge that can be incorporated into the policy-making process and improve the quality of policy decisions. Policy formulation and implementation are inherently social processes. The policies that are formed are human artifacts that have both intended and unintended impacts on society. The science of science policy should not stop at providing academic understanding but, rather, should contribute knowledge that is useful to and used in the formulation of policy.

In this chapter we first outline some important attributes of the practice of science and the practice of policy formulation that will guide an admittedly aspirational vision of the data and analytical tools and methodologies to support the science of science policy and contribute to enhanced policy-making capabilities. We then depict the complex system in which policymakers operate and illustrate how and where connecting the policy-making process to relevant knowledge can result in more informed policy formulation. We also acknowledge the role and limits of data and analysis in formulating good policy, and the implications of such limitations for the science of science policy. Finally, we draw implications for the kind of research that will be useful as part of a science of science policy.

2. Relevant Attributes of the Knowledge Domain of a Science of Science Policy

Science Occurs in a Complex System. We share the view articulated by Powell, Owen-Smith, and Smith-Doerr in this volume that science is a complex system and that science knowledge advances globally through communication networks in which knowledge is generated, shared, and combined to yield incremental and discontinuous advances in basic understanding and applied value. Science ultimately may impact, positively or negatively, strongly or weakly, societal economic, security, and quality of life outcomes. Science policy intervenes into a science system that transcends geographic, disciplinary, institutional, and national boundaries. Complex systems are populated by and shaped through the actions of a multitude of agents, or actors, at different levels of analysis and in different institutional types [1, 2]. The science system includes individual scientists and teams of scientists in and across labs, institutional research settings, such as universities, public and private research institutions, and corporations, formal and informal networks of organizations and of individuals across organizations, professional associations, funding agencies, developers and vendors of scientific equipment and instrumentation, and government policy units. The science system takes shape as these various actors pursue their interests and missions—substantive science focuses, career interests, strategies, constituency demands—and their political, social, and economic values and goals. Because of its allocational and regulatory nature, policy influences the behavior of the different agents as they pursue their interests.

Progress in science has been described as an evolutionary process that advances through the establishment of variation in the science focuses and approaches, the selection of successful science theories and approaches, such as through processes of review, citation, and funding, and the retention of those approaches that become widely accepted and become built into subsequent science activities [3, 4]. Through the same process by which science policy influences the behavior of scientists, it influences the amount of variation in the science system as well as which approaches are selected to continue to receive the resources necessary from the ecosystem to survive and thrive. The combination of these two influences makes policy a strong determinant of what science gets done and toward what purposes it is aimed.

Science Is a Subsystem Deeply Embedded in the Larger Society.   Although the science of science policy must be based on a firm understanding of the nature and processes of science, developing knowledge about how policy can be formulated to apply resources to enhance science output is only one concern. Efficient science allocation may be different when viewed only in terms of science output than when viewed in terms of value to the larger society. The science system is a subsystem of society, and the science of science policy must investigate it using approaches that apprehend its interdependence and embeddedness within its broader societal context. Resources accrue to science through decisions of the larger system, including those made by policymakers but also by other funders of science, based on beliefs about the value that science may deliver. A critical focus of the science of science policy deals with the manner in which science delivers value within the larger society and the formulation of policy that makes this more likely. The science of science policy must therefore focus on the connections of the science subsystem with the other subsystems of society. These include: (1) how science fits into the innovation ecology; (2) how science connects to flows of economic resources through many public and private allocative processes; and (3) science's connections to particular domains of public and private activity, such as those concerned with security, health, and education.

Policymaking Is an Applied, Interdisciplinary Process. Policy formulation allocates resources and regulates activity with the intent to shape behavior to effectively contribute to the well-being, values, and purposes of the larger system. Policymaking cannot be understood nor policies formulated from the perspective of a single disciplinary framework. Because purpose and the definition of well-being are contended among different stakeholders, policy formulation is inherently a political process with political outcomes. Policy formulation is also an economic process with economic constraints, justifications, and outcomes. The flow of economic resources is a major focus of policymakers, and policies shape incentives and impact overall wealth creation, growth, and distribution. Policy is, at its core, a social process, and sociological and psychological forces are integral considerations and determinants of outcomes. Policy formulation occurs through social processes among policymakers and with different stakeholders, and policy substantively affects outcomes, behaviors, and capabilities of the different agents in the system, including influencing collaborations and consequently the shaping of networks of activity. The science of science policy is inherently an interdisciplinary endeavor.

Policy Is Only One of Many Forces Shaping the Behavior and Output of the Science System. Policymakers use the tools available to them to select science investment directions that they expect to contribute to societal purposes and well-being, and to shape the behaviors of the different actors pursuing their own interests to get them to engage in activities that deliver value at a larger system level. The science of science policy must grapple with the questions of how the various actors respond to policy interventions. Individual agents' responses to different policy approaches depend on their personal values and purposes and the whole host of factors influencing them, including science interests, personal aspirations, personal resources, and available options. Organizations' responses similarly depend on their missions and strategies, their existing stocks and flows of science knowledge and capabilities, and their perceived options to secure and exploit resources.

Science Policy Is a Strategic Process with Many Sources of Uncertainty. Science policy consists of forward-looking decisions and actions designed to match resources to opportunities to further the health of the system and to achieve desired system outcomes. Policymaking is probabilistic, uncertain, and dynamic. The scientific method is based on hypotheses and fraught with uncertainty. There are endless options for investment in science, each carrying varying levels and kinds of potential payoff and risk. Investment decisions and science policies are themselves hypotheses. They are based on incomplete knowledge of what avenues of science exploration are likely to yield useful knowledge, what areas of science will be adequately funded without policy intervention, and what dynamics will result from a policy and how they will impact science production and the linking of science to the larger innovation and mission system outcomes. The larger ecology in which the science system operates is so complex, and the feedback loops and interactions so numerous and occurring at so many levels, that it is not possible to model the system sufficiently to predict with certainty (see, e.g., Jaffe, in this volume). The challenge is to infuse knowledge into the policy formulation process that will bolster its ability to deal with uncertainty and to base policy on predictions grounded with evidence. Relevant information is multifaceted, including knowledge about the nature and requirements of the science that is being considered for funding or that is being regulated by policy, about the nature of the system where impact is intended, such as the innovation ecology, about the likely impact of various kinds of policy choices on the dynamics of the system, and on the linkages that lead to intermediate and ultimate outcomes.

Science and the Innovation Ecology Are Characterized by Global Networks That Cannot Be Regulated or Controlled by National Governments. Scientific knowledge circulates through networks that know no national boundaries, scientists move from nation to nation, and knowledge advances are increasingly achieved through cross-national collaborations. Wagner [5] advocates developing a science policy that acknowledges national science activities as part of a larger, interconnected global system and making decisions about where to invest, develop, and assume a leadership role in the creation of knowledge and also about where to link to knowledge that is being developed elsewhere. The innovation ecology is also globally networked (see, e.g., Sapolsky and Taylor, in this volume), with entrepreneurs and corporations seeking knowledge and linking to research wherever it is carried out, open innovation approaches increasingly driving partnerships, supply chains mixing and matching product and technology from around the world, and knowledge- and wealth-sharing arrangements forged globally among companies and other organizations. Corporations fund and locate research near talent and knowledge, anywhere in the world. National policies are in some ways mismatched with the globally networked nature of the work of science and innovation. They are at best one factor affecting the advance of knowledge, shaping the focus of the science within a nation's boundaries, and making it somewhat more likely that such knowledge will promote national interests. At worst, national science policies can predict wrong, place poor "bets" perhaps for political rather than scientific reasons, discourage the conduct of important science in the nation, drive the best scientific minds to do their work in other countries, and divert resources that could have greater impact on societal well-being.

Given these characteristics of science and policy systems and of the larger ecology of which they are part, it is clear that a science of science policy must illuminate the larger ecology in a way that connects with the requisites of the policy-making process.

3. Bridging the Gap: The Data and Analytical Challenge for the Science of Science Policy

Both science and policy are socially constructed processes. Those advocating a science of science policy call for it to produce knowledge that is useful to policymaking, that is, useful to the policy discourse that results in making decisions about investments of resources into science, the regulation of scientific activity and of the resulting knowledge rights, and the pursuit of purposes [6]. Its focus must include but go well beyond the economically framed questions that have driven debate about the value of government investment in science. Policymakers need substantive knowledge about the dynamics of science and the science system, how it advances knowledge, and how science knowledge is combined with other kinds of knowledge, such as technological and organizational innovation, to further societal purposes. How, for example, do basic biological knowledge and physiological knowledge become embodied in drugs, devices, and therapies that then become part of the practices of health care providers? Another substantive contribution of the science of science policy is a reflexive look at policymaking itself, including issues such as how various policy interventions influence the actions of various actors in the science system, how policymakers trade off purposes and make decisions about where and how to intervene, and how they use data in that process.

There is an epistemic gulf between the work of the scholars who study science policy and the practice of science policymakers that yields decisions intended to further certain purposes. The scientists who study science policy are concerned with increasing what is "known" based on theory, empirical testing and experimentation, and their interests are in furthering theoretically based knowledge. The current state of knowledge of science policy is based on narrow studies in which the questions asked are limited by methodological and data capabilities and do not come close to capturing the complexity of the policy domain. Policymakers include politicians, managers, and administrators who are tasked with making decisions and have to deal with the complexity of the system they face. They base decisions on their understanding of the system from their experience, professional knowledge, and often their ideological and pragmatic beliefs about how best to influence behavior to foster outcomes and achieve purposes [7].

Systematic academic knowledge about science policy may or may not be a major consideration in policymakers' decisions. They interpret scientific findings in the context of their experience of the complexity of the social systems they are trying to influence. Imagine that the science of science policy were to rapidly mature in its capability to describe the science and innovation ecologies using sophisticated instrumentation to create ideal data sets and dynamic models broad enough to predict the probable impact of various policy decisions. The actions that policymakers take and the decisions they make will even then necessarily be based on their interpretation of such data and analysis. Policymakers, like producers and adopters of science knowledge (Gero, in this volume), make decisions based on their interpretations that are situated in the context in which they operate. The kinds of data that are compelling to policymakers are those that they see as relevant to their decisions and that fit with the way they make decisions, the way they conceptualize the system they are trying to affect.

For many science policymakers, the advancement of science knowledge is an interim outcome. Policy decisions also embody hypotheses about how advancing science can impact less proximate outcomes, such as fostering innovation and economic growth and contributing to security and the health outcomes of the population. Science policy knowledge includes developing an understanding of the situated decision making of the many other actors, such as corporations, entrepreneurs, innovators, health care delivery systems, defense-oriented agencies, and the population at large, and of how they incorporate (or don't) the knowledge produced by the science that is funded. Effective policy anticipates the behavior of these actors.

Policymaking is a synthetic process that requires a combination of many knowledge bases. Many questions important to policy formation can only be addressed through great leaps forward in methodologies that enable the accumulation and integration of the results of studies from many different discipline perspectives to provide a useful depiction of the complexity facing policymakers.

Because policy intends to guide resources and behavior toward the accomplishment of purpose, data and analytics are not sufficient inputs. Knowledge from the new science of science policy must inevitably be combined with human insight, purpose, ideologies, and wisdom to guide strategic and tactical decisions on science policy. The process by which these are brought to bear on policy decisions is part and parcel of the domain of the science of science policy. Although the science of science policy can elucidate the connection between policy and outcomes, it cannot and should not choose among purposes. That inevitably happens through dynamic political processes that are an inherent dimension of the context of the complex, international system of science.

We have made the case that the aspirations of the science of science policy should go beyond the generation of substantive knowledge about the science system and its context and impact by connecting to the context and practical task of policymaking. To do this requires recognizing the complexity of the policy world and the synthetic nature of policymaking. The science of science policy must incorporate multidisciplinary perspectives and frameworks and address the fundamental nexus in policymaking of human purpose, values, and judgment, with the scientifically knowable elements of the system being influenced through policy. The next section takes a more detailed look at the complex decision-making context being illuminated and served through a science of science policy and examines the knowledge elements, analytical processes, and synthetic methodologies that ideally will inform the policy decision-making process. It then paints an optimistic vision that science policy analysis and decision making can be more science-based.

4. Toward a Scientific Process of Policy Formation

Our vision is that the science of science policy should enable a scientific process and method for analysis and decision making in science policymaking.

We view the work of the policymaker as formulating evidence-based hypotheses to guide decisions aimed at accomplishing desired science and innovation outcomes. The implementation of policy is the ultimate test of these hypotheses, and the source of learning to inform future policy decisions. This section examines the requirements for a science policy process that is evidence based and proactive. We then lay out an agenda for the SOSP to build the knowledge base to inform this process.

A more scientific policy-making process will require clarifying the purpose, gathering contextual information, establishing hypotheses, testing the hypotheses with multiple theories and data sources, calibrating the likely outcomes, given n opportunities, and synthesizing the results to make the policy decision. To describe how to achieve this vision, we first describe the nature of the policy arena and the data requirements for an evidence-based platform supporting science policy formulation. This section is followed by a discussion of the critical aspects of data/information synthesis. An envisioned visual analytic technology suite for science policy decision making is then described, followed by a discussion on moving toward predictive analytics for science policy, which includes the issue of dealing with decision uncertainty. Next is a presentation of the need for testable hypotheses and data in order to increase the scientific basis of science policy decision making. Expected outcomes from such data and analytical tools are discussed. Finally, we provide here a set of recommendations that will lead to analytic capabilities supporting the envisioned ecological context of innovation and a science of science policy.

5. The Varying Contexts of Science Policymaking

In the United States, the Office of Science and Technology Policy (OSTP) provides the overarching policy context for science, and it is where all nationally supported sciences and missions are considered. This office is subject to the vagaries of the societal political processes that influence policies at many levels, through which the purposes of science are debated and shaped. These broad political winds, trade-offs, and directions both constrain and enable the science that is conducted in the nation. Within the broad framework of national policy, local policies and strategies, allocations, and regulations are forged and implemented in many agencies, directorates, institutions, and organizations. The mission focus guiding decision making is far more refined at lower levels than it is at the broad agency level. The translation of broad science policy decisions into operational policies and strategies by agency-, company-, and laboratory-based decision makers is the most proximate determinant of what science is conducted and what societal purposes are achieved. At the national level, policy trade-offs are made across very large science domains and very broad purposes. At lower levels, the decisions that allocate resources and determine the strategies for accomplishing them tend to be focused on specific missions, often within a single-science discipline or cross sections of a few.

Organizations such as national laboratories, universities, and industries that conduct science that contributes to the missions of the government agencies operate within the context of broad governmentally determined science policies. These organizations make science policy investment decisions within some mission, science, or product scope defined by the overall agencies and institutions and their intended client set. These local actors also have their own purposes. For them, a primary goal is to invest in science that can lead to further investments-building technology and products, thus ensuring a resource flow to sustain them institutionally and to sustain the scientists who compose them. It is in these local mission-focused settings, including corporations that carry out self-funded science, that linkages are built across the science system and of the science system to the broader innovation and technology ecologies and societal missions.

The decision-making process varies greatly from organization to organization. In some organizations, decisions are made hierarchically, perhaps reflecting a single leader's views of purpose and the best options to achieve it. Other organizations provide a proposal and review cycle within the mission and science scope, sometimes including peer governance. Still others rely on bottoms-up judgment and provide a great deal of autonomy to scientists to execute the best science within scope with little or no review. Although the organizational context strongly influences the approach and considerations that are applied in developing strategies and specific science recommendations, we argue that increasing the systematic evidence base that is brought to bear on policy decisions will enhance the quality of science policy decisions in all settings.

6. Data Requirements for an Evidence-Based Platform Supporting Science Policy Decisions

The general categories of data required are driven by the policy-making environment and analytic needs illustrated in Figure 13.1. Within these categories, specific data requirements vary for policymakers who are situated in different organizations and science systems. For example, the needs, culture, and infrastructure for a person formulating science policy within a mission organi-

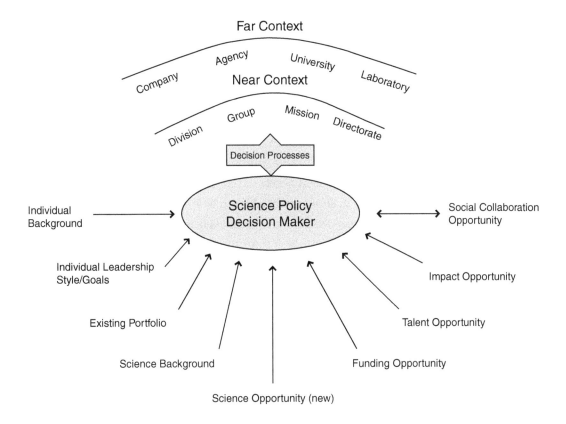

Figure 13.1.
Science policy
decision data and
analytics
considerations.

zation such as the U.S. Department of Homeland Security (DHS) or the National Institutes of Health (NIH) at a directorate or division level may differ from those at a science mission organization such as the National Science Foundation (NSF) or at the broader governmental level where overarching allocative and regulatory policies are made across broad purposes and science domains. Each has its own culture, mission, organizational arrangements, and decision-making processes, as each deals with different domains and breadths of science. Yet they all are faced with the same core policy requirement to make allocative and regulatory decisions to achieve purposes. They are all faced with defining how they fit into the broader science and innovation system and defining their societal purpose.

Evidence is created through the gathering and analysis of data that shed light on the dynamics within the organizational and ecological contexts, on the resources and capabilities available to support various policy options, and about the opportunities for impact. Each of these areas requires the creation of databases and the development of analytical and interpretive tools and methodologies. For the scientists of science policy, the challenge does not stop with the specification of the kinds of data that support a robust, evidence-based science policy decision process. The development of instrumentation and analytical and interpretive methodologies to turn data into information relevant to policy decision making is also an SOSP task. This must then be followed by the process of testing the hypothesis and preparing a story that conveys the context and content in a convincing manner to the desired audience as a likely dynamic report.

6.1. The Institutional Context

Policy decision makers are embedded in Near Context and Far Context, represented in Figure 13.1, that are, either explicitly or implicitly, the sources of much data that provide the fuel for the decision maker. These data concern the broader science policy and allocation environment, client concerns, the structural and mission interconnections between the various actors in the science system, the resources available, and the evaluation criteria that will be applied. These near and far institutional contexts are themselves quite complex (see, e.g., Marburger, in this volume) and present a shifting set of demand criteria as political forces change, the pressures facing society shift, and the science and innovation ecologies unfold through time. An understanding of these contexts enables policy decision makers to shape decisions to position their particular organization within broader contextual directions to enhance their likelihood of securing resources through time.

Once the context of the decision maker is established, many other sources of evidence and opportunities should be considered. These concern the characteristics and trajectories of the relevant science systems and the broader technology and innovation environment that define opportunities to shape science to contribute broader value. Because science and innovation are globally networked systems, relevant data are both global and local. Fundamentally, these data describe the stocks and flows of knowledge, the networks of activity in the science system, and the connections of science with the broader innovation system.

6.2. Talent and Social Capital

Talent and social capital, represented by the Individual Background and Individual Leadership Styles/Goals in Figure 13.1, are core resources that enable various science policies. Creating database approaches and analytic techniques that provide systematic evidence about shifts in the patterns of talent development and availability in different domains of science is an integral part of SOSP. Whether at the national policy level or a more local level, knowledge of the talent that is available or that can be developed to pursue particular policies and directions is critical to the quality of policy decisions. Successful execution of science policies depends on the ability to access needed talent and to align the interests and activities of deep experts with the areas of science that are likely to yield knowledge that can achieve societal purpose. Policymakers need to know where there are concentrations of world-class experts who are carrying out research that is likely to lead to breakthrough knowledge that can catalyze the innovation that will be the foundation for societal progress. They also need to know where imbalances in the stock of talent are developing that may, through time, result in a mismatch with emerging areas and important innovation opportunities of the system. For example, with clear and compelling data and an appreciation of the criticality of the management of the portfolio of science talent in the country, it might have been possible to anticipate and manage the precipitous increase in scientists doing work associated with the arguably unsustainable increase in NIH research funding in recent years as described by Sarewitz and Freeman in this volume.

Science talent resides in expert individuals with relevant training, experience, and accomplishments. Expertise includes deep discipline domain knowledge, cross-discipline capabilities and knowledge, and science leadership capabilities and experience. These are all critical enablers of policy directions, and shortages of these talent areas can constrain policy choices. Given the global nature of science and the importance of being closely connected to the networks of scientists associated with fast-paced scientific domains, social capital is also important. Social capital refers to the connectedness of individuals to others with related knowledge and the consequent ability to achieve knowledge synergy and to collaborate. Thus the data relevant to understanding and tapping into talent go beyond knowledge of individuals and their expertise and experiences and include their collaborations and positions in knowledge networks.

Having a rich picture of the networks of scientists that are contributing to the advancement of particular science domains is integral to understanding what talent is available and to identifying investment directions that optimally build on, leverage, and develop talent. The experience and talent of the policymaker is relevant. A policy decision maker with strong research experience might tend to invest in research that may take some time to result in deployed technology and to look at the acquisition and development of talent longitudinally, while a less experienced individual may consider more conservative research approaches within mission scope that can be rapidly transitioned into products and deployed technologies. Neither direction can be implemented without access to the talent required to carry it out.

The need for data about talent is often an afterthought in science decision making but is a critical consideration in any strategic science decision. The challenge differs depending on the policy context. When decisions are being made within a particular discipline and mission, those making policy choices are generally scientists with a deep understanding of their own discipline and the science process and knowledge about what talent exists in their own organization or where they can find it. Sometimes, however, policy decision makers seek talent in newly developing fields where pipelines of researchers and information about related research experience are both in short supply. They must become aware of the talent, perhaps multidisciplinary, of those focusing on an emergent field. This was the case, for example, as the United States invested in establishing a nanoscience infrastructure during the first decade of this century, and the directors of many of the new centers were faced with staffing up with scientists working in this relatively new area of science who were in great demand and short supply [8]. Some policymakers, such as congressional staff setting budgets for scientific organizations, have little or no science background and have to rely on systematic data and others' input. These last two situations greatly increase the uncertainty of any decision and raise the importance of having solid evidence about the availability of talent to drive decisions.

6.3. Capabilities

Capabilities, represented by the Existing Portfolio and Science Background in Figure 13.1, are the know-how that enables a system to accomplish its intended purposes and outcomes [9]. In a rapidly changing knowledge environment, a system needs the "dynamic capability" to alter its own capabilities over time in order to enact new strategies [10, 11]. Science policy both builds on the existing capabilities of the science system and charts strategies for developing new capabilities. This requires knowledge about the patterns of related science activities at a more global level. At the highest policy level, for example, national policy would in part be determined by where policymakers believe the country can add distinctive value in the context of the global science and technology system and in so doing support policy objectives [5]. The same is true for local policymakers.

The *existing portfolio* is the most common and likely readily available source of information about current capabilities. Data about this portfolio may include proposals, funded projects, and mission, strategic planning, and needs documents. It typically includes well-formed, structured documents as well as documents with unstructured format. Text analysis is the most common approach, taking advantage of structured information, if available, and using unstructured text analytics when the categorical information is not available. However, in many cases, the only representation of the existing portfolio is a set of PowerPoint slides of another person's understanding of the portfolio. Sometimes that person's understanding is quite different from the actual work being conducted within the science programs. For this reason, using formal text analytics on proposals, work plans, progress documents, or review documents that might be available is recommended. Scaling this up to describe broad national and even global portfolios of science is a desirable element of dynamic capability.

Science background data include research and technology papers, reports, patents, and product and/or product descriptions. These usually are collected over time with the temporal aspect being a key analytic component. Young technology with rapid growth will have a typical rapid-growth profile, while well-established technology with a long history will have another profile. Both may be equally valuable as investment candidates, but the decision maker should explicitly consider the state of the background science and technology. Usually these data can be gathered from citation maps or graphics as the result of linking all of the citations at the end of science publications. This graphical representation shows the growth, over time, of a field of science within the constraints of the culture of citations for a publication. Frequently, a well-established field such as chemistry will have a known culture and style of citation, while a rapidly emerging field such as social analytics on the Web will have a very different citation and publication style.

6.4. Opportunities

The opportunities, represented by Science, Funding, Talent, Impact, and Social Collaboration in Figure 13.1, are sometimes the most challenging to represent and deal with in an analytic process. In these areas there is a need to automate tools to support human intelligence and discovery. Science policy-making is an uncertain process. It yields policies that are based on the hypotheses of the policymaker about the connection between the policy and future outcomes. This predictive process is based on knowledge of capabilities with a special analytic focus on new areas that are emerging in science and technology.

Science opportunity data identify long-standing science puzzles that have the potential to move forward fields of knowledge, new concepts, opportunities to shape the development of early-stage sciences, or the combination of inter-disciplinary sciences producing entirely new sciences. A description of the science opportunity is an input to any investment decision, but it is especially difficult to express with any certainty in emerging sciences. Policymakers' hypothesis formulation process establishes a vision of what might be possible in science, and what it would take to get there, and then develops an estimate on the likely investments required. Given the uncertainty inherent in science, policies generally embody multiple science opportunities as hypotheses that can be tested for likely outcomes.

Funding opportunity data describe the likely available resources within an investment portfolio. These data are central inputs to the definition of scope and the aggressiveness of the investment strategy. In many cases, particularly initiatives that entail multiple-year commitments, there will be uncertainty and policymakers will have to think in terms of a range of funding options. Although the quality of a proposal can influence the final funding decision, its scope and the aggressiveness of the proposal are defined by the anticipated range of available funding. For example, funding two scientists' time is very different from funding two hundred scientists' time and will result in a quite different speed and path of knowledge creation. Such considerations strongly influence the amount of leeway in the science policy-making processes.

Impact opportunity data enable a predictive view of what the outcomes of investments might be in terms of jobs and the economy and other societal indicators of well-being. These include benefits that might accrue, such as science-enabled inventions, products, and new companies. The likelihood of achieving these benefits depends on the probability of the success of the science endeavor and also on the behavior of other agents in the system, such as inventors, product developers, entrepreneurs, and venture capitalists. Data about impact opportunities are broad, speculative, and often difficult to collect and provide in computable forms. Current opportunities can be informed by an analogy to models from previous science-technology impacts and by assembling data and models of the current linkages and impacts. Understanding the uncertainty of these data is critical to knowing the certainty of the outcomes of any investment strategy. Uncertainty can be reduced by generating science policies that align various actors in the innovation ecology. Placing new science initiatives near relevant innovation zones and funding proposals that entail cross-sector collaborations are examples of policy approaches aimed at increasing impact probability. Such approaches are predicated on information about the agents and dynamics within the innovation ecology. Having a high degree of uncertainty is not necessarily bad;

the goal is to have a *known* certainty. The many dimensions of these impact opportunity data make them very difficult to qualify in common terms and analysis.

Social collaboration opportunity data provide awareness of groups of investments and of people who are interested in similar technologies and offer the opportunity to craft collaborative and synergistic projects. Knowledge of the current and potential linkages in the global network of science activity often has a strong influence on policy decisions. Decision makers may want to see leverage among several groups that have a part of an investment portfolio. Collaborations may span government agencies, academia, industry, and national laboratories. Increasingly, science policies are being forged that build on opportunities for international collaboration and leverage.

The science policy decision maker must consider the influences of near and far contexts data, the evidential data about talent and capabilities, and the opportunity data. Together these different data types provide the foundations for an ecological decision-making process. While decision makers usually want all of these data, today a complete set of data often is not explicitly included within the policymakers' decision analytical tools. Our view is that an important contribution of SOSP is creating the methodologies to make relevant data more readily available to the science policy-making process.

7. Data Synthesis Requirements

Consistent with the complex nature of the system that science policymakers aim to influence, the multiple sources of information have to be synthesized to provide evidence to guide the making of policy decisions in a scientific manner. For example, collecting data such as publications, proposals, and reports about work in progress is required to establish a good understanding of a portfolio or background of a science. These various forms of information have to be analyzed and synthesized in order to develop a more sophisticated model of how a science field develops to provide guidance to policymakers whose decisions determine how to shape a portfolio for maximum impact.

The various kinds of data discussed in the previous section may be available in some form, whether in measures or text. However, the synthesis of data, defined as establishing a common semantic understanding of all the information, is challenging. Data will not likely have common words, common representations of time, common phrases for discussions, or common methods for describing outcomes. Thus building a common data foundation for analysis is the core scientific challenge in establishing a science for science policy.

Data in numeric tables, graphics, text documents, images, and even videos must all be put within a synthesized framework for analysis. To date, most analysis is conducted on a single-data type, usually from a single source, such as patents or publications. Economic data are usually analyzed with spreadsheet tools, which are separate and distinct from text analysis tools. While the individual forms of data can be analyzed separately, the analytic methods of science policy must enable these data to be considered as a whole.

Some common approaches are to define a common vocabulary, or ontology, that can describe the science area under consideration. Some fields, such as biology and health, have a well-developed set of common terminology. However, even when examples of common terms are available, individuals use the same terms very differently, so full-text analytics is required to establish the meanings of the terms within the context of particular documents.

8. Envisioned Tool/Technology Suites Supporting Science Policy Decision Making

The envisioned analytic tool suite to support the science of science policy does not exist today. The tool suite would allow for inputs of the various kinds of data shown in Figure 13.1. The kinds of data can be expected to be differentially important to different policy domains. For example, while making policy decisions with respect to rapidly developing new science areas around which industries are beginning to form, more weight would be given to talent opportunities and science opportunities to create a unique position in a crowded field. In a mission-oriented science organization, impact opportunity may be more important in a particular decision cycle than the science background. There will be cases where the opportunity to have an impact will dominate funding decisions because it is simply worth the risk, even with known uncertainty, to establish a goal. An example of this is going to the moon—scientists and decision makers worked to reduce the risks of this mission, and yet the uncertain goals in science were clearly appreciated and worth the investments.

Today the justification process for different policy options is dominated by the best persuasive argument as opposed to scientific assessments of known evidence and opportunities. We envision a more scientific method of decision making in science that starts with contextually driven criteria that necessarily stem from the political processes in the larger context that shape the purposes of the science system. Decisions are then systematically justified by illuminating known knowledge and assessing risk and outcome opportunities and probabilities. Most policy decisions will benefit from the juxtaposition of local and global data and analysis, as science organizations strive to achieve and maintain a viable position in proximate and more inclusive ecologies. Given the fact that human purpose operates at all levels and for each agent in the relevant science system, we do not underestimate the extent to which judgment and purpose from different agents in the science system will necessarily and inevitably complement the evidence at all levels where science policy is formulated.

This more scientific policy-making process obviously cannot be automated, but it can apply methodological and content expertise and can be informed by robust data, a dashboard of analyses, and the integration of knowledge about talent, capability, and opportunity. Policy will be determined through human judgment applied to the synthesis of information about contextually determined purposes and constraints, patterns that emerge through the analysis of increasingly sophisticated data sets tested against desired outcomes, and human judgment.

Today there are many, many tools for data-type-specific analytics, such as video analytics, sound analytics, and text analytics. Applying network visualization and analysis to patent and citation analysis is a well-established way of depicting a science field and the collaboration and knowledge flow within it. There are also many tools for mission-specific analytics, such as military command/common operating picture or financial fraud analytics. This envisioned tool suite must first enable strategic decision making and will not likely focus on the deep details of all the data. Although it will take advantage of the detailed analytics tool suites being rapidly developed today through visual analytics, the envisioned tool suite will combine a spreadsheet metaphor with an interactive discourse of context to detail analytics. Spreadsheet approaches are a common methodology for considering alternate approaches and comparing each within context.

Each of the cells within this metaphor will have numbers, categorical data, and text, and it is likely that each will carry weights of emphasis that are appropriate to the policy decisions at hand. The objective is to provide the information to support alternate hypothesis testing. Note that this process will encourage, or force, specific definitions in order to apply science methods to make science policies. It will result in a more uniform standard for policy decision making, even though contexts will differ in the specifics. Neither the development of the methodology nor the mind shifts required among science policymakers will come easily.

Policy impacts the system it intends to regulate, and policymakers require feedback about this impact to test the validity of the assumptions and hypotheses behind the policies. The policy-making process must be self-adjusting, which means the data and analytic suites will of necessity be dynamic and interactive and will allow, through time, the tracking of changes in patterns. The analytic results will be conveyed within active dynamic packages that contain the data, the analytic reasoning, the alternative scenarios, and the recommendations within the context(s) of the organization, as well as the outcomes. The tools themselves should be active, so that the decision makers are able to add information and insight and change weights and priorities to fit what is being learned.

9. Toward Proactive Science Policy Analytics and Dealing with Uncertainty

Our vision goes beyond doing confirmatory analytics on a portfolio of existing programs and science articles. Analyses based on these are primarily retrospective in nature, confirming known facts and putting them into context. Knowledge of science system dynamics and associated outcomes based on retrospective data and cases clearly contributes to core SOSP knowledge and provides the prologue and models to guide today's policy decisions. The proactive approach we are suggesting for developing science policy will require synthesizing information into a knowledge framework to support defining hypotheses of likely scenarios and testing these against likely outcomes. This approach requires exploratory analytic methods to discover patterns and models of the high-dimensional relationships in the knowledge foundations. This exploratory process will enable the creation of hypotheses and make science policy formation a strategic process.

Going toward proactive thinking in the decision-making process requires an analytic process that includes human or computational methods. While human proactive thinking is always critical, computational support in the form of modeling is strongly recommended. The modeling requires multiple human inputs and evaluations and considerable human judgment. However, there is a cost associated with developing such models. Few models of science are available today as compared to models of global change. Even simple models of technology growth would be very helpful. Surely the development of the methodology for proactive science policymaking is an important aspect of the SOSP, and the methodology will be an important element of policymaking.

Uncertainty in decision making in science is the norm. A degree of uncertainty will always exist in any decision about investments in the future. It is easy to claim complete uncertainty and give up on the issue and retreat to a conservative, history-driven portfolio; however, with the data, information, analytic methods, and calibration of testable tools and methods, the uncertainty is reduced.

In the absence of a suite of data and analytic capabilities, an analogous but a very resource-intensive proactive approach to science decision making can be employed that increases the quality of policy decisions. An example is the creation of an international agenda for visual analytics [12]. Workshop teams were used to collect and process information and to achieve some of the same prospective analytic capabilities described earlier. The result has been a success rate of 80 to 90 percent for the associated projects and uncommon advances in science through deployments of early-stage science and technology. The process involved a wide breath of end users, technology providers, and scientists. It used test data scenario sets, evaluations of the state of technology, and debates about plausible outcomes to develop a full agenda now being implemented around the world. If the data and methods environment that we are advocating in this chapter had been available, this process could have been accomplished at a reduced cost. More recent publications illustrate the successes and unmet challenges within the science of visual analytics [13–15].

10. Data to Test and Calibrate Science Policy Decisions

Critical to any scientific method is available test data for calibrating the tools and the results of the decisions. This will be a challenge today, as there are no collected repositories that cover the data described in Section 3. Each decision process will likely require different data, and collecting all data about even one specific science area is not likely useful. Part of the development of such an analytic method will be the collection of some example data and decisions. These must vary in scope and support the contexts of decision making. It is relatively straightforward to collect all science articles and all proposals and to conduct a detailed analysis of a specific science area to determine the background and existing portfolio views for analytics. While large, these are text-based data sources and tools for unstructured text analytics and are readily available. Critical to note is that this is strategic decision making, therefore, information about the broad science picture, the pace of science advancement, the real and likely impact, and economic and other impacts are essential even though they are not easily available. Specific science advancements and mathematical formulas are of less interest.

Collecting or generating synthetic data for other decision-making methods is common. The military collects data from exercises to test their decision-making tools and processes. Homeland security generates synthetic data with

hidden threats to test tools and analytic methods for preparedness and response. Data have been collected for specific technology challenges such as
information retrieval for all to calibrate their advances in science. The concept
is the same in science policy, but the data are in part more abstract.

Data for the science of science policy must be developed at the strategic
level and must enable understanding at both the global and local levels. We
must have some common methods for representing strategic directions in
science, showing the pace of growing science, modeling science development
by demonstrating the dynamics through which science knowledge is translated into societal value, and developing views of the history leading up to
the future in order to go from confirmatory and exploratory into predictive
science policy. Doing predictive analytics on science is not feasible today, but
we believe it is within sight and should be one of the major purposes of SOSP.
We need models of science development to predict plausible futures. While
not available today, we can develop views of science scope and pace of development that provide the human with core concepts supporting predictive
thinking.

11. Expected Outcomes

Policy decision makers need information about the science, state of capabilities, projections of likely advances, and the fit within the context(s) to implement a high-quality strategy that moves science forward, connects it to societal outcomes, and ensures an ongoing flow of resources that makes the
science enterprise viable. Our intent has been to describe the data, the analytics tools, and the analytic methods to enable better decision making in the
policy of science.

In essence, we have laid out an agenda for those in the SOSP community
who are focusing on developing the associated data sets, tools, and methodologies. The expected outputs, vision, and requirements include the following:

- *Collections of data and information* that support the analytics underlying decisions in science. The proposed data and sources are a good
  start.
- *Information representations and synthesis science* that provide scale-
  independent mathematical and semantic knowledge representations
  required for analysis across the multiple data sources and data types.
- *Visual analytic tools* for establishing multiple hypotheses of investment decisions in science and the ability to test and calibrate these
  plausible alternative scenarios.

- *Active analytic products* with data summaries, assumptions, analytic methods, decision weights, and results supporting decision making.
- *Test data sources* that will calibrate the tools and methods for decision making.

We expect that the majority of decision makers will rely on the collection and analytics provided to them rather than doing the collection and analysis themselves. Therefore, the data collection, the tools, and the methods should be available and accessible to a technical staff member who is knowledgeable in the science of science policy to conduct the analytics within the context of the organization and prepare decision packages of analytic results. These are the people Marburger refers to as the "corps of professionals trained in science policy methods and issues" (Marburger, in this volume) who are able to provide support to policymakers.

Human judgment provides the core decision leverage in science policy, and contention about purpose will always underpin the policy-making process. Our vision is not to change that; nor do we believe it can or should be changed. This new process of information and analytic method supporting decision making is expected to significantly increase the quality and degree of known certainty in the decision-making process for science policy. It should better equip policymakers to make the trade-offs and judgments about how best to use scarce resources to accomplish intended purposes.

12. Conclusion—Research, Technology, and Policy Challenges and Opportunities

The envisioned *ecological context of innovation with a science of science* policy is achievable given supportive technology and methods. Many others are actively developing similar science for applications in security and now expanding into health, economy, finance, food/agriculture, transportation, and many other areas of national importance. We should leverage these investments but also consider what is needed to ensure that the data are collectible, that the data are transformable into scalable computation signals, and that science policy analytic methods are computationally supported and enable innovative decision making in science policy with testable results. We expect that each of these areas defined earlier will require investments in core sciences that directly support the envisioned policy-making knowledge foundation and analytics tool suites.

To achieve this vision, a series of pilot case studies should be conducted in differing contexts and organizations to more accurately calibrate and further develop the state of technology and analytic methods in the process of making decisions in science. The experimental science supported by these case studies must be accompanied by continual development of the theoretical science of building science policy methods and tool suites.

We have dealt directly with only one element of the science of science policy: the methodological infrastructure required to enable more scientific and proactive policymaking. SOSP contributions will be required in many substantive arenas developing the models that can frame our understanding of the progression of the science system and its contribution to the larger innovation ecology. Yet academic understanding of a system doesn't necessarily translate directly into decisions. Our vision of the science policymaking process has been based on the assumption that it must fit within the nature of the system it is regulating, and that SOSP must contribute knowledge that can be used by science policymakers. With the vision of enabling a more scientific policy decision-making process and improving human judgment empowered by these methods and tools, we believe that the ability of science policymakers to address the important issues facing the societies they serve will be greatly enhanced.

References

[1]   R. Axelrod. The Complexity of Cooperation: Agent-Based Models of Competition and Collaboration. Princeton (NJ): Princeton University Press; 1997.

[2]   D. Sarewitz. Institutional Ecology and the Social Outcomes of Scientific Research. In: K. H. Fealing (Ed.), Handbook of Science of Science Policy. Stanford (CA): Stanford University Press; 2010.

[3]   D. Campbell. Blind Variation and Selective Retention in Creative Thought as in Other Knowledge Processes. Psychological Review, 67;1960;380–400.

[4]   S. Mohrman, J. R. Galbraith, P. Monge. Network Attributes Impacting the Generation and Flow of Knowledge Within and from the Basic Science Community. In: J. Hage, M. Meeus (Eds.), Innovation, Science and Industrial Change: The Handbook of Research. London: Oxford University Press; 2006, pp. 196–216.

[5]   C. Wagner. The New Invisible College: Science for Development. Washington (DC): Brookings Institution Press; 2008.

[6]   J. Marburger. Keynote Address. Washington (DC): Science of Science Policy Workshop; 2008.

[7]   D. A. Schön. The Reflective Practitioner. New York: Basic Books; 1984.

[8]   S. Mohrman, C. Wagner. The Dynamics of Knowledge Creation: Phase One Assessment of the Role and Contribution of the Department of Energy's Nanoscale Science Research Centers. Washington (DC): NSRC; 2008.

[9]   G. Dosi, R. R. Nelson, S. G. Winter. The Nature and Dynamics of Organizational Capabilities. New York: Oxford University Press; 2000.

[10] M. Ianisti, K. B. Clark. Integration and Dynamic Capability: Evidence from Product Development in Automobiles and Mainframe Computers. Industrial and Corporate Change, 24;1994;521–524.

[11] D. J. Teece, G. Pisano, A. Schuen. Dynamic Capabilities and Strategic Management. Strategic Management Journal, 18;1997;509–530.

[12] J. Thomas, K. Cook. Illuminating the Path: The Research and Development Agenda for Visual Analytics. Los Alamitos (CA): IEEE CS Press; 2005.

[13] J. Thomas, J. Kielman. Challenges for Visual Analytics. Journal of Information Visualization, 8;2009;309–314.

[14] J. Kielman, J. Thomas, R. May. Foundations and Frontiers in Visual Analytics. Journal of Information Visualization, 8;2009;239–246.

[15] P. Wong, J. Thomas. Building a Vibrant and Resilient National Science. Journal of Information Visualization, 8;2009;302–308.

PART THREE

Practical Science Policy
Editors' Overview

Policymakers—whether they are in Congress, federal science and technology (S&T) agencies, or the White House—are the ultimate consumers of data and analysis that drive federal investments in the U.S. innovation economy. As the chapters in this part demonstrate, however, policymakers currently are offered a baffling array of choices when it comes to where they go for investment advice and how they determine which source is the most reliable and will lead to improvements in our nation's economic and social well-being.

Senators and congressmen are inundated by data and advice that come not just from the federal agencies that hope to receive appropriated funds for their research programs but also from armies of special-interest groups who have a stake in the game and local constituents who want to ensure that their university or research park remains or becomes world class. White House officials, whether the science advisor to the president or a budget examiner with the Office of Management and Budget (OMB), meet daily with representatives from federal agencies and science professional societies or take advice from expert panels from the National Academies of Science about federal S&T investment policies. And federal S&T agencies are inundated with requests for data and analysis from the White House, Congress, constituents, professional societies, and other groups interested in gaining insight into how the federal government will spend the more than $140 billion that Congress appropriates each year for research and development (R&D) activities.

Several consistent themes emerge from the chapters in this part by authors who have been intimate observers and participants of this mix of data, analysis, and debate. First, they make the strong case that there currently is an *absence* of a rigorous analytical approach to science policy; second, they state that a *science* of science policy could have an enormous and a positive impact on policy debates that affect millions of people and a significant portion of the nation's economy; third, they identify many of the key institutional *barriers* that prevent or inhibit the spread of data-driven analysis; and, finally, they suggest ways to improve our understanding of science policy. On this last point, the authors are clear that the uncertainty of current science policy debates favors the promotion of agendas that perhaps could not have withstood strong analytical inspection but that align with popular causes and movements.

Kei Koizumi's chapter sets the stage by examining the limited tool set available to federal policymakers as they prepare multibillion S&T agency budgets: retrospective analyses of budget performance and the widespread use of "expert judgment" as the gold standard analytical method; and, a heavy reliance on retrospective analyses that are either aggregated at too high of a level (such as macroeconomic studies) or that study a problem that has been overcome by events that are often unsatisfying when making investment decisions. An absence of prospective data has led to the view in science policy circles that expert judgment, such as peer review and external review panels, is the best (and often only) tool available to policymakers. The resulting mix of retrospective analyses and expert judgments leads to the "default option" for policymakers: "incremental budgeting, whereby the next year's budgets are primarily based on the current year's budgets and decisions on minor increments up and down are based mostly on political priorities and public and political pressures rather than on rigorous program measures or outcome measures." The "time is ripe," Koizumi writes, for the academic community to develop new metrics and analytical methods that "could lead to an improved environment for federal budgeting" that, while still imperfect, would be a major improvement over current practices.

Where Koizumi provides insights into the mind-set of individual policymakers, William B. Bonvillian's chapter focuses on the little studied, but enormously important, process of how institutions are created in "an intense political landscape where sound political design is important to their effectiveness." Bonvillian surveys the design of research organizations, dating from the creation of the Department of Energy (DOE) and the National Aeronautics and Space Administration (NASA) laboratories in the 1940s and 1950s through the Obama administration's efforts to build new research organizations that will transform U.S. energy markets. He notes that the absence of a rigorous analytical framework for the creation of research institutions has led to many false starts and stops in the past, but he proposes nine "rules of political design" that could ensure that future new institutions do not inhibit innovation, that they promote large-front science, and that they will create a strong supporting constituency. Bonvillian concludes by providing examples in emerging sectors, such as advanced manufacturing and health care, to demonstrate how appropriate political design could help policymakers achieve their goals.

"Congress is the ultimate arbiter of federal science policy." David Goldston, with this simple and accurate statement, describes in his chapter how science policy is made in Congress and also provides insights into how institutional ecology, federal budgeting, and political design come together in the cauldron that is congressional policymaking. Goldston notes that Congress makes science policy based "on a largely unexamined mixture of general theories, suppositions, time-honored guesses and just-so stories" because there simply isn't an alternative. This reliance upon guesses and anecdotes can lead to unexpected and negative consequences, Goldston argues, such as the "Malthusian dilemma" facing universities during boom-and-bust periods of the federal S&T budget, and provides much of the rationale for efforts by academia to build a rigorous science policy framework. Goldston notes that a science of science policy could enable Congress and the executive branch to address at least four major issues—science spending, research and risk, jobs creation, and technology policy—that are at the forefront of science policy debates. Doing so would avoid debates that "quickly become almost entirely ideological" and "would be a welcome change, if hardly a panacea."

Daniel Sarewitz picks up on this theme by examining one of the most difficult science policy issues facing policymakers: understanding the relationship between research institutions, their cultures, and the dynamic environments within which they operate, and the accomplishment of major social goals, such as improved health care, increases in national security, and improvements in the environment. This "institutional ecology" has two primary facets: the research organizations that produce the science targeted at specific societal goals, such as improved farm production, and the other organizations that work within that ecology, such as farmers and farm equipment manufacturers, who are most closely associated with the accomplishment of that societal goal. The primary challenge that Sarewitz identifies is the inability by the science policy analysis community to strongly link investments in research to improvements to important societal goals. This absence of rigorous analysis, which Sarewitz argues "has not even achieved a rudimentary capacity," involves the intersection between institutions, such as the National Science Foundation (NSF) and the National Institutes of Health (NIH), that will plan and conduct research and the much larger ecology of institutions and individuals "at which science is often aimed." The solution, Sarewitz writes, is to base research agendas on "noneconomistic thinking and valuation," to include a "significant qualitative component," and to ensure that all members of the institutional ecology critically examine the assumptions underlying a research agenda.

In the last chapter, Janez Potočnik provides an international perspective in how the European Union has overcome ideology to create and advance a science of science policy. The overarching themes stress the importance of stakeholder involvement, data collection, and the translation of findings from the science of science policy to implementation.

The European Union has accelerated progress toward a more integrated research policy through collaborative projects and networks that bring together the different players in each country (universities, laboratories, and enterprises). Cooperation helps, as Potočnik explains, to "build a critical mass of human and financial resources, exploiting complementary competences, sharing expensive infrastructure, and addressing jointly" the societal challenges

Similar to the US, the diversity among the European Union countries also presents challenges, especially due to differences in interests. The European Research Area, which was first adopted at the Lisbon European Council in March 2000, was created to bridge this diversity. This initiative provides lessons for other countries in creating and implementing a science of science policy, especially showcasing the benefits of the cooperation-collaboration-coordination model. This model highlights how bringing resources and complementary competencies together at the European level enhances research into specialized fields as well as allowing 'large science' projects to occur. Examples include the European Space Agency and Observatory (ESA/ESO) in astronomy, AIRBUS for aeronautics, and the European Science Foundation (ESF) for areas that cover many scientific fields. Other examples include fellowships that encourage mobility across borders and grants that allow research teams to choose their own topics. Potočnik notes that these programs allow researchers "to bypass the rigidities or obstacles which exist at the national level" as well as "allow results to be achieved where it would be difficult or even impossible to do so under other conditions. . . ."

The chapters' authors in this part make a strong case that a rigorous science of science policy is at an early stage in its evolution, but they hold out the possibility that significant progress is possible in the immediate future if advances could be made in the limited tool sets that Koizumi describes, in making sense of political decisions that Bonvillian and Goldston discuss, and in understanding, as Sarewitz asks, the "behavior of extraordinarily complex and dynamic sets of actors, institutions, and interactions." Potočnik highlights how the European experience could help the United States to understand this complexity: "The challenges linked with the definition, negotiation, and implementation of international research projects and technological initiatives at world level are therefore precisely those that the Europeans have learned to face through decades of experience."

Above all, the authors suggest that identifying the appropriate research questions will determine if the nascent community of science of science policy analysts will be successful in bringing rigor and relevance to science policy-making. As Sarewitz writes, "The problem of linking science policy decisions to social outcomes is perhaps the central challenge that real-world science policy decision makers must continually confront. If the science of science policy community hopes to prove *its* value to society, then it will need to take this problem seriously."

Science Policy

A Federal Budgeting View

Kei Koizumi

14

1. Introduction

Federal budgeting for research and development (R&D) currently relies on a fairly limited set of science policy tools. While federal agencies, in response to the Government Performance and Results Act (GPRA) and follow-on legislation, have developed and continue to refine performance measures and other evaluation tools, only a few of these tools have relevance to budgeting decisions. The challenge for the science of science policy (SOSP) community is to provide policymakers with more tools, and the right ones, to affect the government's numerous resource allocation decisions.

This chapter starts with a brief overview of the federal budget process, describes some current opportunities for better incorporating SOSP tools in federal budgeting, and concludes with some future opportunities and possible pitfalls in better integrating science policy tools into resource allocation decisions.

2. The Federal Budget Process

Federal budgeting is more of an art than a science, but there are opportunities to make it more scientific. In the federal government, resource allocation decisions are political decisions and will always be political, but data and analysis are important inputs. Policymakers have to balance political demands, output and outcome data, policy goals, and performance data in a complex mix for which there is no set formula. The world of federal budgeting is all about year-to-year decisions and trade-offs at the program level. Nearly all federal programs are funded a year at a time and compete for resources with other programs (both R&D programs and non-R&D programs) in a fiscal environment in which resources are *always* limited. In such an environment for which there are no defined road maps for how to make decisions, the default option is incremental budgeting, whereby the next year's budget is primarily based on the current year's budget, and decisions on minor increments up and down are based mostly on political priorities and public and political pressures rather than on rigorous program measures or outcomes measures. And the default time scale is year by year, in which decisions on next year's budget are based on this year's budget or, perhaps, last year's budget; in such an environment, retrospective data of more than a year or two are of limited value, and near-real-time data are valuable but unfortunately scarce. While the existence of a better and bigger evaluation toolbox is not a guarantee that federal budgeting will change, the use of analytical tools for evaluating R&D investments could make for a richer dialogue and an increased likelihood that political considerations and priorities will be backed up with data and evidence.

The federal government's fiscal year begins on October 1, but federal agencies begin the budgeting process fifteen to twenty months earlier. Generally, federal agencies begin preparing their budget proposals in the spring and summer of the year before the new fiscal year starts. Most of these preparations are based on internal agency evaluations and priorities, but the White House also offers guidance on top-level political priorities and top-level budget constraints in an annual Office of Management and Budget (OMB) memo in the late spring. Most agencies budget for a mix of R&D and non-R&D programs working together toward the agency mission. For R&D investments, the primary form for top-level guidance is the annual Office of Science and Technology Policy (OSTP)-Office of Management and Budget (OMB) R&D priorities memo that articulates the administration's interagency priorities for the federal R&D investment. Agencies take into consideration these interagency priorities when formulating their budgets, as well as the evaluation and performance data showing how programs are performing and what their outcomes are. Performance data are especially valuable toward the end of this stage of the process, when agencies' proposed funding levels are decided and then must be justified.

In September, a year before the fiscal year begins, agencies submit their initial budget proposals to the OMB. These proposals are often accompanied by justifications, including evaluation and performance data. In the fall, the OMB (the president's budget office) and the agencies negotiate over budget proposals through a series of pass backs and appeals as individual agency proposals are molded into a unified federal budget that fits within government-wide spending and revenue targets. The OSTP and other White House offices advise during this process on programs within their domain of expertise. Evaluation tools, such as SOSP tools, are useful during this stage as well in comparing one agency's portfolio to another's or to evaluate cross-agency R&D initiatives against other R&D priorities or non-R&D programs.

The president's proposed budget is released the first week in February and formally goes from the executive branch to the legislative branch. The president's budget is a unified budget proposal encompassing the entire federal government. In addition to specific spending proposals, the president's budget also contains performance measures; for R&D programs, performance can be measured using SOSP tools. The National Science Foundation's (NSF) budget request, for example, contains a performance information chapter describing performance metrics for each NSF portfolio area as well as agency-wide performance measures. The agency-wide measures tend to be process oriented, for example, the average time between the receipt of a proposal and the final decision. Specific portfolios have performance measures of SOSP tools, such as Committees of Visitors, external evaluations, and published results.

After the first week in February, the budget moves to the U.S. Congress. For most of the spring and summer, congressional committees hold numerous hearings on the budget and collect testimony from federal and public witnesses. In the spring, Congress approves a budget resolution for the fiscal year; the budget resolution is Congress' response to the president's budget and establishes high-level budget priorities to guide later congressional action. After a budget resolution is approved by both chambers of Congress, the budget is divided into several pieces and is considered by relevant committees. For R&D spending, nearly all of the spending is controlled by the Appropriations Committees of the House and the Senate. Appropriations provide funding for federal programs that are funded one year at a time, or discretionary programs, through annual appropriations bills. There are currently twelve appropriations bills each year; ideally, each appropriations bill is drafted, debated, and enacted separately before the October 1 start of the new fiscal year. In practice, appropriations bills are often delayed past the start of the fiscal year, and individual appropriations bills are often bundled into omnibus legislation. It is not clear how SOSP tools are used in the congressional decision-making process.

3. Policymakers' Tools for R&D Allocation Decisions

What are a policymaker's current tools when trying to decide budgets for federal R&D programs?

Retrospective data are still the primary tools for policymakers when making budgeting decisions. Right now, the most influential retrospective data are spending data, mainly collected through the NSF's annual surveys on past R&D obligations and expenditures. For example, retrospective data on federal research spending by discipline showed that historically, especially from 1998 to 2003, when the National Institutes of Health (NIH) budget doubled, spending on the life sciences increased dramatically, while federal investments in other science and engineering (S&E) disciplines, especially the physical sciences and engineering, lagged. In response, after prodding by groups such as the National Academies in its *Rising Above the Gathering Storm* report, the Bush administration proposed the American Competitiveness Initiative to double the budgets of three key federal agency supporters of the physical sciences and engineering over a decade, a proposal that has been renamed and continued by the Obama administration. At other times, retrospective data on R&D spending by state have inspired Congress to increase budgetary support to programs such as the Experimental Program to Stimulate Competitive Research (EPSCoR) to build R&D capacity and capabilities in states that have traditionally received less federal R&D funding, and retrospective data on R&D spending by national mission (which show dramatic drops in energy R&D funding from the 1970s) have inspired Congress to increase federal energy-related R&D investments.

Spending data remain the most relevant policy tools for policymakers because they are well understood, relatively easy to obtain, relatively timely (though lagging by a year or two), and directly connected to individual federal agencies and even specific programs. Although spending data only describe the inputs to R&D, they are nevertheless powerful tools for evaluating important characteristics of R&D investments, such as goal, geographic location, science and engineering discipline, performing institution, and immediate economic impact. And these data, because they deal in money (dollars), are the easiest to compare across agencies, disciplines, nations, *and* types of spending. Thus retrospective spending data are continually used to compare the United States to other nations, to compare one federal agency or R&D program to another, and to compare R&D programs against non-R&D programs, and the results of these comparisons have direct impacts on federal budgeting decisions.

There are other forms of retrospective data, but they have traditionally been less used by policymakers. There is an entire body of literature on rates of return for past R&D investments, nearly all showing that R&D investments have substantial social rates of return in percentage terms; other studies trace back economy-changing innovations to federal R&D investments (such as the now-canonical example of the Internet resulting from early Department of

Defense [DOD] and NSF investments), and still other studies show positive contributions of R&D investments to important national goals, such as healthier people or cleaner energy. But these and other retrospective data, while useful and interesting for making the case that R&D investments are good investments in general, are not useful for making allocation decisions *within* the federal R&D portfolio because they are not program specific or, in most cases, agency specific, thus they offer little guidance regarding which programs are better than others in relation to goals. And rates of return studies do not offer *marginal* rates of return at the program level; marginal rates of return data, if available, could help policymakers determine the *right* amount to invest in a particular R&D program and could allow them to shift resources in order to equalize marginal rates of return to some desired return across programs within a broad portfolio.

So while there is a robust literature showing that federal R&D investments offer high rates of return in the aggregate, these highly aggregated results do not offer policymakers the tools to make decisions at the program level because we lack the program-by-program analyses in real time that can answer questions at the level of a portfolio of discrete programs, such as: Which programs offer the highest rates of return? Which programs offer the promise of the greatest progress toward policy goals? And these aggregate tools do not allow us to compare R&D investments with non-R&D investments, despite the reality that nearly all federal R&D programs coexist with non-R&D programs within the budgets of federal departments and agencies.

Policymakers have also been slow to use other retrospective metrics, such as bibliometrics, patent data, citation data, and visualization tools. One problem is the considerable time lag between funding a research project and counting the resulting papers, patents, or other outputs. Although these tools can offer insights into program performance and let program managers know whether their R&D investments are having an impact in scientific terms by marshaling data to indicate whether their past investments resulted in patents, widely cited papers, ripple effects on related disciplines, and so on, the key problem is linking the use of these tools to allocation decisions. Determining whether an R&D program has performed well scientifically in the past is a different question from whether an R&D program is worthy of future support. And most of these tools are still difficult to apply at the program or portfolio level.

When retrospective data are not available, then policymakers and R&D managers are left with "expert judgment" as the best tool, whether in the form of peer review panels, committees of visitors, external review boards, or the judgment of program managers. Ideally, these experts would be able to rely on data to inform these judgments, but this is not guaranteed. Expert judgments are state of the art when it comes to making allocation decisions at the individual project level, the classic example being a peer review panel deciding which grant proposals in a grant competition merit funding, and a different peer panel reviewing these grants' performance later on.

There are examples of prospective allocation decisions based on an expert panel, but they are mostly from one discipline. The astronomy community, for example, provides policymakers with a decadal survey organized under the auspices of the National Academy of Sciences. Every decade, an expert panel of astronomers surveys the field of space- and ground-based astronomy and astrophysics, recommending priorities for the most important scientific and technical activities of the coming decade. The results of the survey guide budget priorities for the NSF and the National Aeronautics and Space Administration (NASA), the two primary federal supporters of astronomy. The earth sciences discipline has a similar decadal survey that presents policymakers with a prioritized list of space programs, missions, and supporting activities to address the key scientific questions on which to focus Earth and environmental observations; the results of this expert panel are a major influence on the structure of NASA's earth science portfolio in the NASA budget. These examples have limitations in that they do not allow NASA astronomy projects to be evaluated against NASA Earth observations projects within the total NASA budget. So expert panels may be able to assess individual programs or portfolios, but it is difficult, if not impossible, to synthesize the assessments of numerous expert panels looking at different programs to come up with a tool that allows for comparisons between programs, across agencies, or within a broad portfolio. How does one compare the judgments of an expert panel of astronomers with a panel of biologists and a panel of mathematicians, for example, to make allocation decisions for a multidiscipline research portfolio?

4. A Road Map for the Science of Science Policy

As this discussion suggests, policymakers would benefit from additional policy tools to assist in allocation decisions, especially if they are real-time tools or prospective tools. So the emerging interdisciplinary field of SOSP has the potential to be highly relevant to policymakers in making budgeting decisions.

The federal government, recognizing the importance of SOSP tools, formed a National Science and Technology Council (NSTC) interagency task group in 2006 to develop a coordinated federal approach to the science of science policy.

This effort, led by the OSTP, resulted in the November 2008 report "The Science of Science Policy: A Federal Research Roadmap" by the NSTC's Subcommittee on Social, Behavioral, and Economic Sciences. For federal policymakers, the good news is that sixteen federal agencies participated in this effort and are now working to fulfill the road map through research on and the development of new SOSP tools. Better still, the interagency group offers a forum for agencies to share best practices and to disseminate analytical tools throughout the government. The not-so-good news (and the ongoing challenge) is that the report found that much work needs to be done before SOSP tools can be fully utilized in federal budgeting and policymaking.

The report is already valuable to policymakers because it inventories the current federal tool kit of quantitative analysis tools, qualitative analysis tools, visualizations tools, data collection tools, outcome metrics, budget and performance metrics, and inputs metrics in a useful grid arrayed along assessments of each tool's potential value, potential cost, and missing elements preventing that tool's full use in policymaking. The identification of missing elements offers an R&D agenda and a clear way of measuring progress toward filling in the missing elements. Not surprisingly, the report found that the most developed tools are the qualitative tools, such as peer review and expert review, the most developed data are survey data, such as the NSF data, and the most developed outcome measures are productivity measures, such as rates of return measures.

But there are significant gaps for other potential tools, including most outcome measures, bibliometrics, and quantitative analysis tools. Making further progress on the road map would give policymakers more and better tools to help inform budgeting decisions. An additional challenge, identified in the NSTC report, is identifying ways of measuring the value of knowledge as it relates to the desired policy outcomes of federal agencies. The primary product of research is knowledge, mediated through outputs such as patents or scientific papers. But to be useful for budgeting purposes across portfolios, there must be standards for evaluating the value of knowledge in terms of outcomes so that policymakers can make decisions about how important an R&D investment might be in gaining the knowledge needed to make progress toward an outcome. There is a promising literature on the "value of information" that attempts to quantify the knowledge that might result from an R&D investment. But more work on this challenge and the other challenges identified in the road map needs to be done to enable R&D agencies to build budgets to maximize the value of outcome-relevant knowledge from their investments.

5. Current Opportunities for Improving SOSP Tools

The time is ripe for advancing progress on SOSP tools, both because of the current U.S. economic and political environment and because of the federal government's policy goals. Globally, national governments have developed stimulus policies and are carefully monitoring their contributions to economic recovery. The U.S. stimulus bill of February 2009 is a prime opportunity to develop and use science policy tools to assess the contribution of R&D spending toward policy goals. One reason is that Recovery Act (U.S. stimulus) spending is designed to be a one-time infusion of federal funds to the economy. Second, Recovery Act spending is segregated from all other federal spending with unique identifiers and tags. Third, Recovery Act spending will be tracked in unprecedented detail through a dedicated federal government website (www.recovery.gov), which integrates spending from throughout the federal government. Taken together, these attributes mean that the Recovery Act is an ideal laboratory of a unique, one-time, well-identified set of R&D investments. If the science policy community can develop and test tools on this group of Recovery Act investments, then the effectiveness of these tools can be evaluated under conditions that are as close as we get to a control group in the messy world of federal budgets.

The Recovery Act is also an opportunity and challenge for the community to demonstrate the (near) real-time relevance of R&D investments to important national goals. As the name implies, the overriding purpose of the Recovery Act is to get the U.S. economy on the road to recovery from an unusually deep and broad recession. Ultimately, the success or failure of the Recovery Act will be judged on how Recovery Act spending did or did not contribute to economic growth. Everything else, such as whether the Recovery Act laid the foundation for long-term economic prosperity or reoriented the economy toward a cleaner energy future, is important but secondary. But the R&D investments contained in the Recovery Act (totaling $18 billion) present an unusual situation, in that they are, in normal discourse, regarded as long-term investments in the future and thus must prove their worth as a short-term stimulus to economic recovery. These R&D investments also are in an awkward situation because the tools to prove their worth are relatively undeveloped. To give one example, policymakers and evaluators can demonstrate easily the short-term economic effects of highway projects, of which there are billions of dollars worth in the Recovery Act; miles of asphalt poured, construction jobs created, and dollars introduced into local economies are well-developed and easily produced measures for these investments. But what are the similar indicators for R&D investments?

In an attempt to come up with good answers, federal agencies are using the Recovery Act as a test bed for new evaluation techniques. One example is the STAR METRICS pilot project (Science and Technology in America's Reinvestment—Measuring the EffecT of Research on Innovation, Competitiveness and Science), a working initiative of the interagency Science of Science Policy group. The project is using spending from the Recovery Act as a test bed to develop a data-driven analytical capability for assessing impacts of federal investments in science and engineering research and education. The initial goal is to provide mechanisms that will allow participating universities and federal agencies to have a reliable and consistent means to account for the numbers of scientists and staff that are supported by federal funds. It is hoped that subsequent generations of the program will allow for measurement of science impacts on economic outcomes such as job creation, on knowledge generation, and on other outcomes. Narrowly, STAR METRICS could offer a consistent, open, and transparent methodology to produce empirical data on economic impacts from R&D investments rather than investigators' or others' estimates of impact or job creation. But broadly, successful STAR METRICS could be a model for studying the current and cumulative impact of science investments on the activities of the nation's R&D workforce and the role of science in the nation's competitiveness, and it could be an inspiration for similar SOSP projects.

6. Opportunities for Future Uses of SOSP Tools and Future Research

How does this translate to policymakers? For one, we know that someday there *will* be another recession, and that policymakers will try to ameliorate its effects through policy. When that next recession comes, policymakers will be able to make better decisions if they have empirical data from the last recession about which investments worked in fostering short-term economic recovery, how well they worked, what the time lags were, and how different investments compared to one another. Maybe we will know that highway investments and R&D investments are comparable in their stimulus effects; maybe we will know that R&D investments are true win-win investments that not only lay the foundations for future economic growth through new knowledge and new technologies but also build an economic recovery in the short term through jobs, new start-up businesses, and other broad economic impacts. Maybe we will know that R&D investments in universities are as effective as R&D investments in businesses to jump-start economic growth if, as we suspect, university investments can lead to start-up businesses and other economic ripple effects.

Second, knowing the short-term impacts of one year's R&D spending would enable policymakers to make better-informed decisions about the next year's R&D budget. In a budget environment in which resources are always limited, data on R&D outcomes and impacts at the portfolio level would enable policymakers to balance better the right mix of R&D investments to make maximum progress toward all of the federal government's goals. How much better it would be if we could make these decisions based on empirical, real-time data rather than on intuition or anecdote or extrapolations from past data.

Another reason the time is ripe for advancing the science of science policy is that for the federal government a key priority is to provide support for "high-risk, high-payoff research" or "transformative research" that can lead to game-changing breakthroughs in knowledge and technologies rather than incremental advances. The R&D priorities memo issued jointly by the OSTP and the OMB in preparation for the FY2011 budget process calls on federal agencies to "describe how they plan to evaluate the success of various techniques to increase support of high-risk research." But this simple instruction carries with it difficult issues. How does one measure the "riskiness" or the "transformativeness" of a research proposal or portfolio? How can one measure whether support for such research is increasing or not? Unlike in financial markets, where there are rating systems in place to give grades or scores on the relative riskiness of financial products or portfolios, however battered those systems may be after recent revelations on the causes of the 2008 financial crisis, there are currently no grades or scores on the riskiness of R&D projects or portfolios. But just as investors are willing to accept higher risk in return for potentially higher returns, R&D policymakers could accept higher risk in research in the hope of more transformative, game-changing breakthroughs if they could balance the degree of risk within a diversified R&D portfolio. If there were grades or scores, then policymakers could act like an investor or a financial planner and choose a mix of R&D portfolios with varying grades of riskiness, and they could raise or lower the riskiness of an agency's R&D portfolio depending on an agency's needs. If there were scores or grades, then agencies could try different policies to increase support for high-risk research (making "riskiness" an explicit review criterion, for example, or selecting projects through project managers explicitly charged with supporting a certain percentage of high-risk projects) and be able to evaluate which policies were the most effective at boosting support. So one tool missing from the science policy tool kit is a tool for measuring the riskiness or potentially transformative character of an R&D proposal or portfolio; while most of us have an intuitive idea of what it means and can judge whether one research proposal is riskier than another, policymakers need metrics to be able to aggregate these judgments and to make comparisons across portfolios.

Another missing but related tool is a metric that could connect the riskiness of a research portfolio with the potential transformations that could result. Again, to use a financial analogy, if by accepting higher risk we can reasonably expect a higher return on investments, then investors can weigh riskiness versus dollars to make an informed allocation decision. Similarly, policymakers would ideally be able to look at riskiness measures and compare them to potential transformations. Of course, the problem is defining what those potential transformations might be and evaluating them in the absence of a common metric like dollars, but for many goals there could be common measures that cut across portfolios: in health, for example, potential life years saved; in energy, reductions in cost per kilowatt-hour; in climate, potential tons of carbon sequestered. Another problem is evaluating the potential transformations that might come out of research: given the unpredictability of research, can we really know what potential transformations might result? To take a historical example, could a DOD manager have looked at a proposal for packet switching research and seen the potential result of today's Internet?

Is it really possible to quantify or predict the potential "transformativeness" of research, or to quantify the chances of success? Maybe not, but the field of economics tells us that we can develop tools and models to predict and quantify unknown future outcomes as a decision tool for making policy decisions. So it's important to try in a federal budgeting context, because without metrics that allow for risks and potential transformations, federal R&D investments are at a disadvantage in competing for scarce resources against established, operational non-R&D programs. And even within the federal R&D investment, the absence of risk/transformation metrics tends to favor incremental, applied R&D over potentially transformative, more basic research.

Such metrics also would be important because they build in a tolerance for "failure." Truly transformative research will result in more failures than successes, so evaluating individual projects will lead us to discourage risky research and instead encourage the safest, most incremental research. We know that failure is not a bad word in research; for every breakthrough, there are likely to be many dead ends or ideas that just don't work. The proper metrics, when used at the proper level (that is, at the broad portfolio level and not at the individual project level), can carve out a place for "failure" and allow research program managers to take risks and allow their programs to stand on their own against more incremental or operational programs that are less risky.

7. Caveats and Conclusions

The possibilities outlined in this chapter could lead to an improved environment for federal budgeting. For programs with a mission of economic competitiveness, future federal budgeting could incorporate new insights and techniques from the STAR METRICS to give policymakers informed estimates of the broad economic impacts of federal basic research spending for various budget scenarios, and new metrics could help gauge whether these scenarios were high risk enough to offer the most transformative research opportunities. Policymakers could balance budget scenarios to maximize these measures if the tools were right. In this example, it is clear what could be lost in the absence of progress on an SOSP agenda: policymakers would be left with their current tools and would be limited in their ability to evaluate potential economic impacts or evaluate the degree of risk. The same types of opportunities are present in other missions, such as health research or energy R&D, as well as the same potential for missed opportunities.

At this point, note the following caveat: in developing and using new science of science policy tools, evaluators and policymakers must always be mindful of how these tools are used. The danger of metrics and other evaluation tools is that they will stifle the thing they measure. Policymakers, and scientists and engineers, understand that the inspiration and creativity flowing into the best research cannot be measured as inputs, and that there will always be something inherently mysterious about the creation of new knowledge that cannot be predicted or measured. The key, of course, is to preserve the serendipity behind the best research but still evaluate the outputs and outcomes. But policymakers and evaluators need to be mindful that defining outputs and outcome measures can lead scientists and engineers to produce the measures instead of producing groundbreaking knowledge.

But with that caveat in mind, the science of science policy community has a nascent tool kit, a research road map, a favorable policy environment, and an interested policymaking community looking for better tools to connect research to policy goals. With these stars aligned, the SOSP community has the opportunity to work on developing, evaluating, and using tools to help inform federal resource allocation decisions.

Of course, better science policy tools will never make budgeting for federal R&D investments completely scientific, not as long as budget decisions continue to involve an idiosyncratic mix of politics, policy, data, and other inputs. We know that R&D investments contribute to multiple goals (economic growth, health, environment, and defense) and that the relative importance of these priorities and the time frames for making progress toward them will be politically determined. Unlike an industrial firm, policymakers cannot just use rate of return or expected profit as a single goal but instead must balance many goals, all of them competing and some of them contradictory. But the appropriate tools for measuring R&D investments' contributions to different goals could help policymakers work toward a more rigorous methodology for evaluating the best uses of scarce R&D resources and could help identify the R&D investments that show the greatest promise for advancing policy goals.

15 The Problem of Political Design in Federal Innovation Organization

William B. Bonvillian

1. Introduction

An overlooked feature in the design of programs and institutions that support our science and technology-based innovation system is political design, as opposed to the factor generally exclusively considered, policy design. This chapter will aim to develop a framework for evaluating political design issues underlying federal innovation institutions, including a perspective of whether the political design model is consciously structured to be supportive, as opposed to contradictory, to the policy design.

Federal science investment doesn't drive itself; of course, science is not divorced from politics, despite the attraction of the ivory tower. Instead, political system demands have been the major driver for the past sixty years for science investment and new science institutions. It was the cold war that drove the growth of science agencies in the postwar period, especially defense science, the Sputnik threat that drove the 1960s science investments, and the competitive economic threat of the 1980s that drove the programs of that era. Given the underlying role of political drivers in science, it should not be surprising that the question of political design requires focus.

During these prior periods of science investment advance, a series of new innovation-oriented federal government organizations was created, offering lessons for the factors to be included in a framework for political design. Particularly illuminating are the experiences of the 1980s generation of innovation organizations designed to cross the "valley of death" between research and late-stage development. A new generation of institutions is now being formed, largely to meet energy technology challenges, thus the political design issue is again timely. Innovation system institutions generally land in an intense political landscape where sound political design is important to their effectiveness. While the contending ideologies around the federal role in science and technology were largely fixed in the period after World War I [1], the political debate in this area, particularly around the public-private partnership role that many of these agencies fill, remains robust and requires program design attention.

2. The First Generation of Federal Innovation Agencies

While the era of innovation is as old as the Industrial Revolution [2], the federal role in innovation didn't truly scale up until the World War II period. While innovation actors[1] [3] were highly connected under the system administered during World War II by Vannevar Bush, President Roosevelt's science czar, he helped dismantle this system at the end of the war and substituted an alternative one.[2]

Bush shaped the two leading organizing entities for wartime U.S. science and technology—the National Defense Research Council (NDRC) and then the Office of Science Research and Development (OSRD). He brought nearly all defense research efforts under these two loose coordinating tents and set up flat, nonbureaucratic, interdisciplinary project teams oriented to major technology challenges, such as radar and atomic weapons, as implementing task forces. He created a "connected science" approach, where technology breakthroughs at the fundamental science stage were closely connected to the follow-on applied stages of government-supported development, prototyping, and production, operating under what can be called a "technology challenge" model.

Then, immediately after the war, as the institutional elements in his connected approach were being dismantled, Bush was able to salvage a residual level of federal science investment. In his 1945 tract *The Endless Frontier* [4], Bush argued that the U.S. government should fund basic research, which would deliver ongoing progress to the country in economic well-being, national security, and health. In other words, he proposed ending his wartime model of connected science research and development, organized around major technology challenges, in favor of making the federal role one of funding only one stage of technology advance: exploratory basic research.[3] Bush's approach became known as the "pipeline" model for science investment. The federal government would dump basic science into one end of an innovation pipeline and early- and late-stage technology development and prototyping would mysteriously evolve inside the pipeline, with new technology products emerging at the end. While Bush proposed to achieve research coherence under a single organizational tent through what became the National Science Foundation (NSF), authorization of the NSF was delayed, and in the interim science agencies multiplied.[4] Bush's pipeline concept of federal funding focused on basic science prevailed, but his loosely centralized science model did not. The result was a new generation of highly decentralized science agencies, each largely adopting his pipeline model for the federal science role.

These twin developments left the federal role in U.S. science fragmented at the institutional level in two ways: overall science organization was split among numerous science agencies, and federal investment primarily was focused on only one stage of the technological pipeline—exploratory basic research[5] [5]. Bush thus left a legacy of two conflicting models for scientific organizational advance: the connected, challenge model of his World War II institutions, and the basic science-focused, disconnected, multiheaded model of postwar U.S. science institutional organization.

Bush's postwar model was a political success, drawing support from cold war concern over American leadership in science. This network of basic research agencies enabled a growing base of American research universities, formed by the turn of the twentieth century but coming into their own under Bush's orchestration of major federal support during World War II and expanding further during the cold war. This was a relatively flexible model of research grant agencies and university recipients, based on competitive grant awards.

3. The Fixed, Large-Scale Lab Model

However, another type of federal first-generation agency emerged from the postwar period, continuing during the cold war period, in parallel with the system of strengthened university research supported by a network of basic science research agencies. This brand of entity featured major in-house research and technology facilities, which provided major regional employment and corresponding political involvement. These institutions were less flexible, fixed in both particular missions and particular locations, with their facilities requiring ongoing infrastructure support. This second institutional type created subsequent political intervention problems for scientific missions.

The Department of Energy's (DOE) national energy labs provide a prime example. They evolved from Los Alamos and Manhattan Project laboratories during World War II, shifted from defense control at the end of the war to the Atomic Energy Commission, and later to the DOE. The DOE laboratory constellation employs one of the largest bases of science PhDs in the world, some 12,000, at its seventeen labs [6]. With the end of the cold war and a rapidly growing need for new energy technologies for energy security and climate reasons, the DOE now faces the task of shifting its lab talent base from its traditional nuclear weapons role to new energy research. Yet over 5,000 of its PhDs are now housed at its three historic nuclear weapons labs, and only 350 are at one of its smallest labs, the National Renewal Energy Laboratory (NREL), which is focused on energy efficiency and renewable energy. The political lock-in buttressing the DOE's established laboratories limits the agency's flexibility in making a shift to the new energy technology challenge that the country now faces.

There is a second political design problem with these types of large-scale research institutions: they tend to become exclusive clubs, isolating and crowding out other researchers working at a smaller scale in other locales. This limits the ability to place a broad base of talent in the field. Arguably, sound policy design requires a broad base of interest and talent for a range of advances. The politics of supporting major institutions with a particular research focus and an accompanying employment base—the narrow front approach—complicates sound organization on the broad front of research. Science advance requires space for both the organized focus of larger-scale teams as well as a wider base of decentralized researchers working at a smaller scale—advance that is both focused and broad based, with a range of talent on a range of tasks. The large-scale research entity, although it offers a strong political base of support, can curtail the broad-front approach.

Although it was created a decade later, the National Aeronautics and Space Administration (NASA) provides a similar example. NASA evolved out of the National Advisory Committee for Aeronautics (NACA), a predecessor prewar aeronautics and engineering research agency [7, 8] and built major research labs and mission facilities with a strong government contractor base during the space race. James Webb, the first NASA director and architect of NASA's organization, understood from his political mentors, Senators Robert Kerr and Lyndon Johnson, the earlier FDR New Deal model of building congressional political support by creating permanent institutions anchored in regional congressional politics [9]. A rare master of political design in science and technology, he consciously created a system of centers and contractors that would enable NASA's space mission to survive long term. The resulting regional employment and procurement contracting base provided NASA with the political support from executive-branch politicians and especially from Congress that helped sustain strong investments during the space race and thereafter. In recent years, however, the regional facilities and powerful supporting contractors have tended to lock in NASA to ever-more expensive manned-space investments, limiting the pace of its scientific and research advance [10, 11]. As the Obama administration attempts to restore NASA's roots as an advanced technology agency, as opposed to the largely operational agency it has become, the regional political base that Webb built has reared up in opposition [12]. Similar problems have afflicted the larger-scale labs (usually organized as FFRDCs–federally funded research and development centers) in the defense research establishment.

Thus while the political support model applied in these agencies initially supported their research and development (R&D) missions, the weight of their established institutional overhead, locked in against significant modification by the political system, has in some cases curtailed these agencies' innovation flexibility in subsequent years. These are first-generation examples of problems in political design that tend to undermine over time evolving agency science and technology missions. What are the political design rules that emerge from these first-generation models?

3.1. Rules of Political Design

Beware of scale: The creation of an excessive personnel mass in a modest number of locations can cause a political design problem. While the corresponding political support that this mass engenders can sustain a science agency over extended periods, it also tends, over time, to limit science and technology mission flexibility.

Don't let narrow front cancel broad front: A second lesson is that a narrow-front, focused advance embodied in large-scale research establishments can cancel out needed parallel broad-front science advance. Both approaches are likely to be needed, and a large-scale entity and the political power it commands by virtue of its size can cancel out a complementary broad-based advance.

4. The Aftermath of the Sputnik Challenge of 1957

Science investments accelerated during the crisis in confidence over U.S. science leadership created by the Soviet launch of Sputnik in 1957. These anxieties over geopolitical developments created a political driver for science support, bringing new institutions and investments. U.S. R&D investment as a percent of GDP reached a postwar height in the mid-1960s, 2 percent by 1964, compared to less than 1 percent today [13]. Both broad- and narrow-front types of science institutional structures received substantial new support. NASA, as discussed earlier, which came to house a network of fixed, large-scale labs, facilities, and centers, was one of the two major new entities created in this period. While the NSF had been formed after much postwar debate in 1950, its budget tripled in one year, between fiscal years 1958 and 1959; by 1968 its budget nearly quadrupled again, to $500 million.[6] The NSF and the Department of Defense (DOD) graduate education programs grew during this period as flexible voucher fellowships, enabling the graduate student recipient to take the award to the graduate program of his or her choice, enhancing competition between university departments, and lending further funding support to the flexible network model of basic research agencies and universities.

The second major new agency created during this period was the Defense Advanced Research Projects Agency (DARPA), which was a particularly interesting model, very different from the Bush-era basic research agency. DARPA's aim was a "right-left" translational approach—decide the technologies you require from the right side of the innovation pipeline, and then nurture breakthrough science advances on the left side of the pipeline to get there.[7] DARPA embodied a return to Bush's earlier World War II "connected science" through a technology "challenge" model. DARPA, perhaps the most successful of the postwar and cold war science and technology agencies, led the information technology revolution [14] and a long series of other major advances [15, 16]. DARPA, as it came into its own in the 1970s and 1980s, marked the beginning of a swing back to a more integrated science model and away from the "pure" basic research approach. While DARPA illustrates the connected science approach, there are also political design lessons to be drawn from this connected model, as discussed in the next section.

5. The Competitiveness Period of the 1970s and 1980s

Vannevar Bush's basic research pipeline model had institutionalized a disconnect between research and later-stage development over large parts of the U.S. innovation system, ensuring that the handoff to the commercialization stage would be a difficult one. Although the Office of Naval Research was the first to explore Bush's basic research model, the arrival of DARPA, as noted, marked a shift in the military away from it. That shift expanded beyond defense in the late 1980s. As the United States entered that period of heightened economic competitiveness over technology advance with Japan and Germany, concerns grew that although the United States was originating the leading technologies, it was limited, due to this pipeline disconnect, in its ability to commercialize them [17].

During the 1980s there was also a significant ideological debate about the policy approach to address this problem. David Hart has traced the origins of this debate to the decades between the world wars.[8] He suggests that the two prevailing policy positions revived in the 1980s were between economic conservatives who wanted to limit federal economic intervention in the innovation system, and what he terms "associationists," a movement originated by

Herbert Hoover, when he was commerce secretary, who envisioned a collaborative, public-private partnership approach to both applied research and follow-on development.[9]

DARPA showed a way to resolve this ideological clash. It operated not only in the basic research space but farther down the innovation pipeline in the development and prototyping spaces—in the parlance of the time, it was "picking technology winners and losers." Yet it defused this debate by tying its intervention in late-stage development to the necessities of its national security mission. It offered a pragmatic solution—the value of technology advance for the national security overrode ideological concerns. In other words, it showed that an agency operating in the science-technology development continuum needs to be tethered to a mission recognized as politically significant to avoid ideological differences. Despite being tied to a security mission, DARPA and the DOD played a significant role in the subsequent resurgence of the U.S. economy.

As noted, in the 1980s the United States was mired in a tough competition with Japan and Germany, which had implemented innovative models for manufacturing and appeared to be having more success in commercializing incremental advances in technology than the United States. Yet the United States had organized its economy in the course of World War II around a comparative innovation advantage, and its innovation system, particularly its capacity for radical or breakthrough innovation, as opposed to incremental innovation, remained the world's leader in the 1980s and early 1990s. After a multidecade gestation period, where, as discussed, DARPA played a keystone role, the United States was able to move out of its confrontation over manufacturing with Japan and Germany and bring on a major innovation wave[10]—the information technology (IT) revolution—in the early 1990s. It was transformative: the U.S. economy created a net 22 million jobs in the 1990s, or 2.2 million a year. On top of IT, the United States also added a biotech wave. By the end of that decade leadership in those waves put the United States strongly ahead of competitive economies; its economy became the envy of the world. As part of its response to its 1980s competitive problems, the United States created the series of new innovation institutions discussed next.

6. The Valley of Death Organizational Models of the Late 1980s

The 1980s problem for the U.S. innovation system became known as the "valley of death" because it focused on the gap between research and late-stage development [18]. Three new institutional models[11] were adopted in this period to bridge this valley, offering instructive illustrations of the challenges of innovation political design; each is discussed in some detail here because each is particularly relevant to the new generation of energy agencies now forming.

The *Manufacturing Extension Partnership* (MEP) was authorized in 1988,[12] based on the success of the long-standing agriculture extension program. It aimed to bring the latest manufacturing technologies and processes to small manufacturers around the nation, since small firms were increasingly dominating U.S. manufacturing. It aided such manufacturers by advising on the latest manufacturing advances to foster productivity gains, thus assisting them across a "valley of death" in this field. The MEP formed extension centers in every state, which states cost share, backed up by a small Commerce Department headquarters staff charged with program evaluations and the transmission of best practices to the centers. The MEP's national network has a federal funding base of around $100 million annually, plus the approximately $200 million this leverages from the state and local resources. It now consists of fifty-nine centers, employing some sixteen hundred manufacturing specialists experienced in small manufacturing needs. For the past twenty years, the centers have worked with thousands of manufacturers, and MEP studies maintain that the centers deliver some $1.44 billion in cost savings annually and $10.5 billion in increased or retained sales a year to small manufacturers.[13] While some centers are inevitably stronger than others, the overall program has received positive evaluations, and it has received solid political support and sustained stable funding from Congress.

Its political support model has worked to sustain its substantive policy design. Small manufacturers have tended to like the program because it keeps them abreast of the latest manufacturing advances in a highly competitive world economy. State governors, who cost share the program, like it because it enables them to connect with small manufacturers, delivering appreciated technology and process advances to employers and employees to keep them competitive. While business consultants initially viewed the MEP as a free rival service that might put them out of business, most found that participation in the MEP generally heightened demand for their own services to introduce further productivity savings. The state MEP programs formed a national association to compare ideas on manufacturing advances, which in turn helped advocate for and sustain the program. Between the governors lobbying their congressional delegations and the association providing information and further backing, there has been solid political support for the program's continuation and expansion. Since this model only worked if the program's quality remained high and valued by its customers, the political support model has generally promoted the substantive policy design for the program.

The *Small Business Innovation Research* (SBIR) program is a second successful "valley of death" program model; however, the political design has not been as optimal. This program offers competitive R&D grant funding to small and start-up companies, administered through the Small Business Administration (SBA) Office of Technology, which also supervises a related program, the Small Business Technology Transfer (STTR) program. These two competitive programs aim to ensure that small, high-tech, innovative businesses are a part of the federal government's R&D efforts. Eleven federal departments participate in the SBIR program; five departments participate in the STTR program. The two programs award over $2 billion to small businesses annually. The SBIR is funded through a modest "tax" (currently 2.5 percent) on the total research budgets of the participating federal agencies (those with extramural research budgets in excess of $100 million), which becomes a set-aside reserved for contracts or grants awarded to small firms by the participating R&D agencies.

The SBIR program was established through the Small Business Innovation Development Act in 1982[14] and periodically reauthorized by Congress (in 1986, 1992, 2000, and 2004, with a reauthorization now pending). The subsequent STTR program funds joint small business and university research efforts with an additional .5 percent set-aside. According to program founder Roland Tibbets, of the NSF, "SBIR was created to address a need that is still critical: to provide funding for some of the best early-stage innovation ideas that, however promising, are still too high risk for private investors, including venture capital firms. . . . In 2005 only 18 percent of all U.S. venture capital invested went to seed and early stage firms while 82 percent went to later stages of development that are lower risk."[15] The SBIR (and the STTR) aim to fill that "valley of death" support gap.

The SBIR has provided initial funding for many of the most noted technology start-up firms of the past twenty-five years; few new firms consider the start-up process without applying. Small business and venture capital communities backed the program politically. However, it has also received sustained support from a group of so-called "SBIR mills," firms that live off repeated SBIR awards and are not particularly focused on commercializing technology, the fundamental SBIR program aim. While small firms with one-time awards have neither the motivation nor the resources to advocate sustaining the program, the mills do. While, overall, the SBIR has played an important role in helping meet the "valley of death" problem,[16] in the past much of the sustaining political support for the program has come from SBIR mills not particularly dedicated to its basic policy goal of technology commercialization. So the political support model, while strong, contradicts an overall substantive policy goal of the program. Thus the political design is problematic: the political support system does not support as strongly as it might one of the key features of the substantive program design, technology commercialization.

The *Advanced Technology Program* (ATP, renamed and restructured in 2007 as the Technology Investment Program [TIP]),[17] is the third of the trio of "valley of death" programs from the 1980s. It was formed in 1988 in the Department of Commerce's National Institute of Standards and Technology (NIST) program to fund a broad base of high-risk, high-reward R&D under-taken by industry. The ATP reached some $200 million in annual grants dur-ing the early Clinton years, with the administration seeking further major increases, but Congress subsequently cut it to half that size, where it remains today, after nearly being shut down in 2007. Widely studied as a strong sub-stantive model for technology innovation,[18] it has faced recurring political survival problems. These issues stem from three political design problems. First, the ATP was not tied to any particular science mission area but instead to a broad base of industry early-stage technology support. Thus it lacked the umbrella of support often extended by political forces to a particular mission focus, such as health (the National Institutes of Health [NIH]) or space (NASA) or defense (DARPA). Second, it had no particular interest group bat-tling for it. It was a highly competitive program, typically making awards at a ratio of only 1 out of 8 or 10 applicants each year,[19] thereby frustrating most of its annual applicants, who were not disposed to support the program be-fore Congress. Those awarded R&D grants were usually small firms and start-ups unlikely to have resources to lobby Congress in the first place; they also knew that the highly competitive award they received would almost cer-tainly be their last. Thus even its limited number of award winners were not likely to support the program on an ongoing basis. It was designed, therefore, without a natural political constituency. It was solely a "good government" venture, strong on substance and performance but without a political sup-port system—it failed political design. The faulty political design, despite the substantive quality of the program, precluded it from rising to a meaningful level of funding, which has prevented it from having a significant economic effect.

In an effort to build political constituency support, the program was re-structured and renamed in 2007, as noted, to allow universities and labs (in consortia with industry) to participate, and it was allowed to focus not simply on a broad range of technology advances but on particular areas around important societal needs.[20] It remains to be seen whether these modifications will create a strong enough political base to sustain and expand the program from its modest funding level.

To summarize, following are three further political design lessons, in addition to those cited earlier, from the three "valley of death" programs:

6.1. Additional Rules of Political Design

Design to ensure a constituency: Ensure in program design that there will be a noteworthy political interest constituency that will support the new agency before the executive and legislative branches on a continuing basis.

Design to ensure that constituency backs program quality: Further ensure that the new program is structured so that it is in the interest of supporting political constituencies to back program quality and the substantive policy behind it, rather than shift or disrupt quality and substance.

Tether the agency to a recognized mission: If a new agency will be involved in late-stage development along with research, then it may face an ideological debate over its role; if it is designed to be tethered to a strong, politically recognized mission area, then it may be able to override ideology.

Of the three 1980s agencies discussed here, only one, the MEP, achieved a political design that aligned both the substantive and political design criteria.

7. New Generation Energy Innovation Institutions

There have been, as discussed earlier, essentially three major innovation policy moments driven by political demands since World War II: (1) the immediate postwar period where the cold war helped drive the formation and expansion of a plethora of science agencies, (2) the Sputnik aftermath with the formation of DARPA and NASA and scaled-up funding for the NSF and for science education, and (3) the competitiveness era "valley of death" programs of the 1980s. We may be on the verge of a fourth: an energy transformation driven by energy security and climate demands. What lessons from these earlier eras are relevant to the institutional elements in the "new generation" energy innovation policy programs now under consideration?

Recent innovation policy has focused particularly on the new energy technology challenge, with policymakers forming new policy and technology implementation institutions to meet the triple problems of energy geopolitics, climate change, and energy economic costs. These problems have been the political drivers for new energy investments in the February 2009 economic stimulus legislation (approximately $34 billion for energy technology implementation and $5 billion for energy R&D at the DOE).[21] There remains a "valley of death" problem in energy technology because of the institutional gaps designed into our energy innovation system. However, there is also a new and larger problem that U.S. innovation policy and legislation have not previously confronted: the "problem of launch": launching new innovations, at the implementation stage, into long-established, mature economic sectors, of which energy is a prime example [19]. In facing innovation issues in such established sectors, a gap analysis is required of the energy innovation system. While Congress and the new administration have not yet conducted this evaluation in detail, four new programs are now being contemplated in the energy arena within the DOE. Each is sketched next, along with the political design rules identified earlier and the ones that follow that may be most relevant to each.

The Advanced Research Projects Agency (ARPA-E). ARPA-E was authorized in 2007 through the America COMPETES Act[22] and received $400 million in FY2010 start-up funding through the 2009 stimulus legislation (the American Reinvestment and Recovery Act). The administration's budget calls for $300 million in FY2011 funding. It is housed in the DOE and reports directly to the DOE secretary. It was based on the DARPA model as a translational research entity, bridging a gap in the energy innovation system between the DOE's Office of Science, a basic research agency supporting university and lab research under a Bush basic research model, and the DOE's Energy Efficiency and Renewable Energy Office and other applied development and demonstration programs that primarily fund industry. It is an institutional fix aimed at the "valley of death" gap between existing DOE research and applied agencies, to expedite technologies from breakthrough research to late-stage development.

It presents the most complex political design issues among the group of new and proposed agencies. First, as a "valley of death" agency, accelerating research advances and then intervening in late-stage development, does it have a strong enough mission justification to survive the ideological issues that afflict entities playing this development role? The DARPA and ATP lessons on the necessity of a mission-based political design (the fifth rule cited

above) appear relevant here. Ongoing bipartisan support for ARPA-E's energy
mission will clearly be needed as a sustaining driver. Second, will the constituency in the energy sector it will serve—university researchers and small
firms and start-ups—be strong enough to sustain ARPA-E as it seeks support
to ramp up its initial funding? It received over 3,600 applications for its broad
initial R&D offering of $150 million but was only able to fund thirty-seven of
these applicants.[23] Like ATP, it ran the risk of disappointing far more applicants for every one it approved, potentially jeopardizing its constituency support base at the outset. More recent ARPA-E offerings have focused on particular energy technology fields, which should narrow interest and avoid
frustrating large numbers of applicants. However, this could be a continuing
problem depending on the level of ongoing funding that ARPA-E achieves.
Recognizing it was funding only a fraction of its qualified applicants, ARPA-E
responded imaginatively, hosting an "ARPA-E Innovation Summit" in March
2010,[24] inviting hundreds of its promising applicants, whether they received
awards or not, and connecting them with venture capitalists and industrial
firms. The event attracted thousands of participants, including an outpour-
ing of venture capitalists, was widely appreciated by the technology sector it
serves, and helped build goodwill in its applicant pool. DARPA was able to
build a loyal constituency, over time, which has sustained it; it's a strong community of interest formed around particular areas of advance it selected for
support. ARPA-E is taking steps to build such a community through its
summit but may have to consider this approach of narrowing its research
focus to build stronger constituency dependence and support. It may also have
to build other services to applicants, such as mentoring systems of technology
experts who can advise rejected applicants on how to improve their future applications. This technique was attempted by the ATP program with some
success.

ARPA-E also faces the additional problem of jealous agencies within the
DOE, such as the energy labs and applied energy agencies that feel threatened
by its role and funding. ARPA-E, like DARPA before it, will have to make a
major effort to cooperate with these potential in-house rivals, involving them
in its projects, and becoming, like DARPA, their agent and supporter whenever possible. Understanding this, ARPA-E has created advisory groups of
other agency representatives within the DOE, trying to foster involvement
and support for its programs among potential DOE rivals. It portrays its program as a complementary one, operating in a "whitespace" of "game changer"
breakthroughs the other agencies aren't working in, not as a funding competitor. It could also consider, as DARPA has, sharing in the cost of joint projects,

enabling rival agencies to leverage their funding with ARPA-E support. ARPA-E's experience to date suggests additional political design rules for science and technology agencies.

7.1. Additional Rules of Political Design

Support your applicant base, don't dismiss it: Grant-making agencies always run the risk of frustrating their potential support community because they must reject the bulk of their grant applications. The realities of grant making usually make the ratio of grantees to awards far too low to appease applicants. This limits their ability to create a political support community. To counter this, the agency can create other reward systems for applicants, such as opportunities for mentoring services, or access to industry support, or as a convener for a new research community.

Co-opt intraagency rivals: Within a large agency, subagencies often compete over funding and missions. A successful new subagency, confronted with powerful competitors, will attempt to integrate with rival agencies and complement their missions, supporting their efforts as well as its own, including the joint funding of common projects.

Energy Frontier Research Centers (EFRCs). These centers, forty-six of which are now funded, evolved after careful study over five years, through workshops and supporting major reports that engaged hundreds of the most prominent energy researchers and thinkers in the country in identifying the most promising areas of energy research. This effort was led by the DOE's Office of Science, which systematically coalesced and then led this national community of energy researchers in examining basic research areas where energy advances were most needed. At the close of the effort an effective report was prepared by an advisory group that made the case for the program in clear, succinct, nontechnical language, in a length (thirteen pages) that enabled time-challenged congressional staff to read and digest it in twenty minutes, justifying this new program and a strong level of investment.[25] The EFRC program proposal was a model for how an agency can effectively create a new program, building careful, in-depth consensus in the research support community, systematically building informed congressional backing, and proposing a sizable enough program to enable the geographical distribution of competitive awards for centers. For FY2010, $277 million in funding for centers was provided through the 2009 stimulus legislation, plus further funds from appropriations, covering a wide range of research areas. The administration budget calls for $140 million in FY2011.[26] The design appears sound—the centers will work in the basic research area so they will not face ideological challenges. They will have a university research constituency, coupled with an energy mission, to sustain them. They are relatively small in scale ($3 to $5 million/year per center) and authorized for five years, so they will not become protected, large-scale enclaves that could isolate other researchers. The carefully organized process for forming EFRCs suggests a further rule:

7.2. Additional Rule of Political Design

Build support for the new agency prelaunch: A new program shouldn't be allowed to descend like a *deus ex machina* into the political world; the creation process should be viewed as an opportunity to build a supporting constituency for the new program in the process of forming and advocating for it. This also offers a chance to create congressional understanding and buy-in. The Energy Frontier Research Centers' launch process serves as a model.

RE-ENERGYSE. REgaining our ENERGY Science and Engineering Edge (RE-ENERGYSE), is an educational effort designed to guide students and workers to pursue careers in science, engineering, technology, and entrepreneurship related to clean energy. This proposed education initiative, which is cross-disciplinary and offers study fellowships, was rushed out by DOE secretary Chu at the beginning of his tenure; he sought funding for it in the FY2010 DOE budget. When the nation began to build an IT revolution, it was aided by the fact that DARPA had early on supported a network of computer science departments within research universities. These blossomed, creating an education element to train new talent that fostered the technology advance. Secretary Chu clearly recognized that the same phenomena could apply in energy— universities had disciplinary stovepipes that encompassed aspects of energy but lacked curricula to look at energy across disciplinary perspectives and from a policy point of view. His proposed "RE-ENERGYSE" program could provide a talent base in the energy field with the foundations to deal with broad energy policy issues and interdisciplinary energy research not possible under the current disciplinary stovepipes. Universities could provide a support constituency for the program, and since it was to be a competitive program, it would be in their interest to ensure program quality.

However, there was no effort to build up constituency support in advance of the announcement of the program through the FY2010 budget. No effort was made to lay the groundwork for the program with congressional committees, and the program was not well defined when announced, consisting of a brief list of ideas. Every new administration is rushed as it comes into office, and in its rush to get the program out the door, the DOE paid a price. Congress did not fund the proposal in FY2010, although the administration has resubmitted it for consideration in FY2011, budgeted at $50 million.[27] Congressional appropriators were unprepared to consider the concept, and since science education is traditionally the territory of the NSF, they were concerned about creating a duplicative new science education agency in the DOE. The DOE tried to accommodate this concern by offering the proposal with an NSF element, but to no avail. Congress was also concerned that the DOE had not budgeted a long-term funding stream that would enable the program to be sustained along with other new energy program elements. The political design issue that the DOE ran into for RE-ENERGYSE amounted to a variation of the rule earlier cited: failure to lay the groundwork for a new program with Congress and to build in advance of launch a constituency for it can jeopardize the new idea. In general, a massive annual budget submission, usually held in secret by administrations until its release by the OMB, is a poor place to announce a new program: it ensures that both the potential support constituency and the congressional committees that will have to fund it are surprised and unprepared.

Innovation Hubs. Secretary Chu, drawing on his personal experiences at Bell Labs and directing the Lawrence Berkeley Laboratory, proposed eight, larger-scale, $25 to $30 million a year labs, to be housed at universities or at national labs, to sponsor research on key areas of energy research. Congress approved initial funding for three of these "hubs" in FY2010, which focused on solar, energy-efficient building design, and advanced nuclear reactors. A fourth hub was proposed in the FY2011 budget to focus on batteries and energy storage.[28] The hubs are to aim at multidisciplinary research in areas ready to be scaled up, to speed R&D and shorten the time from discovery to technology implementation. Because of the larger scale of these efforts, compared to Energy Frontier Research Centers, for example, there is a risk that this scale will lock in political support that could limit the flexibility of future agency research directions, and that could narrow the front of research advance, crowding out a broader front. In other words, while there are large numbers of able researchers starting to engage in energy research advances, the large hubs may capture the funding in key areas and limit support for talent outside the hubs. This is always a risk with scaling up research efforts. These issues of institution building and corresponding research lock-in require careful attention from the DOE as it forms its initial pilot hubs, as the aforementioned

design rules suggest. It should work on designs to find ways to build these research areas in ways that allow a focus on promising technology challenges
that also will bring in more, not less, participants on the tasks the hubs face.

8. The Future

What will future challenges bring for the political design for innovation organization? Ongoing efforts to bring innovation into the energy sector provide a
useful future construct.

All of the DOE's innovation efforts to bring on an energy transformation
have been focused on the front end of the innovation pipeline—on the R&D
side. Proposals on the back end—technology demonstration, commercialization, and deployment—have been neglected, to date, by the Obama administration. There is a further problem, as suggested earlier, in the energy area that
none of the new innovation entities proposed to date by the DOE has focused
on—the problem of technology launch.[29] While the "valley of death" has been
the major preoccupation of science and technology policy for the past two decades, energy, as an established, complex, politically and economically powerful, and technologically locked-in sector, presents an additional problem. The
energy sector operates in an established political-economic-technological paradigm, and that paradigm must be altered if a new reduced carbon energy system is to prevail. Thus even if the valley of death in energy—the gap between
research and development—is surmounted, a deep problem remains. Because
most new energy technologies are components in larger established systems
(for example, advanced batteries are components in cars, enhanced geother-
mal technology must fit into existing utility systems), they must launch into
these established sectors and be price competitive from the moment of launch.
All of the four new agencies proposed by the DOE, as discussed earlier, are
organized around the valley of death problem; none encompasses the technology launch task. As tough as crossing the valley of death in energy is, reaching
the point of market launch is even harder.

A network of additional innovation entities will likely be needed on the
back end of the innovation process, in areas such as demonstration, financing,
and technology road mapping. For example, in financing, the DOE has loan
guarantee authority that it has just started to implement a half decade after it
was first authorized. But loan guarantees are only relevant to some firms;
many start-ups and small firms lack the capitalization and depth to obtain
loans, so guarantees may not solve their problems. A tool box of financing
instruments will be required if the DOE wants to move technology advances
from its new R&D entities into the marketplace. The DOE has had difficulty

in managing commercial-scale demonstrations; it will need new organizational approaches to accomplish this important step. A new energy technology sector will also need test beds, standards, and technology road maps. Each will call for new organizational approaches. The DOE has not yet undertaken the systematic analysis of gaps in the existing energy innovation system to understand which gaps need to be filled. It needs to face the innovation back-end side of the challenge it faces, because innovation in a complex, established sector presents problems very different from standing up technology advances in new, unoccupied breakthrough sectors such as IT or biotechnology [20]. In sum, in energy, additional organizational entities will be needed to meet the challenge of innovating in an established sector. None of the new energy agencies formed to date will prove adequate unless this back-end gap is filled and their efforts are fully coordinated with new programs to fill the launch support mission.

What else will the future of innovation bring? Energy is not the only established, complex sector where innovation is needed; there are at least two other crisis areas. Because there are few incentives in the current system to control costs, and limited effective competition over prices, the nation is faced with out-of-control health care costs. The prospect of health care reforms that will expand the coverage of the existing system will make this task more difficult. Accordingly, there is a significant innovation need in health care service delivery. This innovation demand will need to focus not only on new technologies for more efficient and effective service delivery, such as robotics or the long-discussed introduction of information technologies into medicine at scale, but also on the processes and systems for delivery of that innovation, to try to create incentives for its adaptation. As with energy, we face an established techno-economic-political paradigm that must be overcome for the introduction of efficient health care service delivery. To manage this, a careful gap analysis of that existing system and the introduction of innovation within it must be undertaken, and carefully tailored organizational fixes must be introduced. This is a major pending societal innovation task where political design will be a crucial element.

Similarly, manufacturing is another complex established sector ripe for innovation advances if the United States is to retain a presence in this economic territory. Manufacturing accounts for $1.6 trillion of U.S. GDP, directly employs 11 million people, manufacturing firms account for 70 percent of U.S. R&D funding and 63 percent of science and engineering employment, and manufacturing workers are paid substantially more than service-sector employees [21]. Global wealth continues to be based predominantly on trade in complex, high-value, technology goods; trade in these goods still dwarfs trade in services. While many economists suggest that the United States can shift to a services-only economy, the U.S. deficit in manufactured goods exceeded $500 billion in pre-recession 2007, while its surplus in services trade was less than one-third that number, with the former outpacing the latter. And its surplus in advanced technology goods has now turned into a deficit that exceeded $50 billion in 2008. In other words, U.S. strength in the global economy is being jeopardized by its declining manufacturing performance. While some argue that it can't compete in manufacturing against a low-wage, low-cost economy such as China's, Germany and Japan, which have high-cost, high-wage economies comparable to the U.S. economy, are running major trade surpluses.[30] There is movement in federal agencies to look at innovation in manufacturing, including in the Defense, Energy, and Commerce Departments, through DARPA, EERE (Energy Efficiency and Renewable Energy), and NIST. Two major studies are pending, at PCAST (President's Council of Advisors on Science and Technology) and at the industry-led Council on Competitiveness. Tackling innovation in this complex, established sector will likewise call for a careful gap analysis of its innovation system, which has not been carefully examined since the introduction of the Toyota production system [22, 23]. It also may prove politically difficult; while there is a political consensus on funding basic research, work on manufacturing technologies and processes is inherently applied and more interventionist.

The future of the next generation of U.S. innovation may increasingly fall into the category of innovating in complex, established sectors, such as energy, health care delivery, and manufacturing. In order to confront this existing frontier, new substantive and political designs will be required for effective innovation organization. On the political design side, one design rule already appears apparent.

8.1. Additional Rule of Political Design

Innovation in complex, established sectors requires an innovation gap analysis: Innovation occurs in complex systems of connected institutions; if innovation is to extend into the back end of the innovation pipeline, from demonstration to commercialization, then a gap analysis of the strengths of innovation organizations in those areas must be undertaken, along with the traditional analysis of innovation at the front-end R&D side. Since the applied side and back end are historically dominated by industry, the substantive design of such applied and back-end innovation efforts must be complemented by effective political design, which will involve the careful cultivation of support from established industries that may otherwise oppose such applied or back-end intervention.

9. Conclusion

This chapter has briefly reviewed the history of new U.S. science and technology agencies since World War II. It has identified nine possible rules for political design embedded in the history of the political and policy issues that have afflicted new federal R&D agencies in the four key postwar periods of new innovation investments and institutions. The political design rule set identified here is briefly summarized thus:

First, beware of scale; when an innovation agency reaches a large scale in a particular locality, which multiplies its political support, this may limit future research and mission flexibility.

Second, don't let narrow front advance cancel out the broad front; a large-scale research effort at an entity focused on a particular area of advance may crowd out and limit a broader front for science and technology advance.

Third, science entities will only survive if they are designed to have a strong supporting constituency.

Fourth, when designing constituency support, ensure that the selected constituency base will support, not divert, a quality program consistent with the substantive program design.

Fifth, particularly if a new entity will be involved in late-stage development along with research, it may face an ideological challenge, so it must be tethered to a strong, politically recognized mission area to justify its tasks.

Sixth, because the number of grant applications will significantly exceed the number of grants that can be awarded, this risks alienating the strongest potential political support community for an agency, those that it funds. An agency should offer alternative ways to build its support base, offering additional services aside from grants to its applicant pool, such as mentoring, or connections to industry, or as a convener for a research community.

Seventh, to avoid intra-agency rivalry where a new arrival will inevitably be viewed as a funding competitor, the new entrant program should attempt to integrate rival entities into its deliberations and to complement their missions, supporting their efforts as well as its own, to co-opt the existing programs.

Eighth, the launch process is key to building political support; the agency creation process should be viewed as an opportunity to build a supporting constituency for the new program in the process of forming it, and as a chance to create congressional understanding and buy-in. Congressional and support group launch surprise should be avoided.

Ninth, and finally, innovation in complex established economic sectors, such as energy, health care delivery, and manufacturing, requires an analysis of gaps in those innovation systems, particularly of the applied side and back end of the pipeline, from prototype and demonstration to commercialization. Since industry likely dominates the applied side and back end in these established sectors, careful cultivation of industry support will be required for organizational interventions in this area.

Sound political design along these lines could buttress sound innovation systems. There are, of course, other political design rules; those listed here simply derive from the author's career as a political science practitioner in the science and technology field. Unfortunately, the political design issues that innovation agencies face have rarely received attention, yet we are on the verge of creating a new series of such institutions around the energy challenge and perhaps other areas. Unlearned lessons lead to error repetition. The lessons, for example, of scale, of narrow front advance canceling out broad front advance, or of creating a new entity without a sound support base, remain unrecognized design principles, and we may be facing another generation of design problems in these areas. Recognition of a problem, of course, is the first step to its remedy. A concerted effort to examine the political support systems for science and technology programs and agencies as they are created, including their political strengths and weaknesses, could be a constructive step. Possible ways to resolve these design issues so that the political design better supports the policy design will require conscious attention from policymakers and from the academic community. Otherwise, recurring political design errors could undermine attempts at innovation reforms. The consequences are not minor. Growth economist Richard Nelson was one of the first to articulate that innovation occurs in a system that includes a series of connected innovation institutions and program elements, both public and private.[31] Creating the political design that supports the substantive policy design on the public side of that institutional network could offer a significant enhancement to our innovation system.

References

[1] D. Hart. Forged Consensus. Princeton (NJ): Princeton University Press; 1998, pp. 17–29.
[2] P. Romer. Endogenous Technological Change. Journal of Political Economy, 98; 1990, p. 596.

[3] R. R. Nelson. National Systems of Innovation. New York: Oxford University Press; 1993, pp. 3–21, 505–523.

[4] V. Bush. Science: The Endless Frontier. Washington (DC): GPO; 1945.

[5] D. E. Stokes. Pasteur's Quadrant: Basic Science and Technological Innovation. Washington (DC): Brookings Institution Press; 1997.

[6] V. H. Reis. Nuclear Energy, Nuclear Weapons and Climate Change. Washington (DC): U.S. Department of Energy; 2008, p. 23 (powerpoint slides).

[7] A. Roland. Model Research: The National Advisory Committee for Aeronautics 1915–1958. Washington (DC): NASA (SP-#4103); 1985.

[8] R. Bilstein. Orders of Magnitude: A History of the NACA and NASA, 1915–1990. Washington (DC): NASA (SP #4406); 1989.

[9] P. Bizony. The Man Who Ran the Moon—James Webb and the Secret History of Project Apollo. New York: Thunder's Mouth Press; 2006.

[10] Testimony of Norman Augustine on the Review of U.S. Human Spaceflight Plans Committee. Washington (DC): House Committee on Science and Technology; 2009.

[11] Report of the Advisory Committee on the Future of the U.S. Space Program. Washington (DC): NASA, History Division; 1990.

[12] Long Day on Capitol Hill for OSTP Director John Holdren. FYI: The American Institute of Physics Bulletin of Science Policy News, March 1, 2010.

[13] National Science Board, Science and Engineering Indicators 2008. U.S. R&D Share of GSP 1953–2006, figure 4-17. Arlington (VA): National Science Board; 2008.

[14] M. Waldrop. The Dream Machine, J. C. R. Licklider and the Revolution That Made Computing Personal. New York: Viking Press; 2001.

[15] V. W. Ruttan. Is War Necessary for Economic Growth? Military Procurement and Technology Development. New York: Oxford University Press; 2006, pp. 91–130.

[16] R. VanAtta. Fifty Years of Innovation and Discovery: DARPA: 50 Years of Bridging the Gap. Washington (DC): DARPA; 2008, pp. 20–29.

[17] K. Hughes. Building the Next American Century: The Past and Future of American Economic Competitiveness. Washington (DC) and Baltimore (MD): Woodrow Wilson Center Press and Johns Hopkins University Press; 2004.

[18] L. Branscomb, P. Auerswald. Between Invention and Innovation: An Analysis of Funding for Early-Stage Technology Development. Washington (DC): National Institute of Standards and Technology; November 2002.

[19] C. Weiss, W. B. Bonvillian. Structuring an Energy Technology Revolution. Cambridge (MA): MIT Press; 2009, pp. 37–56.

[20] W. B. Bonvillian, C. Weiss. Taking Covered Wagons East. Innovations, 4; Fall 2009.

[21] G. Tassey. Rationales and Mechanisms for Revitalizing U.S. Manufacturing R&D Strategies. Journal of Technology Transfer, 35; June 3, 2010.

[22] M. Dertouzos, R. Lester, R. Solow. Made in America: Regaining the Productive Edge. Cambridge (MA): MIT Press; 1989.

[23] J. P. Womack, D. T. Jones, D. Roos. The Machine That Changed the World. New York: HarperCollins; 1991.

Notes

1. The term refers to the network of R&D and related innovation institutions and support mechanisms that constitute the ecosystem that Nelson and other growth economists view as a prerequisite for strong innovation capability [3].

2. The discussion in this section is drawn from William B. Bonvillian, "The Connected Science Model for Innovation–The DARPA Model," *21st Century Innovation Systems for the U.S. and Japan* (Washington, DC: National Academies Press, May 2009), 206–235. See also G. Pascal Zachary, *Endless Frontier—Vannevar Bush, Engineer of the American Century* (Cambridge, MA: MIT Press, 1999); George Mazuzan, *NSF: A Brief History (1950–1985)* Pub. #86-16 (Washington, DC: NSF, 1986), 1-25, www .nsf.gov/pubs/stis1994/nsf8816/nsf8816.txt; William A. Blanpied, "Inventing U.S. Science Policy," *Physics Today*, vol. 51, no. 2 (February 1998): 34–40, www.nsf.gov/about/ history/nsf50/science_policy.jsp.

3. The pipeline model was initially institutionalized at the Office of Naval Research. See Harvey M. Sapolsky, *Science and the Navy—The History of the Office of Naval Research* (Princeton, NJ: Princeton University Press, 1990), 9–81. It provided the foundational model for exploratory, basic research that evolved at the National Science Foundation, the National Institutes of Health, and the Department of Energy's Office of Science.

4. Bush attempted to organize postwar science under a single tent, the National Science Foundation, but a veto confrontation with President Truman over the role of the President in senior science appointments delayed that agency's creation by five years, and other agencies evolved in the interim. See Blanpied, "Inventing U.S. Science Policy"; Mazuzan, *NSF.*

5. The problems with this model are explored in [5].

6. Matzuzan, *NSF,* chap. 3.

7. Bonvillian, "The Connected Science Model."

8. See Hart [1].

9. It is possible to push this debate even further back into American history to ideological battles between Hamilton, arguably the parent of the modern commercial American economy, and his anti-economic intervention opponents Jefferson and later Jackson. See William B. Bonvillian, "The Innovation State," *The American Interest* (July/August 2009): 78.

10. Innovation wave theory is explored in Carlota Perez, *Technological Revolutions and Financial Capital* (Cheltenham, UK: Edward Elgar, 2002), 3–46; Robert D. Atkinson, *The Past and Future of America's Economy—Long Waves of Innovation That Power Cycles of Growth* (Cheltenham, UK: Edward Elgar, 2004), 3–40.

11. Although not an institution, as part of the same 1980s competitiveness response Congress passed the Bayh-Dole Act (35 U.S.C. 200–212) in 1980, which transferred ownership of federally funded research from the federal government to the universities, where the research was executed, giving universities a stake in its commercialization. The act is generally viewed as a transformative success, enhancing the role of universities in what is termed here "connected" science and giving them a stake in their regional economies. See, for example, Birch Bayh, Joseph P. Allen, and How-

ard W. Bremer, "Universities, Inventors and the Bayh-Dole Act," *Life Sciences Law and Industry Report*, vol. 3, no. 24 (BNA, December 18, 2009); David Roessner, Jennifer Bond, Sumiye Okubo, and Mark Planting, *The Economic Impact of Licensed Commercialized Inventions Originating in University Research 1996–2007: Final Report to the Biotechnology Industry Organization* (Washington, D.C.: BIO, September 3, 2009), www.bio.org/ip/techtransfer/BIO_final_report_9_3_09_rev_2.pdf.

12. See PL 100-519, Title I, Sec. 102(d) (October 24, 1988); 102 Stat. 2590; 15 USC chap. 7, sec. 278k (Regional Centers for the Transfer of Manufacturing Technology); 15 CFR sec. 290.6, www.mep.nist.gov/about-mep/legislative-history.htm.

13. NIST, MEP, About MEP (program description on website as of 2010), www.mep.nist.gov/about-mep/index.htm.

14. P.L 97-219, 97th Cong., 2d Sess. (July 22, 1982), 96 Stat. 217, Report on HR 4326, 97th Cong., 1st Sess., House of Representatives, No. 97-349, pt. 1; Report, 97th Cong., 2d Sess., House of Representatives, No. 97-349, pt. 2-7; as amended through PL 108-447, 108th Cong., 2d Sess. (December 8, 2004).

15. Roland Tibbetts (SBIR Program Manager, 1976–1996, and program founder, National Science Foundation), *Reauthorizing SBIR: The Critical Importance of SBIR and Small High-Tech Firms in Stimulating and Strengthening the U.S. Economy* (May 28, 2008), www.nsba.biz/docs/tibbetts.pdf.

16. See the series reports on SBIR programs at federal agencies from the National Research Council, Board on Science, Technology and Economic Policy, Committee for Capitalizing on Science, Technology, and Innovation, including *An Assessment of the Small Business Innovation Research Program at the Department of Defense* (Washington, DC: National Academies Press, 2009), www.nap.edu/catalog.php?record_id=11963; *An Assessment of the Small Business Innovation Research Program at the National Institutes of Health* (Washington, DC: National Academies Press, 2009), www.nap.edu/catalog.php?record_id=11964; *An Assessment of the Small Business Innovation Research Program at the National Aeronautics and Space Administration* (Washington, DC: National Academies Press, 2009), www.nap.edu/catalog.php?record_id=12441; *An Assessment of Small Business Innovation Research Program at the Department of Energy* (Washington, DC: National Academies Press, 2008), www.nap.edu/catalog.php?record_id=12052.

17. Section 3012 of the America Creating Opportunities to Meaningfully Promote Excellence in Technology, Education, and Sciences (COMPETES) Act, Pub. L. 110-69, 110th Cong., 1st Sess. (August 9, 2007), repealed the Advanced Technology Program (ATP) and reformed it as the Technology Investment Program (TIP).

18. See, for example, National Research Council, Board on Science, Technology, and Economic Policy, *Advanced Technology Program: Challenges and Opportunities* (Washington, DC: National Academies Press, 1999), www.nap.edu/openbook.php?isbn=0309067758; Rosalie Ruegg and Irwin Feller, *A Toolkit for Evaluating Public R&D Investment Models, Methods, and Findings from ATP's First Decade* (NIST GCR 03-857 2003), www.atp.nist.gov/eao/gcr03-857/contents.htm; studies and data referenced in NIST, Advanced Technology Program, Impacts of ATP Funding, www.atp.nist.gov/; "ATP Gems and Success Stories (through 2007)," www.atp.nist.gov/gems/list gems.htm.

19. NIST, Advanced Technology Program, "ATP Applications, Awards & Participants by State—45 Competitions (1990–September 2007)," www.atp.nist.gov/eao/02aap_state.htm.

20. NIST, Technology Investment Program, "About TIP, Key Features," www.nist.gov/tip/about_tip.html.

21. American Recovery and Reinvestment Act (ARRA), HR 1, P.L. 111-5, 111th Cong., 1st Sess. (signed into law February 17, 2009), Title IV.

22. America COMPETES Act, Sec. 5012, Pub. L. 110-69, 110th Cong., 1st Sess. (August 9, 2007). See discussion of ARPA-E in William B. Bonvillian, "Will the Search for New Energy Technologies Require a New R&D Mission Agency?" *Bridges* (July 14, 2007), www.ostina.org/content/view.2297/721/; Erica R. H. Fuchs, "Cloning DARPA Successfully," *Issues in Science and Technology* (Fall 2009): 65–70.

23. DOE–ARPA-E, "Bold Transformational Energy Research Projects Win $151 Million in Funding," October 26, 2009, http://arpa-e.energy.gov/NewsMedia/News/tabid/83/vw/1/ItemID/20/Default.aspx.

24. ARPA-E, "Energy Innovation Summit Materials, March 1–3, 2010," http://arpa-e.energy.gov/ConferencesEvents/InnovationSummitMaterials.aspx.

25. DOE–Basic Energy Sciences (BES) Advisory Committee, *New Science for a Secure and Sustainable Energy Future* (Washington, DC: DOE-BES, December 2008), www.sc.doe.gov/BES/reports/files/NSSSEF_rpt.pdf.

26. DOE–Office of Science, Overview—Appropriation Summary by Program, FY2009–FY2011 (2010), 10, www.er.doe.gov/bes/archives/budget/SC_FY2011budget_overview.pdf; DOE, Office of Science, Energy Frontier Research Centers, *Tackling Our Energy Challenges,* re: FY2011 budget (2010), www.er.doe.gov/bes/EFRC/index.html.

27. DOE, FY2011 Congressional Budget Request—Budget Highlights (Washington, DC: DOE/CF-0046, February 1, 2010), 30, www.mbe.doe.gov/budget/11budget/Content.FY2011Highlights.pdf.

28. Ibid., 2.

29. See discussion on the issues raised in this section in reference [19], 2, 28–36, 151–161, 167–171 and [20].

30. OECD Stat. Extracts, Balance of Payments (MEI)(2009 data), http://stats.oecd.org/index.aspx?datasetcode=MEI_BOP.

31. See [3].

Science Policy and the Congress

David Goldston

16

1. Introduction

Congress is the ultimate arbiter of federal science policy. While it often defers, or delegates, to the executive branch, Congress has the final say on the size of agency science budgets, the focus of science programs, and the selection of science projects. Yet members of Congress, even more than other federal policymakers, tend to base decisions about science policy (i.e., policy for science) on a largely unexamined mixture of general theories, suppositions, time-honored guesses, and just-so stories. Little information is available to help them do otherwise. And while the research enterprise that has resulted has certainly been of great benefit to the nation, there is no systematic way to determine whether it is optimal or how best to reshape it to handle new challenges. The most fundamental questions, when asked, go begging for answers.

This chapter will point out some of the primary questions that Congress would need to have answered to guide science policy more systematically. In some cases, these are matters that Congress has explicitly raised, but more often they are the questions that are implicit in congressional deliberations—the questions that would arise if Congress dove beneath its surface assumptions. Without answers to these questions, it is difficult, if not impossible, for Congress to project with any precision the consequences of its most basic decisions about science policy. And those decisions help determine the parameters of the U.S. research enterprise—its overall size, which scientific fields are emphasized, how research proposals are reviewed, and what kinds of scientific inquiries are pursued.

2. How Congress Handles Science Policy

While the U.S. Constitution vests Congress with ultimate authority, it is largely a reactive body. The congressional agenda is shaped primarily by presidential priorities and the concerns of national interest groups. This may be especially true in the case of science policy: the institutional structure of the

Congress, the arcane nature of science, the relative obscurity of science policy issues, and even the long-standing consensus in favor of federal research spending all tend to limit congressional initiative and to keep critical science policy questions beneath the surface of public discussion.

The congressional structure fragments jurisdiction over science policy. Numerous committees have authorizing responsibilities for one or more science agencies, that is, they oversee and can direct an agency's operations through hearings and legislation, and through more informal means, such as letters. The House Committee on Science and Technology, which was established in 1958 to oversee the National Aeronautics and Space Administration (NASA), is the only committee in Congress that has science as its primary focus, but it does not exercise legislative control over several major agencies, such as the National Institutes of Health (NIH).

In any event, authorizing committees do not provide funding to science agencies; that is the province of the Appropriations Committee (which can also provide policy direction), and spending control over the science agencies is distributed among the Appropriations subcommittees. Each subcommittee has its own pot of money that it allocates among the agencies in its purview, so science agencies do not necessarily compete directly with each other for funds in the appropriations process; rather, they compete against the agencies that happen to share the subcommittee to which history has assigned them. Sometimes the agencies that report to a subcommittee share a common theme—most energy-related programs are in one subcommittee, for example—but this can also be a bit of a grab bag.

In many ways, this disaggregated, overlapping, and somewhat random arrangement of jurisdictions has turned out to serve science well. It has encouraged diversity in the federal research establishment; different agencies can take differing approaches to scientific questions, and they have different methods for reviewing proposals. (As noted later, this can provide a natural experiment for science policy research.) Having more committees with their fingers in the science pie has also meant that more representatives and senators have some familiarity with, and interest in, the health of the science agencies. At the same time, the dispersal of authority makes it difficult to attack science as an overall enterprise. But a downside, relevant to this chapter, is that few members of Congress or the congressional staff focus enough on science to make it their defining issue or to pursue deeper questions about how to shape or organize science policy.

Moreover, many—if not most—of the members of Congress who actively engage in science policy issues are concerned primarily with furthering the interests of specific institutions in their home state or district, a university or a federal laboratory, for example. Such concerns do not lead to probing questions about how best to support the research establishment nationally. Beyond that, members of Congress often feel uneasy about dealing with questions that would involve making judgments about the value of a particular field of science, and they tend to defer to the executive branch on issues that seem to draw directly on scientific expertise.

Finally, the interest groups that work to influence the congressional science policy agenda—universities, disciplinary societies, and business groups, for example—are essentially on the same page on the broadest issues; they work to increase research spending, and they resist federal mandates and changes to the status quo. Perhaps uniquely among areas of public policy, science policy is characterized by consensus; there are no standing armies in opposing camps of lobbyists. Science policy is rarely a topic in political campaigns, and when it is, the issue is usually which candidate would provide more generous support for research. Rarely do disputes erupt that can be parsed or reconciled only by reexamining first principles.

The one exception to this broad agreement is the long-standing debate—going back almost to the nation's founding—over the proper role of the federal government in promoting technology. But the periodic disputes over the extent the federal government can subsidize research and financing on specific technologies do not usually prompt Congress to raise questions of science policy, that is, practical questions about which programs might work to achieve a particular goal. Rather, the debates over technology just send members of Congress back to the comfort of their philosophical corners; they retreat to their ideological predisposition for or against federal activity generally.

What all this means is that Congress has little incentive to raise (or even recognize) the most salient questions about science policy. The congressional structure, the abstruse character of science, the nature of local and national interests, and the postwar U.S. record of scientific, technical, and economic success all create a sense of comfort with the status quo. When Congress does seek guidance, it is often looking to have its assumptions vindicated. The legislators who asked the National Academy of Sciences to undertake the study that produced *Rising Above the Gathering Storm*, for example, were seeking ammunition for their existing efforts to increase science spending.

But if anything, this state of affairs makes it more important that the academic community develop a science of science policy that could have direct application and relevance to congressional policymakers. They are unlikely to seek out or interpret studies that appear to be tangential to their decision making. But a science of science policy could be highly influential if a handful of key leaders in Congress (and the executive branch) found such work to be helpful in achieving their goals for science—making the United States a leader in research, promoting economic growth, improving human health, strengthening national defense, and so on. The questions that a science of science policy might help answer are too vital to the nation's future to be left to chance.

3. Science Spending

This is certainly true of the overarching question in federal science policy: How large should the federal research budget be? Science advocates, both inside and outside the Congress, regularly answer that question simply by arguing that more must be better and then settling on some campaign goal—most commonly, doubling science agency budgets, returning to the real-dollar equivalent of some previous appropriations peak, or spending a percentage of gross domestic product (GDP) that is at least equal to that of other industrial nations. Such spending targets have the advantage of being concrete and sounding like they have a basis in economics, but they are actually about as arbitrary as the goals for a fund-raising telethon; they're as much a guess about how much money can successfully be sought from the Congress as they are a precise calculation of what the research system needs.

There is, of course, a kernel of analysis behind such goals. Studies have shown that U.S. economic growth has been driven by innovation, and that federally funded research has contributed, and continues to contribute, to that innovation. But except rhetorically, such economics research is not enough to assume that any specific increase in federal research spending is the best use of a marginal federal dollar, or even that it will be salutary. Indeed, it's not even clear that overall federal (or national) spending on research, or on research and development (R&D), is a useful barometer of anything, given the disparate nature of the spending. In any event, despite all the head-scratching in the science policy community about how much money to seek for research, the primary determinant of annual federal science spending turns out to be the size of the federal budget as a whole. Macroeconomics and macropolitics are the primary drivers of the science budget, and given how little "science of science policy" there is to draw upon, it's hard to imagine how it could be otherwise.

Moreover, the federal research budget is only an after-the-fact calculation. Neither the executive branch nor (as noted earlier) the Congress put together a science budget per se; decisions about individual agencies and programs are made by different policymakers and then later added together and displayed as a science budget. Science policy experts often express regret at this state of affairs and periodically propose to remedy the situation by, for example, putting all research spending under one congressional Appropriations Subcommittee. But there is no reason to assume that this would result in higher spending levels,the goal of those proposing such reorganizations—in fact, the opposite would be far more likely. More relevant here, there is little intellectual justification for bringing science budgeting under one roof when we lack the analytical tools to debate what the impact of different overall spending levels would be.

The intellectual underpinnings for other broad science policy debates are even shakier than those for discussing overall budget levels. For example, advocates for the physical sciences (again, both inside and outside the government) have argued in recent years that the federal budget has become "unbalanced," pointing to the sharp rise in the percentage of federal funding going to the biomedical sciences. "Balance" sounds like an inherently benign attribute, but little, if any, research has been done that could help policymakers determine what an optimal spending mix among scientific fields would be. The only fact that is adduced to argue for balance is that biomedical research depends in part on advances in the physical sciences. But that is a far cry from being able to claim that a particular level of investment in the physical sciences is inadequate (or adequate). And no one then talks about shaping a physical sciences agenda around aiding biomedical research. Rather, the argument about balance is primarily visceral: funding for one set of fields has grown rapidly, while funding for others has stagnated (although this is somewhat distorted by the inclusion of the *sui generis* Apollo program in the physical sciences base). This feels as unfair to partisans of the physical sciences as a parent serving different portions of dessert to siblings (even if they may be of different ages and have different dietary needs). The disproportionate growth of biomedical research, and especially of the NIH, is worth debating; the problem is that little more than hunches and extrapolations are available as a basis for argument once the issue is joined.

4. Research and Risk

Policymakers need a more scientific basis for making decisions, not only about spending levels but also about the nature of the research to be funded. For example, in recent years, several prominent reports and a number of members of Congress have called for federal agencies to give greater emphasis to "transformational research" or "high-risk, high-return research." This summons is based largely on an amorphous sense on the part of some scientists and policymakers that agencies have increasingly been playing it safe when deciding which grant proposals to approve, driven, perhaps, by tight budgets. Agencies have responded with some new programs targeted at riskier projects but just as often have claimed that all the research they fund is transformational. This is another important debate that is being conducted with virtually no intellectual grounding. What is transformational research (the term might cover a number of categories of research, if it means anything at all), and has it become less likely to receive funding? Can it be identified in advance (i.e., at the proposal stage), and could proposal review processes be designed to increase the likelihood of such research being funded? These questions have barely been raised, let alone answered. The word "paradigm" is often thrown around in these debates, but it's a safe bet that most people using it have not read Thomas Kuhn's *The Structure of Scientific Revolutions,* where this use of the term originated, and Kuhn's work would lead one to think that transformations tend to arise gradually from developments in "normal science," not from a research project that is labeled "high risk" a priori.

The debate over transformational research points to a whole area of social science research that could use more work—the nature of peer review and how to improve it. Different agencies use different forms of grant review, and such diversity is healthy, but none of the systems seems to have been subjected to rigorous evaluation. It is simply taken as a given that peer review has its foibles but is the "worst system except for all the others," to apply Winston Churchill's quip about democracy. But different methods of peer review and different methods of selecting peer reviewers can have different results. Developing some systematic ideas about what kinds of peer review work best for what kinds of programs would be enormously helpful.

5. Jobs

The impact of research spending on employment is arguably the murkiest area of all, even though jobs are what Congress wants to see result first and foremost from research spending. All of this became especially clear when Congress was debating economic stimulus legislation in early 2009. Research spending was included in the bill largely because the stimulus legislation was a convenient vehicle for winning long-sought budget increases for federal science agencies. But the inclusion of science in a stimulus package immediately raised questions no one could answer very well about how many and what kinds of jobs such spending could create, particularly in the short run—this despite years of universities positioning themselves politically as economic development tools and members of Congress earmarking funds for their home schools with that in mind. The direct and indirect shorter-term employment effects of science spending warrant intellectual investigation, preferably before a backlash is prompted by an anecdote about federal money just creating jobs for Chinese postdoctoral students or some such thing.

But the questions related to employment go far beyond the matter of short-term impacts. Paralleling questions about the size of the overall research budget are questions about the optimal size of the scientific workforce, particularly in academia. Just as the reigning assumption about science budgets is that more is always better, policymakers tend to argue that, or at least act as if, a larger academic sector is always better. This has created a Malthusian dilemma in which increases in research spending lead universities to expand their faculty and research staffs, creating a demand for more research funding that inevitably grows more quickly than the federal budget.

The *reductio ad absurdum* of this dilemma occurred when the NIH budget was doubled between 1998 and 2002, leading universities to bring on large numbers of new researchers, some of them funded entirely with "soft money" (i.e., the universities did not use any of their own internal funds for salaries). Universities also went on a construction spree, usually without setting aside any funds for the research that would take place in the new buildings. This would probably have created an unsustainable demand for dollars, even if the NIH budget had kept growing instead of flattening out. Research is needed on how large the academic sector needs to be or, better, on how to evaluate the impacts of having an academic sector of different sizes, but also on how to increase research funding in a way that does not produce unwarranted or unsustainable growth. Perhaps simpler, but equally important, would be the development of models or tools to think through how increases in spending would likely affect the size and scope of the research establishment and how to shape those effects. For example, the NIH boom did relatively little to help younger researchers or to reshape the aging biomedical research workforce. Could the money have been spent in a way that would have refreshed the research enterprise (in a sustainable way)?

The concern about young faculty points to a more specific question about the size of the academic sector: How many PhDs does the United States need to be awarding each year in the natural and physical sciences and engineering? Since not all PhD students go into, or should expect to go into, academic jobs—and since not all of them remain in the United States—this question involves more than concerns about academia. Here too the complaint for years has been that the United States is not producing enough PhDs, particularly those who are U.S. citizens (or, some claim, even enough baccalaureate degrees in the physical sciences and engineering). Here as well the analytical framework is rickety. The argument generally comes down to an assumption that producing more PhDs will inevitably be helpful, regardless of market demand; indeed, the assumption seems to be that the supply will create the demand. Proponents of increasing PhD production, like those pushing higher budgets, also point to international comparisons, but as with budgets, it's unclear why the United States is necessarily disadvantaged if China is producing more engineers than the United States, whether in terms of percentage or absolute numbers, or regardless of how an engineer is defined. Additionally, no one can seem to explain satisfactorily why, if there is such a shortage of scientists and engineers, their salaries are not higher. The whole array of questions on the labor market for scientists and engineers seems to be relatively open intellectual territory.

This is true even for questions narrower than those related to the overall size of the educational enterprise. A flash point in discussions of human capital is the role of immigration, particularly whether the United States needs to bring in foreign scientists and engineers under the H1-B visa program. In this case, even some of the basic data are lacking; it has been hard to get a sense of who is being brought in and for what kinds of jobs. But beyond that, high-tech companies argue that they cannot find the talent they need within the United States. Their antagonists point to seemingly qualified scientists and engineers who cannot find jobs. And there does not seem to be a consensus on how the availability of H1-B visas affects salary levels, and how salaries, in turn, are affecting domestic supply. The recurring debates over H1-B visas tend to be fought more on the basis of instinctive reactions to immigration and loyalties to high-tech companies than on the limited research that has been conducted so far on the relevant questions.

6. Technology

So far this chapter has focused primarily on debates related to what is generally regarded as basic research. But discussions related to more targeted or applied research are just as likely to amount to fumbling around in the dark. Take for example, congressional efforts to create programs to foster innovation in the energy sector. Both data and theory are lacking to answer some of the most basic questions that energy debates raise: What are the most significant barriers to energy innovation in the United States? In what particular areas are U.S. research efforts inadequate? Is the United States, in effect, falling short when it comes to ideas, to understandings about the fundamental science, to firms that bring ideas to the prototype stage, to financing for prototypes or scaling up or initial or full-scale production, to demand for new products? (These categories, of course, are not mutually exclusive.) What do we know about how to make applied research programs work? How and when can such programs be evaluated? Perhaps more critically, what do we know about how to set up a successful demonstration program? Right now, virtually the only answers to these questions are instincts and ideologies (e.g., the government should not "interfere" with the market) and mythologized anecdotes (e.g., some previous program, such as Synfuels or clean coal, was a success or failure). There do not appear to be any useful studies even to inform the much narrower but essential questions about the strengths and weaknesses of the national laboratories and what role they could reasonably play in an energy innovation strategy.

The problems and knowledge gaps that characterize the energy innovation discussion are magnified when Congress is debating innovation policy more generally—a debate that can quickly become almost entirely ideological. But those who seek more analytical information are likely to come away disappointed, if not empty handed. More work is needed on the time-honored and broad questions of what makes nations successful innovators, and on the relationship between fundamental research and innovation, and innovation and jobs. But work on narrower questions would also help. What R&D programs have been successful at fostering innovation, and why? There is even surprisingly little work exploring everyone's favorite success stories, such as the Defense Advanced Research Projects Agency (DARPA, or, sometimes ARPA) work that led to the Internet, in a way that thinks through the lessons for future programs.

This chapter has touched upon only some of the most basic questions raised by congressional debates that a more robust science of science policy could usefully inform. But the overall point comes down to this: As noted earlier, the federal government funds scientific research primarily to get tangible results—more jobs, greater economic growth, improved health, strengthened security, and a cleaner environment. This has always been the case. Vannevar Bush's groundbreaking 1945 report *Science: The Endless Frontier* did not argue that federal research funding was needed to keep scientists happy or to satisfy human curiosity. The report opens by describing the life-saving impact of penicillin. A science of science policy needs to help policymakers figure out how to shape the research enterprise to get the desired and expected results.

7. The Future

A science of science policy program should start by formulating the key questions, such as the ones raised in this chapter. It can then solicit researchers from a wide variety of fields for different approaches to answering them, including those offered in the earlier chapters. But a science of science policy program should not start with a "bottom-up" approach; the questions need to be driven by policymakers' concerns and needs, not by the internal dynamics of researchers' subfields. But just making progress on the research agenda, while a gargantuan task, will not be enough. An effort will be needed to bring together recent findings in a way that makes sense to policymakers. Perhaps some broad interdisciplinary group, along with some policymakers, could be brought together periodically by the National Academy of Sciences, or some other respected convener, to review and summarize the state of the field for policymakers. An analogy might be the Intergovernmental Panel on Climate Change (IPCC) and its "Summary for Policy Makers." The equivalent effort in science policy would presumably be much smaller and less controversial—although it might involve more fields and a more disparate set of research—but the IPCC processes may be worth looking at in deciding how such a summary might be put together. Such a summary could be structured around the kinds of fundamental questions raised in this chapter, and perhaps each report could focus on only a few of the questions, with reports being updated in a rotating cycle.

Science of science policy research will never be definitive, and Congress certainly always would and should draw on more than social science results in making its decisions. But there is plenty of room to improve the current state of affairs. In other areas of policy—macroeconomics, health care, and environmental protection, to name a few—at least a semblance exists of an ability to project the outputs that will result from a given set of inputs, and a range of studies to draw upon in discussing what has worked and what has failed. Reaching a similar level of understanding for science policy would be a welcome change, if hardly a panacea.

Institutional Ecology and the Social Outcomes of Scientific Research

17

Daniel Sarewitz

1. Introduction

Science policymaking faces a difficult dilemma. On the one hand, public support for a robust national investment in scientific research depends on the plausibility of the claim that investments in particular areas of research will lead to social benefits that people desire. On the other hand, scientific knowledge is rarely more than one of many factors that will influence a society's capacity to make progress toward resolving a problem. Progress in science and progress in society are related, but the links are indirect and difficult to discern.

To the extent that the science of science policy has faced this problem, it has done so indirectly, by treating the *outputs* of scientific research (publications, patents, prizes, etc.) as proxies for social problem-solving capacity, and by viewing the contribution of scientific knowledge to economic growth (itself of course very difficult to assess, as discussed in several chapters in this volume) as a proxy for the contribution of science to societal well-being more generally. There are many reasons—mostly obvious ones—these proxies are poor guides for science policy decision making [1, 2]. In this chapter I emphasize the importance of one key aspect of the problem: the complex institutional settings (and the interactions within and among these settings) for science and its use in society. To capture this dynamic complexity I use the term "institutional ecology." Institutions provide the structures—the rules, resources, physical settings, social networks, and so on—for the creation and use of scientific knowledge. An ecological view of institutions provides a synoptic lens for considering the diversity of pathways available to science policymakers, scientists, and other actors in seeking to address social problems.

A key challenge for the social science of science policy, then, ought to be the elucidation of the interactions that link knowledge creation and societal problem solving, and the institutional ecologies within which these interactions occur. Indeed, if publicly funded science aims at fostering societal well-being, then it is difficult to see how good science policy decisions can be made without a deep understanding and awareness of the interactions between research and use, both for assessing past science policy decisions and for making effective decisions investments in the future. Yet the social science of science policy has not developed theories, methods, models, cases, and data that can allow science policy decision makers to understand and assess, either prospectively or retrospectively, the institutional factors that mediate between science policy decisions and societal outcomes. My goal here is to describe why the problem is crucially important, and why science policymaking will remain a dark art until it is informed by a deeper, more formal, and more rigorous set of insights into the institutional contexts for science and its use in society. I end with one brief example of the type of research that can help build such insights.

2. Science Institutions

The research and development (R&D) budget for the United States was $147 billion in FY2010.[1] This budget was allocated among more than twenty federal agencies, which spent the money in many different ways: by contracting with corporations, making grants to universities, providing support for in-house government laboratories, and so on. Funding agencies, corporations, universities, and government laboratories are all examples of science institutions, and any particular science institution will be characterized by a unique set of internal attributes and external relationships.

Particular sets of science institutions aggregate and evolve around particular social problems. The oldest government R&D institutions in the United States are those related to the social problem of ensuring sufficient food at affordable prices for the nation. These include the U.S. Department of Agriculture, the land grant colleges, agricultural experiment stations, agricultural extension programs, and corporations that manufacture seeds, fertilizers, pesticides, and farm equipment. The relations among these institutions strongly influence the types of knowledge that are created, the avenues along which such knowledge diffuses, and the capacity of the knowledge to contribute to solving social problems. For example, since their inception in 1887, the agricultural experiment stations have forged close linkages between farmers and scientists who in turn have had to negotiate between the desire of scientists to explore nature and the desire of farmers to improve practice [3]. Importantly, there is no privileged frame of reference from which to view the institutional ecology of agricultural science; each of the individual institutions—with its own internal ecology—provides a distinctive place to look at the whole. (Moreover, "the whole" could of course be further expanded to encompass farmers and corporate farms, food distribution networks and companies, consumers, economic and trade policies, and the rest of the world.)

Similar aggregations of science institutions have grown up around public health, biomedicine, national defense, environmental protection, energy, academic disciplinary research, and so on. As with agriculture, the ecology of institutions within each of these areas of social priority will strongly influence the types of scientific knowledge that are created, the manner in which this knowledge will be diffused into and used by other institutions, and the likelihood that desired social outcomes will be effectively pursued. The institutional ecology of an agency such as the National Institute of Standards and Technology (NIST), with its mission to foster private-sector innovation, is substantially different from that of the National Science Foundation (NSF), whose primary mission is to foster university research and education.

As science policy decision makers seek to productively mobilize R&D investments to address social problems, they will therefore be doing so within a particular context of institutional ecology. For example, reducing the nation's dependence on hydrocarbon fuels is today a national priority for converging reasons of global climate change, energy security, and energy economics. The U.S. Department of Energy (DOE) is the principal R&D institution for implementing new investments aimed at decarbonizing the U.S. energy system. Historically, the DOE has focused on weapons development, basic research in physics, advancing nuclear power, disposing of nuclear waste, and R&D related to fossil fuels, especially coal. Each of these priorities brings with it a set of institutional relationships and priorities. As science policymakers seek to move the DOE toward a significant reordering of its priorities, will the institutional ecologies inherited from the past be appropriate for the evolving mission? Congressional decision makers, bolstered by recommendations from the National Academy of Sciences [4], created a new science institution: the Advanced Research Projects Agency-Energy (ARPA-E), a branch of the DOE aimed at fostering high-risk, high-benefit R&D. Arguments in favor of ARPA-E were principally based on superficial, if apparently sensible, analogies with institutions from very different ecological settings, especially the Defense Advanced Projects Agency in the Department of Defense [4]. Yet the capacity of ARPA-E to meet the goals that justified its creation—especially in the context of the larger institutional ecology in which it must operate—remains largely unexamined (but see reference [5] for a partial exception). In particular, little, if any, rigorous analysis from the science of science policy community was brought to bear on the creation of ARPA-E.

3. The Problem: Many Disjunctures

How are the ends of science (whether basic or applied) related to the ends of policymaking? In particular, what can we say about the relations between the institutions and cultures within which science is planned and carried out, and the potentially very different institutions and cultures within which the solutions to complex social problems are sought? The challenge for science policy-makers is to better understand how the decisions they make (about science priorities; about resource allocation; about institutional arrangements) can influence and improve the value of science for making progress on problems facing society. The challenge for the science of science policy community is to foster this better understanding.

Consider health care. Public expenditures on biomedical research through the U.S. National Institutes of Health (NIH) have grown from about $7 billion in 1976 to $28 billion in 2008 (in constant 2008 dollars),[2] about half of the entire nondefense federal R&D expenditure. This investment is justified by claims that it will yield significant benefits to the public in terms of improved health. Yet it is also obviously true that improved health depends on the behavior of extraordinarily complex and dynamic sets of actors, institutions, and interactions—and that science and technology are only one factor within such a dynamic complexity. (Were that not the case, the U.S. Congress and the Obama administration would not have just engaged in a politically bruising year-long battle to enact health care policy legislation that had little, if anything, to do, directly at least, with science policy.) Indeed, as is well known, the United States already enjoys world preeminence in biomedical research, in levels of funding for such research, *and* in per capita expenditures on health care delivery, yet national health outcomes are mediocre at best by the standards of the affluent world and are exacerbated by an inflationary spiral that coexists with continual scientific and technological advances. Given that other nations that invest less money in health research and spend less on health care may have significantly better health outcomes than the United States, one may at the least say that there is no very obvious connection between marginal increases in funding for science and the achievement of improved health outcomes.

Research supported by public funding is almost always publicly justified as instrumental to larger social goals (for example, "better [health care] outcomes for all at lower cost . . . deploying S&T for poverty eradication, development, and voluntary fertility limitation . . . combating [*sic*] preventable and pandemic disease . . . transforming the global energy system and land-use practices to avoid catastrophic climate change . . . [and] reducing risks from nuclear & biological weapons" [6]). Yet the institutions that plan and conduct research are always trying to accomplish many different things at the same time. For example, universities perform research to, among other things, create knowledge, generate indirect cost returns from federal grants, generate revenue from intellectual property, build institutional prestige in the competition for students, faculty, and resources, and train the next generation of researchers. Similar lists of motives could be offered for government R&D agencies and corporate R&D programs. Each of these institutional settings may be viewed by scientists and administrators who work inside them (as well as people who observe them from the outside) as existing to help solve social challenges, yet that role is at best indirectly linked to the daily motives and activities of people in such settings.

Moreover, the institutions of science experience their own parochial and internal challenges with which they must cope, such as: increasing competition for funding, increasing privatization of knowledge, increasing globalization of the scientific workforce, an allegedly decreasing pool of future scientists and engineers, increasing administrative burdens (for academic researchers and government research administrators), increasing political scrutiny (for some government researchers), increasing public skepticism (about some avenues of private research), decreasing time horizons to demonstrate results, decreasing role of individual investigators, increasing pressure to hype results, increasing pressure and incentives to work across disciplinary, institutional, and sectoral boundaries, and increasing competition from abroad. These internal challenges may wax and wane in terms of their relative importance within any particular institutional setting and time frame, but they are significant influences on the behavior and the knowledge products of institutions that "do" science—influences that may be entirely unrelated to the broader social challenges that motivate the production of knowledge in the first place.

A social science of science policy that can improve the social value of science policy decisions (and, thus, of science) must therefore be able to grapple with two very complex institutional systems that may at best be weakly coupled. The first system encompasses the ecology of science institutions—those that plan and conduct research. The second system encompasses the much broader ecology of institutions that may use scientific knowledge to pursue a social outcome—the complex health care delivery system, for example. There is no reason to believe that improving the scientific productivity of the research system—biomedical research, for example—will necessarily or automatically lead to improved outcomes in the larger social system. We may have a well-developed theoretical and empirical framework for the "innovativeness" or "productivity" of the research activities that go on within institutions that do research (citation rates and impact, collaboration networks, patents and patent citations, stakeholder input, etc.), but we have little reason to be confident that the metrics of healthy research institutions are also the metrics of potential social benefit.

Let me provide a concrete, if coarse-grained, example. Several years ago I was contacted by a member of the board of regents of a large, Midwestern, research-intensive state university that is known for excellence in agricultural research (and football teams). The regent was interested in how to think about connections between the research carried out at his university and the outcomes of that research in society. "We need to find ways to be strategic about planning and stimulating research to address social need," he wrote to me. "Most of our agricultural research has ultimately led to rural decline" in the state. He went on to note that his "interest in this issue is met with significant apprehension" by the university's president and other regents.

The regent's concerns highlight a difficult tension. His university's success as a research institution is strongly dependent on its ability to compete on the basis of internal measures of scientific quality—the sort of quality that ensures federal grant support, excellent faculty and graduate students, and a national reputation. For a state university in the nation's rural agricultural heartland, a prime reason scientific quality is important is that it is supposed to advance the larger instrumental goal of regional economic and social development via improvements to agricultural practice. Yet such improvements contribute directly to an undesirable outcome—rural decline—that is in many ways the opposite of what was intended. Institutional success is accompanied by—is even implicated in—social failure. Moreover, those who are accountable for the university's performance, to the extent that they are aware of this tension, probably see themselves as having no avenues for reconciliation. After all, it is hard enough to maintain the excellence and productivity of a research university without having to worry about being judged based on outcomes over which the university may have little control—thus the regent's observation about the "significant apprehension" of his colleagues. If local communities understood that advances in agricultural science were at the core of large-scale trends in industrial agriculture that render long-standing rural economic and social arrangements increasingly untenable, why would they tolerate the role that their own university (and their own tax dollars) plays in such trends?

4. It's Not Just the Economy, Stupid

The main intellectual agendas of the social science of science policy have reinforced, rather than challenged, the radical incoherence of this situation. First, much "research on research" aims to provide metrics and causal inferences about scientific practice and productivity; institutional leaders use such information to assess the performance and competitive standing of their institutions on the basis of criteria that are largely internal to science itself. Second, most research aiming at assessing the social contributions of research takes an economic perspective, either at the macro scale, in trying to understand the contribution of R&D to economic growth, or in viewing marginal economic benefit as a surrogate for social utility [7, 8].

Neither of these dominant approaches concerns itself with the problem at hand; indeed, these approaches conceal it. If agricultural research is excellent by the light of criteria that are internal to science, if it is effective in contributing to agricultural productivity and wealth creation, then it is successful. Yet these broad criteria of success say nothing at all about either the distribution of benefits or about the possibility that scientific excellence and economic growth could be accompanied by other undesirable outcomes, such as the ongoing dissolution of rural communities.

My point here is not to promote the preservation of the family farm or good-old-small-town American values but simply to show that the institutional ecology of science does not and can not automatically act to reconcile the complex linkages between the conduct of science and the achievement of the public values [9] that often explicitly justify public investments in science. To date, the main thrusts of social science research related to revealing and assessing knowledge production, value, and use are not directed at clarifying this tension and end up having the effect of camouflaging it, as already mentioned, via the vague proxies of scientific and economic "productivity."

Moreover, while economists of innovation have done a pretty good job of specifying the roles that research institutions play in national and global innovation activities as part of the wealth creation process [10, 11], wealth creation is not the only thing we ask from science. Let me briefly raise two examples to illustrate the breadth of the problem. The first is global climate change. Over the past twenty years or so, the United States has spent upward of $30 billion on research to understand the behavior of the global climate system as a basis (according to those who advocate for such research, and according to the government documents that explain and justify the programs) for creating appropriate public policies to protect the nation against the adverse consequences of climate change [12, 13]. One result of this investment has been the creation of a world-class scientific capability housed within a variety of academic and governmental research institutions. While these institutions face challenges and undergo transitions, they are nevertheless highly productive and have considerably expanded our understanding of climate behavior.

On the other hand, the United States—and the world, too, but that's another point—has failed to implement policies that lead to decisive action to reduce human harm from climate. This of course is not the fault of our climate research institutions, but if we measure success on the basis of those promises upon which the research is justified, then it is empirically the case that the advancing science has not been matched by the advancing societal capability to prevent and respond to climate change [14–17]. The reasons this is the case are immaterial to my argument. A sophisticated institutional critique of climate science would need to assess where research institutions fit into an institutional ecology that includes, among many other entities, utility, natural resource, and manufacturing corporations, government regulatory bodies, international trade organizations, and political decision-making bodies at the local, regional, national, and international levels. A sophisticated science policy would integrate that ecological knowledge into its decision processes. Its central focus would not be on the capacity of research institutions to generate scientifically excellent knowledge but on their capacity to generate knowledge that was useful and valuable for the broad set of institutions that, in one way or another, find themselves in the position of confronting various aspects of the climate problem.

An institutional example from another domain that powerfully illustrates this problem is the California Institute for Regenerative Medicine (CIRM), funded in 2004, through a California voter initiative,[3] to support stem cell research. CIRM was promoted to the public on the basis of the potential for stem cell research to contribute to curing a wide variety of diseases and disabilities, such as Alzheimer's, spinal cord injury, and type 1 diabetes. Crucial to the point I am making here, *by design* CIRM was to be a completely insular research institution, exempted through the language of the referendum [18] from any meaningful public accountability or need to interact or integrate with institutions that are responsible for what presidential science advisor Holdren termed "better [health] outcomes for all at lower cost" [6]. Those who conceived CIRM sought to simplify its institutional ecology by guaranteeing a stream of funding for an extended period of time, and by protecting researchers from the political institutions that could act to restrict or direct the types of research that CIRM would be doing, and, in so doing, from any mechanism or metric of accountability not internal to science itself. The institutional structure codified through the referendum equates CIRM's scientific performance with the achievement of particular social needs. Left out of the equation is the complex and troubling institutional ecology within which health care gets delivered. Any plausible assessment of CIRM's capacity to achieve its promises should have included an analysis of institutions (and their interactions) ranging from HMOs and hospitals to pharmaceutical companies to the U.S. Patent Office to the Medicare and Medicaid programs to the private insurance industry and its public regulatory bodies. Moreover, if the desired end goal is improved health outcomes, and the question is how California could best spend $3 billion to support that end, then one would need not only to assess CIRM's potential in light of the broader institutional context of health care delivery but also in comparison to other possible interventions (scientific or otherwise) that could lead to better health.

As long ago as 1964, philosopher Stephen Toulmin recognized that discussions of science policy were aggregating around two important themes: the "economists view, according to which science is basically deserving of support because it is the handmaid of industrial growth; and a scientists view, representing technology as a kind of scientific roulette in which those who plunge deepest tend to win the biggest prize" [19]. Toulmin's insight came in the very earliest years of serious research on science policy, and the dichotomy that he documented turned out to define the boundary conditions for most of the science policy research in the decades that followed [19]. These boundary conditions help explain why, despite some significant progress in understanding the social setting, scientific impacts, and, to a lesser extent, economic value of scientific research, the ability to connect these insights to social and public values has not even achieved a rudimentary capacity. In particular, the capacity to evaluate, either prospectively or even retrospectively, the potential for particular research priorities and institutional arrangements to achieve stipulated noneconomic goals and values remains primitive at best.

5. The Future
The absence of capacity in applying the science of science policy to problems of noneconomic assessment cannot be explained simply by pointing out the difficulty of the problem (although it *is* difficult). Plausible research agendas for making progress are easy to imagine and have been proposed by various

people working in the field (for example, McNie's literature summary of research on the problem of improving the usability of scientific research for decision making [20]). Such agendas will necessarily have three related attributes that will be in tension with the institutional ecology of the universities that would carry out the research, and the federal agencies that would support it. First, they will be rooted in noneconomistic thinking and valuation. Second, they will have a significant qualitative component. And third, they will hold up to critical scrutiny the very assumptions that justify the existing institutional ecologies of the sponsors and performers of scientific research.

The brief examples I have raised here should make clear why the science of science policy needs to attend closely to the problem of how science investments may connect to social outcomes. One looks at huge, long-term public investments in areas such as cancer research and climate change research and sees at best modest returns in terms of meeting the public aspirations that have driven decades of investments. Federal R&D budgets are likely to be tight for the foreseeable future, yet challenges to public well-being remain daunting. Decision makers need to be smart about how they allocate scarce resources in the face of urgent problems, and part of being smart is making sure that funds are spent in institutional settings that are appropriate for the tasks at hand.

The NSF's program on Science of Science and Innovation Policy (SciSIP)[4] has funded public policy scholar Barry Bozeman and me to study the institutional capacity of a number of research programs to advance the public values that the programs are supposed to advance. One important preliminary insight from this project, which seems to be consistent across many of our case studies, is that the logical coherence of the public values a research program uses to justify its activities is related to the capacity of the program to achieve those values [8]. In other words, when science institutions are organized around logic models and value hierarchies that make sense in the real world, they may be more likely to achieve desired outcomes than when they are not so organized. This is, perhaps, thoroughly unsurprising. When the process of knowledge creation is tightly linked to the process of knowledge use via appropriate institutional arrangements, we would expect some commonality and coherence of value structures among those producing and those using the knowledge (e.g., see many of the articles cited in McNie [20]). More broadly, if this sensible hypothesis continues to hold up, then perhaps it can begin to guide the development of a variety of research approaches regarding the identification, classification, and interrelations among values that motivate research within a complex institutional ecology, as a foundation for assessing a science institution's potential to achieve desired social outcomes.

As preliminary and modest as these results may now be, the larger point is this: there is no intellectual obstacle to formulating researchable questions that begin to get at the relations between the institutional ecology and social outcomes of research. Intrinsic difficulty cannot be the main reason science policy researchers have failed to seriously confront this domain. Rather, for a variety of historical, cultural, political, and of course institutional reasons, researchers have simply avoided these questions, focusing instead on problems of scientific productivity and economic valuation. Yet the problem of linking science policy decisions to social outcomes is perhaps the central challenge that real-world science policy decision makers must continually confront. If the science of science policy community hopes to prove *its* value to society, then it will need to take this problem seriously.

References

[1]   P. Kitcher. Science, Truth, and Democracy. New York: Oxford University Press; 2001.

[2]   D. Sarewitz. Frontiers of Illusion: Science, Technology, and the Politics of Progress. Philadelphia (PA): Temple University Press; 1996.

[3]   C. Rosenberg. Science and Social Values in Nineteenth-Century America: A Case Study in the Growth of Scientific Institutions. In: No Other Gods: On Science and American Social Thought. Baltimore (MD): Johns Hopkins University Press; 1961, pp. 135–152.

[4]   National Academy of Sciences. Rising Above the Gathering Storm: Energizing and Employing America for a Brighter Economic Future. Washington (DC): National Academy Press; 2007.

[5]   J. A. Alexander. An Energy Future Transformed: The Advanced Research Projects Agency-Energy—R&D Pathways to a Low-Carbon Future. Washington (DC): ARPA-E; 2009.

[6]   J. Holdren. Science and Technology Policy in the Obama Administration. Business Higher Education Forum, Washington, D.C., 16 June 2009.

[7]   B. Bozeman. Public Value and Research Evaluations in Enhancing Public Research Performance Through Evaluation, Impact Assessment and Priority Setting. Directorate for Science, Technology and Industry, Committee for Scientific and Technology Policy Organisation for Economic Cooperation and Development, Paris; 2009.

[8]   B. Bozeman, D. Sarewitz. Public Value Mapping: The Marriage of Choice and Evaluation. Minerva; 2011.

[9]   B. Bozeman. Public Values and Public Interest: Counterbalancing Economic Individualism. Washington (DC): Georgetown University Press; 2007.

[10] C. Freeman, L. Soete. The Economics of Industrial Innovation. 3rd ed. Cambridge (MA): MIT Press; 1997.

[11] R. Nelson. National Innovation Systems: A Comparative Analysis. New York: Oxford University Press; 1993.

[12] R. Pielke Jr. Policy History of the U.S. Global Change Research Program: Part I. Administrative Development. Global Environmental Change, 10;2000;9–25.

[13] R. Pielke Jr. Policy History of the U.S. Global Change Research Program: Part II. Legislative Process. Global Environmental Change, 1;2000;133–144.

[14] J. Pielke Jr., D. Sarewitz. Wanted: Scientific Leadership on Climate. Issues in Science and Technology, 2003;27–30.

[15] D. Sarewitz. Curing Climate Backlash. Nature, 464;2010;28.

[16] G. Prins, S. Rayner. The Wrong Trousers: Radically Rethinking Climate Policy. Oxford: Oxford Institute for Science, Innovation and Society; 2007.

[17] D. Sarewitz, R. A. Pielke Jr. The Steps Not Yet Taken. In: D. Kleinman, K. Cloud-Hansen, C. Matta, J. Handelsman (Eds.), Controversies in Science and Technology, vol. 2, From Climate to Chromosomes. New York: Mary Ann Liebert; 2008, pp. 329–351.

[18] D. Sarewitz. Stepping Out of Line in Stem Cell Research. Los Angeles Times, October 25, 2004, p. B11.

[19] S. Toulmin. The Complexity of Scientific Choice: A Stocktaking. Minerva, 2;1964; 343–359.

[20] E. McNie. Reconciling the Supply of Scientific Information with User Demands: An Analysis of the Problem and Review of the Literature. Environmental Science and Policy, 20;2007;17–38.

Notes

1. See table "R&D in the FY 2010 Budget by Agency" at www.aaas.org/spp/rd/.

2. See Historical Table 2: R&D by Agency, 1976–2009, in Constant Dollars (revised 3/2008), at www.aaas.org/spp/rd/guihist.shtml (viewed November 1, 2009).

3. For background information, see www.smartvoter.org/2004/11/02/ca/state/prop/71/; www.lao.ca.gov/ballot/2004/71_11_2004.htm.

4. For program information, see www.nsf.gov/funding/pgm_summ.jsp?pims_id =501084.

Science Policy in a Complex World

Lessons from the European Experience

Janez Potočnik

1. What Does "European Research Policy" Mean?

What does the history of research policy in Europe teach us? Are there particular lessons to be drawn from the European experience in this field? To what extent could such lessons be of some interest to the rest the world? One cannot begin to answer these questions without having previously clarified the complicated picture of research policy in Europe. And, in reality, such an effort of clarification will itself provide many of the clues and indications, the elements that will eventually provide us with the answers.

The European landscape in research and science policy is notoriously rich and complex, in a way that mirrors the complexity of Europe and of Europe's history. Such a complexity can generate many ambiguities and misunderstandings.

Inside and outside Europe, for instance, many observers speak about "European research policy." But what do they mean by that exactly? The expression is intrinsically very ambiguous. It can either refer to all research policies in Europe, both at the national and European levels, or only to research policies that are undertaken in this respect in European cooperation within the different policy frameworks, including the various intergovernmental ones or those specifically designated as research policy of the European Union (EU). The less those who use this expression are familiar with Europe and European science, the more they are prone to confuse these distinct realities.

2. A Complex and Disparate Whole

Let us consider each of these three different realities, starting with the first. Europe is composed of many countries that are extremely diverse in terms of geography, population, economic power, language, and history, as well as in its political, social, and cultural traditions. Of those countries, twenty-seven are joined within the EU, the most obvious expression and, by far, the most powerful instrument of European integration. This does not mean that the countries that don't belong to the EU are separate from its activities. In many fields, not least in research and technology, they are often "associated" with the EU through various technical and legal agreements.

This high level of diversity among European countries is clearly mirrored in the area of research and science policy. In terms of research capacities and infrastructures, the number of researchers, the volume and respective proportions of public and private financial effort, forms of public support, the nature of research programs, the structure and organization of research, university landscape, and so on, the picture presented throughout the different countries is highly heterogeneous. The range of situations is tremendously broad: from an overall research effort of less than 0.5 percent of GDP to almost 4 percent; from close to 70 percent of funding from the public sector to close to 70 percent from industry; from a few thousand researchers to several hundred thousand, and so on. In some countries the bulk of research is performed in universities; in others, public laboratories; and in others, enterprises [1].

Of course, there is no shortage of common features. Despite the persistence of national traditions and preferences originating in history or as a result of particular regional or national peculiarities, because science is so often asked to find the answer to the same global questions, research priorities are becoming more and more drawn together in all European countries. Successful or fashionable models, structures, and modus operandi are spreading. And practices in science policy tend to align with each other.

Such commonalities and the fact that, as we will see, national research activities and policies in Europe are today conducted less in isolation than they were in the past are beyond doubt. However, this trend is not significant and substantial enough to allow us to use the expression "European research policy" meaningfully to refer to the sum of national research policies in Europe.

3. Facets of European Scientific Cooperation

This is certainly not the case for the second reality: European scientific cooperation in its different forms. As I have already mentioned, European cooperation in science and technology is implemented within different frameworks. Most of the cooperation schemes used are intergovernmental in nature and associate countries through "variable geometry": the number of participating countries varies, as does the overall composition. Often these schemes were set up in specialized fields: the European Organization for Nuclear Research (CERN) in particle physics, the European Molecular Biology Organization

(EMBO) and the European Molecular Biology Laboratory (EMBL) in molecular biology, the European Southern Observatory (ESO) in astronomy, and the European Space Agency (ESA) for space and AIRBUS for aeronautics. There are exceptions: the European Science Foundation (ESF) covers the whole range of sciences, and the EUREKA initiative[1] deals with all technologies.

Due to the high visibility of the activities that these schemes operate, they are (relatively) well known by "outsiders." CERN, for instance, is famous among American physicists, as is AIRBUS in the American aeronautical industry and economic circles throughout the world. In Europe, they are perceived as emblematic of European scientific cooperation and rightly considered as an eloquent demonstration of what European countries can achieve when they join forces. Indeed, in their respective areas, they are clear manifestations of a "European research policy," an expression that fully deserves to be applied to them.

4. Joining Forces: The EU Research Policy

What people often have in mind when they talk about "European research policy" is something else: the research policy of the European Union. Indeed, since its creation under the name "Common Market" (later replaced by "European Community"), the European Union, as it is called now, implements its own research policy.

Limited at the very beginning to some particular fields, EU research policy extended progressively to the whole area of science and technology, including, more recently, the social sciences and humanities. Its budget has grown progressively, passing from several hundreds of millions of euros annually forty years ago to almost 10 billion euros annually today [2]. The mechanisms and schemes of financial support it uses have diversified and evolved continuously to meet a changing range of various and specific needs. Its basic principle is that the EU undertakes what cannot be achieved (at least as efficiently and successfully) at a national level, "national level" here meaning by the member states, acting independently.

For this reason, the bulk of research activities implemented within the EU framework takes the form of collaborative projects or networks associating laboratories, universities, and enterprises from different countries. There are also different kinds of cooperative and coordination ventures at the larger scale. Indeed, cooperation, collaboration, and coordination allow results to be achieved where it would be difficult or even impossible to do so under other conditions, by helping build a critical mass of human and financial resources, exploiting complementary competences, sharing expensive infrastructures, and addressing jointly—at the European level—issues that arise at a European level and scale, in the fields of health, environment, or energy, to take but a few examples.

However, this so-called "European added value" can take other forms. Among the most successful and popular of the EU's support schemes are the "Marie Curie" individual fellowships,[2] which encourage the mobility of researchers across borders and the grants allocated by the recently created European Research Council (ERC),[3] a kind of "European NSF," since it supports projects carried out by single research teams on subjects and topics chosen by the researchers themselves. Together with other different mechanisms of collaboration and coordination, these two schemes compose a complete and diversified panoply of tools, giving the European Union the means of supporting research as such (which is necessary in any case) while creating the right conditions to allow the best of each member state's resources to be maximized.

In financial terms, the combined budget of all intergovernmental research initiatives and the European Union research policy represents less than 20 percent of the total public research effort in Europe [1]. But it would be a mistake to underestimate their importance and their impact based on a simple percentage. To a large extent, for instance, the activities performed by CERN influence and determine research in particle physics and astrophysics in national laboratories in Europe. When you consider the element of funding from the EU, not within the total of national research expenses but only within the funding of projects, the proportion is much more significant: varying according to the countries and the fields concerned, it can represent up to 50 percent of the "free funding," even in some of the biggest countries. Moreover, the mobilization of large quantities of money on specific themes at the European level has a clear impact on the definition of national research priorities.

5. Toward a "European Research Area"

There is not, therefore, a clear-cut separation between the three aspects identified as possible elaborations of the expression "European research policy." The picture is far more complex than seen at first glance, and all the more because these old distinctions, which have prevailed for years, have recently became blurred by an important policy development: the desire to create a "European research area" (ERA).

The idea of the ERA was first adopted at the Lisbon European Council of March 2000 (the European Councils gather together the EU's heads of state and governments) as a major component of the so-called "Lisbon strategy."[4] This aims at stimulating the development, in Europe, of a knowledge-based economy, with the view to promoting sustainable social and economic development. This ambitious project has three major complementary components: improving the coordination of national research activities, programs, and policies in Europe; creating a "European internal market" for knowledge, research, and technology; and launching research-dedicated funding initiatives conceived and set up to work at the European level.

In such an intellectual and political framework, the distinctions between the three orders of reality I have described here tend to blur, or even fade: activities and policies taking place at the national level start to be designed and implemented (to a certain extent) as part of a European context; intergovernmental research initiatives and organizations are redefined and come closer to the EU framework (an additional reason for that is financial, since scientific research is ever more expensive); and the EU research funding system and research policy acquire a broader and deeper dimension.

One year after having agreed to create this ERA, and as a natural complement to the project, Europeans added a further objective of devoting 3 percent of EU GDP to research and technological development [3]. Progress achieved so far toward this goal has been unfortunately limited. For years now, despite significant efforts accomplished by the least advanced countries in this respect, the overall European research effort is becalmed at around 1.8 percent of GDP [1]. Nevertheless, although harder than we first would have anticipated to reach the Lisbon target of 3 percent, it has never been abandoned. It is, in fact, an indisputable goal.

Today the ERA is far from the reality we would like it to be, but it is no longer a vague idea or some intangible objective to strive for. It is here to stay, and the process of its final realization has recently restarted through new initiatives in five key areas: career and mobility of researchers, research infrastructures, intellectual property rights, "joint programming" between EU member states, and international science and technology cooperation. Of course the full achievement of this project will take time, particularly because there are issues that bear heavily on its development that are broader than research policy; social security, for instance, or fiscal regimes, but if progress is slow, then we are moving in the right direction and have no intention of turning back.

All of these remarks concern basic and applied science. As far as European industrial and technological policy is concerned, the picture is very different. In some areas, such as aeronautics and space, Europe, as we used to say, obviously "speaks with one voice." In other fields this (still) is far from being the case, with each country supporting its own "national champions." The recent launch, at the EU level, of a series of large projects in various industrial fields (energy, for instance) could help improve the situation in this respect.

6. Lessons from Particular Experience

"What does the history of research policy in Europe teach us?" This was the question I asked at the beginning of this chapter. For Europeans, the answer is that it has taught them a lot, including the creation of the conditions that will allow them to act together, using the best and the most effective instruments to do so.

And, to a large extent, these lessons are useful and valuable for the rest of the world. Let us start with the mechanisms. One of the most obvious results of forty years of EU research policy, for instance, is the definition of a new range of schemes of collaboration. They were invented and used to overcome a series of practical limitations and political obstacles stemming from the simple but important fact that Europe is made up of many different countries.

It is clear that such mechanisms do have value in themselves and can fruitfully be used in other contexts, but the reality is that, more often than not, no one has enough financial and human resources, knowledge, and know-how to go it alone. Even in the United States, the world's scientific superpower, comparable instruments are being used. And, significantly, while Europeans have borrowed successful schemes and mechanisms, such as the NSF-type grants for individual projects, from Americans, the Americans themselves have introduced specifically different kinds of support to encourage collaboration between universities and research centers.

But these lessons also concern, possibly above all, the decision-making process. As I wrote at the beginning of this chapter, Europe (and the European Union) brings together many individual countries, diverse in terms of economic and technological development, social traditions and interests, ethical values, and so on. In such an environment, the process of decision making is particularly challenging. But for this very reason, both the successes and failures achieved under these conditions are illuminating.

Why do different countries have different preferences, objectives, and priorities? The most obvious source of this diversity is their respective interests. When the moment comes to decide on a priority or a mechanism, countries will choose the one that best corresponds to some specific need linked to their specific economic, social, geographical, or political situation. They can fight to obtain funding in areas where they are already particularly strong, in order to become even stronger, or, conversely where they are especially weak, to acquire the competences they do not already have. They can also defend the creation, at the European level, of mechanisms allowing them to bypass those rigidities or obstacles that exist at the national level.

Another important factor is the variety of social and ethical values that different countries will have on "sensitive" subjects. Significantly and typically, during negotiations for the EU research programs, the two most controversial issues, the subjects which, totally out of proportion to the budget allocated to them, lead to the longest and toughest discussions, were research on human embryonic stem cells and in nuclear energy. For two subjects, agreement at the EU level was never easy to reach. However, at the end of the day, solutions were almost always found, which allowed common issues to be addressed with the common good in mind.

Such features of science policy in Europe are of particular relevance for other parts of the world and for science policy in the world, in particular, for a clear reason. In an increasingly interconnected world, major issues in areas such as public health, environment and climate change, and energy or space are more and more a global concern. And in science and technology, international ventures are clearly likely to become the rule rather than the exception. Yet the diversity of situations, scientific and economic capacities, needs, interests, views, and values that exist at world level, mirrors, at a broader scale and even to a higher degree, what can be observed in Europe. The challenges linked with the definition, negotiation, and implementation of international research projects and technological initiatives at the world level are therefore precisely those that the Europeans have learned to face through decades of experience. For this reason, the experience that Europe has earned in this respect is of the highest relevance. I hope, and I am sure, that we will be able to share it with everyone, for the benefit of the entire international community.

References

[1] European Commission, Directorate-General for Research, A More Research-Intensive and Integrated European Research Area, Science, Technology and Competitiveness Key Figures Report, 2008/2009. Office for Official Publications of the European Communities, Luxembourg 2008.

[2] Decision No. 1982/2006/EC of the European Parliament and of the Council of 18 December 2006 Concerning the Seventh Framework Programme of the European Community for Research, Technological Development and Demonstration

Activities (2007–2013). Official Journal of the European Union L 412/1, 30 December 2006.

[3] Presidency Conclusions-Barcelona European Council, 15 and 16 March, 2002, SN 100/1/02. Council of the European Union, Brussels 2002.

Notes

1. EUREKA was established by a conference of ministers of seventeen countries and members of the Commission of the European Communities. Since its inception in 1985, substantial public and private funding has been directed to support the research and development carried out within the EUREKA framework. EUREKA's mission is to support market-oriented R&D by "raising the productivity and competitiveness of European businesses through technology." See http://www.eurekanetwork.org/about.

2. These are called Marie Curie actions and cover four broad areas: initial training networks, lifelong training, international dimensions, and industry-academia. See http://cordis.europa.eu/fp7/mariecurieactions/home_en.html.

3. The European Research Council (ERC) is established by the European Commission and funded through the EU 7th Research Framework Program. See http://erc.europa.eu/index.cfm.

4. See http://ec.europa.eu/growthandjobs/objectives/index_en.htm.

Contributors

William B. Bonvillian is the director of the Massachusetts Institute of Technology's (MIT) Washington, D.C., office. Prior to that position, he served for seventeen years as a senior policy advisor in the U.S. Senate. His legislative efforts included science and technology policies and innovation issues. He worked extensively on legislation creating the Department of Homeland Security, on intelligence reform, on defense and life science research and development (R&D), and on national competitiveness and innovation legislation. His book, with Distinguished Professor Charles Weiss of Georgetown University, entitled *Structuring an Energy Technology Revolution*, was published in 2009. His chapter "The Connected Science Model for Innovation—The DARPA Role" appears in the book *21st Century Innovation Systems for the U.S. and Japan* (2009). He teaches on the adjunct faculty at Georgetown and Johns Hopkins–SAIS.

Michael Darby currently serves as the Warren C. Cordner Distinguished Professor of Money and Financial Markets at the University of California, Los Angeles, Anderson School of Management and in the Departments of Economics and Public Policy at UCLA, and also serves as director of the John M. Olin Center for Policy at UCLA, Anderson. Concurrently, he holds appointments as chairman of the Dumbarton Group, research associate with the National Bureau of Economic Research, and adjunct scholar with the American Enterprise Institute. Darby served in a number of senior positions during the Reagan and Bush administrations, including Assistant Secretary of the Treasury for Economic Policy, Member of the National Commission on Superconductivity, Under Secretary of Commerce for Economic Affairs, and Administrator of the Economics and Statistics Administration. During his appointment, he received the Treasury's highest honor, the Alexander Hamilton Award.

Kaye Husbands Fealing is a professor at the Hubert H. Humphrey School of Public Affairs, University of Minnesota, where she received the distinction of

"Teacher of the Year" for academic years 2008–9 and 2009–10. Prior to coming to the Humphrey, she was the William Brough Professor of Economics at Williams College, where she began her teaching career in 1989. Dr. Husbands Fealing developed the National Science Foundation's Science of Science and Innovation Policy Program in 2006 and cochaired the Science of Science Policy Interagency Task Group from June 2006 through January 2008. She also served as a program director in NSF's Economics Program. Dr. Husbands Fealing was a visiting scholar at Massachusetts Institute of Technology's Center for Technology Policy and Industrial Development, where she conducted research on NAFTA's impact on the Mexican and Canadian automotive industries, and research on strategic alliances between aircraft contractors and their subcontractors. Dr. Husbands Fealing also participates on several panels and boards at the National Science Foundation, including the Advisory Committee for Social, Behavioral and Economic Sciences and the AAAS Committee on Science, Engineering and Public Policy. Dr. Husbands Fealing is the Midwest representative for the American Economic Association's Committee on the Status of Women in the Economics Profession. Dr. Husbands Fealing received her BA in mathematics and economics from the University of Pennsylvania and her PhD in economics from Harvard University.

Irwin Feller is professor emeritus of economics at Pennsylvania State University, where he has been on the faculty since 1963. Dr. Feller's current research interests include the economics of academic research, the university's role in technology-based economic development, and the evaluation of federal and state technology programs. He is the author of *Universities and State Governments: A Study in Policy Analysis* (1986) and of over one hundred refereed journal articles, final research reports, and book chapters, as well as of numerous papers presented to academic, professional, and policy audiences.

Richard B. Freeman holds the Herbert Ascherman Chair in Economics at Harvard University. He is currently serving as faculty director of the Labor and Worklife Program at Harvard Law School. He directs the National Bureau of Economic Research/Sloan Science Engineering Workforce Projects and is senior research fellow in Labor Markets at the London School of Economics' Center for Economic Performance. He received in 2006 the Mincer Lifetime Achievement Prize from the Society of Labor Economics. The following year he was awarded the Institut zur Zukunft der Arbeit (IZA) Prize in Labor Economics. His recent publications include the following: *What Workers Want* (2007, 2d ed.), *Can Labor Standards Improve Under Globalization?* (2004), *Emerging Labor Market Institutions for the 21st Century* (2005), *America Works: The Exceptional*

Labor Market (2007), and *What Workers Say: Employee Voice in the Anglo American World* (2007). His IZA Prize book is entitled *Making Europe Work: IZA Labor Economics Series* (2009). Coedited books include *Reforming the Welfare State: Recovery and Beyond in Sweden* (2009); *Shared Capitalism: The Economic Issues* (2009); *International Comparison of the Structure of Wages* (2009), and *Science and Engineering Careers in the United States* (2009).

Fred Gault is a professorial fellow at the United Nations University–Maastricht Economic and Social Research and Training Centre on Innovation and Technology (UNU-MERIT). He is also a professor at the Tshwane University of Technology (TUT) in South Africa and a member of the TUT Institute for Economic Research on Innovation. Prior to joining UNU-MERIT, he was a visiting fellow at the Canadian International Development Research Centre (IDRC), where his principal objective was making innovation part of the development agenda. In addition, he was a member of the management team responsible for the Innovation Strategy of the Organization for Economic Cooperation and Development (OECD), delivered in May 2010. Until April 2008, he was the director of the Science, Innovation, and Electronic Information Division at Statistics Canada and was responsible for the development of statistics on all aspects of research, development, invention, innovation, and the diffusion of technologies, as well as on related human resources. He also was responsible for the development of statistics on telecommunications and broadcasting, Internet use, and electronic commerce.

John S. Gero is a research professor at the Krasnow Institute for Advanced Study and at the Volgenau School of Information Technology and Engineering, George Mason University. Formerly he was professor of Design Science and codirector of the Key Center of Design Computing and Cognition at the University of Sydney. He is the author/editor of forty-eight books and over six hundred papers and book chapters in the fields of design science, design computing, artificial intelligence, computer-aided design, design cognition, and cognitive science. He has been a visiting professor of architecture, civil engineering, cognitive science, computer science, design and computation, and mechanical engineering at MIT, University of California (UC), Berkeley, UCLA, Columbia, and Carnegie Mellon University (CMU) in the United States, at Strathclyde and Loughborough in the United Kingdom, at Institut National des Sciences Appliquées de Lyon (INSA) and Provence in France, and at École Polytechnique Fédérale de Lausanne (EPFL) in Switzerland. His former doctoral students are professors in the United States, United Kingdom, Australia, India, Japan, Korea, Singapore, and Taiwan.

David Goldston has been the director of government affairs for the Natural Resources Defense Council since July 2009. He worked on science policy and environmental policy in the U.S. House of Representatives for more than twenty years. From 2001 through 2006, he served as chief of staff of the House Committee on Science, which oversees most of the federal civilian research and development enterprise. After leaving Capitol Hill, he was a visiting professor at Princeton and Harvard and wrote a monthly column on science policy for *Nature*.

Adam B. Jaffe, the Fred C. Hecht Professor in Economics, has served since 2003 as dean of the College of Arts and Sciences at Brandeis University. He also has held the position of chair of the Economics Department and chair of the Intellectual Property Policy Committee at Brandeis University. Prior to joining the university in 1993, Jaffe was an assistant and associate professor at Harvard University and a senior staff economist for the President's Council of Economic Advisers. Jaffe's research focuses on the economics of innovation. His highly acclaimed book *Innovation and Its Discontents: How Our Broken Patent System Is Endangering Innovation and Progress, and What to Do About It*, coauthored with Josh Lerner of Harvard Business School, was released in paperback in 2006.

Kei Koizumi is assistant director for federal research and development at the White House Office of Science and Technology Policy (OSTP). Before joining the OSTP, Koizumi served as the longtime director of the R&D Budget and Policy Program at the American Association for the Advancement of Science (AAAS). Koizumi received his master's degree from the Center for International Science, Technology, and Public Policy program at George Washington University and his bachelor's degree in political science and economics from Boston University. He is a fellow of the American Association for the Advancement of Science.

Julia I. Lane is the program director of the Science of Science and Innovation Policy program at the National Science Foundation, former senior vice president and Director, Economics Department at NORC/University of Chicago, Director of the Employment Dynamics Program at the Urban Institute, senior research fellow at the U.S. Census Bureau and assistant, associate and full professor at American University. She is an American Statistical Association Fellow. She has been the recipient of over $20 million in grants; from foundations such as the National Science Foundation, the Sloan Foundation, the MacArthur Foundation, the Russell Sage Foundation, the Spencer Foundation, the National Institute of Health; from government agencies such as the Departments of Commerce, Labor, and Health and Human Services in the United States, the ESRC in the United Kingdom, and the Department of Labour and Statistics in New Zealand, as well as from international organizations such as the World Bank. She is one of the founders of the Longitudinal Employer-Household Dynamics (LEHD) program at the U.S. Census Bureau, which is the first large scale linked employer-employee dataset in the United States.

Robert E. Litan is the vice president for research and policy at the Ewing Marion Kauffman Foundation in Kansas City, where he oversees the foundation's extensive program for funding data collection and research relating to entrepreneurship and economic growth. Dr. Litan also writes frequently with the foundation's president, Carl Schramm. Their book, *Good Capitalism, Bad Capitalism, and the Economics of Growth and Prosperity*, coauthored with William Baumol (2007), has been translated into ten languages and is used as a college text around the world. Dr. Litan is also a senior fellow in economic studies at the Brookings Institution, where he previously was vice president and director of economic studies.

John H. Marburger III is the vice president for Research at Stony Brook University. He served as the Science Advisor to President George W. Bush and director of the Office of Science and Technology Policy from 2001–8, and was previously director of Brookhaven National Laboratory from 1998, and president of the State University of New York at Stony Brook (1980–94). From 1967 he was consecutively professor of Physics and Electrical engineering, Physics Department chairman, and dean of the College of Letters, Arts and Sciences at the University of Southern California where he performed research in nonlinear and quantum optics and cofounded the USC Center for Laser Studies.

Susan Albers Mohrman is a senior research scientist at the Center for Effective Organizations at the University of Southern California. She researches organization design and effectiveness issues, knowledge and technology management, and useful research methodologies. She is the coauthor and/or editor of *Large-Scale Organizational Change* (1995); *Self-Designing Organizations* (1989); *Designing Team-Based Organizations* (1995); *Organizing for High-Performance* (2002); *Handbook of Collaborative Management Research (2007);* and *Useful Research: Advancing Theory and Practice* (in press).

M. Granger Morgan is the Lord Chair Professor in Engineering, professor and department head of Engineering and Public Policy, and professor of

Electrical and Computer Engineering at Heinz College. His research interests are focused on policy problems in which technical and scientific issues play a central role. Methodological interests include problems in the integrated analysis of large complex systems, problems in the characterization and treatment of uncertainty, problems in the improvement of regulation, and selected issues in risk analysis and risk communication. More recent works include his multiauthored book with Baruch Fischhoff, Ann Bostrom, and Cynthia Atman entitled *Risk Communication: A Mental Models Approach* (2002) and an edited book with Jon Peha, entitled *Science and Technology Advice to the Congress* (2003).

Jason Owen-Smith has held faculty appointments since 2002 in the Department of Sociology and the Organizational Studies Program at the University of Michigan. He is the recipient of a National Science Foundation Faculty Early Career Development (CAREER) award and an Alfred P. Sloan Foundation Industries Studies fellowship in biotechnology. He received in 2008 the University of Michigan's Henry Russel Award, which recognizes mid-career faculty for their exceptional scholarship and conspicuous teaching ability. He received his MA and PhD degrees in sociology at the University of Arizona and his BA in sociology and philosophy from the New College of Florida.

Janez Potočnik is the European Commissioner for the Environment. Prior to that, he was the European Commissioner for Science and Research and "shadow Commissioner" for the European Union enlargement. He was formerly Slovenia's Minister for European Affairs, head of the negotiating team for the accession of Slovenia to the European Union, and minister councillor at the office of the Prime Minister of Slovenia. He served as assistant director (1984–87) and director (1993–2001) at the Institute of Macroeconomic Analysis and Development in Ljubljana and obtained his PhD in economics at the University of Ljubljana. He was awarded the honorary degree of Doctor of Science by London Imperial College in 2008 and from Ghent University (Belgium) in 2009.

Walter W. Powell is professor of education and (by courtesy) sociology, organizational behavior, management science and engineering, and communication at Stanford University. He is also an external faculty member at the Santa Fe Institute and codirector of the Stanford Center on Philanthropy and Civil Society. He joined the Stanford faculty in July 1999, after previously teaching at the University of Arizona, MIT, and Yale. Professor Powell works in the areas of organization theory and economic sociology. He is the coauthor of *Books:*

The Culture and Commerce of Publishing (1982), an analysis of the transformation of book publishing from a family-run, craft-based field into a multinational media industry, and the author of *Getting Into Print* (1985), an ethnographic study of decision-making processes in scholarly publishing houses. He edited *The Nonprofit Sector* (1987, referred to by reviewers as "the Bible of scholarship on the nonprofit sector"). The second edition of this book, coedited with Richard Steinberg, was published in 2006. Powell is also coeditor with Elisabeth Clemens of *Private Action and the Public Good* (1998).

E. J. Reedy is a manager in research and policy at the Ewing Marion Kauffman Foundation, where he also oversees grants and conducts academic and policy research in the field of entrepreneurship. He has been significantly involved in the coordination of the foundation's entrepreneurship and innovation data-related initiatives, including the Kauffman Firm Survey and the foundation's multiyear series of symposiums on data, as well as in many Web-related projects and initiatives.

Harvey M. Sapolsky is professor of public policy and organization, emeritus, at MIT and the former director of the MIT Security Studies Program. He has written extensively on science, health, and defense policy. His recent work includes *US Defense Policy: The Origins of Security Policy* (2008), written with E. Gholz and C. Talmadge and *US Military Innovation Since the Cold War: Creation Without Destruction* (2009), edited with B. Friedman and B. R. Green.

Daniel Sarewitz is codirector of the Consortium for Science, Policy and Outcomes, and professor of science and society in the School of Life Sciences and School of Sustainability at Arizona State University. Sarewitz's published work includes *Frontiers of Illusion: Science, Technology, and the Politics of Progress* (1996), *Prediction: Science, Decision Making, and the Future of Nature* (2000), and *Living with the Genie: Essays on Technology and the Quest for Human Mastery* (2003). He is a regular columnist for *Nature* magazine.

Stephanie S. Shipp is a senior research analyst for economics, energy, and environment, at the IDA Science and Technology Policy Institute. Her primary focus is on evaluation of federal science and technology funding. She also conducts research on high risk, high reward programs at NIH and other government programs. She is currently conducting a study on the commercialization landscape of federal labs. From 2000 to 2007, Dr. Shipp was the director of the Economic Assessment Office in the Advanced Technology Program at the National Institute of Standards and Technology. In that position she directed economic research and program evaluation that examined individual project and overall program performance. She was one of the founders of the NORC Data Enclave, which permits researchers to remotely access microdata in a secure way and also allows replication of results by other researchers. Prior to that, Dr. Shipp was the assistant division chief in the Housing and Household Economic Statistics Division at the Census Bureau, Chief of Information and Analysis of the Consumer Expenditure Survey, Bureau of Labor Statistics, and an economist at the Federal Reserve Board. She is a fellow of the American Statistical Association (ASA) and the recipient of the ASA Pat Doyle Award. She is a member of the International Advisory Board of Vinnova, the Swedish Innovation Agency.

Laurel Smith-Doerr is an associate professor of sociology at Boston University. Her research has examined the tensions in the institutionalization of science, including an examination of networks in the biotechnology industry, commercialization in the university, contributions of immigrant entrepreneurs, gendered organizations, and scientists' responses to ethics education requirements. Her book *Women's Work: Gender Equality vs. Hierarchy in the Life Sciences* (2004) explains how network forms of organization are more conducive to gender equity than are more rule-bound hierarchical settings.

Mark Zachary Taylor is an assistant professor at the Sam Nunn School of International Affairs at the Georgia Institute of Technology. He was a solid-state physicist who now specializes in international relations, political economy, and comparative politics. His research seeks to explain why some countries are better than others at science, technology, and innovation. His research has been published in the journals *Foreign Affairs, International Organization, Harvard International Review, Journal of Health Politics, Policy and Law, Journal of Political Science Education,* and *Review of Policy Research.*

Michael S. Teitelbaum is program director at the Sloan Foundation and was a demographer educated at Reed College and at Oxford University, where he was a Rhodes Scholar. Over the course of his career, Dr. Teitelbaum has served in numerous high-profile academic and public policy positions. More recent coauthored books include *Political Demography, Demographic Engineering* (2001) and *A Question of Numbers: High Migration, Low Fertility, and the Politics of National Identity* (1998).

Jim Thomas was the founding director of the Department of Homeland Security's National Visualization and Analytics Center and a laboratory fellow at Pacific Northwest National Laboratory. With a career spanning thirty years of contributions in information technology, Thomas specialized in the research, design, and implementation of innovative information and scientific visualization, multimedia, and human computer interaction technology. Thomas was internationally recognized for his contributions to the field of information visualization. He received several international science awards and was honored for transferring research technology to industry. Thomas sat on several national and international science and technology boards for universities, states, and industry. He was a member of the Association for Computing Machinery and Institute of Electrical and Electronics Engineers.

Lynne Zucker is a professor in the Department of Sociology at the University of California, Los Angeles. Her current major interests are on processes and the impact of knowledge transmission from basic science to commercial use, especially the impact on the economic performance of firms, the creation of new organizational populations (some of which become new industries), and productivity growth.

Index

Small Business Innovation Development Act of 1982, 310
Small Business Innovation Research (SBIR) program, 310–11
Small Business Technology Transfer (STTR) program, 310
Smith-Doerr, Laurel, 5, 24–25, 28, 60, 258
Social, Behavioral and Economic Research in the Federal Context (NSTC), 157–58
Social, Behavioral and Economic Sciences Subcommittee of the Committee on Science, 3
social capital in decision analysis, 267*f*, 268–70
social collaboration opportunity data, 267*f*, 273
social influence, 111–12
social rates of return, 100, 195, 200, 206n4, 292
social science community, 15
sociological approach, 5, 7, 23, 56–80, 59
  to institutions, 24–25, 56–61, 64–65, 69–70, 72–73
  to interactions between innovators and adopters, 27
  to network dynamics, 24–25, 56–58, 61–62, 65–66, 70–71, 73
  to policy contentions, 58, 72–76, 77
  to policy conundrums, 68–72, 77
  to policy mandates, 57–63, 76–77
  to policy restrictions, 58, 63–68, 77
  to power relations, 24–25, 56–58, 61–62, 65, 72
  to transformative practices, 78–79
  to unanticipated consequences, 56, 61, 66, 67–69
SOI Tax Stats–Corporation Tax Statistics database, 238*t*
Solow, R. M., 132, 141, 193, 205
Sony Corporation, 251*t*
SOSP ITG/SciSIP website, 4
Spector, Arlen, 99

spillovers and clusters, 8*t*
  measurement of, 26, 142, 198, 200–201
  types of, 100, 195, 200
Sputnik program, 14, 98, 302, 306–7
stability in measurement, 197
stakeholders, 8*t*, 25, 28
  engagement in innovation policy of, 167–69
  in politics of distribution, 33–34, 40, 54n2
  See also power relationships
Standard Occupational Classification (SOC) system, 230n2
standards, 176
  See also measurement processes
STAR METRICS project, 190, 242, 249, 297, 300
star scientists, 204, 267*f*, 268–70
  impact of, 252–54
  patents of, 242–46
statistical infrastructure. *See* measurement processes
stem cell research. *See* human embryonic stem cell (hESC) research
STEM education. *See* education and training
Stephan, P., 252–53
Stiglitz, J., 143
Strategy for American Innovation, 141
"A Strategy for Assessing Science" (NRC), 138
structural modeling, 199–200
structure of an artifact, 109–10
The Structure of Scientific Revolutions (Kuhn), 332
Summers, Lawrence, 90
supply of engineers and scientists, 86–94, 210, 333–34
  foreign scientists in, 91–92, 187, 214–16, 224
  impact of educational policies on, 88–89, 103n2
  impact of financial incentives on, 86–88, 92–93

impact of investment on, 89–90, 186–87

impact of teamwork and collaboration in, 93–94

in international contexts, 173

women's representation in, 90–91

See also workforce in S&E occupations

Survey of Business Owners (SBO), 219*t*, 225

Survey of Consumer Finance, 219*t*

Survey of Doctoral Recipients (SDR), 187, 213*t*, 219*t*

Survey of Earned Doctorates, 187, 238*t*

Survey of Federal Funds for Research and Development, 236*t*

Survey of R&D Expenditures at Universities and Colleges, 221*t*, 222, 226*t*

Survey of Small Business Finance, 221*t*, 225

sustainable growth, 8*t*

synthesis of data, 267*f*, 273–74

systems models and applications, 8*t*, 28–29

talent. *See* star scientists

Task Force on the Future of American Innovation, 14

Taylor, Mark Zachary, 4–5, 23–24

teamwork. *See* network structures

TECH-Net database, 238*t*

technological modularity, 48

technological opportunity, 198, 244

technological spillovers. *See* spillovers and clusters

technology assessment, 122

Technology Investment Program (TIP), 311–12

technology launch, 318

Teitelbaum, Michael S., 186–87, 188–89, 204–5

theoretical basis of science policy. *See* evidence-based platform of science policy

Thomas, Jim, 188–90

Thomson, James, 63–64, 65, 67

Thomson/Reuters ISI, 234*t*, 237*t*, 247, 250

Thursby, J., 244

Thursby, M., 244

Tibbets, Roland, 310

top-down approaches, 132

Topical Guide to this Handbook, 8*t*

Toulmin, Stephen, 345

Toyota, 320

transformational research, 8*t*, 74, 298–300

government debates on, 331–32

social science study of, 78–79

trends, 196

triple-helix partnerships, 8*t*

Truman, Harry, 324n4

unanticipated consequences, 56

in human embryonic stem cell research, 66, 67–68

in interdisciplinary networks, 73–75

of mandatory ethics education, 61

of regional high-tech clusters, 68–69

uncertainty models, 26, 123, 261

United Nationals Educational, Scientific, and Cultural Organization (UNESCO), 28, 164, 169, 178

University of Minnesota Healthcare Partners, 93

unobservables, 185–86

U.S. Congress. *See* Congress

U.S. Patents Citations Data File, 238*t*, 247

U.S. Patents Full-Text and Full-Page Image Databases, 238*t*

U.S. Supreme Court, 69, 245

user-driven innovation, 174

valley of death programs, 308–12, 313, 318

"value of information" literature, 295

Lightning Source UK Ltd.
Milton Keynes UK
UKHW030033120321
380214UK00004B/241

9 780804 770781